Jamaica

WORLD BIBLIOGRAPHICAL SERIES

General Editors:
Robert L. Collison (Editor-in-chief)
Sheila R. Herstein
Louis J. Reith
Hans H. Wellisch

VOLUMES IN THE SERIES

1 *Yugoslavia*, John J. Horton
2 *Lebanon*, Shereen Khairallah
3 *Lesotho*, Shelagh M. Willet and David Ambrose
4 *Rhodesia/Zimbabwe*, Oliver B. Pollack and Karen Pollack
5 *Saudi Arabia*, Frank A. Clements
6 *USSR*, Anthony Thompson
7 *South Africa*, Reuben Musiker
8 *Malawi*, Robert B. Boeder
9 *Guatemala*, Woodman B. Franklin
11 *Uganda*, Robert L. Collison
12 *Malaysia*, Ian Brown and Rajeswary Ampalavanar
13 *France*, Frances Chambers
14 *Panama*, Eleanor DeSelms Langstaff
15 *Hungary*, Thomas Kabdebo
16 *USA*, Sheila R. Herstein and Naomi Robbins
17 *Greece*, Richard Clogg and Mary Jo Clogg
18 *New Zealand*, R. F. Grover
19 *Algeria*, Richard I. Lawless
21 *Belize*, Ralph Lee Woodward, Jr.
23 *Luxembourg*, Carlo Hury and Jul Christophory
24 *Swaziland*, Balam Nyeko
25 *Kenya*, Robert L. Collison
26 *India*, Brijen K. Gupta and Datta S. Kharbas

27 *Turkey*, Meral Güçlü
28 *Cyprus*, P. M. Kitromilides and M. L. Evriviades
29 *Oman*, Frank A. Clements
30 *Italy*, Emiliana P. Noether
31 *Finland*, J. E. O. Screen
32 *Poland*, Richard C. Lewański
33 *Tunisia*, Allan M. Findlay, Anne M. Findlay and Richard I. Lawless
34 *Scotland*, Eric G. Grant
35 *China*, Peter Cheng
36 *Qatar*, P. T. H. Unwin
37 *Iceland*, John J. Horton
38 *Nepal*, Dina Nath Wadhwa
39 *Haiti*, Frances Chambers
40 *Sudan*, M. W. Daly
41 *Vatican City State*, Michael J. Walsh
42 *Iraq*, Abdul Jabbar Abdulrahman
43 *United Arab Emirates*, Frank A. Clements
44 *Nicaragua*, Ralph Lee Woodward, Jr.
45 *Jamaica*, K. E. Ingram
46 *Australia*, I. Kepars
47 *Morocco*, Anne M. Findlay, Allan M. Findlay and Richard I. Lawless
48 *Mexico*, Naomi Robbins
49 *Bahrain*, P. T. H. Unwin

VOLUME 45

Jamaica

K. E. Ingram

CLIO PRESS

OXFORD, ENGLAND · SANTA BARBARA, CALIFORNIA

British Library Cataloguing in Publication Data

Ingram, K. E.
Jamaica. — (World bibliographical series; 45)
1. Jamaica — Bibliography
I. Title II. Series
016.97292 Z1541

ISBN 0-903450-82-8

Clio Press Ltd.,
55 St. Thomas' St.,
Oxford OX1 1JG, England.

ABC-Clio Information Services,
Riviera Campus, 2040 Alameda Padre Serra,
Santa Barbara, Ca. 93103, U.S.A.

Designed by Bernard Crossland
Computer typeset by Peter Peregrinus Ltd.
Printed in Great Britain by
Billing & Sons Ltd., Worcester

THE WORLD BIBLIOGRAPHICAL SERIES

This series will eventually cover every country in the world, each in a separate volume comprising annotated entries on works dealing with its history, geography, economy and politics; and with its people, their culture, customs, religion and social organization. Attention will also be paid to current living conditions – housing, education, newspapers, clothing, etc. – that are all too often ignored in standard bibliographies; and to those particular aspects relevant to individual countries. Each volume seeks to achieve, by use of careful selectivity and critical assessment of the literature, an expression of the country and an appreciation of its nature and national aspirations, to guide the reader towards an understanding of its importance. The keynote of the series is to provide, in a uniform format, an interpretation of each country that will express its culture, its place in the world, and the qualities and background that make it unique.

SERIES EDITORS

Robert L. Collison (Editor-in-chief) is Professor Emeritus, Library and Information Studies, University of California, Los Angeles, and is currently the President of the Society of Indexers. Following the war, he served as Reference Librarian for the City of Westminster and later became Librarian to the BBC. During his fifty years as a professional librarian in England and the USA, he has written more than twenty works on bibliography, librarianship, indexing and related subjects.

Sheila R. Herstein is Reference Librarian and Library Instruction Coordinator at the City College of the City University of New York. She has extensive bibliographic experience and described her innovations in the field of bibliographic instruction in 'Team teaching and bibliographic instruction', *The Bookmark*, Autumn 1979. In addition, Doctor Herstein co-authored a basic annotated bibliography in history for Funk & Wagnalls *New encyclopedia*, and for several years reviewed books for *Library Journal*.

Louis J. Reith is librarian with the Franciscan Institute, St. Bonaventure University, New York. He received his PhD from Stanford University, California, and later studied at Eberhard-Karls-Universität, Tübingen. In addition to his activities as a librarian, Dr. Reith is a specialist on 16th-century German history and the Reformation and has published many articles and papers in both German and English. He was also editor of the *American Society for Reformation Research Newsletter*.

Hans H. Wellisch is Associate Professor at the College of Library and Information Services, University of Maryland, and a member of the American Society of Indexers and the International Federation for Documentation. He is the author of numerous articles and several books on indexing and abstracting, and has also published *Indexing and abstracting: an international bibliography*. He also contributes frequently to *Journal of the American Society for Information Science*, *Library Quarterly*, and *The Indexer*.

To

Sir Philip Manderson Sherlock, K.B.E.
Formerly Vice-Chancellor, University of the West Indies
Author and Interpreter of Jamaican Life

Contents

Contents

Contents

Contents

Preface

In keeping with the general purpose and theme of the *World Bibliographical Series* this bibliography of Jamaica seeks to interpret the history and culture of the country and to draw attention to those characteristics, those qualities and those events which distinguish it as a country and which account for its particular contribution to the tapestry of world history.

The intention of interpreting and illumining has governed the selection of material for inclusion in this bibliography more so than that of being merely comprehensive. Regard has also been paid to the historical aspects of all the facets of the country's life and achievement and to this end a modicum of older publications reflecting the views and *status quo* at various periods of the country's history have been included. However, the emphasis has been on contemporary or near-contemporary material in the form of either books or periodical articles. Dissertations available in published form and government and technical reports have been included when they seemed to cover aspects of subjects which are inadequately represented in the book trade literature or where they seemed to add a further dimension to subjects represented in this literature.

While every attempt has been made to include authentic and informed works, no claim is made for all the works represented by entries, that they have achieved the same high standards of authenticity or accuracy. Some works have been included because they alone covered some aspect of the subject, irrespective of other considerations, and others have been omitted for the reason that it has not been possible to examine a copy personally for annotation. The selection of works by individual authors in the Literature section does not necessarily represent the best work from a purely literary viewpoint, although in many instances the works chosen are fine literary creations, but rather, they have been chosen because they best illustrate some aspect or aspects of Jamaican life.

Preface

Several of the titles included relate to the Caribbean, or the Commonwealth Caribbean, rather than to Jamaica only, for the reason that they deal adequately with the part, while treating of the wider subject, and because they help to place the study and understanding of Jamaican culture and history within the context of the wider geographical and cultural grouping to which they belong. For this reason the bibliography may serve as a partial guide to the parallel literature of the Caribbean area.

Shorter periodical articles have been included on some subjects adequately covered by monographic publications, on the grounds that they may be more readily available to the reader than the latter, or because they may meet the needs of a reader who prefers a short and summary treatment of the subject.

Within each chapter or sub-section entries have been arranged alphabetically by the name of the author, or, when there is no author, by the first word of the title exclusive of the article, definite or indefinite, except that entries for periodical titles have been arranged alphabetically by title at the end of the chapter or sub-sections to which they relate.

The great majority of the works described in this bibliography are to be found in the Library of the University of the West Indies, Mona, Jamaica, where they were examined for purposes of bibliographical description and annotation. However, a substantial minority of entries were prepared on the basis of examination of copies located in the libraries of the Institute of Commonwealth Studies (University of London); the Royal Commonwealth Society; the University of Florida, Gainesville; the University of Miami and Florida International University, Miami, the last three having been especially resorted to in connection with periodical articles published outside the West Indies.

In the preparation of a work such as this which has extended over many years one accumulates debts to many persons. In particular I wish to thank the staff of the University of the West Indies Library, Mona, Jamaica, in its various branches, departments and sections, for so many kindnesses in bringing books to my attention, in fetching books from the shelves, in checking the Library's periodical holdings for specific references and, in a few instances, in preparing for me draft entries for works which in nearly every instance I examined subsequently. Grateful acknowledgement is also made of the help given me by the University of Miami Library in the final stages of this bibliography by obtaining for my use a considerable number of titles on inter-library loan or as photocopies.

xiv

Preface

I also wish to thank the University of the West Indies for granting me leave in 1978 to take up a United Kingdom Commonwealth Travel Grant which enabled me to spend three months in England seeking out material and working on this bibliography, and for a research grant which assisted me with its preparation; the Institute of Commonwealth Studies Library, University of London, for the use of an office and its Library during my stay in London in 1978; the Central Research Fund of the University of London for a grant towards the preparation of the bibliography; and my wife, not only for her support and encouragement and her patient acceptance of the demands of this work on my time but for accurately typing the entire script submitted to the publishers from an amended manuscript which would have been almost indecipherable to anyone else.

The views expressed in the annotations and responsibility for the accuracy of the work remain solely mine.

Coral Gables, Florida
17th July 1983

Introduction

Jamaica is one of a chain of islands — the West Indian archipelago — which encircles the Caribbean Sea, being the tops of a submerged mountain range linking the Americas. Its mountainous interior rises to over 7,400 feet in the Blue Mountain range which runs from east to west, and whose high mountain peaks are for the most part covered with verdant vegetation, falling steeply to a coastal plain which contracts or expands as the foothills approach or retreat from the sea.

Its recorded story begins with its discovery by Columbus in 1494, when it was inhabited by the Arawak Indians who had been moving northward from South America through the archipelago under the pressure of attack from that other tribe of Indians from whom the neighbouring sea took its name — the Caribs. Nothing remains of the reputedly gentle Arawak inhabitants except several kitchen middens, some burial caves, potsherds, stone implements, a few effigies and some place-names. They were exterminated under harsh Spanish rule and possibly by exposure to European diseases against which they had no immunity, having disappeared before the end of the period of Spanish rule. Spain had no more interest in Jamaica than as a supply base for ships bound for the gold and silver mines of the former Aztec and Inca empires and it is not surprising therefore that having eliminated the indigenous population the period of Spanish colonial rule has bequeathed to us nothing more than a few place-names, some intriguing lapidary remains and a site or two of archaeological interest.

In 1655 Jamaica was captured by an English force under the command of Admiral Penn and General Venables and the small body of African slaves belonging to the Spaniards took the opportunity of the defeat of their masters to flee to the mountainous interior and to become the nucleus of that group known as the Maroons. Later, joined by runaways from the English planters, they fought successfully against the English and eventually established their right to be free to enjoy a measure of self-rule in their mountainous townships and settlements.

Introduction

The English brought with them their customs and their religious and political traditions and set to work to develop the island as a colony of small settlers dependent on their own labour and that of a small number of African slaves and indentured whites. However, by the end of the 17th century the attraction of the more lucrative sugar trade from sugar-cane grown on extensive plantations requiring a large labour force (then consisting of slaves) had led to the eclipse of small settler planting, and even of buccaneering, which had reached its peak at Port Royal prior to the destruction of that city by the earthquake of 1692.

Africa, and more particularly, West Africa was to supply the insatiable appetite of the sugar plantations for slave labour so that soon the African-derived population of Jamaica was to far outnumber the original white settlers. From the mixture of the two was to spring the sizeable segment of the population known as coloured or, at an earlier date, mulatto.

Shortly after the English conquest, Spanish and Portuguese Jews fleeing persecution settled in Jamaica, mainly in the towns, from which many engaged in trade.

After the union of England and Scotland many Scots came to Jamaica to serve as bookkeepers and overseers on the sugar estates and in time rose to positions in government as well as being property owners and attorneys.

Thus, for nearly two centuries Jamaican society was founded upon a structure of plantation slavery which was formally ended by the emancipation of the slaves in 1838. It was to create in effect 'Two Jamaicas' — a community of masters and a community of slaves, the orbit of whose interests rarely coincided, although in the course of time a type of accommodation, a sort of creole stasis was arrived at which allowed for coexistence when there was not open conflict and which was to become the nucleus of a creole culture. The increasing prosperity of the planters in the 18th century was matched by a growing resistance on the part of the slaves who were determined to vindicate their right to freedom, a resistance which continued right up to the eve of emancipation. It was the strength of this resistance in its varied manifestations which, coupled with the humanitarian movement in England, brought about the abolition of slavery.

The immediate post-emancipation era was one of declining prosperity as sugar growing suffered from the loss of a protected market with a series of enactments including the Sugar Duties Equalization Act of 1846 and the final repeal of the British Navigation Acts in 1849, and also from the lack of labour as the new freedmen refused to work for the small wages which were offered by their erstwhile masters. This

Introduction

period, however, saw the rise of an independent indigenous peasantry and of a politically aware predominantly coloured middle class, the fear of whose potential for exercising political power led the predominantly white planter assembly to immolate the two-centuries old constitution and system of representative government after the Morant Bay Rebellion of 1865. This outbreak was in essence a protest of the peasantry against the unfair administration of justice by the planter class. In the immediate post-emancipation period the lot of the newly-freed class was tempered by the work of Christian missionaries who built chapels, schools and purchased land for the resettlement of the landless.

The passing of the old constitution made way for the introduction of Crown Colony government and for a measure of administrative and social reform though the social amelioration achieved by these measures was totally inadequate to the human needs which had been created by the brutal and dehumanizing effects of the slave system. The steady decline of the sugar industry, notwithstanding the introduction of large numbers of Indian indentured labourers and a smaller number of Chinese indentured labourers during the 19th and, in the case of the former, even as late as the early 20th century, did not help with the amelioration of social conditions.

The growth of the banana trade from 1870 under the stimulus of the activities of Lorenzo Dow Baker and the Boston Fruit Company was to improve significantly the lot of the small landowners as well as that of the large landowners and companies which held lands suitable for banana cultivation. The revival of agriculture in Jamaica was reflected in the formation of the Jamaica Agricultural Society in 1895 and by the subsequent formation in the early 1930s of the Jamaica Banana Producers Association which aimed at the co-operative marketing of Jamaican bananas in the United Kingdom. The banana industry was the most important but not the only example of the diversification of Jamaican agriculture during the 20th century. Sugar growing also was to regain a modest prosperity with the reversion of the British Government to a protectionist system in 1932 and with the adoption of quotas which provided a guaranteed market. Jamaican agriculture, however, has never reached the peaks of productive prosperity which it attained in its 18th and early 19th century heyday and remains highly sensitive not only to world economic conditions but to local hazards such as Panama disease which formerly decimated the banana industry, or lethal yellowing which in recent years has wiped out the tall and graceful coconut palms which were part of the tourist stereotype of the tropical paradise.

Introduction

The latter decades of the 19th century were to see the foundation of the educational system which prevailed until after Jamaican independence, a system which has been justly berated for trying to lead out the Jamaican Man in the mould of his English rulers but which also set certain standards of achievement in both primary and secondary education which were to form a stable basis upon which later institutions such as the University of the West Indies could build.

The Institute of Jamaica was founded in 1879 for the encouragement of literature, art and science and has carried out this mission according to the varying lights and vision of the times, perhaps one of its best known achievements being the formation of the West India Reference Library which, since 1978, has been reconstituted as the National Library of Jamaica.

The economic and social quickening of the later decades of the 19th century were also accompanied by political stirrings albeit of limited strength. The growing middle class were not content to have no voice in the government of the country and under pressure from them an elective element was introduced into the constitution in 1884. From then onwards there followed a series of constitutional amendments which allowed for increased representation and responsibility in the exercise of government until 1962 when the country became independent as a monarchic state within the Commonwealth, the Queen of Great Britain being head of state in her capacity as Queen of Jamaica.

The movement towards nationhood and the emergence of Jamaica as a country with a sense of its identity were to receive a filip from the labour disturbances which erupted in Jamaica in 1938, being part of the expression of social discontent and malaise which manifested itself in the West Indies throughout the middle to late 1930s. Although the Second World War delayed political change until 1944 when a constitution based on universal adult suffrage was introduced, a new national spirit and the awareness of a need for social change found expression in a cultural renewal. Artists and writers emerged, who looked at the Jamaican scene with a fresh vision and who apprehended the human condition in Jamaica with greater understanding and greater empathy. There had always been a strand of interest, albeit a somewhat attenuated and precious one, in Jamaican folklore and dialect. This was to find fuller expression both in creative writing and the performing arts, especially the annual pantomime which from the early 1940s when it began, increasingly became a vehicle for popular culture. So that when Jamaica became an independent country in 1962 there existed the beginnings of indigenous institutions which were able to develop cultural expressions in the fine arts, music and dance.

Introduction

Since 1962 there has been a growing interest in Jamaica's African roots and in the survivals of African culture into the present. Marcus Garvey, the first of our national heroes, had been among the earliest also to summon Jamaicans to a sense of pride in their African connection, as expressed in the back-to-Africa movement, the Universal Negro Improvement Association and the idea of an independent Africa. His ideas were to influence strongly the Rastafarian movement whose most popular vehicle of expression has been reggae music and song. Others, from a more intellectual perspective, have sought to discover the survivals of the African past and to make these part of a Jamaican cultural expression rather than hearing in them voices calling us to return to a lost continent, an irredentist dream.

Jamaica's African roots have not so much been rediscovered as they have been allowed to flourish in a favourable climate where previously they had been cribbed, cabined and confined by cultural restraints imposed by the colonial ethos. It would be a mistake however to believe that a country which had been exposed for more than three centuries to European culture and, to a lesser extent, to Asiatic and Middle-Eastern influences, would either wish to, or could withdraw itself wholly from these influences. While Jamaica now busily redresses the cultural and social negligences of the past, it is but another stage in that journey of discovery towards an equipoise resulting from the perfect balance of her varied human and historical experience.

The discovery of bauxite in the 1940s and the subsequent development of the bauxite/alumina industry linked with the phenomenal if mercurial rise of the tourist industry from its early beginnings in this century have brought Jamaica more and more into the mainstream of world consciousness as they have bolstered its agricultural economy. The country's achievements in the field of athletic sports have focused the eyes of the outside world on her from time to time.

Jamaicans also have looked outwards from their island home often seeking opportunities of economic betterment and employment as long as immigration laws permitted their admission to other countries — thus today the descendants of that diaspora are to be found in Panama, Costa Rica, Cuba, the United States and Britain. These doors are now almost completely closed in a world increasingly conscious of the need to protect the interests of its own nationals. With the safety valve of emigration removed and with increased life expectancy from better medical services augmenting population, unemployment has created serious social problems.

In the 1970s Jamaica was launched on a socialist experiment in the midst of a world recession stemming from the oil crisis and the result

Introduction

was an economic débâcle from which the country is not yet recovered. It remains to be seen whether the free enterprise economic policies endorsed in the 1980 general elections will be able to create the economic and social climate within which a free society can survive. In the global village created by the communications revolution, the peoples of less developed countries, especially such as Jamaica set full in the face of North American technological civilization, have expectations which far exceed the material means at their disposal. Although their survival, in part, depends upon the support they look for from an interdependent world, their peculiar contribution to that global village will depend on the extent to which they conserve and develop their own indigenous culture and resources while remaining open to fresh currents of thought.

Abbreviations & Acronyms

(Acronyms for names in languages other than English are rendered in English)

CARDI	Caribbean Agricultural Research and Development Institute
CDCC	Caribbean Development and Co-operation Committee
CEPAL	Economic Commission for Latin America
CFNI	Caribbean Food and Nutrition Institute
CLADES	Latin American Centre for Economic and Social Documentation
CRESALC	Regional Committee on Family Life and Sex Education for Latin America and the Caribbean
CTC	Centre for Transnational Corporations
DANIDA	Danish International Development Agency
FAO	Food and Agriculture Organization
IDB	Inter-American Development Bank
IICA	Inter-American Institute for Cooperation on Agriculture
ILO	International Labour Office
IOC	Intergovernmental Oceanographic Commission
ISER	Institute of Social and Economic Research
JAS	Jamaica Agricultural Society
MAL	Ministry of Agriculture and Lands
OAS	Organization of American States
ODA	Overseas Development Administration
PAHO	Pan American Health Organization

Abbreviations & acronyms

s.l.	Without place of publication
s.n.	Without name of publisher
UNDP	United Nations Development Programme
UNEP	United Nations Environment Programme
UNICA	Association of Caribbean Universities and Research Institutes
UWI	University of the West Indies
WHO	World Health Organization

The Country and Its People

General

1 Jamaica: an island mosaic.
Peter Abrahams. London: HM Stationery Office, 1957. 284p. map. bibliog. (Corona Library).

A many-faceted portrait of Jamaica by a prominent South African writer, who later became a citizen of Jamaica. His account spans both past and present - from discovery by Columbus to the threshold of West Indian Federation. The series to which the work belongs 'has been designed to fill the place between official Blue Books on the one hand and the writings of occasional visitors on the other, to be authoritative and readable, and to give a vivid yet accurate picture.' Although sponsored by the Colonial Office, the views expressed are personal to the author.

2 A descriptive account of the island of Jamaica: with remarks upon the cultivation of the sugar-cane, throughout the different seasons of the year, and chiefly considered in a picturesque point of view; also observations and reflections upon what would probably be the consequences of an abolition of the slave-trade, and of the emancipation of the slaves.
William Beckford. London: T. & J. Egerton, 1790. 2 vols.

The author resided in Jamaica as a man of property for thirteen years though at the time of writing he was confined to the Fleet prison for debt. In addition to describing picturesque scenes of natural beauty, he devoted much of his narrative to the details of sugar planting, the management of estates and the condition of the slaves, concerning which he wrote with some sympathy.

The Country and Its People. General

3 **Jamaica in 1850: or, the effects of sixteen years of freedom on a slave colony.**
John Bigelow. New York, London: George P. Putnam, 1851. Reprinted, Westport, Connecticut: Negro Universities Press, 1970. 214p.

The author states his purpose thus: 'He has not presumed to write a history or a geography of Jamaica, nor to present a scientific statement of its resources, neither has he written a book of travels. He has limited the personal narrative almost exclusively to such incidents as seemed necessary to an intelligible analysis of the causes which have reduced Jamaica to her present deplorable condition, and of the means which are in operation for her ultimate restoration.' (cf. Preface, p. ii). His prescription for restoring Jamaican prosperity anticipated in some measure the policies of a later period, viz., redistribution of land in smaller holdings, more efficient agricultural management thereby effecting economies and enabling the payment of better wages, establishment of central sugar mills and development of manufacturing resources.

4 **Jamaica.**
Clinton V. Black. In: *The New Encyclopaedia Britannica,* 15th ed. Chicago: Helen Hemingway Benton. 1974, Macropaedia, vol. 10, p. 15-19. map. bibliog.

A concise account of the land, its people, history, economy, administration, cultural life and institutions.

5 **Beautiful Jamaica.**
[Written and edited by Evon Blake]. Port Antonio, Jamaica: Vista Publications, 1978. 4th ed. 207p. end-paper maps. photos.

First published 1970. A pictorial record of the natural and human resources of Jamaica, past and more particularly present, in 250 photographs, in colour and black-and-white, by fourteen outstanding photographers; with a matching narrative by a notable Jamaican journalist. Among the subjects to which sections are devoted are the arts, historic landmarks, the human faces, the government, the land, religion, culture and recreation.

6 **A description of the island of Jamaica; with the other isles and territories in America, to which the English are related... taken from the notes of Sr. Thomas Linch, Knight, Governour of Jamaica.**
Richard Blome. London: printed by T. Milbourn, sold by J. Williams, Jr., 1672. 192p. 3 maps.

Pages 1-63 are devoted to Jamaica. A fine early map of Jamaica (1671) showing towns and indicating the extent to which the interior remained forested and unsettled at that time, is the first of three maps.

The Country and Its People. General

7 The cruise of the _Port Kingston_.
W. Ralph Hall Caine. London: Collier, 1908. 352p.

An account of a voyage and visit to Jamaica, with the author's extended observations on the social, religious and economic condition of the island. He gives expression to his inveterate objections to interracial marriages. However, the most interesting part of the work is his account of the earthquake which destroyed Kingston on 14 January 1907 and which occurred three days after the _Port Kingston_ arrived in Kingston harbour.

8 Ian Fleming introduces Jamaica.
Edited by Morris Cargill. London: Andre Deutsch, 1965. 240p. end-paper map. bibliog.

An entertaining and informed account of Jamaica in its varied aspects, written by a team of writers including specialists in their particular fields. In separate chapters the book treats of the country, its people, politics, religion, archives, historic houses, natural history, literature, art, recreation and cooking. The volume was inspired by Ian Fleming who lived for part of the year in Jamaica from 1946 until his death in 1964 and who contributed an introductory chapter.

9 Jamaica farewell.
Morris Cargill. Secaucus, New Jersey: Lyle Stuart, 1978. 224p.

In the words of the sub-title of the dust-jacket, 'a witty and affectionate remembrance' of Jamaica - its people, its social life and customs, family connections, persons notable and otherwise encountered there - by the author, a Jamaican planter and well-known journalist, written on the eve of his departure from Jamaica in 1977, after concluding that 'for now, I have been too long in Babylon.'.

10 Jamaica: the old and the new.
Mary Manning Carley. New York: Frederick A. Praeger, 1963. 212p. 2 maps. bibliog.

A condensed, informative and knowledgeable general account of Jamaica in which the past and the present are pleasingly woven together. The style is terse and enlivened by keenness of observation.

11 Jamaica: the making of a nation.
[Prepared by the Reference Division, Central Office of Information, London]. London: HM Stationery Office, 1962. 35p. map. bibliog. (Central Office of Information Reference Pamphlet, 51).

A summary official view of the political development and economic and social progress of Jamaica on the threshold of gaining independence.

The Country and Its People. General

12 Pleasure island: the book of Jamaica.
Edited by Esther Chapman. Kingston: Arawak Press, 1968.
7th ed. 306p. bibliog.

First published in 1951, this work has retained a considerable popularity. It is by an English journalist long resident in Jamaica and provides a wide-ranging account of the country and its people, with numerous illustrations and concluding with a tourist guide, now partially outdated.

13 Twentieth century Jamaica.
H[erbert] G[eorge] DeLisser. Kingston: Jamaica Times, 1913. 208p.

A Jamaican middle-class view of social, economic and political conditions at the start of the century, with particular reference to colour, class, popular attitudes to religion and marriage, commercial ties with North America and England and the political attitudes engendered by these ties. The author perceived a Jamaican identity, a sense of organic unity moving towards a levelling of class and colour differences, with Jamaica taking its place as a homogeneous people in the mainstream of Western civilization.

14 Daguerian excursions in Jamaica, being a collection of views of the most striking scenery, public buildings and other interesting objects taken on the spot with the daguerrotype by Adolphe Duperly; and lithographed under his direction by the most eminent artists in Paris.
Kingston: published by A. Duperly (printed by Thierry Brothers, Paris), [1844?]. 24 plates.

Twenty-four numbered plates depicting urban and rural life, buildings and equipages in the immediate post-emancipation period in Jamaica. A work of great scarcity and value. The work was projected to comprise 48 views in 12 numbers to appear periodically but only four numbers of four plates each appear to have been published. The British Museum Catalogue ascribes an uncertain publication date of 1850, while Cundall states that the work is believed to have been published in 1844.

15 Jamaica in pictures.
Anne Egan. New York: Stirling Publishing, 1977. 64p. map. (Visual Geography Series).

An attractive, concise account of Jamaica - its history, the land and the people - with well-chosen illustrations. It is intended for juveniles.

16 Jamaica: an island microcosm.
Barry Floyd. New York: St Martin's Press, 1979. 164p. 15 maps. bibliog.

A concise, informative, up-to-date general description, exceptionally strong on the physical features and economic resources of Jamaica, by a former head of the Geography Department, University of the West Indies. The illustrations complement the text and include diagrams and maps which cover a wide range of subjects.

4

The Country and Its People. General

17 The English in the West Indies: or, the bow of Ulysses.
James Anthony Froude, with illustrations engraved on wood by G. Pearson (after drawings by the author). New York: Charles Scribner's, 1888. Reprinted, New York: Negro Universities Press, 1969. 373p. map.

Though a prejudiced observer, believing in the native inferiority of the Negro and obsessed with the dangers he saw arising from Negro political ascendancy, Froude's fluent style is engaging and he writes perceptively on some aspects of colonial policy, the social and political life of the island and of the general climate of belief in his time. Pages 189-287 and 350-61 relate to the author's stay in Jamaica and his reflections thereon.

18 A winter in the West Indies, described in familiar letters to Henry Clay, of Kentucky.
Joseph John Gurney. London: John Murray, 1840. Reprinted, New York: Negro Universities Press, 1969. 2nd ed. 282p.

An account of a missionary visit undertaken in the company of his fellow Quaker Mahlon Day and another, written to show 'the beneficial working of freedom among the negroes of the West Indies in a pecuniary, civil and moral point of view', in the hope of influencing opinion in the slave states of the United States of America. The main burden of his writing is that freedom is the true catalyst of prosperity. Various towns, estates and mission stations visited are described and the names of individuals connected therewith mentioned. Pages [88]-176; [237]-252 and two plates relate to Jamaica.

19 A picturesque tour of the island of Jamaica, from drawings made in the years 1820 and 1821.
James Hakewill. London: Hurst & Robinson; E. Lloyd, 1825. 16p.+21p. coloured plates each with 1 leaf of text.

A charming colour plate work, engraved in aquatint, of town and country (mainly sugar estates) scenes in Jamaica shortly before the collapse of plantation slavery, based on observations made during a two-year residence in Jamaica. In his introduction the author gives a favourable picture of the social condition of the slaves and of their personal contentment. The book is dedicated 'to the noblemen and gentlemen, proprietors of estates in the West Indies; to the resident gentlemen, (from many of whom the author received so much kindness); and to the merchants of the United Kingdom, connected with those valuable colonies...'. The work is now a scarce and valuable one and no doubt the fact that the plates are often framed separately and sold as collectors' items have contributed to the scarcity of the published volume. It was issued in seven parts of three plates each from 1824 to 1825.

20 Jamaica.
Hans W. Hannau. Munich: Wilhelm Andermann, 1962. 60p. map. (Panorama Books).

A brief, accurate and attractive account of Jamaica - its history, its people and its countryside - as it was on the eve of becoming an independent country in 1962. The text is complemented by 30 excellent colour photographs.

5

21 **Jamaica in 1866: a narrative of a tour through the island, with remarks on its social, educational and industrial condition.**
Thomas Harvey, William Brewin. London: A. W. Bennett, 1867. 126p. map.

Documentary report, prompted by the Morant Bay Rebellion and made on behalf of the Society of Friends, England, by two of its members, one of whom, Thomas Harvey, had visited Jamaica previously with Joseph Sturge and had collaborated with him in a published account entitled *The West Indies in 1837* (London: 1838).

22 **Jamaica.**
Painted by A. S. Forrest, described by John Henderson. London: Adam & Charles Black, 1906. 179p. (Black's Smaller Series of Beautiful Books).

An account of Jamaica, the land and people, their social life and customs illustrated with 24 coloured plates of water-colour paintings of scenes and persons. There are chapters on the army, politics, the railway, alligator shooting and the race-course. The author foresaw the rise of nationalism among the countries of the West Indies and 'the inevitable struggle for supremacy between the white man and the black' (p. 179) though he had no sympathy with the latter's aspirations.

23 **Jamaica viewed; with all the ports, harbours, and their several soundings, towns, and settlements thereunto belonging.**
Together with the nature of its climate, fruitfulnesse of the soile and it's suitablenesse to English complexions...
[Edmund Hickeringill]. London: John Williams, 1661. 106p.

Possibly the earliest example of a work written to promote the island as a place of settlement, shortly after it had been captured by the English in 1655. As a general account it fulfils the sentiments expressed in the couplet of some prefatory lines addressed to the author on his return from Jamaica - 'And this epitomized urn shall retain/ The Indies memory when they're dead again.' The work is one of exceptional rarity, the copy described here being of the first edition in the University of the West Indies Library, Jamaica. The author was an English visitor to Jamaica.

24 **Jamaica.**
[London: Commonwealth Institute], 1978. 14p. bibliog. map. (Commonwealth Fact Sheet).

A handy fact sheet intended to be used for reference purposes.

25 **The Negro in the New World.**
Sir Harry Johnston, with a new introduction by George Shepperson. London: Methuen, 1910. Reprinted, New York; London: Johnson Reprint Corporation, 1969. 499p. 2 maps.

A pioneering work in race relations and Afro-American studies, comprising a notable body of facts and several illustrations of Negro social and domestic life and of the contemporary environment. The chapter on Jamaica (p. 239-93) is a concise essay on the social history of Jamaica, as well as a description of the

The Country and Its People. General

countryside as it appeared in the early 20th century when the author visited the island and was helped by Sir Sydney Olivier, the governor, and other public officers, in gathering information for this work.

26 Jamaican interlude.
R. Gerallt Jones. Swansea, Wales: Christopher Davies, 1977. 196p.

A lively, impressionistic account of Jamaica and the workings of its educational system, by a Welshman who spent two years there, from 1965 to 1967, as first principal of the Mandeville Teachers' Training College, Jamaica. 'This book was written in the main as a page of autobiography, and some part of it was published in the Welsh language in 1974.' (Introduction, p. 9).

27 Area handbook for Jamaica.
Irving Kaplan, Howard I. Blutstein, Kathryn Therese Johnston, David S. McMorris. Washington, DC: US Government Printing Office, 1976. 332p. 3 maps. bibliog.

'This volume is one of a series of handbooks prepared by Foreign Area Studies (FAS) of the American University, designed to be useful to military and other personnel who need a convenient compilation of basic facts about the social, economic, political and military institutions and practices of various countries' (p. iii). A comprehensive general account, for which the research was completed in April 1975, representing the work of the authors and FAS and not representing the official view of the United States government.

28 Jamaica gallery: a documentary of the island of Jamaica, West Indies.
Philip Kappel, introduction by John P. Marquand. London: Macmillan, 1961. 56p.

Pages of descriptive and historical text alternate with the 25 etchings of country life, in which 'it was the intention of the artist to race against time, to arrest the charm of Jamaica before further changes inflicted upon the quintessence of the island's simplicity the modifications that they impose upon the character of the land.' (p. 54). 'The chief concern of the artist is with the romance of people and not with their bitterness.' (p. 26).

29 West Indian scenery. Illustrations of Jamaica in a series of views comprising the principal towns, public buildings, estates and most picturesque scenery of the island.
Joseph B. Kidd. London: Smith, Elder, Kingston: James Wallace, 1838 [-1840]. 50 plates.

Fifty coloured lithograph plates, originally issued in ten parts of five plates each, all marked 'from nature and on stone by J. B. Kidd, SA', except plate 27 which is marked, 'on stone by J. B. Kidd from a sketch by his brother William'. The finest large-scale plates on Jamaica, they convey the brilliance of tropical light and colour and the lushness of tropical foliage far more faithfully than do Hakewill's engravings with their subdued northern light. The work is now an exceptionally rare one and, as in the case of Hakewill's work, the plates are often sold as separately framed pieces. J. B. Kidd was a member of the Scottish Academy and visited his brother Thomas P. Kidd in Jamaica 1835-36 and 1837-38 when, doubtlessly, he made the sketches from which these lithographs were made. The prospectus on the wrappers of the separate parts states descriptive letterpress would be issued separately to purchasers at the conclusion of the work, but neither this nor a title-page appears to have been published.

30 **Through Jamaica with a Kodak.**
Alfred Leader, with introductory notes by His Grace the Archbishop of the West Indies and Sir Alfred L. Jones. Bristol, England: John Wright; London: Simpkin, Marshall, Hamilton, Kent & Co., 1907. 208p. map.

Remembrances of a four-month visit to Jamaica in 1905 in which the author captures by keen observation, anecdote and photography, pictures of a Jamaica which has passed. The 129 illustrations are an important feature of the volume.

31 **The land of look behind: a study of Jamaica.**
Mona Macmillan. London: Faber & Faber, 1957. 224p. map.

A lively expatriate account of Jamaica about a quarter of a century ago. Based on personal observation and discussion with informed residents, it is strongest in its perception of social life and institutions below the surface and weakest in matters of historical detail and interpretation. The author states that from working with her husband on an earlier book on social and economic conditions of the West Indies (i.e. *Warning from the West Indies*, 1936), she knew 'that there were other things besides sun and sea and luxury in Jamaica, that there were people who had troubles and problems.' (Introduction, p. 12).

32 **Caribbean nights.**
William J. Makin. London: Robert Hale, 1939. 287p.

An English newspaperman's account of the Caribbean after a year's stay in Jamaica as first editor of the *Jamaica Standard*. With lively reportage he directs some penetrating shafts of light upon social and economic conditions at the time and gives a particularly interesting firsthand account of the riots of 1938 in Jamaica. He also treats of pocomania, obeah, folklore and the Maroons.

33 **Not by sun alone.**
George Mikes, drawings by William Papas. London: Andre Deutsch, 1967. 142p.

Jamaica through the eyes of an internationally known humourist - often tolerant, sometimes perceptive and occasionally patronising. The illustrations match the humour.

34 **Rose Hall, Jamaica: story of a people, a legend and a legacy.**
Text by Rex Nettleford (editor), T. A. L. Concannon, John W. Rollins, Linda Ashland, Olive Senior, photographs by Slim Aarons, Arnold Newman. Jamaica: Rose Hall in association with Kingston Publishers, 1973. xix, [84]p.

Includes text and 42 numbered coloured plates portraying an historic house restored, also the people and scenes from contemporary life on the surrounding estate and in the community. A fine example of a Jamaican coffee-table book and a beautiful memento of a house whose legend continues to be a great tourist attraction.

35 Jamaica: the island and its people.
A. J. Newman. Kingston: printed by Jamaica Times (Press), [1948?]. 141p. 7 maps.

This is the fifth edition of a work published originally in 1935 under the title of *The Times geography & history of Jamaica*. Its aim is to provide a textbook for students being prepared as primary school teachers but it is also a useful compendium of historical and geographical information.

36 Jamaica: the blessed island.
Lord Olivier. London: Faber & Faber, 1936. Reprinted, New York: Russell & Russell, 1971. 466p. 3 maps. bibliog.

The author was governor of Jamaica from 1907 to 1913. He describes his book as 'a highly condensed survey', and this it is, encompassing the early history of the island followed by a more detailed account of its physical features and of its social, economic and political life in the century following the emancipation of the slaves. It presents a very definite and independent view of Jamaican development, informed by a strong sympathy for the Jamaican peasantry and expressed in a fluent and engaging style. The combination of Fabian socialist and colonial administrator makes for a most unusual and perceptive study.

37 Jamaica: its past and present state.
James M. Phillipo, with a new introduction by Philip Wright. London: John Snow, 1843. Reprinted, London: Dawsons of Pall Mall, 1969. 487p. (Colonial History Series).

A general account, with especial reference to the social, moral and religious condition of the black and coloured population before and after emancipation, designed to show the great improvement in their condition since that event and the part played by the missionaries in that improvement. 'Appendix. Plan of a college in Jamaica': p. 477-85.

38 Waters of the west.
Kenneth Pringle, foreword by the Rt. Hon. Lord Olivier. London: Allen & Unwin, 1938. 325p.

The first chapter of the book (p. 1-126) relates to Jamaica, where the author resided for some time as a secondary school teacher. Lord Olivier's remarks are particularly apt: 'Mr Pringle's observations... appear to me... exceptionally perspicacious, sympathetic and informative. It is the most interesting book of its kind that I have recently seen, and its method and style form a pleasant change from those of the ordinary book-making tourist or journalist.' It presents a highly individual view of West Indian life and the descriptions of Caribbean scenes are informed with a penetrating and sensitive vision.

39 Letters from Jamaica 'the land of streams and woods'.
[Charles J. G. Rampini]. Edinburgh: Edmonston & Douglas, 1873. 182p.

Attributed to Charles J. G. Rampini, stipendiary magistrate of Jamaica and sheriff of Shetland, these '... sketches... of a traveller's impressions of Jamaica

The Country and Its People. General

and its people,' are mainly sketches of Negro character, social life and customs, and in particular, folklore. Includes one of the earliest published collections of anansi stories and 'Negro proverbs'.

40 **Jamaica: the portrait of an island.** W. Adolphe Roberts. New York: Coward-McCann, 1955. 247p.

The first half of the book is a short history, the other half is a general description of Jamaica, including some guidebook information. A number of chapters are devoted to towns or places of special interest. The author was born in Jamaica and having spent several years as a journalist and war correspondent, devoted himself to the study and writing of Caribbean history.

41 **Jamaica, as it was, as it is, and as it may be: comprising interesting topics for absent proprietors, merchants, &c. and valuable hints to persons intending to emigrate to the island: also an authentic narrative of the negro insurrection in 1831, with a faithful detail of the manners, customs and habits of the colonists and a description of the country, climate, productions, &c., including an abridgment of the slave law.** [Bernard Martin Senior?] A Retired Military Officer. London: T. Hurst, 1835. Reprinted, New York: Negro Universities Press, 1969. 312p.

Attributed to Bernard Martin Senior who had resided for twenty years in Jamaica when this work was originally published. The first part of the book is an interesting, concise general account of the geography, people and institutions of Jamaica. The second half is a detailed account of the slave rebellion of 1831, which preceded emancipation, during which the author served in the militia operations against the rebels. He describes Gardiner and Dove, two of the rebel leaders.

42 **Jamaica today: a handbook of information for visitors and intending residents, with some account of the colony's history, being a new and revised edition of the late Mr. Frank Cundall's 'Jamaica in 1928'.** Edited by Philip M[anderson] Sherlock. [Kingston: Institute of Jamaica with the assistance of the] Tourist Trade Development Board of Jamaica, 1940. 204p. fold. map. bibliog.

A handbook prepared with the assistance of a number of well-informed Jamaican residents and of the Department of Agriculture, the Jamaica Agricultural Society and the Director of Education. Much of the information has ceased to be current but the chapters on the history, geography and natural history of the country are still very informative and useful.

10

The Country and Its People. General

43 A view of the past and present state of the island of Jamaica; with remarks on the moral and physical condition of the slaves, and on the abolition of slavery in the colonies.
J[ohn] Stewart. Edinburgh: Oliver & Boyd, 1823.
Reprinted, New York: Negro Universities Press, 1969. 363p.
The work was first published anonymously and in a shorter form, in 1808. It covers the physical features, the social, economic and political life of all classes of inhabitants. It is one of the more objective and factual accounts of pre-emancipation Jamaica, the author having lived in Jamaica for 21 years.

44 Jamaica: photographs.
Francis Stoppelman. London: Ernest Benn, 1962. [140]p. end-paper map.
Two hundred and fifty-two photographs, including a few in colour, of the land and its people, with sections devoted to Kingston, beliefs, sports and pastimes, industry and tourism. In his foreword, Victor Stafford Reid says, 'Stoppelman's *Jamaica* is a camera essay that speaks with a craftsman's eloquence in his tools. He has not "classified" but has allowed authority to his camera, to look life in the eye, or at the nape of the neck, and to speculate. So his story has turned out well rounded; and more, a joy to possess.'.

45 The West Indies and the Spanish Main.
Anthony Trollope. London: Chapman & Hall, 1859.
Reprinted, London: Frank Cass, 1968. 2nd ed. 395p. map.
First published 1859. In chapters 2 to 9 (p. 11-130) a well-known Victorian novelist, with deft style, gives his impressions of the débâcle of post-emancipation Jamaica - impressions coloured by prejudiced notions of Anglo-Saxon superiority but expressive of insights into the Jamaican society and its classes at that time and prophetic of future social and political developments.

46 The West Indies: their social and religious condition.
Edward Bean Underhill. London: Jackson, Walford & Hodder, 1862. Reprinted, Westport, Connecticut: Negro Universities Press, 1970. 493p.
An account of a tour undertaken on behalf of the Baptist Missionary Society to investigate the condition of the Baptist churches in the West Indies since the passing of the Emancipation Act. More than half the volume is devoted to Jamaica and contains much useful information on the social and economic life of the country. It is a vehicle for the opinions of the newly freed peasantry and labouring classes and presents a more optimistic and enthusiastic view of post-emancipation 19th-century Jamaican society than either Trollope or Froude.

47 A tour through the island of Jamaica, from the western to the eastern end, in the year 1823.
Cynric R. Williams. London: printed for Hurst & Clarke, 1826. 352p.
A very personal account, relying more on anecdote than on observation and liberally illustrated with classical and literary allusions. The numerous reported speeches of persons encountered reflect strong anti-sectarian and pro-slavery

views, 'The author himself disavows every intention of attempting ridicule... and appeals for the fidelity of his picture to the proprietors and dwellers of Jamaica.' (Preface, p. vi). Ragatz regarded it as a very unreliable account, but it has been used as a source by a number of recent West Indian historians. The work is illustrated with the following plates: Port Royal harbour; view near Maroon Town; Diana; interior of a negro house; Port Antonio - lithographs; all of which, with the exception of the third are subscribed: 'Printed by C. Hullmandel'.

48 Jamaica boy.
Bernard Wolf. New York: Cowles Book Co., 1971. 48p.
Written and photographed by a well-known photographer, this book includes some excellent photographic studies of Jamaican boyhood.

The Caribbean, Bermuda, and the Bahamas, 1982.
See item no. 83.

Jamaica guide.
See item no. 84.

Jamaica.
See item no. 85.

Jamaica.
See item no. 86.

Jamaica: a Benn holiday guide.
See item no. 87.

This is Jamaica: an informal guide.
See item no. 88.

Stark's Jamaica guide (illustrated) containing a description of everything relating to Jamaica of which the visitor or resident may desire information.
See item no. 89.

Exploring Jamaica: a guide for motorists.
See item no. 90.

Jamaica.
See item no. 91.

Fielding's Caribbean 1983.
See item no. 92.

Periodicals

49 Report on Jamaica for the Year...
Great Britain, Colonial Office. London: HM Stationery Office, 1887-1961/62. annual. (not issued 1939-1945).
A reliable and informative publication by the British Colonial Office, providing not only a report on government activities during the year but a summary account of the country and its people in chapters which treat of various aspects of the economic, social, political and cultural life of Jamaica.

Geography and Geology

General and political

50 A complete geography of Jamaica.
R. M. Bent, Enid L. Bent-Golding. London, Glasgow: Collins, 1966. 128p. 32 maps.

Covers the physical, human and economic geography of Jamaica. It is written principally for the use of senior pupils in post-primary schools but may also be used by tourists and the general reader. The authors are a former Chief Education Officer and a geography teacher in Jamaica.

51 A human geography of Jamaica.
R. M. Bent, Enid L. Bent-Golding. [Kingston]: Wm. Collins & Sangster (Jamaica), 1978. 2nd ed. 64p. maps.

This book is drawn in great part from the authors' earlier work, *A complete geography of Jamaica*. It is pitched at a junior secondary level but is also intended to give the general reader and visitor a picture of Jamaica and how its people occupy themselves at work and play.

52 The Caribbean islands.
Helmut Blume, translated by Johannes Maczewski, Ann Norton. London: Longman, 1974. 464p. 89 maps. bibliog.

Originally published as *Die Westindischen Inseln*, 1968. A geographic survey of the West Indies which includes a concise account of the physical geography, regional devisions and economy of Jamaica (Chapter 17, p. 176-207), to which 7 of the maps relate.

53 A first geography of Jamaica.
F. C. Evans. Cambridge, England: Cambridge University
Press, 1968. 48p. 14 maps.

An elementary text for use in schools, primarily concerned with human and
economic geography. A second edition was issued in 1973.

Economic and regional

**54 Kingston, Jamaica: urban development and social change,
1692-1962.**
Colin G. Clarke. Berkeley, Los Angeles, London: University
of California Press, 1975. 270p. 86 maps. bibliog.
(American Geographical Society Research Series, no. 27).

'This book examines two interconnected themes. The first is concerned with the
analysis of the city's spatial, demographic, and economic change; the second refers to the social
relationship between social and economic change; the second refers to the social
structure of the city and, in particular, to the changing relationship between race,
culture and status.' (Preface, p. x). Nearly half the population of Jamaica lives in
Kingston and its environs, the largest city in the non-Hispanic Caribbean. Based
on a doctoral dissertation accepted in 1967, a final chapter has been added
summarizing conclusions concerning the post-1962 period arrived at in the course
of subsequent visits by the author between 1964 and 1972. The text is complemented by detailed cartographic analyses, statistical tables and photographs of
urban scenes.

55 Geographic aspects of population dynamics in Jamaica.
L. Alan Eyre. Boca Raton, Florida: Florida Atlantic
University Press, 1972. 172p. 30 maps. bibliog.

A geographic study based on field surveys of four rural communities; it is also of
equal interest as a demographic study.

56 The shanty town - a reappraisal.
L. Alan Eyre. [Mona, Jamaica]: Geography Department,
University of the West Indies, [1970 or later]. 17p. bibliog.
(Research Notes, no. 3).

A reappraisal of how shanty towns develop and of their problems. A shanty town
is defined as a 'peri-urban collection of dwellings erected on land to which the
occupants, or at least a majority of them, possess no title, and which, at least
initially, is not subdivided for housing purposes.' The work is based on a case
study of shanty towns around Montego Bay.

Geography and Geology. Economic and regional

57 **Shantytown stage development: the case of Kingston, Jamaica.**
Gerald Thomas Hanson. PhD thesis, Louisiana State University, Department of Geography and Anthropology, Louisiana, 1975. 232p. map. bibliog. (Available from University Microfilms, Ann Arbor, Michigan, 1978).

A detailed analysis of the development of shanty towns, low-income housing areas of the poor, as a part of the urban structure of Kingston, using the following eight indices to monitor change in the shanty town landscape: relative location, land use, tenure, population characteristics, housing, public services, commercial activities and vegetative patterns. This study is based on field-work done in Kingston from July to March 1974.

58 **The growth and spatial structure of Kingston, Jamaica.**
Bruce Edgar Newling. PhD thesis, Northwestern University, Evanston, Illinois, 1962. 182p. maps. bibliog. (Available from University Microfilms, Ann Arbor, Michigan, 1973).

A geographer studies the relationship between urbanization, as reflected in the growth of Kingston, and economic development, as reflected in rising per capita income levels and levels of literacy. This study is copiously illustrated with sketch maps, diagrams and tables and is based on field-work undertaken in Jamaica from June 1960 to January 1961. In 1979 the author presented a paper to the Seventy-fifth Annual Meeting of the Association of American Geographers, Philadelphia, Pennsylvania, entitled: 'Growth cycles: primary and rank-size arrays, with special reference to the city of Kingston and the towns of Jamaica' (36 leaves).

59 **Shanties or skyscrapers: growth and structure of modern Kingston.**
Ann Norton. Mona, Jamaica: Institute of Social and Economic Research, University of the West Indies, 1978. 108p. 12 maps. (University of the West Indies, Institute of Social and Economic Research. Working paper, no. 13).

A study of population growth and internal migration with respect to the expansion and residential structure of Kingston for the years 1942 to 1968. Includes 20 statistical tables relating to migration, housing and residential patterns. The author was formerly lecturer in the Department of Geography, University of the West Indies.

Special features

60 Estimates of maximum 24-hour rainfall amounts for return periods from 5 to 100 years.
C. J. Evans. *Journal of the Scientific Research Council of Jamaica*, vol. 3, no. 1 (April 1972), p. 25-45. 10 maps. bibliog.

'This paper reports a project in which annual extreme observation-day falls were analysed for 139 points in Jamaica. Maximum 24-hour rainfall amounts to be expected in specified periods were then estimated using statistical techniques. The results were used to construct isopluvial maps of the island.' (p. 34).

61 Water water everywhere: the surface water resources of Jamaica.
Thorant Hardware. *Jamaica Journal*, vol. 7, no. 3 (Sept. 1973), p. 20-22.

A brief sketch of the amount of surface water passing through the Jamaican river systems, by a hydrologist in the employ of the government. A companion article entitled 'Bringing forth water from the rock (the geology of ground water)' by Raymond M. Wright, appears in the same issue of *Jamaica Journal*, p. 23-25, 44.

62 The climate of Jamaica.
Prepared by the Climatology Branch of the Jamaican Meteorological Service. Kingston: [Jamaican Meteorological Service], 1973. 68p. 31 maps.

An overview of the climate of Jamaica, discussing rainfall, temperature, wind, relative humidity, evaporation, sunshine and pressure.

63 Spatial and seasonal distribution of rainfall and runoff in Jamaica.
Lawrence C. Nkemdirim. *Geographical Review*, vol. 69, no. 3 (July 1979), p. 288-301. 5 maps. bibliog.

Analyses based principally on rainfall and streamflow data from eleven drainage basins, including all major geographical regions in the island. The author is a professor of geography at the University of Calgary, Alberta, Canada.

64 The rainfall of Jamaica.
Jamaica: Scientific Research Council, November 1963. 6p. 14 maps.

This brochure, including a topographical and annual and monthly rainfall maps of Jamaica, was published with a view to making up-to-date information on rainfall available, the previously available rainfall maps having been compiled some 70 years before. The project was initiated by Michael Nancoo. Acting Assistant Director, Jamaica Division, West Indies Meteorological Services and sponsored by the Scientific

Research Council. The rainfall maps were prepared by L. E. Saunders, Chief Survey Draughtsman, under the direction of O. B. Rogers, Director of Surveys.

Geology

65 Remarks on the geology of Jamaica.
H. T. De la Beche. *Transactions of the Geological Society of London*, 2nd series, vol. 2. 1829, p. 143-94.

The earliest geological study of Jamaica by the founder of the Geological Survey of England, who was born in Jamaica.

66 Copper prospects of Jamaica: a geological review.
Compiled by A[llison] D. Fenton. Kingston: Geological Survey Division, Ministry of Mining and Natural Resources, 1979. 225p. maps. bibliog. (Bulletin no. 9).

Based on a survey undertaken from 1974 to 1978 to collate and review the information available from all sources, on copper mineralization in Jamaica, in order that the true potential of the many showings could be evaluated.

67 Jamaica underground: a register of data regarding the caves, sinkholes and underground rivers of the island.
Alan G. Fincham. Kingston: Geological Society of Jamaica, 1977. 247p. map. bibliog.

The only comprehensive compilation of information of its kind, prepared with the assistance of members of the Jamaica Caving Club. It includes 'The geology of Jamaican caves' by Geoff Wadge and Gren Draper. In recording details of the caves, a major feature of the landscape of Jamaica, the author hopes 'that the information will assist all of those people concerned with the academic or economic aspects of the caves and also provide for those who find sport, excitement and interest in the underground world.' (p. 2).

68 The structure, evolution and sedimentology of the reef, beach and morass complex at Negril, western Jamaica.
Malcolm D. Hendry. Kingston: Petroleum Corporation of Jamaica, 1982. 185 leaves. maps. bibliog.

A study undertaken to provide necessary geological information on the structure of the coastal margins and adjacent marine areas at Negril, western Jamaica, and to assess the possible impact of cutting peat from the morass on the beach and offshore region.

69 The geology and mineral resources of Jamaica.
H. R. Hose. *Overseas Geology and Mineral Resources (Colonial Geology and Mineral Resources)*, vol. 1 (1950), p. 11-36. map.

The author, a geologist, was formerly Managing Director of Jamaica Bauxites Ltd.

70 Mineral resources of Jamaica.
Compiled by I. G. Hughes, revised and edited by Allison [D.] Fenton. [Kingston, Jamaica]: Ministry of Mining and Energy, Geological Survey Division, 1981. 2nd ed. 104p. 23 maps. bibliog. (Bulletin no. 8).

An invaluable source of information on the mineral resources of Jamaica, of which the first edition appeared in 1973. This revised edition reflects the several developments in geoscience and related fields in Jamaica during the decade 1970-80, during which the Jamaica Bauxite Institute, the Petroleum Company of Jamaica, the Energy Division in the Ministry of Mining and Energy and the Mineral Resources Development Committee were established. Five sections cover the following subjects: geology, mining regulations, metallic minerals, non-metallic minerals, potential energy sources, mineral springs and therapeutic waters.

71 Minerals and rocks of Jamaica: a guide to identification, location, occurrence and geological history.
Anthony R. D. Porter, Trevor A. Jackson, Edward Robinson. Kingston: Jamaica Publishing House, 1982. 174p. 6 maps. bibliog.

The only work of its kind, intended as a guide to identification, it includes illustrations, some in colour, with a concluding chapter on the geological history of Jamaica. The authors are geologists engaged in industry or university teaching and research.

72 Physiography of the sea floor east of Jamaica.
E[dward] Robinson, F. W. Cambray. In: *Symposium on Investigations and Resources of the Caribbean Sea and Adjacent Regions*. Willemstad, Curaçao, Netherlands Antilles, 18-26 November 1968. Paris: UNESCO, 1971, p. 285-89. map. bibliog.

This paper presents the bathymetric results of the first phase of a study by the Department of Geology of the University of the West Indies, carried out during two short cruises in 1967 and 1968, and from inshore work. The symposium at which it was presented was organized jointly by UNESCO and FAO.

Geography and Geology. Geology

73 A review of the thermal and mineral springs of Jamaica.
M. T. Royall, J. Banham. *Journal of the Geological Society of Jamaica*. Special issue: Proceedings of Industrial Minerals Symposium (Sept. 1981), p. 83-93. map. bibliog.

A short account of their geology and chemistry, their occurrence and their potential for development, by geologists attached to the University of the West Indies and the Ministry of Mining and Energy, Jamaica.

74 Reports on the geology of Jamaica; or, Part II of the West Indian survey.
James G. Sawkins, with contributions from G. P. Wall, Lucas Barrett, Arthur Lennox, C. B. Brown, appendix by Robert Etheridge. London: Longman, Green, 1869. 339p. 3 maps. (Memoirs of the Geological Survey [London]).

The first geological survey of Jamaica and the basis of all later geological study of the island. The only comprehensive work on both the geology and mineral resources of Jamaica. Among the illustrations is an excellent large-scale geological map. (scale: 1 mile=¼ inch) and five sectional diagrams illustrating the geological structure of the parishes of the island. Among the appendices are, 'Outline of the flora of Jamaica', by Nathaniel Wilson (Appendix II, p. 263-91) and 'Summary of the palaeontology of the Caribbean area,' by Robert Etheridge (Appendix V, p. 306-39).

75 Field guidebook to the modern and ancient reefs of Jamaica.
Jeremy [D.] Woodley, E[dward] Robinson. Miami Beach, Florida: Atlantic Reef Committee, University of Miami, 1977. 33p. 5 maps. bibliog.

Prepared for the Third International Symposium on Coral Reefs, 1977, by a marine biologist and a geologist of the University of the West Indies.

76 Field guide to selected Jamaican geological localities.
Edited by R. M. Wright. Kingston: Mines and Geology Division, Ministry of Mining and Natural Resources, 1974. 57p. 5 maps. bibliog. (Special publication, no. 1).

This guide was prepared for the Joint Geological Society of America/Geological Society of Jamaica field trip, 21-23 November 1974. Although it does not present a comprehensive statement on the geology of Jamaica, it incorporates the current state of knowledge of the areas to be visited. The introductory chapter provides a useful synopsis of the geology of Jamaica. It supplements the *International Field Institute's guide to the Caribbean island-arc system* (1970) which includes a paper entitled 'Field guide to aspects of the geology of Jamaica', by E. Robinson, J. F. Lewis and R. V. Cant. An excerpt of the latter work may be found in *West Indies island arcs*, edited by Peter H. Mattson (Stroudsburg, Pennsylvania: Dowden, Hutchinson & Ross, 1977. Benchmark Papers in Geology 33, p. 210-21. 3 maps. bibliog.). The Benchmark series contain key papers in their respective fields.

Periodicals

77 **Journal of the Geological Society of Jamaica.**
Kingston: Geological Society of Jamaica, Geology
Department, University of the West Indies, 1958- . annual.

The journal first appeared in 1958 under the title *Geonotes: quarterly journal of
the Jamaica Group of the Geologists' Association*. In 1965 the name was
changed to the present title. In addition to the regular volume, seven special
issues have appeared, as follows: 'Proceedings of the Bauxite/Alumina Symposium' (June 1971), 94p; 'Proceedings of Bauxite Symposium II' (Oct. 1973), 40p;
'Proceedings of Bauxite Symposium III' (May 1975), 59p; 'The origin of bauxite'
(Aug. 1977), 67p; 'Proceedings of Bauxite Symposium IV' (June 1980), 370p;
'Proceedings of the Industrial Minerals Symposium' (Sept. 1981), 312p; and
'Proceedings of Bauxite Symposium V' (June 1982), 382p. The 1982 issue of the
journal records the proceedings of a recently concluded one-day seminar on the
theme 'The International Seabed Authority and Its Implications for Jamaica',
held in Kingston on 20 November 1982 just three weeks before the historic
signing of the Convention on the Law of the Sea on 10 December at Montego
Bay, Jamaica.

Maps and atlases

78 **Caribbean history in maps.**
Peter Ashdown. Trinidad, Jamaica: Longman Caribbean,
1979. 84p.

With the aid of over 175 individual maps and diagrams accompanied by concise
explanatory captions this work illustrates the historical development of the Caribbean basin from the period of discovery to the late 1970s, focusing on various
aspects of that development - economic, political and religious. The maps treat
generally of the region as well as of the individual countries comprised therein.
Among tables of current as well as historical interest are those of the major
political parties and of notable West Indians old and new. The work has been
prepared with a view to the needs of students and teachers of the new CXC
(Caribbean Examinations Council) History syllabus and in such a way that it
may be used alongside the companion history *Caribbean story* by William Claypole and John Robottom (Longman Caribbean, 1980-81. 2 vols.).

79 **Atlas for Jamaica and the Western Caribbean.**
[Kingston]: Collins, Longman, 1971. 57p.

A general atlas, in which approximately half the number of plates relate to
Jamaica and the Caribbean, prepared with the advice of members of staff of the
Departments of Geography of the University of the West Indies and the University of Guyana. A useful teaching aid which places Jamaica in its Caribbean and
world context.

80 Jamaica in maps.

Colin G. Clarke, cartography by Alan G. Hodgkiss. London: University of London Press, 1974. 104p. 42 maps. bibliog.

Each of the 42 sheets of maps is prefaced by a short essay relating to the wide range of topics covered: geography, geology, demography, education, employment, housing, rural and urban settlement, electoral patterns, agriculture, industry, tourism, communications and external trade. This study, by a senior member of the Department of Geography of the University of Liverpool, 'is the outcome of more than a decade's research on Jamaica - much of it devoted to Kingston....'. A useful compendium, which fills a real need.

81 The national atlas of Jamaica.

Kingston: Town Planning Department, Ministry of Finance and Planning, November 1971. 79p. 50 maps. diagrs.

This atlas attempts to include all the major characteristics of the country's natural environment and of its physical, human and economic resources. The maps are complemented by the text and numerous diagrams. The atlas was in preparation from 1967 to 1971 with the assistance of the United Nations Development Programme Physical Planning Project.

82 Maps and plans in the Public Record Office. 2. America and West Indies.

Edited by P. A. Penfold. London: HM Stationery Office, 1974. 835p.

Lists 142 manuscript and printed maps of Jamaica or Jamaican counties, towns and estates, mainly of the 18th and 19th centuries. Particularly valuable for the study of the military and naval history of Jamaica with regard to defences and fortifications.

Historic Jamaica from the air.

See item no. 132.

Travel guides

83 The Caribbean, Bermuda, and the Bahamas, 1982.

Edited by Stephen Birnbaum. Boston, Massachusetts: Houghton Mifflin, 1981. 692p. maps. bibliog. (Get 'Em and Go Travel Guides).

Includes a number of general sections on preparations for travel, cultural and historical perspectives, diversions, as well as individual sections on each country. The chapter on 'Jamaica' comprises a map, an introductory essay, a 'site-by-sight' survey of the most important sights, a concise compilation of local tourist information and a selection of places to stay on a variety of budgets.

84 Jamaica guide.
Clinton V. Black. [Kingston]: William Collins & Sangster (Jamaica), 1973. 128p. 6 maps (incl. end-paper map).

Particularly interesting for its information on the history, social life and customs and natural history of Jamaica. Includes a substantial section on chief places of interest, with plans of the principal towns, indicating many of the places of interest mentioned. Illustrated with coloured and black-and-white photographs.

85 Jamaica.
Prepared by the staff of Editions Berlitz. Lausanne, Switzerland: Editions Berlitz, 1981. 128p. 8 maps. (Berlitz Travel Guides).

A concise pocket-size guide, with pictures and maps in colour, giving current information principally on sightseeing, shopping and eating out in Jamaica. There are extra sections on Haiti, the Dominican Republic and the Cayman Islands, which are conceived of as excursions from Jamaica.

86 Jamaica.
George Hunte. London: B. T. Batsford, 1976. 216p. 2 maps. bibliog.

Slightly more than half the book consists of an historical account of Jamaica. The latter part consists of a general account of the principal towns and sites of historic or current interest, with a digest of particulars for travellers, listed by parish.

87 Jamaica: a Benn holiday guide.
Ian Sangster. London: Ernest Benn, 1973. 96p. maps.

A concise and well-written guide including interesting photographs and an account of the geography, natural products, people, social life and history of Jamaica together with a detailed guide to nine routes, which comprehend the entire island.

88 This is Jamaica: an informal guide.
Philip [Manderson] Sherlock. London: Hodder & Stoughton, 1968. 160p. 7 maps.

In addition to the usual guidebook information on routes, places of interest, shopping, food and drink, this book deals briefly with the country's history, government, educational system, recreation, folklore, literature and investment opportunities.

89 Stark's Jamaica guide (illustrated) containing a description of everything relating to Jamaica of which the visitor or resident may desire information..

James H. Stark. Boston, Massachusetts: James H. Stark; London: Sampson, Low, Marston; Jamaica: Aston W. Gardner, c.1902. 209p. 3 maps.

One of a well-known series of guides to the islands of the West Indies, replete with interesting historical information and illustrations. The work also reflects some of the prejudiced notions on race prevalent at that time.

90 Exploring Jamaica: a guide for motorists.

Philip Wright, Paul F. White. London: Andre Deutsch, 1969. 253p. 8 maps.

An excellent guide, written in an entertaining style, replete with historical facts and anecdotes. The eight routes described and their maps cover the greater part of the main road system and many secondary roads. 'Since the book is intended primarily for visitors, the emphasis is on places and routes most easily accessible from the north coast resorts...' (Introduction, p. 11).

91 Jamaica.

Directed and designed by Hans Johannes Hoefer, produced and edited by Paul Zach. [Singapore]: Apa Productions (HK) in association with Kingston Publishers, Jamaica, 1983. 313p. 6 maps. bibliog. photos. (Insight Guides, 16).

An exceptionally interesting and reliable guidebook in respect of both its text and its superb photographic illustrations which bring to life the beauty, the colour and the detail of the Jamaican countryside, as well as the character and diversity of the Jamaican people. It has been written and produced by a team of journalists, photographers, and others experts in the fields of history, literature, political science, communication, public relations and sport, drawn from the Apa Productions editorial and publishing staff abroad and from the world of scholarship, creativity; business and government in Jamaica. The work falls into five parts: Introduction, History and Politics; People; Places; Features (sections on reggae, the performing arts, the fine arts, cricket, food and drink, ganja and Jamaica dialect); and Guidebook information in brief.

92 Fielding's Caribbean 1983.

Margaret Zellers. New York: Fielding in association with William Morrow, 1982. 852p.

In addition to providing information on the politics, customs and tourist requirements of each country and on hotels, restaurants, interesting sites and recreational facilities in the tourist areas, the author expresses views on the most recent trends in the Caribbean. She was the recipient of an award from the Caribbean Tourism Association in 1977. There is a substantial section on Jamaica on p. 424-80.

Geography and Geology. Travel guides

93 **The inn way... the Caribbean.**
Margaret Zellers. Stockbridge, Massachusetts: Berkshire
Traveller Press, 1978. 192p.

A choice of inns, including eight in Jamaica (based on the author's experience of
travel in the Caribbean), which offer the opportunity of unique and enjoyable
holidays, forms the subject of this travel guide.

Pleasure island: the book of Jamaica.
See item no. 12.

Flora and Fauna

94 The Blue Mahoe & other bush: an introduction to plant life in Jamaica.
C. Dennis Adams. Kingston: Sangster's Bookstores; Singapore: McGraw-Hill Far Eastern Publishers (S), 1971. 159p. illus.

An entertaining and informed book written for the general reader, in which botanical description is mixed with relevant details of history and geography. The coloured photographs beautifully and faithfully present the plants.

95 Flowering plants of Jamaica.
C. D[ennis] Adams, with contributions by G[eorge] R. Proctor, R. W. Read (and others). Mona, Jamaica: University of the West Indies, 1972. 848p.

This comprehensive reference work, by the Reader in Botany at the University of the West Indies, is intended to complement the definitive work, *Flora of Jamaica*, by Fawcett and Rendel, which is still being published. It omits illustrations but includes 'useful field and ecological data which the other Flora did not have.' (cf. Preface, p. 9).

96 Medicinal plants of Jamaica.
G. F. Asprey, Phyllis Thornton. Kingston: [s.n.], 1953-55. 2 vols.

Plants are listed alphabetically by family and then by species, with the addition of common names. Medicinal properties and uses are described, with occasional citation of authors referring to such uses. The second volume is furnished with indexes of botanical names, common names and of disorders, with the plants stated to be used as remedies. Reprinted from *The West Indian Medical Journal*.

97 **Flora & fauna of the Caribbean: an introduction to the ecology of the West Indies.**

Peter R. Bacon. Port-of-Spain, Trinidad: Key Caribbean Publications, 1978. 319p. map. bibliog.

Deals generally with the physical background of the Caribbean, the natural environment - forests, sea shores, rivers and swamps, savannas, caves, desert islands and dry environments - and with man-made environments. Illustrated with numerous line-drawings and photographs, black-and-white and coloured. The author is Senior Lecturer in Zoology at the St. Augustine campus of the University of the West Indies.

98 **The Culicidae of Jamaica (Mosquito studies. XXI).**

John N. Belkin, Sandra J. Heinemann, William A. Page. Kingston: Institute of Jamaica, 1970. 458p. bibliog. (Bulletin of the Institute of Jamaica. Science Series, no. 20).

The most recent and comprehensive review of the mosquitoes of Jamaica, including the subfamilies *Chaoborinae* and *Dixinae* which were not treated in the two previous reviews (Theobald, 1905a; Hill & Hill, 1948). There are 126 illustrations, which, with the exception of six figures, are original.

99 **Birds of the West Indies.**

James Bond, with colour illustrations by Don R. Eckelberry, Arthur B. Singer, line drawings by Earl L. Poole. London: Collins, 1979. 4th ed. 256p. end-paper maps.

The most comprehensive field guide to species in Jamaica and elsewhere in the West Indies. The author was Associate Curator at the Academy of Natural Sciences, Philadelphia and, in 1952, received a Musgrave medal from the Institute of Jamaica.

100 **Jamaica and its butterflies.**

F. Martin Brown, Bernard Heineman, illustrated by Marjorie Statham Favreau. London: E. W. Classey, 1972. 478p. 5 maps. bibliog.

A comprehensive and thorough description of 133 species of butterflies to be found in Jamaica, including sections on taxonomy, life history, habits, habitats, the distribution for each species and 10 coloured plates depicting 157 specimens. The work is based on twenty years' collecting experience by Bernard Heineman during annual visits (except for three years) from 1946 to 1965. The technical aspects of the work were done by F. Martin Brown, Head of the Science Department of the Fountain Valley School, Colorado Springs, USA. The work includes interesting historical information on earlier natural history collectors in Jamaica and is concluded with a detailed bibliography.

101 **The civil and natural history of Jamaica.**
Patrick Browne. London: 1756. Reprinted New York: Arno Press, 1972. 503, [44]p. 2 maps. (Research Library of Colonial America).

Reprinted from a copy of the original edition of this work, with a reprint of the complete Linnaean index from the 3rd ed. of 1789. The most celebrated early study of Jamaican natural history, after that by Sir Hans Sloane. Illustrated by 49 black-and-white plates of drawings by G. D. Ehret, eminent botanical illustrator of the 18th century, and others. R. P. Stearns in *Science in the British Colonies of America* (Urbana: University of Illinois Press, 1970) says of this work that it 'was, scientifically speaking, the most up-to-date treatment of the natural history of any of the British colonies in America before the end of the Old Colonial Era.'.

102 **Marine and freshwater fishes of Jamaica.**
David K. Caldwell. Kingston: Institute of Jamaica, 1966. 120p. bibliog. (Bulletin of the Institute of Jamaica. Science Series, no. 17).

The most comprehensive listing of Jamaican fishes. It is a technical work, listing species and localities where found, with remarks on earlier published references to these species. The author, who is Curator of Ichthyology, Los Angeles County Museum, prepared this report with a view to providing a modern starting point for further studies on Jamaican fishes.

103 **Flora of Jamaica, containing descriptions of the flowering plants known from the island.**
William Fawcett, Alfred Barton Rendel. London: Trustees of the British Museum. 1910-36. vols. 1, 3-5, 7 published to date. bibliog.

The definitive work on the flora of Jamaica, the publication of which has remained incomplete for several decades. The contents include: Volume one, 'Orchidaceae'; Volume three, 'Dicotyledons Part one'; Volume four, 'Dicotyledons, Part two'; Volume five, 'Dicotyledons, Part three'; Volume seven, 'Dicotyledons, Part five'. When published, Volume six will complete the account of the Dicotyledons and Volume two will complete the Monocotyledons, excepting the orchids which were the subject of the first volume. The text is illustrated with numerous drawings done in fine detail.

104 **The birds of Jamaica.**
Philip Henry Gosse, assisted by Richard Hill Esq. of Spanish Town. London: John Van Voorst, 1847. 447p.

Published as a result of Gosse's visit to Jamaica (1851), which also resulted in his book *A naturalist's sojourn in Jamaica* (1851), this work remains a readable and reliable guide despite the passage of time. The *Dictionary of National Biography* states that his collections of birds and insects were made for the British Museum. An exceptionally rare companion piece is his *Illustrations of the birds of Jamaica* (London: John Van Voorst, 1849) which comprises 52 deftly executed and delicately coloured ornithological lithographs, depicting their subjects in characteristic stances or actions. According to R. B. Freeman and Douglas Wertheimer, compilers of *Philip Henry Gosse: a bibliography* (London: Dawson, 1980), the *Illustrations* depicts only those birds newly described or those considered not to have been previously properly delineated and was issued in 13 monthly parts of four loose plates from April 1848 to April 1849.

105 **A naturalist's sojourn in Jamaica.**
Philip Henry Gosse, assisted by Richard Hill. London: Longman, Brown, Green & Longman, 1851. 508p.

Not only is this a comprehensive and detailed account of the island's natural history by an eminent naturalist of his day, written as a result of a sojourn in Jamaica from December 1844 to July 1846, but it attempts, as the author states, 'to describe... somewhat of the glory and loveliness of the scenes in which they [i.e. the objects of his study] dwell; and he has endeavoured to do this with a kind of panoramic effect so that the reader might have before his mind a succession of pictures, as it were, of a beauteous tropic island.' (Preface, p. x).

106 **Wild flowers of Jamaica.**
Alex D. Hawkes, illustrated by Brenda C. Sutton. [s.l.]: Collins, Sangster, 1974. 96p.

An excellent guide, describing and illustrating 174 species of plants, written by an authority on horticulture and illustrated by a qualified Jamaican designer. The descriptions include interesting details as to the indigenous habitats of plants, their introduction to Jamaica and the particular localities where they occur. It is furnished with a glossary of botanical terms and indices of botanical and vernacular names.

107 **Sea shells of the West Indies: a guide to the marine molluscs of the Caribbean.**
Michael Humfrey. New York: Taplinger Publishing Co., 1975. 351p. map. bibliog. (Taplinger World Wide Field Guide).

The author is an amateur conchologist of high repute who spent many years in the police force in Jamaica, where he did most of the collecting for this work, which describes and illustrates 497 shells of the Caribbean from Bermuda to Brazil. Most of the habitats described are Jamaican and among the author's purposes was that of providing a census of all known Jamaican marine molluscs. There are coloured illustrations.

108 **Bird-watching in Jamaica.**
May Jeffrey-Smith, illustrated by Ivy Jeffrey-Smith, with new colour photographs for this edition by Lisa Salmon. Kingston: Bolivar Press, 1972. enlarged ed. 167p.

This book, first published in 1956, is written for the bird-lover or curious visitor, by a resident of Jamaica and a keen observer of birds over very many years. Included are anecdotes, historical and literary allusions and bits of folklore.

109 **Island biology illustrated by the land birds of Jamaica.**
David Lack. Oxford, England: Blackwell Scientific Publications, 1976. 445p. 58 maps. bibliog. (Studies in Ecology, vol. 3).

The most detailed study of Jamaican birds since that published by Gosse in 1847. Part I develops an ecological theory of island avifaunas based on Part II, which discusses in some detail the habitats, feeding habits and systematics of the Jamaican land birds, illustrated by fine line-drawings done by Kay Kepler. The author, who died before the completion of his book, was a Fellow of the Royal Society and spent the year 1970-71 as a visiting professor at the University of the West Indies, Jamaica.

110 **The herpetology of Jamaica.**
W. Gardner Lynn, Chapman Grant. Kingston: Institute of Jamaica with the assistance of the Dept. of Science and Agriculture, 1940. 148p. bibliog. (Bulletin of the Institute of Jamaica. Science Series, no. 1).

Treats of amphibians and reptiles in separate sections. The most comprehensive general study of this subject, bringing together most of the known information on Jamaican reptiles and amphibians at that time. This work is supplemented by *Contributions to the herpetology of Jamaica: studies on Anolis Reconditus Underwood and Williams*, by J. D. Lazell (Kingston: Institute of Jamaica, 1966. 15p. Bulletin of the Institute of Jamaica. Science Series, no. 18, pt. 1).

111 **A field guide to shells of the Atlantic and Gulf coasts and the West Indies.**
Percy A. Morris, 3rd edition edited by William J. Clench, sponsored by the National Audubon Society, National Wild Life Federation. Boston, Massachusetts: Houghton Mifflin, [1973]. 330p. illus. photos. bibliog. (Peterson Field Guide Series).

First published in 1947, the third edition has been enlarged to include the West Indies. It describes a total of 1,035 species, all but two of which are illustrated by one or more photographs, including the more common shells of the Caribbean area, giving English common names as well as Latin scientific names.

112 **Glimpses of Jamaican natural history.**
Members of the Natural History Society of Jamaica. [Kingston]: Institute of Jamaica, 1946-49. 2nd ed. 2 vols.

As the editor, C. Bernard Lewis, formerly Curator of the Museum of the Institute of Jamaica, tells us in the preface to the first volume, this work was prepared in order to provide the people of Jamaica and in particular the teachers, with simply written factual information on various aspects of Jamaican natural history. The subjects discussed cover a wide range of animal and plant life, and the material is based upon articles written for *Natural History Notes*, the mimeographed journal of the Natural History Society of Jamaica, and on radio talks sponsored by the Society. The first chapter of volume one is an excellent introduction to earlier work done in the study of natural history in Jamaica. The first edition, in a single volume, was issued simultaneously with the opening of the Natural History Gallery of the Institute of Jamaica Museum in July 1945.

113 **Flowering trees of the Caribbean: 30 paintings.**
   Bernard Pertchik, Harriet Pertchik, introduced by William C. White. New York, Toronto: Rinehart, 1951. 125p.

Although the book is not a scientific treatise but is intended for the tourist and visitor, expert advice was obtained from those in the fields of botany, forestry and horticulture to ensure accuracy. The text is an interesting blend of history, plant lore and descriptive and economic botany. Although all the specimens described were not selected from Jamaica, all, or very nearly all, occur there. Among those responsible for guidance with the selection of trees to be included were L. V. Burns, a former conservator of forests in Jamaica and E. J. Downs, former Superintendent of Public Gardens of Jamaica. The title is somewhat of a misnomer in that the illustrations only depict the flowers and leaves, rendered in superb coloured reproductions of original paintings. The text is by Paul Knapp of the Aloca Steamship Company, which underwrote the cost of art and engraving.

114 **The voyage of the plant nursery, H.M.S. Providence, 1791-1793.**
   Dulcie Powell. Kingston: Institute of Jamaica, 1973. 69p. bibliog. (Bulletin of the Institute of Jamaica. Science Series, no. 15, pt. 2)

A short historical account, incorporating the text of original correspondence relating to Captain William Bligh's voyage from the South Seas to St. Vincent and Jamaica, with lists of plants brought to Jamaica and sent from Jamaica to Kew, England.

115 **More additions to the flora of Jamaica.**
   George R. Proctor. *Journal of the Arnold Arboretum*, vol. 63, no. 3 (July 1982), p. 199-315. maps. bibliog.

This publication summarizes new information collected by the author since 1972 when C. D. Adams' *Flowering plants of Jamaica*, a milestone in the history of Jamaican botany, was published; it also includes a few overlooked or unpublished older records. It can be considered an informal supplement to Adams' volume.

116 **Birds and flowers of Jamaica.**
   Illustrated and described by Margaret K. Rhodes. Kingston: Novelty Trading Co., 1961. 73p.

Includes 36 illustrations from original watercolours done by an artist who had spent 18 years in Jamaica. The first such collection of bird portraits in colour since Philip Gosse's *Illustrations of the birds of Jamaica* (London: 1849). Each bird is shown in association with a flowering plant.

117 **The shell book [of Jamaica]: the complete guide to collecting and identifying with a special section on starfish and other sea creatures.**

Sandra Romashko. Miami, Florida: Windward Publishing, 1974. 2nd ed. 64p.

The cover-title only attributes a Jamaican connection but the work relates to the shells of the waters of Florida and the Caribbean. The shells are illustrated in colour and the booklet is furnished with indices to common names and scientific names.

118 **A voyage to the islands Madera, Barbados, Nieves, S. Christophers and Jamaica, with the natural history of the herbs and trees, four-footed beasts, fishes, birds, insects, reptiles, &c. of the last of those islands; to which is prefix'd an introduction, wherein is an account of the inhabitants, air, waters, diseases, trade, &c. of that place, with some relations concerning the neighbouring continent and islands of America. Illustrated with the figures of the things describ'd, which have not been heretofore engraved; in large copper-plates as big as the life.**

Hans Sloane. London: printed by the British Museum for the author, 1707-25. 2 vols. map.

A celebrated work on the natural history of Jamaica, by the renowned naturalist, collector and physician, Sir Hans Sloane, who was later to become Secretary of the Royal Society and whose collections formed the nucleus of the British Museum. It comprises 274 numbered plates exquisitely executed and accurately depicting the flora and fauna of Jamaica, 264 pages of text devoted to natural history description and 154 pages of introduction devoted to the history and geography of Jamaica and to an account of the medical symptoms of his patients in Jamaica, Sloane having gone out to Jamaica as personal physician to the Duke of Albemarle, during his governorship from 1687 to 1689.

119 **Familiar trees and cultivated plants of Jamaica: a traveller's guide to some of the common trees, shrubs, vines and crop plants.**

Written and illustrated by Dorothy P. Storer. [Kingston]: Institute of Jamaica; London: Macmillan; New York: St. Martin's Press, 1958. 81p.

A simply written guide, with clear line-drawings, intended for visitors to Jamaica. The Director of the Arnold Arboretum, Harvard University, who writes the introduction, says 'the visitor to Jamaica... will find it extremely useful in learning more of the plant life around him.'.

120 Introduction to the birds of Jamaica. Lady Taylor, illustrated by William Reeves. London: Macmillan in association with Institute of Jamaica, 1955. 114p.

An elementary guide to the commoner birds of the island, written with clarity and illustrated with excellent black-and-white line-drawings of almost every bird described.

121 A history of the Jamaican fauna. J[eremy] D. Woodley. *Jamaica Journal*, vol. 2, no. 3 (Sept. 1968), p. 14-20. map.

A popular account of the origins and present state of the vertebrate fauna of Jamaica, with suggestions for their conservation.

The history of Jamaica: or, General survey of the antient and modern state of that island: with reflections on its situations, settlements, inhabitants, climate, products, commerce, laws and government. *See* item no. 161.

Prehistory and Archaeology

General

122 **Aboriginal Indian remains in Jamaica.**
J. E. Duerden. *Journal of the Institute of Jamaica*, vol. 2, no. 4 (July 1897), p. [309-64]. map. bibliog.

Issued as a separately paged number (51p.). The sequence of paging in the volume has been deduced from its contents page. Despite the passage of time this remains an authoritative work, which discusses the kitchen middens, burial caves, implements, pottery, images, amulets, ornaments and petroglyphs of Jamaica's aboriginal Indian inhabitants and the sites where these remains have been found. Several illustrations are included. The author was Curator of the Museum of the Institute of Jamaica. The article also includes a 'Note on the craniology of the aborigines of Jamaica' by A. C. Haddon.

123 **The archaeology of Jamaica and its position in relation to circum-Caribbean culture.**
Robert Randolph Howard. PhD thesis, Yale University, New Haven, Connecticut, 1950. 485p. fold. map. bibliog. (Available from University Microfilms, Ann Arbor, Michigan, 1969).

The first section of this dissertation is devoted to a survey of the archaeology of the island of Jamaica based on two summers of field-work in 1947 and 1948. The second section is concerned with the bearing of Jamaican archaeology on the larger problems of circum-Caribbean culture. The work provides a concise assessment of archaeological work done to 1950 in Jamaica, a useful survey list of sites reported and a description of artifacts collected from these sites.

124 Central American and West Indian archaeology; being an introduction to the archaeology of the states of Nicaragua, Costa Rica, Panama and the West Indies.

Thomas A. Joyce. New York: G. P. Putnam's Sons, 1916. Reprinted, New York: Hacker, 1973. 270p. 2 maps. bibliog.

Nearly one half the volume is devoted to the West Indies, with numerous references to Jamaica, in chapters dealing with the government, marital and martial customs, religion, amusements, food, habitations, dress and manufactures of the Indian inhabitants at the time of the discovery of the New World. A good general study by a recognized expert on the subject.

125 Exploring the drowned city of Port Royal.

Marion Clayton Link, kodachromes by Luis Marden. *National Geographic Magazine*, vol. 117, no. 2 (Feb. 1960), p. 151-83.

A popular account of the first scientific expedition - the Geographic-Smithsonian-Link Expedition - to explore the site of the sunken city of Port Royal. Its significance was that it demonstrated the richness of the site as a field for further archaeological exploration and produced a chart of the 17th-century town which was to prove useful to later explorers.

126 Origins of the Tainan culture, West Indies.

Sven Lovén. Göteborg, Sweden: Elanders Bockfryckeri Akfiebolag, 1935. 696p. map.

The first comprehensive modern treatise on the Arawaks of the Greater Antilles, dealing with their artifacts, culture, domestic and social life. Interesting for its comparative treatment of the various island cultures. Translated from a revised second edition of an earlier treatise in Swedish (Göteborg: 1924), with alterations and additions.

127 Port Royal rediscovered.

Robert F. Marx. Garden City, New York: Doubleday, 1973. 304p. end-paper plan. bibliog.

A very personal account of the author's experience as a marine archaeologist in the employ of the Government of Jamaica, engaged in salvaging artifacts from the sunken city of Port Royal. Its interest lies in the day-to-day account of operations, in the description of the remarkable variety and quantity of 17th-century artifacts and Spanish coins retrieved, and in the author's candid comments on his dealings with officialdom, on the obstacles encountered in the course of his employment from 1966 to 1968 and in his expression of final disappointment as to the outcome of his efforts, as a result of a return visit to Jamaica in 1971. A shorter, less controversial account of the same subject, excellently illustrated, appeared as *Pirate port: the story of the sunken city of Port Royal* by Robert F. Marx (London: Pelham Books, 1967). There are also a number of technical reports by Marx, published by the Jamaica National Trust Commission, on artifacts discovered.

Prehistory and Archaeology. General

128 **History from the earth: archaeological excavations at Old King's House.**
R. Duncan Mathewson. *Jamaica Journal*, vol. 6, no. 1 (March 1972), p. 3-11. bibliog.

An account of the initial investigation of the Old King's House site in Spanish Town, undertaken in July 1971 under the auspices of the Institute of Jamaica. The site chronologically spans some 400 years of Jamaican history, embracing the Arawak, Spanish and English periods of settlement. A more specialized account of this investigation is pursued by the author in his 'Archaeological analysis of material culture as a reflection of sub-cultural differentiation in 18th century Jamaica,' *Jamaica Journal*, vol. 7, no. 1-2 (March-June 1972), p. 25-29. bibliog.

129 **Port Royal, Jamaica: excavations 1969-1970.**
Philip Mayes. Kingston: Jamaica National Trust Commission, 1972. 136p. 15 maps.

This report summarizes the results of the first major land excavation ever attempted at Port Royal, which was destroyed by earthquake in 1692. The author was seconded from the University of Leeds and appointed by the British Government to serve as Head of the British Archaeological Mission to Port Royal, Jamaica. The work is a detailed and technical account, illustrated with copious scale drawings of the artifacts and structures brought to light. Included is a summary account of earlier attempts to excavate the site, together with a history of the site.

130 **Anthropology and archaeology in Jamaica.**
Don Robotham. *América Indígena*, vol. 40, no. 2 (April-June 1980), p. 355-66.

A brief survey of work completed and in progress in these disciplines in Jamaica and of the institutional framework for research and teaching, including museums.

131 **The aborigines of Jamaica.**
Philip M[anderson] Sherlock. Kingston: Institute of Jamaica, 1939. 20p. map.

Though outdated as to the state of current archaeological investigation this is still a useful short account of the artifacts and life-style of the Arawaks of Jamaica.

132 **Historic Jamaica from the air.**
Photographs by Jack Tyndale-Biscoe, text by David Buisseret. Barbados: Caribbean Universities Press, 1969. 73p. 26 maps.

Aerial photographs matched with old plans from various sources, including the British Museum, the Hispanic Society of America, the Institute of Jamaica, the Jamaica Archives and the Public Record Office (London). The photographs by Tyndale-Biscoe constitute possibly the more important part of the volume.

Jamaica: conservation and development of sites and monuments. [Final report of UNESCO Mission to Jamaica] September 1968-April 1969.
See item no. 779.

Periodicals

133 Archaeology - Jamaica.
[Mandeville, Jamaica]: Archaeological Society of Jamaica, 1965-. monthly, later quarterly.

First published in January 1965 as the monthly bulletin and newsletter of the Archaeological Club of Jamaica, this publication became a regular organ of the Archaeological Society of Jamaica, which was constituted on 5 September 1970. The contents comprise short articles by amateur and professional archaeologists, reports of site surveys, field trips and society meetings.

History and Collective Biography

General and social

134 The story of Jamaica from prehistory to the present.
Clinton V. Black. London: Collins, 1965. 255p. end-paper maps. bibliog.

This book is based on the author's shorter *History of Jamaica*, first published in 1958, with some revision and additions to bring the story up to the attainment of political independence in 1962. The text, with a changed format and many more illustrations, was issued as a special edition for schools in 1973, entitled *A new history of Jamaica*. The author, who is Government Archivist of Jamaica, states in the foreword that he has concentrated on telling the island's story in as much detail as possible rather than interpreting that story for his readers. The illustrations match the text of this wide-ranging though compact story of Jamaica's development from prehistory to the attainment of independence in 1962.

135 Tales of old Jamaica.
Clinton V. Black. London: Collins, 1966. Reissued, [Kingston]: Collins Sangster, 1979. 127p.

Ten tales, based on historical fact for the most part, intended to illuminate the first 200 years or so of Jamaica's history under British rule. Illustrated.

136 The development of creole society in Jamaica, 1770-1820.
Edward [Kamau] Brathwaite. Oxford, England: Clarendon Press, 1971. 374p. 2 maps. bibliog.

This book is in substance a doctoral thesis of the same title accepted by the University of Sussex in 1968. It is a study of the adaptation of European and African derived cultures within the framework of slavery. The author describes it as 'an historical study with a social-cultural emphasis'. (Introduction, p. xiv). In it, he attempts not only 'to understand the workings of a "creole" society during the central period of West Indian slavery' but to point to the directions in which creolization at a later stage led and may yet lead.

137 The annals of Jamaica.

George Wilson Bridges. London: John Murray, 1827-28. Reprinted, London: Frank Cass, 1968. 2 vols. (Cass Library of West Indian Studies, no. 1).

This is a history conceived and written in a highly polemic vein, in which invective against all who opposed the planter interest of Jamaica is clothed in sonorous and sometimes pompous language. It was a most popular work in its day and mirrors the most extreme views in support of the establishment under slavery.

138 Slaves in red coats: the British West India regiments, 1795-1815.

Roger Norman Buckley. New Haven, Connecticut; London: Yale University Press, 1979. 210p. map. bibliog.

'The present study which is based on a doctoral dissertation submitted to McGill University in 1975, attempts to explore the effects of war on slavery by focusing on the British government's controversial decision of 1795 to defend its West Indian possessions with regiments of slaves...' (Preface, p. viii). The author, who is Professor of History at Vanier College, Montreal, explores a little studied area. Chapter three is devoted to 'The Jamaican experience and the policy of purchase' (p. 43-62).

139 The dynamics of change in a slave society: a sociopolitical history of the free coloreds of Jamaica, 1800-1865.

Mavis Christine Campbell. Rutherford, New Jersey: Fairleigh Dickinson University Press; London: Associated University Presses, 1976. 393p. 2 maps. bibliog.

The most detailed study of this subject published to date, particularly informative on the role of the free coloureds as an opposition group in the House of Assembly in the years between emancipation and the final dissolution of the House in 1865. Polemic rather than dispassionate in style, with some of the quality of an indictment.

140 Caribbean story.

William Claypole, John Robottom. Trinidad; Jamaica: Longman Caribbean, 1980-81. 2 vols. 55 maps. bibliog.

Book one, entitled 'Foundations', covers the period from the coming of the Amerindians to emancipation in 1834. Book two, entitled 'The inheritors', covers the period from emancipation to the post-independence era. This history was written to provide a Caribbean perspective for the CXC (Caribbean Examinations Council) History syllabus. The selection of illustrations, which includes some little-known items, provides a good visual complement to the text. A number of learning exercises are included at the end of each volume.

History and Collective Biography. General and social

141 Historic Jamaica.
Frank Cundall. London: West India Committee for the Institute of Jamaica, 1915. Reprinted, New York: Johnson Reprint Corporation, 1971. 424p.

A well-recognized account of the historic buildings, monuments and sites of Jamaica, arranged by parish.

142 Jamaica under the Spaniards.
Abstracted from the archives of Seville by Frank Cundall, Joseph L. Pietersz. Kingston: Institute of Jamaica, 1919. 115p.

One of the few source books for the history of Jamaica under the Spaniards and the only one in the English language. The documents abstracted consist of letters from Spanish governors of Jamaica and communications from the Crown and from royal and ecclesiastical officials and secular individuals to persons in Jamaica, or concerning Jamaica. The documents were transcribed by Miss. I. A. Wright, translated by J. L. Pietersz and the transcripts are preserved in the National Library of Jamaica.

143 Richard Hill.
Frank Cundall. *Journal of Negro History*, vol. 5, no. 1 (Jan. 1920), p. 37-44.

A biographical sketch of one of Jamaica's most famous sons - anti-slavery fighter, stipendiary magistrate and savant. This account is taken in great measure from a biographical notice by the writer which appeared in the *Journal of the Institute of Jamaica*, July 1896.

144 Sugar and slaves: the rise of the planter class in the English West Indies, 1624-1713.
Richard S. Dunn. Chapel Hill, North Carolina: University of North Carolina Press, 1972. Reprinted, New York: W. W. Norton, 1973. 359p. 7 maps. bibliog. (Norton Library).

Although a general study of the English West Indies, numerous examples are drawn from Jamaican history. In addition, a single chapter is devoted entirely to Jamaica. A readable and balanced account of the establishment of the plantation system and of domestic and social life in the Caribbean tropics. Useful also, in that unlike many studies of the West Indies in the 17th century it does not concentrate unduly on buccaneering. The author is Professor of History at the University of Pennsylvania.

145 The hero as murderer: the life of Edward John Eyre, Australian explorer and governor of Jamaica, 1815-1901.
Geoffrey Dutton. Sydney: Collins; Canberra: Cheshire Publishing Pty., 1967. 416p. 3 maps. end-paper maps. bibliog.

An interesting and sympathetic biography of Eyre and a successful one, in that the author succeeds in showing him, although a quite unprepossessing character as governor of Jamaica, in a tragic light. All that could be said in favour of Eyre has been said here. The author, at one time Lecturer in English at the University of Adelaide, has carefully researched his study in the archives of Australia, Britain, Jamaica and New Zealand.

146 **The history, civil and commercial, of the British West Indies.** Bryan Edwards. London: G. & W. B. Whitaker, 1819. Reprinted, New York: AMS Press, 1966. 5th ed. 5 vols.

An esteemed work by a Jamaican planter historian who achieved an unusual degree of objectivity for one so placed in his time. The history of Jamaica is treated separately in substantial sections of the work, as well as in the chapters which treat generally of slavery, agriculture, government and commerce. The plates and maps of the original work are not included in the reprint.

147 **The buccaneers of America: a true account of the most remarkable assaults committed of late years upon the coasts of the West Indies by the buccaneers of Jamaica and Tortuga (both English and French).** John Esquemeling, with a new introduction by Percy G. Adams. New York: Dover Publications, 1967. 506p.

A re-publication of the edition published by Swan, Sonnenschein & Co., in 1893. The first three parts of this volume, written in Dutch, were originally published in 1678. It is a classic of the literature of piracy and the chief source of information on the buccaneers of that period.

148 **The narrative of General Venables, with an appendix of papers relating to the expedition to the West Indies and the conquest of Jamaica, 1654-1655.** Edited for the Royal Historical Society by C. H. Firth. London: Longman, Green, 1900. xli, 180p.

The original narrative of the commander of the land forces which captured Jamaica for the English, written as an apologia for his conduct, published *in extenso*. The appendices include two contemporary accounts, useful as comparative evidence in evaluating Venables' narrative. This work makes available a number of historic accounts (existing for the most part as original MSS. only) of a major event in Jamaican history.

149 **A history of Jamaica from its discovery by Christopher Columbus to the year 1872: including an account of its trade and agriculture, sketches of the manners, habits and customs of all classes of its inhabitants, and a narrative of the progress of religion and education in the island.** W. J. Gardner. London: T. F. Unwin, 1909. Reprinted, London: Frank Cass, 1971. 510p. fold. map. (Cass Library of West Indian Studies, no. 17).

First published in 1873. The most detailed of the histories of Jamaica written in the post-emancipation period. The author spent 25 years of his life as a Congregational missionary in Jamaica, of which 23 were spent prior to the publication of his history. Five major periods of the country's history are identified and under

History and Collective Biography. General and social

each there are chapters devoted to historical events, commerce and agriculture, religion and education, manners and customs.

150 **Where the twain meet.**
Mary Gaunt. London: John Murray, 1922. 335p.

An interesting and sympathetic account of the story of Jamaica from its discovery by Columbus, told by recounting the events as seen through the eyes of a series of historical writers and interspersed with observations on the contemporary scene by the author.

151 **British slave emancipation: the sugar colonies and the great experiment 1830-1865.**
William A. Green. Oxford, England: Clarendon Press, 1976. 449p. 3 maps. bibliog.

This is a general study of British imperial policy in the West Indies which draws heavily on the history of Jamaica; the author summarizes it as a contrasting case study of Barbados and Jamaica - 'the former having fulfilled to a large extent the aspirations of the metropolitan emancipators of 1833, the latter having confirmed many of their apprehensions.' (p. 404).

152 **The ex-colonial society in Jamaica.**
Douglas Hall. In: *Patterns of foreign influence in the Caribbean*. Edited by Emanuel de Kadt. London: Oxford University Press for the Royal Institute of International Affairs, 1972, p. 32-48.

A perceptive outline of the social, political and economic development of Jamaica between 1838 and the end of the decade of the 1960s.

153 **The buccaneers in the West Indies in the XVII century.**
C. H. Haring. Hamden, Connecticut: Archon Books, 1966. 298p. maps. bibliog.

In addition to its interesting style, the work is based on hitherto neglected sources. It was originally presented to the University of Oxford as a BLitt thesis in History in 1909.

154 **The life of George William Gordon.**
Ansell Hart. [Kingston]: Institute of Jamaica, [1971 or 1972]. 144p. map. (Cultural Heritage Series, vol. 1).

An able defence of Gordon, National Hero, which leaves one in no doubt that he was judicially murdered. The account is a reversal of the view of Gordon held in Jamaica during the latter part of the 19th and the early 20th century. The author was a scholarly lawyer with an interest in Jamaican history and an intense fascination with the period of the Morant Bay Rebellion.

155 Between black and white: race, politics and the free coloreds in Jamaica, 1792-1865.
Gad J. Heuman. Westport, Connecticut: Greenwood Press, 1981. 231p. map. bibliog. (Contributions in Comparative Colonial Studies, no. 5).

The author examines the role of the free coloureds in Jamaican life under slavery and after emancipation, with particular reference to their struggle for full legal rights and their role in the factious politics of the Jamaican Assembly until it immolated itself in 1865. It is the second such study to treat this subject in detail, but unlike the earlier work, Mavis Campbell's *The dynamics of change in a slave society* (1976), Heuman presents a more favourable view of the free coloureds as a creole group displaying positive values and attitudes. The author is a lecturer in the Department of History and the School of Comparative American Studies at the University of Warwick, England.

156 Jamaica: a historical portrait.
Samuel J. Hurwitz, Edith F. Hurwitz. London: Pall Mall Press, 1971. 273p. bibliog.

'This is an account of Jamaica from its historical origins to the present day. An attempt has been made throughout to stress the factors that have contributed to the making of contemporary Jamaica. Although the broad framework is chronological, emphasis has been placed on the major themes of Jamaica's development'. (Preface, p. ix). The author spent a year as Visiting Fulbright Professor of History at the University of the West Indies, 1969-70, accompanied by his wife, the joint author.

157 A token of freedom: private bill legislation for free negroes in eighteenth-century Jamaica.
Samuel J. Hurwitz, Edith F. Hurwitz. *William and Mary Quarterly*, 3rd ser., vol. 24, no. 3 (July 1967), p. 423-31. bibliog.

An account of the historical factors which surrounded this legislation whereby free Negroes in Jamaica sought to acquire rights which were denied them because they were not born white.

158 Sixty years of change, 1806-1866: progress and reaction in Kingston and the countryside.
H. P. Jacobs. [Kingston]: Institute of Jamaica, 1973. 122p. map. (Cultural Heritage Series, vol. 2).

An interesting study, full of curious anecdotal information though rather inconclusive as a study of historical change and ideas. The object of the work, in the words of the author, is 'to show how classes and persons reacted to particular situations. Attention [is] paid to the personalities and backgrounds of governors, because... the Governor had a task of great delicacy'. (p.11). The author came to Jamaica in 1926 and has since been active as a teacher, journalist and commentator on public affairs. He is a past president of the Jamaican Historical Society and past editor of the *Jamaican Historical Review*.

History and Collective Biography. General and social

159 **A new history of Jamaica, from the earliest accounts, to the taking of Porto Bello by Vice-Admiral Vernon. In thirteen letters from a gentleman to his friend..**
[Charles Leslie]. London: J. Hodges, 1740. 340p. 2 fold. maps.

The first professed general history of Jamaica, written by a visiting Scot with some claim to objectivity. A somewhat shorter account comprising twelve letters, with a dedication to the Earl of Eglinton signed by the author, was published as *A new and exact account of Jamaica* (Edinburgh: R. Fleming, 1739. 358p.). This edition includes an additional letter, numbered 10, relating to Trelawny's governorship and Admiral Vernon's attack on Porto Bello. In addition to the political, social and natural history, letter 7 consists of an abstract of laws then in force. The map of Jamaica shows the location of towns, churches, plantations and plantation works.

160 **Jamaica and the new order: 1827-1847.**
Anton V. Long. Jamaica: Institute of Social and Economic Research, University College of the West Indies, 1956. 167p. bibliog. (Special Series, no. 1).

A perceptive study of the emergence of a new social order in the decades before and after emancipation. The work is based on a BLitt thesis accepted by the University of Oxford.

161 **The history of Jamaica: or, General survey of the antient and modern state of that island: with reflections on its situations, settlements, inhabitants, climate, products, commerce, laws and government.**
Edward Long, with a new introduction by George Metcalf. London: T. Lowndes, 1774. Reprinted, London: Frank Cass, 1970. new ed. 3 vols. maps. (Cass Library of West Indian Studies, no. 12).

The most celebrated and monumental history of Jamaica in respect of historical detail, literary style and partisan polemics. It is more than a history, it is a wide ranging compilation on the political, civil, economic, ecclesiastical and natural history of Jamaica. George Metcalf speaks of it as 'a book with many fascinations; it is a work of art, it is splendid source material for the historian, and lastly, it is a political tract...' (new introduction, p. 14). Volume three is essentially devoted to natural history. In addition to drawing heavily from the earlier work done in this field by Sloane and Browne, Long provides much additional information, hitherto unpublished, the source of which is obscure. At the end of volume three is a detailed list of the contents of the three volumes but the lack of an index is a disadvantage.

162 Jamaica española. (Spanish Jamaica.) Francisco Morales Padron, [introduction by] Vicente Rodríguez Casado. Seville, Spain: Escuela de Estudios Hispano-Americanos de Sevilla, 1952. 497p. 15 maps (incl. end-paper map). bibliog. (Publicaciones de la Escuela de Estudios Hispano-Americanos de Sevilla, Serie 2a, no. 67).

The only thorough history of Jamaica under Spanish rule, based very largely on source material in Spanish archival repositories.

163 Letters to Jane from Jamaica, 1788-1796. Edited by Geraldine Mozley. London: West India Committee for the Institute of Jamaica [193-?]. 157p.

Letters, or extracts of family letters, written to Jane Brodbelt, a schoolgirl in England, by members of her family in Jamaica. They are principally concerned with life in Spanish Town, where her father practised as a physician, and are of interest for the light they throw on social life at that time.

164 Lady Nugent's journal of her residence in Jamaica from 1801 to 1805. A new and revised edition by Philip Wright. Kingston: Institute of Jamaica, 1966. 331p. map.

This edition of the journal, which was privately printed in 1839 and first published in 1907, restores a few entries relating to Jamaica which had been omitted from earlier editions edited by Frank Cundall, and abridges those parts dealing with life in England. It is equipped with a well-informed and well-written introduction dealing with the principal historical concerns which form a background to the journal, and with a most interesting collection of illustrations. Lady Nugent's diary 'has been recognised as one of the most interesting of the contemporary accounts of colonial society in the West Indies,' and the American scholar Ragatz has described it as 'an utterly inimitable and imperishable picture of planter society.' (Introduction, p. xi).

165 Harry Morgan's way: the biography of Sir Henry Morgan, 1635-1684. Dudley Pope. London: Alison Press, Secker & Warburg, 1977. 379p. 3 maps. bibliog.

The author, a naval historian, having spent eleven years in the Caribbean cruising in the wake of the buccaneers, was prompted to write this book which he says 'answers most of the questions about Morgan and the buccaneers, although a few are beyond a positive answer' (p. xiv).

166 Sir Henry Morgan: buccaneer and governor. W. Adolphe Roberts. Kingston: Pioneer Press, 1952. 165p. West Indian ed.

A popular but authentic biography.

History and Collective Biography. General and social

167 'The notorious riot'. The socio-economic and political base of Paul Bogle's revolt.

Don Robotham. Kingston: Institute of Social and Economic Research, University of the West Indies, 1981. 95p. bibliog.

'This paper is an attempt to provide factual and interpretative support' for a view of the Morant Bay Rebellion and of Bogle's role in that event which, the writer states, is 'beginning to emerge in the scientific literature' and which is different from that of the historians. The works of Geoffrey Dutton and Douglas Hall are rejected in some detail. Scholarly historical literature is said to minimize Bogle's role which is not in keeping with the popular esteem in which he is held.

168 Jamaican blood and Victorian conscience: the Governor Eyre controversy.

Bernard Semmel. Boston, Massachusetts: Houghton Mifflin, 1963. Reprinted, Westport, Connecticut: Greenwood Press, 1976. 188p. bibliog.

First published in London under the title: *The Governor Eyre controversy*. An interesting account directed at the general reader. The Jamaica insurrection is examined in the light of conflicting ideas of imperialism and liberal democracy in the Victorian period.

169 Dictionary of place-names in Jamaica.

Inez Knibb Sibley. Kingston: Institute of Jamaica, 1978. 184p.

Includes names of towns, districts, properties, historic sites and even streets, often giving brief histories of properties and the families which owned them in the past. Illustrated with photographs. Compilations completed in 1972.

170 The western design: an account of Cromwell's expedition to the Caribbean.

S. A. G. Taylor. London: Solstice Productions, 1969. 2nd ed. 242p. 2 fold. maps.

First published in 1965 in Kingston by the Institute of Jamaica and the Jamaica Historical Society, this is a detailed account not only of the expedition, but of the five-year struggle of the English conquerors against the Spanish settlers in Jamaica. The author bases his account not only on the written and printed sources but on an extensive familiarity with and knowledge of, the terrain on which the battles and skirmishes took place. He uses knowledge of Jamaican topography and other local factors to interpret anew the historical sources of this account.

171 The tragedy of Morant Bay.

Edward B[ean] Underhill. London: Alexander & Shepheard, 1895. Reprinted, Freeport, New York: Books For Libraries Press, 1971. 219p.

A narrative of the events leading up to and during the disturbances known as the Morant Bay Rebellion. The author had previously visited Jamaica in 1859-60 and, as Honorary Secretary of the Baptist Missionary Society, received numerous reports on the social and economic conditions of Jamaica from Baptist missionaries closely connected with and sympathetic to the peasantry. The publication of this letter to the Secretary of State for the Colonies on conditions in Jamaica, known as the 'Underhill Letter', and the public and official reactions to it, are closely associated with the circumstances immediately preceding the outbreak.

172 **Monumental inscriptions of Jamaica.**
Compiled by Philip Wright. London: Society of Genealogists, 1966. 361p.

The most complete collection of its kind. Does not include inscriptions from Jewish burial grounds.

Twentieth century Jamaica.
See item no. 13.

The Negro in the New World.
See item no. 25.

The civil and natural history of Jamaica.
See item no. 101.

A voyage to the islands Madera, Barbados, Nieves, S. Christophers and Jamaica, with the natural history of the herbs and trees, four-footed beasts, fishes, birds, insects, reptiles, &c. of the last of those islands; to which is prefix'd an introduction, wherein is an account of the inhabitants, air, waters, diseases, trade, &c. of that place, with some relations concerning the neighbouring continent and islands of America. Illustrated with the figures of the things describ'd, which have not been heretofore engraved; in large copper-plates as big as the life.
See item no. 118.

The West Indian trade of an English furniture firm in the eighteenth century.
See item no. 598.

Tom Cringle's log.
See item no. 964.

Periodicals

173 **Jamaican Historical Review.**
Kingston: Jamaican Historical Society, June 1945- . irregular.

The official organ of the Jamaican Historical Society, it originally was published at about yearly intervals but later issues have been at longer intervals. Contributions are by professional as well as amateur historians and, at first, were principally concerned with topics relating to the history of Jamaica. From vol. 4 (1964) to vol. 7 (1967) editorial policy was to fashion the review into an academic journal of Caribbean history in its widest sense. Since vol. 8 (1971) this enlarged theme was abandoned and the journal reverted to its original purpose as a review of Jamaican history. The *Journal of Caribbean History* founded at about that time by the Department of History of the University of the West Indies has taken over the task of publishing historical articles of general Caribbean interest. The Society's mimeographed *Bulletin*, which appears quarterly, publishes articles of a less substantial nature.

History and Collective Biography. Slavery and the Maroons

174 **Jamaican Historical Society Bulletin.**
Kingston: Jamaican Historical Society, Aug. 1952- . quarterly.

The principal aim of the Bulletin is to stimulate and increase the interest and participation of members in the activities of the Society. In addition to accounts of lectures, notes on field trips and society activities, the Bulletin includes short articles on Jamaican historical subjects including much information not readily found in any other source.

Slavery and the Maroons

175 **Apprenticeship and emancipation.**
Kingston: Department of Extra-Mural Studies, University of the West Indies, Jamaica, [after 1977]. 67p.

Four essays (three of which relate to Jamaica) reprinted from out-of-print issues of *Caribbean Quarterly*, in order to make them easily available to students. The three relevant essays are authoritative works on aspects of labour in Jamaica during and after the apprenticeship period. They are: 'The apprenticeship system in Jamaica, 1834-1838' by D. G. Hall; 'Sir Charles Metcalfe' by D. G. Hall; and 'The free village system in Jamaica' by Hugh Paget.

176 **Emancipation and apprenticeship in the British West Indies.**
W. L. Burn.   London: Jonathan Cape, 1937. Reprinted, New York; London: Johnson Reprint Corporation, 1970. 398p. bibliog. (Reprints in Social and Economic History).

A thorough and detailed study of British governmental policy in the enactment and implementation of emancipation and apprenticeship, not only as it was conceived in Britain but as it was modified by the working of the system in Jamaica and the British West Indies. 'It was inevitable that much of this book should be devoted to Jamaica... A study of the Colonial Office Records shows that Jamaica affairs received an amount of close attention which was never given to those of the other West India colonies... Our reward is that in Jamaica the problems of apprenticeship were presented in their most acute form, the contrasts were the sharpest, the evidence the most complete.' (Preface, p. 10).

177 **A Jamaican plantation: the history of Worthy Park, 1670-1970.**
Michael Craton, James Walvin.   London: W. H. Allen, 1970. 344p. 14 maps. bibliog.

A tercentenary history of a Jamaican sugar estate, based mainly on the estate's records and on primary sources preserved in Jamaican and English repositories. In addition, it has a wider and more general interest for the history of slavery and of the sugar industry.

48

History and Collective Biography. Slavery and the Maroons

178 Jamaican slave mortality: fresh light from Worthy Park, Longville and the Tharp estates.
Michael Craton. *Journal of Caribbean History*, vol. 3 (Nov. 1971), p. 1-27. map.

On the basis of a comparative study of a select group of estate records the author concludes that 'considerable revision is called for in the accepted notions of plantation slavery in Jamaica, particularly in respect of the expectation of life among the slaves'. (p. 26).

179 Searching for the invisible man: slaves and plantation life in Jamaica.
Michael Craton, with the assistance of Garry Greenland. Cambridge, Massachusetts; London: Harvard University Press, 1978. 439p. 14 maps. bibliog.

The contents are: a prologue, 'Worthy Park and its context, 1670-1975'; part one, 'The slave population at large'; part two, 'Individuals in slave society, selected biographies; part three, 'The sons of slavery': appendixes; and notes (including bibliographical references), p. 401-439. The authors claim that ... its aim is to bring to the plantation slaves of the British Caribbean and their descendants something like the degree of visibility which similar studies have recently restored to the blacks of the United States' (p. xi). In this respect the book is most successful in part three, where the personal record, be it oral or written, exists, rather than in the earlier parts where the reconstruction depends largely upon the use of statistics and 'cliometric methods'. The enlarged illustrations of details from William Clark's *Ten views on the island of Antigua* and other illustrations of slavery and plantation life reveal aspects of the 'Invisible Man' which might otherwise have been overlooked.

180 The history of the Maroons from their origin to the establishment of their chief tribe at Sierra Leone including the expedition to Cuba for the purpose of procuring Spanish chasseurs and the state of the island of Jamaica for the last ten years with a succinct history of the island previous to that period.
R. C. Dallas. London: Longman & Rees, 1803. Reprinted, London: Frank Cass, 1968. 2 vols. 2 fold. maps (Cass Library of West Indian Studies, no. 5).

'The gentleman, to whom I have dedicated the work [i.e. William Dawes Quarrell] and who was indeed the friend that suggested it, is the chief source of my information; an authority that will have full weight when it is known that he served in the Maroon War; that he was the commissioner sent to Cuba for the Spanish chasseurs; and afterwards the commissary entrusted with the removal of the Maroons from Jamaica to Nova Scotia, where he remained some time with them.' (Preface, p. iv-v).

181 Slaves who abolished slavery.

Richard Hart. Jamaica: Institute of Social and Economic Research, University of the West Indies, 1980. 2 vols. (vol. 1 only published to date). bibliog.

Volume one is entitled 'Blacks in bondage' and volume two, 'Blacks in rebellion'. The author informs us in his preface that, as originally conceived, his work was to have consisted almost entirely of the subject of the second volume - the struggle of the slaves in Jamaica against their enslavement - but, subsequently, he wrote the more general study which constitutes volume one, to give background and place the subject of volume two in its context. The work was in gestation for thirty-five years. 'My initial interest in the subject... was unashamedly political. But the subject... is such an absorbing one that its pursuit develops in the researcher a momentum of its own.' (Preface, p. ii). The author is a founder member of the People's National Party of Jamaica and, since 1965, has practised as a solicitor in England. Includes some uncommon illustrations.

182 Slave population and economy in Jamaica, 1807-1834.

B. W. Higman. Cambridge, England: Cambridge University Press, 1976. 327p. 2 maps. bibliog.

This work attempts a factual and statistical analysis of the slave population and economy of Jamaica for the period between the abolition of the slave-trade and emancipation of slaves, based on contemporary systematic records, and it establishes relationships between demographic and economic changes. The core of this book is a PhD thesis in History presented to the University of the West Indies in 1970.

183 Slavery remembered: the celebration of emancipation in Jamaica.

B. W. Higman. *Journal of Caribbean History*, vol. 12 (1979), p. 55-73. bibliog.

The author traces the history of the anniversary of the abolition of slavery in Jamaica, 1 August, in order to study the place of slavery in post-emancipation social thought, and, in conclusion, notes the recent revival of the idea of slavery as an explanation for, or model of, modern West Indian society.

184 The Maroons of Jamaica: an ethnohistorical study of incomplete polities, 1655-1905.

Barbara Klaymon Kopytoff. PhD thesis, University of Pennsylvania, Philadelphia, Pennsylvania, 1973. 392 leaves. 2 maps. bibliog. (Available from University Microfilms, Ann Arbor, Michigan, 1975).

A study of the Jamaican Maroons which attempts to examine their political organization and institutions over a period of 250 years. The research was based on extensive documentary sources and on field-work visits to Maroon settlements in Jamaica in 1966-67.

185 Journal of a West India proprietor, 1815-17. M. G. Lewis, edited with an introduction by Mona Wilson. London: John Murray, 1834. Reprinted, London: George Routledge, 1929. 356p. (Broadway Diaries, Memoirs & Letters).

Lewis's journal, kept during a residence on his estates in Jamaica, is a lively account of the social life and customs of Blacks and Whites, as well as a reflection of the reaction of a sensitive mind to the brutalities of slavery and to the ownership of slaves. Coleridge thought it was 'by far his best work...' (cf. *Table Talk*, 20 March 1834).

186 A twelvemonth's residence in the West Indies, during the transition from slavery to apprenticeship: with incidental notices of the state of society, prospects and natural resources of Jamaica and other islands. R. R. Madden. Philadelphia, Pennsylvania: Carey, Lea & Blanchard, 1835. Reprinted, Westport, Connecticut: Negro Universities Press, 1970. 2 vols.

The author was one of six special magistrates sent out to supervise the transition from slavery to apprenticeship. During his stay in Jamaica, with which island his book is largely concerned, he resigned his position due to differences with the Jamaica House of Assembly and proceeded to America. His book is important for the light it sheds on the apprenticeship system and is also a mine of anecdotal information and observations on the social life and customs of the time. It is written in the form of letters.

187 The sociology of slavery: an analysis of the origins, development and structure of Negro slave society in Jamaica. H. Orlando Patterson. Great Britain: MacGibbon & Kee, 1967; Jamaica: reprinted for Sangster's Book Stores in association with Granada Publishing, 1973. 310p. 2 fold. maps. bibliog.

This work, a revised version of a doctoral thesis written at the London School of Economics in 1965, is of both sociological and historical interest. It covers a wide spectrum of social customs and institutions. The analyses are incisive, the conclusions are often bold and the presentation always forthright.

188 The fighting Maroons of Jamaica. Carey Robinson. [Kingston]: William Collins & Sangster (Jamaica), 1969. 160p. 6 maps. bibliog.

A well-written popular account.

189 **Remarks on the condition of the slaves in the island of Jamaica.**
William Sells. London: J. M. Richardson, 1823. Reprinted, Shannon, Ireland: Irish University Press, 1972. 50p.

A defence of the planters against the charges made by the Anti-Slavery Leaders in Britain. The author based his case on the knowledge gained during twenty years of medical practice in the parish of Clarendon, Jamaica, from 1803 to 1823. A pro-planter more than a pro-slavery view.

190 **Nanny - Maroon chieftainess.**
Alan Teulon. *Caribbean Quarterly*, vol. 19, no. 4 (Dec. 1973), p. 20-27.

An attempt to unravel some of the mystery surrounding Nanny, the latest declared National Hero of Jamaica, by an English surveyor who led an expedition to the site of Nanny Town in 1967 and later in 1973.

191 **Slaves and missionaries: the disintegration of Jamaican slave society, 1784-1834.**
Mary Turner. Urbana, Illinois: University of Illinois Press, 1982. 223p. map. bibliog. (Blacks in the New World).

A study of the role of the missionaries in the developments leading to the emancipation of the slaves in Jamaica. The author, a lecturer on the staff of Dalhousie University, Nova Scotia, has made considerable use of missionary archives, especially those of the Wesleyan Methodist Missionary Committee in London, as sources for this work.

192 **The Maroons of Jamaica.**
Joseph J. Williams. Chestnut Hill, Massachusetts: Boston College Press, 1938. 379-480p. bibliog. map. (Anthropological Series of the Boston College Graduate School, vol. 3, no. 4).

A study compiled largely from historical sources, with some contemporary investigation carried out by the author, a Jesuit priest who spent many years in Jamaica. Includes a concluding chapter on the Maroons of Moore Town, by I. E. Thompson.

193 **Knibb 'the notorious' slaves' missionary 1803-1845.**
Philip Wright. London: Sidgwick & Jackson, 1973. 264p. map. bibliog.

An account of the later anti-slavery struggle in Jamaica and England distilled from an engaging and sympathetic study of Knibb the polemicist and missionary, written with a fine command of language and subtle irony. The author, an Englishman, lived and worked in Jamaica from 1949 to 1961.

A descriptive account of the island of Jamaica: with remarks upon the cultivation of the sugar-cane, throughout the different seasons of the year, and chiefly considered in a picturesque point of view; also observations and reflections upon what would probably be the consequences of an

abolition of the slave-trade, and of the emancipation of the slaves.
See item no. 2.

A picturesque tour of the island of Jamaica, from drawings made in the years 1820 and 1821.
See item no. 19.

Jamaica: its past and present state.
See item no. 37.

A view of the past and present state of the island of Jamaica; with remarks on the moral and physical condition of the slaves, and on the abolition of slavery in the colonies.
See item no. 43.

The development of creole society in Jamaica, 1770-1820.
See item no. 136.

Slaves in red coats: the British West India regiments, 1795-1815.
See item no. 138.

The dynamics of change in a slave society: a sociopolitical history of the free coloreds of Jamaica, 1800-1865.
See item no. 139.

Sugar and slaves: the rise of the planter class in the English West Indies, 1624-1713.
See item no. 144.

British slave emancipation: the sugar colonies and the great experiment 1830-1865.
See item no. 151.

Marly; or, a planter's life in Jamaica.
See item no. 948.

Regions and cities

194 Port Royal: a history and guide.
Clinton V. Black. Jamaica: Bolivar Press, 1970. 87p. end-paper maps.
A reliable guide for the general reader.

195 Spanish Town: the old capital.
Clinton V. Black. Spanish Town, Jamaica: Parish Council of St. Catherine, 1974. 2nd ed. 78p. end-paper maps.
A concise account of the town's history and historic buildings, excellently illustrated with photographs, for the general reader and the tourist. This second edition incorporates new historical information not included in the first edition which was published in 1960.

196 **A short history of Portland.**
Beryl M. Brown. Kingston: Ministry of Education, Publications Branch, 1976. 47p. 3 maps.

Pitched at a juvenile level, this nevertheless contains much useful information not readily available otherwise. A simple, clear narrative, well illustrated by photographs and drawings by Meryl McCallum.

197 **The fortifications of Kingston 1655-1914.**
David Buisseret, illustrated with line drawings by Susan Judah. Jamaica: Bolivar Press, 1971. 51p. bibliog.

This work is based on a series of articles contributed to the *Bulletin* of the Jamaica Historical Society, vol. 4 (1965-68), where full bibliographical citations may be found. It is the only work on the subject published in this century and was published as a limited edition of 500 copies signed by the author and the illustrator.

198 **A popular history of the port of Kingston.**
David Buisseret. [Kingston]: Shipping Association of Jamaica, [1972]. 30p. 6 maps.

Thirty plates comprising aerial, 19th-century and more recent photographs, and plans both old and new, with brief historical text for each plate. A revised edition (35p.) was issued in August 1976.

199 **Kingston: a hundred years a capital, 1872-1972.**
Thomas L. Graham. [Jamaica: published by the author (?), 1972?]. 158p.

A volume of textual and pictorial material intended to mark the centenary of Kingston. Includes, *inter alia*, historical information as well as information on current developments, buildings, institutions and services.

200 **A full account of the late dreadful earthquake at Port Royal in Jamaica; written in two letters from the minister of that place. From a/board the *Granada* in Port Royal harbour, June 22, 1692.**
[Rev. E. Heath]. London: Printed for Jacob Tonson, sold by R. Baldwyn, 1692. 2p.

The second letter is dated 28 June 1692. A vivid contemporary account of the first of two extremely destructive earthquakes in Jamaica's history. The destruction of Port Royal led to the rise of Kingston as the principal port and seat of trade.

201 **A short history of Kingston.**
H. P. Jacobs. Kingston: Ministry of Education, Publications Branch, 1976. vol. 1 only. 72p. bibliog.

Part 1, 1692-1871, only, published to date. For juveniles. Informative.

54

202 **Historic Saint Thomas: a list of the monuments in St. Thomas protected by the Jamaica National Trust Commission.**

Jamaica National Trust Commission. [Kingston]: Jamaica National Trust Commission, 1978. 20p. maps.

Contains brief descriptions, with illustrations, of monuments arranged under the following headings: sites of historical significance; industrial remains; military and naval installations; churches and burial grounds; public buildings; and domestic structures.

203 **Port Royal, Jamaica.**

Michael Pawson, David Buisseret. Oxford, England: Clarendon Press, 1975. 204p. 12 maps. bibliog.

A reconstruction of the history and topography of the town, drawing on all the available evidence from various sources - manuscript, printed and archaeological.

204 **The capitals of Jamaica: Spanish Town, Kingston, Port Royal.**

Edited by W. Adolphe Roberts. Kingston: Pioneer Press, 1955. 112p.

A collection of historical articles by local historians. The contents include a preface; 'Our unique city' by W. Adolphe Roberts; 'Spanish Town' by Sybil Williams; 'Port Royal' by S. A. G. Taylor; 'The founding of Kingston' by J. G. Young; 'Kingston in the 18th century' by Clinton V. Black; 'Kingston in the 19th century' by F. L. Casserly; 'From 1901 to the earthquake' by E. V. Clarke; and 'From the earthquake to 1944' by H. P. Jacobs.

205 **In old St. James (Jamaica): a book of parish chronicles containing the story of the Jamaica ancestry of Mrs Barrett Browning; the true tale of Rose Hall; what an estate slave-book tells, etc.**

Compiled by Joseph Shore, edited by John Stewart. London: Bodley Head, 1952. new ed. 118p.

First published 1911, the work is based on information culled from old records. A particular interest of the work is that Shore's account of the identity of the Mrs Palmer of the Rose Hall legend became the basis for H. G. DeLisser's popular novel *The white witch of Rose Hall*, first published in 1929.

206 **A short history of Clarendon.**

S. A. G. Taylor. Kingston: Ministry of Education, Publications Branch, 1976. 50p. 8 maps (incl. 2 on end-papers).

For juveniles. Clear, simple and informative text. Illustrated by Meryl McCallum.

207 Early Kingston.
Wilma Williams. *Jamaica Journal*, vol. 5, nos. 2-3 (June-Sept. 1971), p. 3-9.

An historical and geographical study of the growth of Kingston from 1692-1838.

Collective biography

208 Nanny, Sam Sharpe and the struggle for people's liberation.
Edward Kamau Brathwaite. Kingston: Agency for Public Information for the National Heritage Week Committee, 1977. 64p. bibliog. Cover title: *Wars of respect, Nanny and Sam Sharpe.*

Contents include: 'Jamaican history and the national heroes'; 'Nanny and Sam Sharpe as historical figures'; 'Maronage'; 'The nature and basis of Maroon resistance'; 'Nanny'; 'Nanny as National Hero'; 'Slave rebellions'; 'The Black churches'; 'The rebellion'; and 'Sam Sharpe as National Hero'.

209 National heroes, honours and awards.
[Edited by] Hazel D. Campbell. Kingston: Agency for Public Information, 1974. 52p. bibliog.

Contains short biographical sketches on the national heroes, a description of the national honours and awards and their insignia and a list of those honoured 1970-73.

210 The governors of Jamaica in the seventeenth century.
Frank Cundall. London: West India Committee, 1936. 177p. 2 maps.

A collection of biographical sketches of the first fifteen governors of Jamaica, with portraits of as many as could be found.

211 The governors of Jamaica in the first half of the eighteenth century.
Frank Cundall. London: West India Committee, 1937. 229p.

These thirteen short biographies continue the account of the British imperial presence in Jamaica as reflected in its gubernatorial history. This, together with the earlier volume on the 17th century, provides the most comprehensive coverage of this aspect of Jamaican history.

212 **The Jamaica directory of personalities 1981-82.**
[Edited by] Roy Dickson. Kingston: Gleaner Co., 1982.
386p. map.

A biographical dictionary of persons prominent in various fields of activity such
as government, business, the professions, religion, sport, culture and social
services, largely compiled from information supplied in response to questionnaires
by the persons invited. Some of the biographical entries are illustrated with
portrait photographs.

213 **Women of distinction in Jamaica: a record of career women
in Jamaica, their background, service and achievements.**
Compiled and edited by Henry A. Guy, Lavern
Bailey. Kingston: Caribbean Herald, 1977. 164p.

The only compilation on this subject. Includes many portrait photographs.

214 **Personalities Caribbean: the international guide to who's who
in the West Indies, Bahamas, Bermuda.**
Founder editor-in-chief and managing director 1963-75
Owen Lancelot Levy, editor-in-chief and managing director
1975- Anthony Lancelot Levy. Kingston: Personalities,
1977. 6th ed. 1,064p.

The announced intention of the publishers was that the work should be revised
every two years. It embraces the countries stretching from Bermuda to Surinam
with a distinct section devoted to each. In addition to the biographies (some with
portrait photographs) each section is furnished with a classified list of biographies
by avocation or profession and a classified list of selected advertisers. The coverage is selective but embraces a fairly wide spectrum of interests and gives
evidence of being compiled with the co-operation of a number of institutions,
groups and persons with official connections as well as those acting in a purely
private capacity. The section on Jamaica comprises p. 225-515.

215 **A small corner of the Jamaican tapestry.**
Sydney E. Patterson. [Montego Bay, Jamaica]: the author,
1972. 64p.

Mini-biographies of 31 Jamaicans, some well-known others less so, illustrative of
the wide spectrum of ethnic types and avocations represented in their compatriots
- 'stable, worthy citizens, quietly helping to build their small nation.' Portrait
photographs are by Brook Cuddy of Montego Bay.

216 **Six great Jamaicans: biographical sketches.**
W. Adolphe Roberts. Kingston: Pioneer Press, 1951. 122p.

The biographies include: Edward Jordan; George William Gordon; Enos Nuttall;
Robert Love; Thomas Henry MacDermot; and Herbert George DeLisser. This
selection includes native-born as well as those not born in Jamaica but who were
identified with it through length of service given in the country. 'The six have not
been chosen haphazardly. Considered together their lives exemplify the chief
trends in Jamaican history for a century and a quarter, from the fight for the
abolition of slavery to the eve of the... self-government movement.' (Foreword,
p.2).

56

Population and Fertility

General

217 **Sex, contraception, and motherhood in Jamaica.**
Eugene B. Brody. Cambridge, Massachusetts: Harvard University Press, 1981. 278p. bibliog. (A Commonwealth Fund Book).

A study of how Jamaicans feel, think and act about sexual intercourse, childbearing and child-rearing and how these affect their attitudes to and use of contraception. The research for this book was carried out with the support of the Smithsonian Institution's Interdisciplinary Communications Project, which funded the Jamaican interviewers and with that of the Jamaican Government's National Family Planning Board, the Jamaica Family Planning Association and the University of the West Indies, the latter two organizations having recruited the interviewers.

218 **Preliminary analysis of population growth and social characteristics in Jamaica, 1943-60.**
George E. Cumper. Jamaica: Census Research Programme, Institute of Social and Economic Research, University of the West Indies, [1963]. 39p.

This is a first attempt to interpret such of the 1960 census data for Jamaica as had been published in early 1963, for the use of persons interested in the social sciences but without training in demography.

219 The people of modern Jamaica.
O. C. Francis. Jamaica: Department of Statistics, 1963. 1 vol. (variously paged). bibliog.

A summary of and commentary on the main results of the 1960 census, for the use of individuals and groups who would not resort to the extensive tabulations and reports on the census, by the Director of Statistics and Census Officer for Jamaica.

220 Population dynamics and prospects: a 1981 assessment for Jamaica.
Tomas Frejka. New York: Population Council, June 1981. 52p. bibliog. (Population Council. Center For Policy Studies. Working Paper, 74).

This paper discusses mortality, fertility and population growth prospects. It was prepared by an Associate of the Center for Policy Studies as a background document for the Jamaica Population Policy Development Conference organized by the Population Policy Task Force, Ministry of Health, in collaboration with the National Family Planning Board, Kingston, Jamaica, 18-19 June 1981.

221 The Jamaican censuses of 1844 and 1861: a new edition, derived from the manuscript and printed schedules in the Jamaica Archives.
Edited with an introduction by B. W. Higman. Mona, Jamaica: Social History Project, Department of History, University of the West Indies, 1980. 58p. map.

More data which have recently come to light are reproduced herein. The new data provide important material for a more detailed picture of post-emancipation Jamaica than had previously been available. The Jamaican population censuses are basic documents for the study of the country's social history.

222 Jamaica population census 1970 classified by constituencies and type of household (preliminary data).
Jamaica. Department of Statistics, Division of Censuses and Surveys. Kingston: Department of Statistics, 1971. [4]p. (Commonwealth Caribbean Population Census 1970).

A tabulation of preliminary information on population in fifty-three constituencies, prior to the final and more detailed reports becoming available, classified mainly by sex and by a distinction between private and non-private households.

223 Jamaica population census 1970: preliminary report.
Jamaica. Department of Statistics, Division of Censuses and Surveys. Kingston: Department of Statistics, 1970. 32p. 5 maps. (Commonwealth Caribbean Population Census 1970).

Preliminary estimates of the count of population in Jamaica in April 1970, tabulated by parish and selected towns and an estimate of the number of dwellings enumerated by parish. Maps and descriptions of five selected towns are included.

224 Jamaica fertility survey 1975/76: country report.
Kingston: Department of Statistics, 1979. 2 vols.

A survey conducted as part of the World Fertility Survey Programme, designed to meet Jamaica's needs for fertility data as well as to provide data comparable with other countries participating in the WFS. Volume one contains chapters on the background, organization, conduct and substantive findings of the survey; also, some tables and appendices, including a glossary in English, Spanish and French. Volume two contains statistical tables.

225 Base research document: submission to Population Policy Task Force.
Population Policy Research Officer. Kingston: Planning and Evaluation Unit, Ministry of Health, Jamaica, June 1981. 1 vol. (variously paged) 9 maps. bibliog.

Written by the Population Policy Research Officer, 'The purpose of the study was to identify and assess the Jamaican demographic situation in context of history, policies affecting population and linkages to social institutions, economic activities and the national environment. Further, to outline consequences of the population trends. The study in this way, contains information from which policies can be developed.' (Introduction, p. 2). A useful compilation, with the sources of data indicated after each table or diagram with which the work is amply furnished. The wide range of social and economic data reflect an holistic approach to demographic study and all are related to the demographic situation.

226 Contraceptive use in Jamaica: the social, economic and cultural context.
Dorian Powell, Linda Hewitt, Prudence Woo Ming. Mona, Jamaica: Institute of Social and Economic Research, University of the West Indies, 1978. 88p. bibliog. (University of the West Indies. Institute of Social and Economic Research. Working Paper, no. 19).

This study is intended to provide a reliable basis for family planning policy and programmes and some understanding of 'the sociological dynamics of fertility and contraceptive behaviour.'.

227 The population of Jamaica.
George W. Roberts, with an introduction by Kingsley Davis. Cambridge, England: Cambridge University Press for the Conservation Foundation, 1957. 356p. map. bibliog.

A thorough demographic analysis of Jamaica based on censuses up to 1943 and on records of fertility and mortality kept by the Registrar General up to 1952. The author, until recently Professor of Demography at the University of the West Indies, delineates the historic growth of the population, describes its major characteristics, quantifies and assesses the currents of external and internal migration, analyses patterns of mortality and fertility and indicates the prospects of population growth.

228 **Recent population movements in Jamaica.**
G[eorge] W. Roberts (and others). Paris: Comité
International de Coordination des Recherches Nationales en
Démographie, 1974. 189p. (CICRED Series).

This is intended to supplement G. W. Roberts' *The population of Jamaica*
(1957), basing itself on the censuses of 1960 and 1970.

229 **Population trends and housing needs.**
P. Simms. [Kingston]: Department of Statistics, Jamaica,
1974. 43p.

A brief study of the basic demographic characteristics of the population of
Jamaica, relating them to the housing situation and evaluating housing needs in
Jamaica. It is based on data from the 1960 and 1970 population censuses and the
information is presented on a parish-by-parish basis. The treatment is cursory and
the work is intended as background for more detailed studies. This review was
prepared by a statistician on contract to the Government of Jamaica and assigned
to the Department of Statistics.

230 **Population and vital statistics, Jamaica, 1832-1964: a
historical perspective.**
Kalman Tekse. [Kingston]: Department of Statistics, 1974.
340p. bibliog.

Chiefly tables, bringing together data on population censuses from 1844 to 1960
and on vital events from 1879 to 1964. The United Nations Technical Assistance
Programme assigned the author to work in Jamaica for a period in 1967-68 as
UN Operational Expert in Demography. The partial contents include Dexter L.
Rose's 'History of census taking in Jamaica' (p. 289-94) and E. V. G. Wilks 'The
history and mechanics of registration in Jamaica' (p. 295-303).

231 **A study of fertility in Jamaica.**
Kalman Tekse. Jamaica: Department of Statistics,
Demography and Vital Statistics Section, 1968. 27p. bibliog.

A study based on data from population censuses and sample surveys, supplementary to work done by George W. Roberts and by others, such as Back and
Stycos, of a decade before. The author is a United Nations demographic expert.

232 **The English-speaking Caribbean.**
United Nations Fund for Population Activities. New York:
United Nations Fund for Population Activities, 1978. 45p.
(Population Profiles, no. 10).

An outline of national family planning programmes in Jamaica (p. 1-18) and
other countries of the region.

233 **Economic development and population control: a fifty year projection for Jamaica.**
B. Thomas Walsh. New York: Praeger, 1971. 134p. bibliog. (Praeger Special Studies in International Economics and Development).

The objective of this study was to gather and analyse support for the thesis that economic growth in a developing country can be substantially increased and accelerated by reductions in fertility rates, and thereby has a direct bearing on national policies with regard to population growth. The author was Associate Professor of Demography at the Graduate School of Public Health, University of Pittsburgh.

The effects of the population explosion on Jamaica's international relations.
See item no. 243.

Internal migration in Jamaica.
See item no. 253.

Women in Jamaica: patterns of reproduction and family.
See item no. 367.

Periodicals

234 **Demographic Statistics.**
Kingston: Department of Statistics, 1972 - . annual.

Begun in 1970 as a quarterly, the frequency changed to annual since the issue for 1972. Statistical tables for vital registration, international migration and related statistics of divorces and family planning are included.

Migration, Nationalities and Minorities

Migration

235 **The Colonial Land and Emigration Commission and immigration to Jamaica, 1840-1860.**
George Brizan. *Caribbean Quarterly*, vol. 20, no. 3 & 4 (Sept.-Dec. 1974), p. 39-58. bibliog.

An outline of British government policy on immigration as a means of solving labour shortages in Jamaica.

236 **Caribbean immigration to the United States.**
Edited by Roy S. Bryce-Laporte, Delores M. Mortimer. Washington, DC: Research Institute on Immigration and Ethnic Studies, Smithsonian Institution, 1976. 257p. bibliog. (RIIES Occasional Papers, no. 1).

A collection of studies, in the majority prepared by scholars of Caribbean ancestry, which focuses on the characteristics and patterns of Caribbean migration to the United States since the 1965 Immigration and Nationality Act. In the view of the Research Institute, the new immigration represents the newest extension of the continued historical process of the peopling of the United States.

237 Emigration of high-level manpower and national development: a case study of Jamaica.

Jay Ralph Buffenmeyer. PhD thesis, University of Pittsburgh, Pennsylvania, 1970. 232p. bibliog.

Part one of this study is designed to establish an analytical framework to evaluate the impact of emigration of high-level manpower on development efforts of less developed countries. Part two, which constitutes the greater part of this work, is a Jamaican case study with chapters as follows: 'Development of an independent Jamaica'; 'General migrations'; 'Migration of Jamaican high-level manpower'; 'Emigration of university graduates'; 'Transfer of educational inputs'; 'Effects of emigration on Jamaica's development inputs'; 'Special aspects of the impact'; 'Summary and conclusions'; and appendices.

238 The Chinese in Latin America: a preliminary geographical survey with special reference to Cuba and Jamaica.

Ching Chieh Chang. PhD thesis, University of Maryland, 1956. 167 leaves. 14 maps. bibliog. (Available from University Microfilms, Ann Arbor, Michigan, [1956?]).

The approach of this study is systematic rather than regional and hence much of the information relating to the Chinese in Jamaica is incorporated with that of the rest of Latin America. It concerns the historical, demographic, economic and social aspects of Chinese immigration. The author is a Chinese scholar who spent about six weeks in Jamaica in 1953 conducting interviews and library research on his topic.

239 Jamaican migrant.

Wallace Collins. London: Routledge & Kegan Paul, 1965. 122p.

An unusual autobiography, written with clarity and perception, giving an account of the life of a Jamaican artisan (cabinet-maker), from his boyhood through early manhood in Jamaica to migration to Britain and of his experience there from 1954 to 1962, after which he migrated to Canada. A human account of the maturing of a Jamaican in his homeland and as a migrant in an alien milieu.

240 Black British: immigrants to England.

R. B. Davison. London: Oxford University Press for the Institute of Race Relations, 1966. 170p.

Although this survey embraces all black Commonwealth immigrants, it focuses primarily on Jamaicans, having started with a random sample from interviews with prospective Jamaican migrants at the Kingston Passport Office which were later followed up after arrival of the immigrants in London. These data were further amplified by details extracted from the census records of seven London boroughs which showed the largest proportion of Jamaicans in the borough population. The final chapter, 'Flight to disenchantment', is written as a series of individual case studies by Mrs Betty Davison (the project secretary) and is based upon tape-recorded interviews taken in the London homes of people she first met in the Kingston Passport Office.

241 **Caribbean migration: contract labour in US agriculture.**
Joseph DeWind, Tom Seidl, Janet Shenk, NACLA-East
Labor Migration Project. *NACLA Report on the Americas*,
vol. 11, no. 8 (Nov.-Dec. 1977), p. 1-37. bibliog.

An examination by participants in the North American Congress on Latin
America (NACLA), of the role of West Indians (primarily Jamaicans and, to a
lesser extent St. Lucians and Kittitians) in harvesting Florida's sugar-cane and in
the apple orchards of the eastern seaboard, the conditions under which they work,
and the effect of their employment on domestic workers in the United States. The
report concludes that the contract programme denies foreign workers their legal
and trade-union rights while depressing the wages and working conditions of
domestic workers.

242 **Jamaica farewell: Jamaican migrants in London.**
Nancy Foner. Berkeley, Los Angeles: University of
California Press, 1978. 262p. bibliog.

Although written as an academic analysis, the lucid style and informative nature
of this work also commend it to a wider readership. As a study in migration it
looks at how various types of status change - as characterized by colour, sex,
occupation, class, age and education - affect the lives of Jamaican migrants in
London, and how the migrants' perceptions of their social position are rooted in
the social, economic and political realities of Jamaican life. It is based not just on
research into the experiences of migrants in London but on field-work in rural
Jamaica for fifteen months in 1968-69.

243 **The effects of the population explosion on Jamaica's
international relations.**
Irene Green. Johannesburg: South African Institute of
International Affairs, University of Witwatersrand, 1966.
85p. bibliog.

This very summary treatment is of interest for its focus on the effects of Jamaican migration on Jamaica's relations with a number of host countries - the
United Kingdom, the United States and Canada. It was written as a thesis for a
first degree in international relations at the University of Witwatersrand.

244 **Jamaican letters from nineteenth-century Australia.**
[Edited by Barry Higman]. Mona, Jamaica: Caldwell Press,
1975. 19p.

Reproduces extracts from five letters which appeared originally in the Jamaican
press, written by emigrants from Jamaica to Australia, following the discovery of
gold in Eastern Australia in 1851. A slender work dealing with a little-studied
aspect of Jamaican emigration.

245 **Jamaican Blacks and their descendants in Costa Rica.**
Charles W. Koch. *Social and Economic Studies*, vol. 26,
no. 3 (Sept. 1977), p. 339-61. bibliog.

A contribution to a neglected field of study by an Assistant Professor of Geography, University of Nebraska at Omaha, United States of America. He reviews
the settlement of Jamaicans in Costa Rica, beginning in 1871, with particular

Migration, Nationalities and Minorities. Migration

reference to employment practices there, the political influence of Blacks and the maintenance of separate Black culture.

246 'Going foreign' - causes of Jamaican migration.
Joanne Koslofsky. *NACLA Report on the Americas*, vol. 15, no. 1 (Jan.-Feb. 1981), p. 1-31. 2 maps. bibliog.

The writer traces the phenomenon of Jamaican migration since the mid-19th century up to the present time, representing the fundamental causes which give rise to this migration as the introduction and expansion of capitalist development, particularly as directed by the transnational corporations and, in the case of the most recent exodus of persons from the managerial and professional ranks, the trials experienced under the attempt of the People's National Party government to introduce democratic socialism into Jamaica. Those trials are attributed 'to international capital's low tolerance for reforms, particularly in underdeveloped countries where they have tended to breed demands for even more radical social change.' The North American Congress on Latin America (NACLA), founded in 1966, is a non-profit organization focusing on the political economy of the Americas, and its journal appears bimonthly.

247 Population movements in the Caribbean.
Malcolm J. Proudfoot. Port-of-Spain, Trinidad: Caribbean Commission, 1950. Reprinted, New York: Negro Universities Press, 1970. 187p. bibliog.

Although this is a comparative study, the generalizations made are based largely on data for Puerto Rico and Jamaica, which were the only two countries where considerable work on the subject had been done. The study was done for the Caribbean Commission by the author, a Professor of Geography at Northwestern University, Evanston, Illinois.

248 Endless pressure: a study of West Indian life-styles in Bristol.
Ken Pryce. Harmondsworth, England: Penguin Books, 1979. 297p. bibliog.

This is an attempt to depict life-styles based on real-life situations and experiences rather than from the viewpoint of academic theories of race relations. The community studied is made up almost entirely of Jamaicans, mainly from the parish of St. Thomas, and reflects the life-styles of a wide spectrum of citizens which the author classifies as belonging to two main categories - workers and 'hustlers'. The work reflects some of the the social problems of Jamaica in a metropolitan context. It is based on data and research conducted in Bristol between 1969 and 1974. The author is a Lecturer in Sociology at the University of the West Indies, Trinidad.

249 Study of external migration affecting Jamaica; 1953-55.
G[eorge] W. Roberts, D. O. Mills. [Kingston]: Institute of Social and Economic Research, University College of the West Indies, Jamaica, 1958. 126, xvip. bibliog. (*Social and Economic Studies*, supplement to vol. 7, no. 2).

An authoritative study of one of the peak periods of migration from Jamaica to the United Kingdom, undertaken at the request of the Government of Jamaica, with a view to providing some indication of the magnitude and composition of that migratory movement and of its possible effects on Jamaica's labour force. It is based principally on the migration records of the Jamaican Immigration Department. In the Foreword by the then Chief Minister, N. W. Manley, it is referred to as a companion study to one on the same subject undertaken by Clarence Senior and Manley (i.e. Douglas Manley) in England in 1955.

250 Black Britain's dilemma: a medico-social transcultural study of West Indians.
John Royer. Roseau, Dominica: Tropical Printers, 1977. 399p. bibliog. vol. 1 only published to date.

An interestingly written and carefully researched study of Blacks in Britain, relating migration and its attendant problems to studies of West Indian culture, mental health and criminality. It covers a wide range of interests and contains a great deal of information. The text is marred by an excessive number of misprints and by amateurish typography. It is difficult to consult until the index is published in volume two, to come. The author is a psychiatrist resident in Jamaica.

251 'Alas, Alas, Kongo'. A social history of indentured African immigration into Jamaica, 1841-1865.
Monica Schuler. Baltimore, Maryland; London: Johns Hopkins University Press, 1980. 186p. 3 maps. bibliog. (Johns Hopkins Studies in Atlantic History and Culture).

This is not only a contribution to the study of migration but also to that of African cultural survivals in Jamaica, based in part on contemporary oral sources. The work had its origins in a PhD dissertation at the University of Wisconsin-Madison.

252 A report on Jamaican migration to Britain.
Clarence Senior, Douglas Manley. Kingston: printed by the Government Printer, 1955. 67p. bibliog.

The report of a fact-finding mission, sponsored by the Government of Jamaica and led by the Head of the Migrant Services in New York of the Puerto Rican Government, on the Jamaican emigration experience in the United Kindom, with recommendations on services to assist the migrants in adjusting after arrival. The Honourable Norman Manley, Chief Minister of Jamaica, writes a foreword.

253 Internal migration in Jamaica.
Kalman Tekse. Jamaica: Department of Statistics, Demography and Vital Statistics Section, 1967. 42p. 7 maps. bibliog.

A preliminary study of migration from rural areas to the towns, comprising estimates of migration between parishes, sex and age differences of migrants, factors such as unemployment which affect migration and indicating problems for further research. Includes 23 statistical tables.

Migration, Nationalities and Minorities. Nationalities and minorities

254 **Jamaica and voluntary laborers from Africa, 1840-1865.**
Mary Elizabeth Thomas. Gainesville, Florida: University Presses of Florida, 1974. 211p. 2 maps. bibliog.

A detailed study of the administrative and governmental efforts to secure voluntary immigrants from Africa to meet the shortage of plantation labour in Jamaica, after the emancipation of the slaves. Based on official publications and on colonial records in British and Jamaican archives.

Ethnicity in the Americas.
See item no. 260.

The United States and West Indian unrest, 1918-1939.
See item no. 495.

Canada-West Indies economic relations.
See item no. 503.

Nationalities and minorities

255 **They came from the Middle East.**
Nellie Ammar. *Jamaica Journal*, vol. 4, no. 1 (March 1970), p. 2-6.

A descendant of Lebanese origin writes of early Lebanese immigration to Jamaica from her conversations with some of the earliest immigrants.

256 **A record of the Jews in Jamaica from the English conquest to the present time.**
Jacob A. P. M. Andrade, [edited by Basil Parks]. Kingston: Jamaica Times, 1941. 282p. 2 maps.

Embodies information collected over seventeen years and drawn from various sources - the printed books and manuscripts in the Institute of Jamaica, the records of the Island Record Office, newspapers, interviews and correspondence with many persons. The lack of an index makes this valuable compilation difficult to use.

257 **Emigrés, conflict and reconciliation. The French émigrés in nineteenth century Jamaica.**
Patrick Bryan. *Jamaica Journal*, vol. 7, no. 3 (Sept. 1973), p. 13-19. bibliog.

An historical study of the integration into Jamaican society of the French émigrés and their slaves from Saint Domingue following the outbreak of revolution in that colony. The author is a Lecturer in History at the University of the West Indies, Jamaica.

258 **East Indian cane workers in Jamaica.**
Allen S. Ehrlich. PhD thesis, University of Michigan, 1969. 247 leaves. bibliog. (Available from University Microfilms, Ann Arbor, Michigan, 1972).

An anthropological study based on the sugar labouring population of a village in the parish of Westmoreland, Jamaica. The author focuses on interpersonal relationships between Indians and those of African origin, the measure of social and cultural differentiation of the Indian population and the measure of their identification with the political parties and organs of government. It helps to fill a gap in a neglected area of ethnographic study.

259 **Bountied European immigration into Jamaica with special reference to the German settlement at Seaford Town up to 1850.**
Douglas Hall. *Jamaica Journal*, vol. 8, no. 4 (Dec. 1974), p. 48-54; vol. 9, no. 1 (March 1975), p. 2-9. bibliog.

An historical account by the former Professor of History, University of the West Indies, Jamaica.

260 **Ethnicity in the Americas.**
[Edited by] Frances Henry. The Hague, Paris: Mouton, 1976. 456p. bibliog. (World Anthropology).

Contributions to the IXth International Congress of Anthropological and Ethnological Sciences, including the following which relate, in whole, or in part, to Jamaica: 'The social adjustment of returned migrants to Jamaica', by Edward Taylor (p. 213-29); 'Remnants of all nations: Rastafarian attitudes to race and nationality', by C. D. Yawney (p. 231-62); 'The repairer of the breach: Reverend Claudius Henry and Jamaican society', by A. Barrington Chevannes (p. 263-89); 'West Indian radicalism in America: an assessment of ideologies', by Dennis Forsythe (p. 301-32); and 'Some comments on race and ethnicity in the Caribbean', by Coleman Romalis (p. 417-27). The last article includes a commentary on the first three articles mentioned, being studies by sociologists on sub-cultures and minority groups in Jamaica. Forsyth's contribution relates substantially to the ideological role of migrants such as W. A. Domingo, David Grange, Claude McKay and Marcus Garvey, all Jamaicans, as well as other West Indians. Includes biographical notes.

261 **The New World sets an example for the Old: the Jews of Jamaica and political rights, 1661-1831.**
Samuel J. Hurwitz, Edith F. Hurwitz. *American Jewish Historical Quarterly*, vol. 55, no. 1 (Sept. 1965), p. 37-56. bibliog.

An historical account of the process whereby the Jews were granted full rights of citizenship in Jamaica in 1831. The author was Professor of History at the Brooklyn College of the City University of New York and spent the year 1963-64 as Fulbright Visiting Professor at the University of the West Indies. Mrs Hurwitz was also a teacher and was engaged in historical research.

Migration, Nationalities and Minorities. Nationalities and minorities

262 **The Chinese in Jamaica.**
[Edited by] Lee Tom Yin. Kingston: Chung San News, 1963. rev. ed. 55, 260p.

Text in English and Chinese. The first part is a compilation in English of information primarily on Chinese societies and institutions in Jamaica. The greater part of the work, which is in Chinese, consists of biographical information on the Chinese in Jamaica.

263 **Adjustment patterns among the Jamaican Chinese.**
Andrew W. Lind. *Social and Economic Studies*, vol. 7, no. 2 (June 1958), p. 144-64. bibliog.

Provides historical and other information on a sparsely documented ethnic group in Jamaica. The work was undertaken during a seven-month period in 1955 when the writer was on leave of absence from his regular responsibilities as a sociologist and student of race relations at the University of Hawaii.

264 **East India (Indentured Labour): report to the Government of India on the conditions of Indian immigrants in four British colonies and Surinam. Part II - Surinam, Jamaica, Fiji and general remarks.**
James McNeill, Chimman Lal. London: HM Stationery Office, 1915. 151-334p. (Command Papers, Cd. 7745).

A basic document on the social conditions of Indian immigrants after the turn of this century. Pages 201-43 are devoted to Jamaica.

265 **Indian heritage in Jamaica.**
Lakshmi Mansingh, Ajai Mansingh. *Jamaica Journal*, vol. 10, nos. 2-4 (Dec. 1976), p. 10-19. bibliog.

A review of Indian cultural survivals, set in the historical context of the migration of Indian indentured labour to Jamaica in the 19th century, illustrated with several photographs. The authors are both Indians on the staff of the University of the West Indies and are actively promoting the revival and propagation of Indian culture in Jamaica.

266 **The Jews of Jamaica: a historical view.**
Benjamin Schlesinger. *Caribbean Quarterly*, vol. 13, no. 1 (March 1967), p. 46-53. bibliog.

A brief, readable account by the author when he was Visiting Professor of Social Work at the University of the West Indies.

267 **Spanish & Portuguese Jews of Jamaica.**
Rosemarie DePass Scott. *Jamaica Journal*, no. 43 (March 1979), p. 90-100. bibliog.

A concise historical account.

268 **German immigrants in Jamaica 1834-8.**
Carl H. Senior. *Journal of Caribbean History*, vols. 10 &
11 (1978), p. 25-53. bibliog.

A thoroughly researched historical study.

269 **A panorama of Jamaica Jewry: the tercentenary of the
official founding of the Jewish community of Jamaica B. W.
I.; 5415-5715, 1655-1955.**
Henry Phillips Silverman. Kingston: Gleaner Co., [1955].
19p. map.

An illustrated brochure of historical and biographical data relating to the Jews in Jamaica, by the then Spiritual Leader of the Jewish community.

Language and Dialect

270 Jamaican creole syntax: a transformational approach.
Beryl Loftman Bailey. Cambridge, England: Cambridge University Press, 1966. 163p. map. bibliog.

An analysis of Jamaican creole grammar by a Jamaican linguist and pioneer of research into the subject. Her primary concern was to prove that the dialect was a language and that the recognition of this had implications for the system of education. A readable account of a technical subject, though it is doubtful that it is successful in its primary objective.

271 A language guide to Jamaica.
Beryl Loftman Bailey. [?Jamaica: University College of the West Indies], 1962. 75p.

A guide written specifically for the use of the members of the United States Peace Corps prior to their arrival in Jamaica. It treats of the major features of Jamaican creole and is intended as a companion handbook to Frederic G. Cassidy's *Jamaica talk* (Macmillan, 1961), which the author regards as the basic text on language in Jamaica. The title-page carries no imprint statement but the Preface is signed and dated: 'University College of the West Indies, February 1962'.

272 Dictionary of Jamaican English.
Edited by F[rederic] G. Cassidy, R. B. Le Page. Cambridge, England: Cambridge University Press, 1980. 2nd ed. lxiv, 509p. bibliog.

An historical and descriptive dictionary of the English language in all its forms in Jamaica. This edition brings the first edition of 1967 up to date with a supplement (p. 491-509) and a revision of the introductory chapters and the bibliography, including the linguistic introduction on the historical phonology of Jamaican English.

273 Jamaica talk: three hundred years of the English language in Jamaica.
Frederic G. Cassidy. London: Macmillan, [in association with the] Institute of Jamaica, 1961. 468p. map. bibliog.

'This book seeks to give an account of the language, both past and present, of Jamaicans of all ranks.' (Preface, p. vii). Part one deals with history, pronunciation and grammar and Part two with vocabulary, by topics, e.g. work and occupations, seasons and places, etc. Though written specially for the layman, the book is also of interest to linguists. Research for the book was done during the tenure of a Fulbright Research Fellowship at the University College of the West Indies, 1951-52.

274 Language and social change in Jamaica.
Pauline Christie. *Journal of Caribbean Studies*, vol. 3, no. 3 (winter 1983), p. 204-28. bibliog.

An analysis of linguistic trends becoming increasingly evident in Jamaica at the present time and of the extent to which their social meaning is identifiable. In particular, it discusses language developments as reflected in the usage of newspapers and the electronic media and in formal written and spoken expression. The author is a member of the Department of Linguistics and the Use of English, University of the West Indies, Mona, Jamaica.

275 Language and dialect in Jamaica.
Jean D'Costa. *Jamaica Journal*, vol. 2, no. 1 (March 1968), p. 71-74.

Discusses Jamaican speech under the threefold varieties of creole language, dialect and standard English and indicates how the usage of any of these may be governed by social and psychological factors.

276 Jamaican creole: an historical introduction to Jamaican creole.
R. B. Le Page, and four Jamaican creole texts with introduction and phonemic transcriptions and glosses by David De Camp. London: Macmillan, 1960. 182p. map. bibliog. (Creole Language Studies, no. 1).

The earlier part represents perhaps the first attempt to write a settlement history of Jamaica as an indispensable introduction to the linguistic studies which are to follow.' The four creole texts which follow are of stories tape recorded during visits to the Maroons at Accompong.

277 The development of bilingualism in Jamaica, W. I., as a function of inter- and intra-societal forces.
Nila Laborde Nicolas. PhD thesis, Rutgers University, New Brunswick, New Jersey, 1978. 189 leaves. bibliog. (Available from University Microfilms, Ann Arbor, Michigan).

An analysis of individual and group attitudes toward the Spanish language and bilingualism in the context of social change. The study focuses mainly, though not exclusively, on high-school student attitudes and is based on field-work and surveys carried out in Jamaica during the 1970s. There is considerable attention given to the historical background literature as well as to studies of contemporary Jamaican society.

278 Jamaican pronunciation in London.
J. C. Wells. Oxford, England: Basil Blackwell for the Philological Society, 1973. 150p. bibliog. (Publications of the Philological Society, 25).

Although this is primarily a phonological study of Jamaicans in the London area, it discusses their socio-linguistic background and is relevant to the study of Jamaican creole. The work is based on a PhD thesis for the University of London.

From research to action: language policy in Jamaica.
See item no. 819.

Communication and politics in Jamaica.
See item no. 1119.

Religion

General

279 The Rastafarians: the dreadlocks of Jamaica.
Leonard E. Barrett. Kingston: Sangster's Book Stores in association with Heinemann, 1977. 257p. bibliog.

The aim of the book is to 'show the emergence and development of the Rastafarians cult from its inception in 1930 to the present... [with] particular attention... to the socioeconomic conditions from which this cult emerged; its ideology; its function as a socioreligious movement... and its impact on the Western world'. The author, a Jamaican, is a member of the Faculty of Religion and Inter-Cultural Studies at Trinity College, Hartford, Connecticut.

280 Handbook of churches in the Caribbean.
Edited by Joan A. Brathwaite. Bridgetown, Barbados: Christian Action for Development in the Caribbean (CADEC), 1973. 234p.

A handbook of historical, statistical, descriptive and directory information compiled with the co-operation of twenty-four denominations and others, specially prepared for the inaugural assembly of the Caribbean Conference of Churches, 13-16 November 1973.

281 God's people: West Indian Pentecostal sects in England.
Malcolm J. C. Calley. London: Oxford University Press, 1965. 182p. bibliog.

Although primarily an anthropological study of Pentecostal sects among West Indian immigrants in Britain, the work includes some useful factual and historical information on the sects in Jamaica and elsewhere in the West Indies which cannot readily be found in other published sources. Issued under the auspices of the Institute of Race Relations, London.

282 **Caribbean Catholic directory 1980.**
Kingston: printed by Wayne Ho Sang for the Caribbean
Catholic Directory, [1980]. 189p.

Published with the approval of the Antilles Episcopal Conference giving the status (as received up to December 1979) for the dioceses of the Roman Catholic Church in Belize, Bridgetown-Kingston [i.e. Kingston] (Barbados; St. Vincent), Castries (St. Lucia), Georgetown (Guyana), Hamilton in Bermuda, Kingston in Jamaica, Montego Bay (Jamaica), Nassau (Bahamas), Paramaribo (Suriname), Port-of-Spain (Trinidad and Tobago), Roseau (Dominica), St George's Grenada, St. John's (Antigua), Willemstad (Curaçao and Dutch Islands), French dioceses in the Caribbean and St. Thomas in the Virgin Islands of the USA. It provides information on Church offices, committees and institutions. Pages 56-91 are devoted to the archdiocese of Kingston and the diocese of Montego Bay, Jamaica. The previous edition of the directory appeared in 1977.

283 **Rastaman: the Rastafarian movement in England.**
Ernest Cashmore. London: Allen & Unwin, 1979. 263p.
bibliog.

Although this is a sociological study of the movement in England it analyses the genesis of the movement in Jamaica and throughout relates it to the reggae Rasta culture of Jamaica, thereby giving new insights into that movement. The author is an English university lecturer who did doctoral research on the subject.

284 **For ever beginning: two hundred years of Methodism in the Western area.**
Donald S. Ching [and others]. Jamaica: Literature Department of the Methodist Church (Jamaica District), 1960. 96p.

A commemoration of the bicentenary of the Methodist Church in the West Indies.

285 **Christ for Jamaica: symposium of religious activities.**
Compiled by the Jamaican Christian Council, edited by J. A. Crabb, preface by the Reverend John Poxon. Kingston: Pioneer Press, 1951. 102p.

A handbook for Church members, issued by the Jamaican Christian Council, to provide accurate information about the Church and what it stands for, what it is and what it does. Part one deals separately and briefly with thirteen Christian denominations and related organizations. Part two deals generally with the Church and wider topics such as social services, education, youth, etc.

286 **The potential of Ras Tafarianism as a modern national religion.**
George E. Cumper. New Delhi: printed at Recorder Press, 1979. 18p.

This article examines the principles and distinctive practices of Ras Tafarianism to determine whether they are consistent with the sound functions of a major religion in the context of a developing Jamaican nation state and concludes that some of these would be seriously dysfunctional and divisive.

287 **The life of Enos Nuttall, Archbishop of the West Indies.**
Frank Cundall, with a foreword by the Archbishop of
Canterbury. London: Society for Promoting Christian
Knowledge, 1922. 256p. fold. map.

An authoritive biography, written under the auspices of a committee appointed
by the Synod of the Church of England in Jamaica meeting in 1920, 'based in a
great measure on the diaries which he kept [from 1866 almost to the day of his
death] and the copies of his letters, over thirty-five thousand in number, filling
over eighty volumes'. (cf. p. viii). Archbishop Nuttall (1842-1916) was not only
an outstanding churchman in the Anglican communion at large, as well as in
Jamaica, but was closely identified during his long sojourn in Jamaica, from 1862
until his death and especially during the years of his episcopate beginning 1880,
with efforts to advance education and ameliorate social conditions in Jamaica.

288 **Roots and blossoms.**
Edmund Davis. Bridgetown, Barbados: Cedar Press, 1977.
124p. bibliog.

An analysis of the development of theological education in the Church of England
in Jamaica from 1655 to 1966, calling for the development of a theology more
aware of the social and cultural environment of the Jamaican people.

289 **The Church in the new Jamaica: a study of the economic and
social basis of the evangelical church in Jamaica.**
J. Merle Davis. New York; London: Department of Social
and Economic Research & Counsel, International
Missionary Council, 1942. 100p.

This survey does not attempt a detailed analysis of economic and social conditions
in Jamaica, but rather was a timely attempt to relate the Church to the social
and economic realities of Jamaica at a crucial period of national change and
development and to point the course which might be followed in the future. The
author was particularly perceptive in seeing the need for the established churches
to come to terms with the Jamaican psychology as expressed in the independent
religious sects, in so far as the 'enduring elements of Jamaican psychology'...
could...if better understood, be seen as assets and used in the development of a
more harmonious and natural Christian community' (p. 93). The author was
director of the department which published the work and spent some time in
Jamaica in 1941 helping to establish the Jamaican Christian Council.

290 **Caribbean Quakers.**
Harriet Frorer Durham. Hollywood, Florida: printed by
Dukane Press, 1972. 133, xxxviiip. bibliog.

A panoramic view of the unevenly documented history of the Society of Friends in
the Caribbean.

291 **Street preachers, faith healers and herb doctors in Jamaica,
1890-1925.**
W. F. Elkins. New York: Revisionist Press, 1977. 99p.

The growth of revivalism is related to the social aspirations and needs of the
broad mass of the Jamaican people and to the social protest and nationalist
activities which give expression to these aspirations and needs. 'The first part of

the book consists of historical vignettes, most of which sketch the doings of messianic healers... The second part... traces the careers of Alfred Mends and Samuel Radway, leaders of the Reform Club, the most militant nationalist organization on the island before the formation of political parties in the 1930's.' (Chapter 1, p. 6).

292 **Decolonizing theology: a Caribbean perspective.**
Noel Leo Erskine. Maryknoll, New York: Orbis Books, 1981. 130p. bibliog.

An examination of theology from the perspective of a Caribbean spirituality based on the author's experience as a Baptist pastor in his native Jamaica. The author is now Associate Professor of Theology and Ethics, Candler School of Theology at Emory University in Atlanta.

293 **A history of the Diocese of Jamaica.**
E. Lewis Evans. [Kingston: Diocese of Jamaica, 1976?]. 136p. end-paper maps.

A concise, factual account, covering in less detail the period dealt with by the Reverend J. B. Ellis in his *Diocese of Jamaica*, published in 1913 and recording the history of the later period down to 1973. It is characterized by clarity of style and economy of expression, with some engaging and perceptive thumb-nail sketches of persons and events. The author served for more than twenty years in Jamaica, becoming Suffragan Bishop of Kingston and, later, Bishop of Barbados.

294 **The 150th anniversary of the diocese of Jamaica, yesterday, today and tomorrow, 1824-1974.**
Compiled by Bishop [E.] Lewis Evans (and others). Kingston: published by the Church in Jamaica, [1974]. 44p.

In addition to congratulatory messages and numerous photographs, this work provides a brief history of the Church of England in Jamaica - its establishment and its missionary, social and educational work.

295 **Troubling of the waters.**
Edited by Idris Hamid. San Fernando, Trinidad: [St. Andrew's Theological College], 1973. 206p. bibliog.

A collection of papers and responses presented at two Conferences on Creative Theological Reflection held in Jamaica and in Trinidad during May 1973. The principal concern of the papers is the development of a Caribbean Theology as part of the Caribbean identity currently being sought.

296 **Seedtime and harvest: a brief history of the Moravian Church in Jamaica, 1754-1979.**
S. U. Hastings, B. L. MacLeavy. Kingston: Moravian Church Corporation, 1979. 264p. map. bibliog.

The latest history of the Unitas Fratrum in Jamaica, based on printed and archival sources and oral traditions, written to commemorate the Church's 225th anniversary. The authors are respectively, Bishop of the Moravian Church in Jamaica and former principal of the Moravian training college.

297 **Leonard P. Howell and millenarian visions in early Rastafari.**
Robert Hill. *Jamaica Journal*, vol. 16, no. 1 (Feb. 1983),
p. 24-39.

An account of the emergence of the millenarian visions in early Rastafari religion. The author is a Jamaican who teaches in the History Department of the
University of California, Los Angeles.

298 **Jamaican religions: a study in variations.**
Donald William Hogg. PhD thesis, Yale University, New
Haven, Connecticut, 1964. 466 leaves. map. bibliog.
(Available from University Microfilms, Ann Arbor,
Michigan, 1973).

An anthropological study of historical changes and modern variations in Jamaican
religion, based on field research into pocomania and other cults in urban and
rural communities in Jamaica in 1955 and 1956.

299 **The Society of Friends in Jamaica.**
Prepared by the Jamaica Yearly Meeting of
Friends. Richmond, Indiana: American Friends Board of
Missions, 1962. 66p. map.

An account of the foundation and activities of the various groups of Friends in
Jamaica, since their return to Jamaica in 1881 through the initiatives of the Iowa
Yearly Meeting of Friends. For an account of the Society of Friends in Jamaica
during the latter half of the 17th century, after which the Society disappeared
from our history, see *Caribbean Quakers* by Harriet Frorer Durham (Hollywood,
Florida: Dukane Press, c.1972, p. 50-56).

300 **United Free Church of Scotland. The story of our missions:
the West Indies.**
George McNeill. Edinburgh: Foreign Mission Committee,
United Free Church of Scotland, 1911. 93p. map.

An historical outline of the Jamaica mission from the arrival in 1800 of three
missionaries despatched by the Scottish Missionary Society; an undenominational
body representing the Scottish Churches. Among the appendices is a brief account
of the Trinidad mission.

301 **Obeah, Christ and Rastaman: Jamaica and its religion.**
Ivor Morrish. Cambridge, England: James Clarke, 1982.
122p. 2 maps. bibliog.

A synopsis of religious cults and movements in Jamaica. The approach to the
subject is both historical and sociological and the development of religion in
Jamaica is viewed against the historical background and origins of the Jamaican
people.

302 **Disciples of Christ in Jamaica 1858-1958.**
Robert G. Nelson. St. Louis, Missouri: Bethany Press, 1958. 200p. bibliog.

The author spent several years in Jamaica as a missionary of the United Christian Missionary Society based in Indianapolis, Indiana.

303 **Rastafari: a way of life.**
Text by Tracy Nicholas, photographs by Bill Sparrow. New York: Anchor Press, Doubleday, 1979. 92, [72]p. map. bibliog.

The purpose of the book 'is to reflect some portions of Rastafarian reality as it is lived in Jamaica rather than to provide a definitive, structured or clinical study.' (cf. Introduction, p. 2). The several chapters of text deal with the historical background, Rastafarian beginnings, the Rasta world view, ganja, food, domestic life and the arts. The second half of the book comprises some superb portrait photographs of Rasta individuals and groups.

304 **History of the Catholic Church in Jamaica.**
Francis J. Osborne, S. J. Aylesbury, England: Caribbean Universities Press, Ginn, 1977. 210p. map. bibliog.

This work is the fruit of seventeen years of research and writing, drawing on materials in the principal archive repositories of Jamaica and the United Kingdom and in Catholic missionary archives in Kingston, Rome and London. It spans the entire period of Jamaican history from the island's discovery in 1494 up to 1970. Although marred by several typesetting errors, omissions and gaffes on the part of the publisher and the printer, the work is the most detailed and informative account of the subject, enlivened by a number of documented anecdotes relating to persons and events of the period and embracing a good deal of the civil and political history of Jamaica. Those desiring a more concise account of the Church, omitting much of the detail of secular history included in this work, may profitably consult an earlier work, *A history of the Catholic Church in Jamaica, B.W.I., 1494 to 1929* by Francis X. Delany, S. J. (New York: Jesuit Mission Press, 1930. 292p.). This latter work reproduces a few documents which complement the work by Osborne. It stops forty years short of Osborne's history.

305 **Dread: the Rastafarians of Jamaica.**
Joseph Owens, with an introduction by Rex Nettleford. Kingston: Sangster, 1976. 282p.

The book is a vehicle of authentic Rastafarian belief and practice wherein the author lets the Rastafarians speak through quotations from their recorded utterances. No attempt is made to set these ideas within a framework of critical thought or judgement and the author's views, when he does express or imply them, are wholly sympathetic. The author is a Jesuit priest and social worker who worked and lived in West Kingston from 1970 to 1972, during which time he came into close contact with the Rastafarians.

306 **Daybreak in Jamaica.**
Frederick Pilkington. London: Epworth Press, 1950. 220p.

A general account of the rise of Methodism and its present-day practice against the background of slavery and post-emancipation social and economic conditions.

307 Revival cults in Jamaica: notes towards a sociology of religion.
Edward Seaga. *Jamaica Journal*, vol. 3, no. 2 (June 1969), p. 3-13.

A concise account, in non-technical language, of the practices and beliefs of Jamaican revivalist cults, with numerous illustrations by the Jamaican artist Osmond Watson. This article was reprinted in 1982 and issued as a 20-page offprint along with two other contributions to the same issue of *Jamaica Journal*, namely 'Cult music' by Olive Lewin and 'River maid (poem)' by Edward Seaga, under the title of the first article.

308 The Baptists of Jamaica: 1793-1965.
Inez Knibb Sibley. Kingston: Jamaica Baptist Union, 1965. 91p. bibliog.

The author has based her account on earlier histories and historical sources and has produced a condensed work which brings to light new material on the establishment of Baptist churches in the various parishes.

309 Black religions in the New World.
George Eaton Simpson. New York: Columbia University Press, 1978. 415p. 3 maps. bibliog.

A comparative study of the religions of blacks in the Caribbean, and in North and South America. Chapter two, 'The Caribbean: blacks in the historical churches,' is based largely on earlier published accounts. Chapters three and four, which deal with Neo-African, Revivalist, and other cults of the Caribbean, are based on the author's observations during field-work in Western Kingston in 1953, in Port-of-Spain and its environs in 1960, and in the course of several shorter visits to the Caribbean in the years 1936 to 1972.

310 Jamaican Revivalist cults.
George Eaton Simpson. Kingston: Institute of Social and Economic Research, University College of the West Indies, Jamaica, 1956. 321-442p. bibliog. (*Social and Economic Studies*, vol. 5, no. 4).

A detailed study of the organization, beliefs and functions of Revivalist cults, based on field-work in West Kingston, a poor urban area, done in 1953 by the Head of the Department of Sociology and Anthropology of Oberlin College, Ohio. The work occupies a single issue of the periodical *Social and Economic Studies*.

311 Pentecostalism in Jamaica: a challenge to the established churches & society.
Ashley Smith. Kingston: Literature Committee of the Methodist Church, 1975. 20p. bibliog. (William Hammett Lecture, 1975).

Pentecostalism, which is viewed from a combination of theological, sociological and related perspectives, is seen not merely as a form of religious expression but also of social protest. The author was minister of the Hope United Church, Kingston.

312 **The Rastafari movement in Kingston, Jamaica.**
M. G. Smith, Roy Augier, Rex Nettleford. Mona,
Jamaica: Department of Extra-Mural Studies, University of
the West Indies, 1960. 41p. bibliog. Reprinted 1968.
First published in 1960, this was the first serious investigation of the movement
by a team of scholars appointed by the then University College of the West
Indies.

313 **From shore to shore: soundings in Caribbean theology.**
William Watty. Kingston: [s.n.], 1981. 96p. bibliog.
A collection of addresses, lectures and papers delivered at various times, being the
fruits of the author's Caribbean theological reflection. The author is Principal of
the United Theological College, Kingston, Jamaica.

314 **Psychic phenomena of Jamaica.**
Joseph J. Williams. New York: Dial Press, 1934. 309p.
bibliog.
'It has been my constant purpose to forward a scientific study of such unusual
phenomena as might be regarded as psychic' (p. 4). The author, a Jesuit priest,
spent in all nearly six years in Jamaica, at times in remote country districts, and
his study is based on personal experience and observation, first-hand accounts of
others, including priests, and conversations with Jamaicans of every class, both
practitioners of obeah and disillusioned clients of the obeahman. Against a background discussion of Ashanti cultural influence in Jamaica he examines Jamaican
witchcraft, popular belief in ghosts, funeral customs and poltergeist manifestations
and concludes that some preternatural occurences must be 'attributed to spirit
control, which, judged from the consequences, are of diabolic origin'. The work is
carefully documented.

Periodicals

315 **Jamaica Churchman.**
Kingston: Anglican Diocese of Jamaica, Province of the
West Indies, 1877- . monthly.
The official organ of the Diocese of Jamaica.

Society and Social Conditions

Social theory and cultural identity

316 **Black roadways: a study of Jamaican folk life.**
Martha Warren Beckwith. Chapel Hill, North Carolina:
University of North Carolina Press, 1929. Reprinted, New
York: Negro Universities Press, 1969. 243p. fold. map.
bibliog.

One of the first publications based on a serious analysis and study of the social
life, religious beliefs and artistic expression of the Jamaican peasantry, made in
the course of four visits to Jamaica between the summers of 1919 and 1924.

317 **Which Jamaican identity?**
Gloria Cumper. [s.l.: the author?], 1979. (New Delhi:
printed at Recorder Press). 12p.

A critique of the Rasta-reggae-ganja culture and identity of the new Jamaica
which the author regards as 'tailored for and directed to the adolescent male' and
mediated notably by the electronic media. She offers no substitutes except the
jettisoning of a physical national image and the 'cultivation of a realistic understanding of ourselves'.

318 **Two Jamaicas: the role of ideas in a tropical colony,
1830-1865.**
Philip D. Curtin. Cambridge, Massachusetts: Harvard
University Press, 1955. Reprinted, Westport, Connecticut:
Greenwood Press, 1968. 270p. map. bibliog.

An illuminating study of the formative role of European and African ideas in
Jamaican society and of their interaction in that society.

Society and Social Conditions. Social theory and cultural identity

319 **Race crossing in Jamaica.**
C. B. Davenport, Morris Steggerda, in collaboration with F. G. Benedict, Laurence H. Snyder, Arnold Gesell, Inez Dunkelberger Steggerda (and many residents of the colony of Jamaica). Washington, DC: Carnegie Institute of Washington, 1929. Reprinted, Westport, Connecticut: Negro Universities Press, 1970. 516p. map. bibliog.

An anthropometric and psychological study of three groups of rural Jamaican adults: Blacks, Whites and hybrids between them.

320 **The Jamaican cultural identity.**
Neville Dawes. *Jamaica Journal*, vol. 9, no. 1 (March 1975), p. 34-37.

The author, who was manager of the Institute of Jamaica, attempts to answer the questions 'Who is a Jamaican?' and what is a 'culture', relating these to the role of the Institute of Jamaica, past and present, in cultural development. Originally delivered as an address to the Lions Club of Montego Bay, it has been reprinted from *The Daily Gleaner*.

321 **Journey to Accompong.**
Katherine Dunham. New York: Henry Holt, 1946. Reprinted, Westport, Connecticut: Negro Universities Press, 1971. 162p.

Field notes, in diary form, of a famous dancer, during a visit to the Maroon town of Accompong while she was a student of anthropology. Records in detail impressions of her stay and, in particular, her discovery of a secret Koromantee war dance. Illustrated with drawings by Ted (i.e. Proctor Fyffe) Cook, journalist.

322 **Brown face, Big Master.**
Joyce Gladwell. London: Inter-Varsity Press, 1969. 126p.

A coloured Jamaican, 'brown face', writes a readable, forthright story of her experiences growing up in Jamaica where she attended school, afterwards going to England to study at university and there marrying an Englishman. A sensitive account of growth in personal development and social awareness as she comes to face the reality of racial differences and prejudices, both in her home environment and in England, against the wider concern of her search for God, or 'Big Master'.

323 **Jamaica heritage.**
[Edited by] Alex Gradussov. [Kingston]: published by the Government of Jamaica under the auspices of the Minister of Finance and Planning, [1969]. 64p.

A composite work including historical articles, literary extracts, short biographies, reproductions of art works and several unusual illustrations of Jamaican life in the past, prepared to mark Heritage Week. The publishers acknowledge their debt to the staff of the Institute of Jamaica from whose West India Reference Library much of the historical information and many of the illustrations derived.

324 Our heritage.

John Hearne, Rex Nettleford. [Kingston]: Department of Extra-Mural Studies, University of the West Indies, 1963. 56p. biblig. (Public Affairs in Jamaica, no. 1).

This volume contains: 'European heritage and Asian influence in Jamaica', by John Hearne and 'The African connexion: the significance for Jamaica', by Rex Nettleford. A summary view.

325 Cultural policy in Jamaica: a study.

Institute of Jamaica. Paris: UNESCO, 1977. 53p. (Studies and Documents on Cultural Policies).

Outlines the historical background to Jamaica's cultural development, colonial and post-colonial cultural policies and the nature of the institutions and organizations whereby policies have been and are being implemented. Since 1972 the government's major proposals for cultural decolonization have been implemented, in general, through the Institute of Jamaica.

326 Personality and conflict in Jamaica.

Madeline Kerr. Liverpool, England: Liverpool University Press, 1952. Rev. ed., London: Collins; Jamaica: Sangster's Book Stores, 1963. 220p.

The theme of this book is culture conflict. It is the conflict, in an emergent society, between groups of people exposed in varying degrees to diverse cultures associated with different ethnic types. The author, a social psychologist, found that the degree of social and psychological frustration of the people inhibited their development. The main body of the work comprises a survey of the peasantry in three field centres, in chapters dealing with birth customs, children's work and play, parental and family relations, school, sex and marriage, class and colour, religion, folklore and politics. Although the book is based on field-work and a survey carried out from 1947 to 1949 it is still considered a basic work in its field.

327 Social change and images of the future: a study of the pursuit of progress in Jamaica.

James A. Mau. Cambridge, Massachusetts: Schenkman Publishing Co., 1968. 145p. map. biblig. (International Studies in Political and Social Change, 4).

This study of the relative strength of the belief in progress for Jamaica among Jamaicans is based on research done in Jamaica during 1961 to 1962, when the author was a Social Science Research Council Pre-Doctoral Fellow. It was brought up to date by additional field-work in the Caribbean during 1966-67. He found that 'those leaders who were egalitarian, powerful, and knowledgeable, were more likely to believe in progress than those who did not favour equality, were less powerful and less knowledgeable about the discontents of the lower-class people' (p. 115).

Society and Social Conditions. Social theory and cultural identity

328 Self and identity problems in Jamaica.
Errol Miller. *Caribbean Quarterly*, vol. 17, nos. 3 & 4 (Sept.-Dec. 1971), p. 15-35; vol. 19, no. 2 (June 1973), p. 108-42. bibliog.

A statement on the nature of the problem and on possible solutions, by a well-known educator.

329 Caribbean cultural identity: the case of Jamaica. An essay in cultural dynamics.
Rex Nettleford. Kingston: Institute of Jamaica, 1978. 238p.

The author proposes the following themes for discussion in this work: cultural pluralism and national unity; the preservation and further development of cultural values; the cultural dimension of development and the possibility of cultural integration and co-operation between the territories of the Anglophone Caribbean and the wider Caribbean and Latin America. The discussion of these themes is rooted in a wide-ranging survey of aspects of Caribbean art, literature and theatre and of the Jamaican government's policy with regard to cultural agencies such as the media, the Institute of Jamaica, libraries, the JAMAL Foundation, the Jamaica Festival Commission and the Jamaica Agency for Public Information, as well as private cultural groups. The conclusion of the work may be summarized in the words of the author: 'There is a revolution apace in Jamaica and the Caribbean... a continuing dynamic revolt... [constituting] a process of decolonisation of self and society and the constructive act of articulation of the collective self in terms of the variety of experience...' (cf. p. [181]).

330 Mirror mirror: identity, race and protest in Jamaica.
Rex Nettleford. Jamaica: Collins & Sangster (Jamaica), 1970. 256p. bibliog.

A collection of essays which seek to record and interpret the anxieties and uncertainties of Jamaican society in the 1960s. An informed exposition. The contents include: 'National identity and attitudes to race in Jamaica'; 'African redemption: *The Rastafari and the wider society 1959-1969*'; 'Jamaican Black Power or, Notes from the horn'; 'The melody of Europe, the rhythm of Africa'; and 'Mirror, mirror: a postscript'.

331 Jamaica: the search for an identity.
Katrin Norris. London: Oxford University Press, under the auspices of the Institute of Race Relations, 1962. 103p.

Although this work is characterized by an oversimplified view of the dynamics and structure of Jamaican society, the author packs into its slender compass a number of penetrating insights into the social and cultural life of the society and awareness of the needs of the society on the threshold of becoming an independent nation. The burden of her book is that 'the overpowering cultural image of Britain must be diluted and replaced by new ideas rooted in Jamaica herself' (cf. p. 101). The author is British and was at the time of writing a journalist.

86

Society and Social Conditions. Marcus Garvey and Garveyism

332 **The groundings with my brothers.**
Walter Rodney, with an introduction by Richard Small, and
a new introduction by Omowale. London:
Bogle-L'Ouverture Publications, 1975. 68p. map.

Lectures on Black power and African history in relation to the Jamaican situation, given by the author during the ten months prior to, and immediately following, his exclusion from re-entering the country by the government of Jamaica, in October 1968. This ban triggered off civil disturbances in Kingston indicative of great social malaise. First published 1969.

333 **Essays on power and change in Jamaica.**
Edited by Carl Stone, Aggrey Brown. [Kingston]: Jamaica
Publishing House, 1977. 207p.

A collection of essays by Jamaican-based social scientists of the University of the West Indies, designed to stimulate thought in the wider Jamaican society. Part one, entitled 'Political economy', covers topics such as Jamaican élites, patterns of ownership and economic control, agrarian relations, Black nationalism and the growth of the trade union movement. Part two concentrates on policy issues with particular reference to government programmes since 1972, including a national minimum wage, Project Land-Lease, sugar co-operatives, bauxite and national development, worker participation, price control and the control and function of the mass media. 'No attempt has been made to orchestrate the material to reflect any particular ideology... It is obvious, however, that the authors share a largely socialist view of development in the country...' (Introduction).

Jamaica farewell: Jamaican migrants in London.
See item no. 242.

Endless pressure: a study of West Indian life-styles in Bristol.
See item no. 248.

**Black Britain's dilemma: a medico-social transcultural study of West
Indians.**
See item no. 250.

Decolonizing theology: a Caribbean perspective.
See item no. 292.

Troubling of the waters.
See item no. 295.

Marcus Garvey and Garveyism

334 **Marcus Garvey and the vision of Africa.**
Edited with an introduction and commentaries by John
Henrik Clarke, with the assistance of Amy Jacques
Garvey. New York: Vintage Books, 1974. 496p. bibliog.

This reader, selected with catholicity, shows Garvey in all his dimensions. Each period of his life and activity is introduced by a commentary followed by excerpts

Society and Social Conditions. Marcus Garvey and Garveyism

from the writings of others, favourable and critical, and from Garvey's own writings.

335 Black Moses: the story of Marcus Garvey and the Universal Negro Improvement Association.

Edmund David Cronon. Madison, Wisconsin: University of Wisconsin Press, 1969. 278p. bibliog.

First published 1955. The first full-length biography of Garvey, in the writing of which the author made a 'thorough search for all the surviving Garvey material...'. A standard work.

336 Marcus Garvey.

Edited by E[dmund] David Cronon. Englewood Cliffs, New Jersey: Prentice-Hall, 1973. 176p. bibliog. (Great Lives Observed). (A Spectrum Book).

This volume includes: an introduction, 'Chronology of the life of Marcus Garvey'; part 1, 'Garvey looks at the world'; part 2, 'The world looks at Garvey'; and part 3, 'Garvey in history'. The latter includes a hitherto unpublished paper, 'Garveyism in Jamaica', by Rupert Lewis. 'Each volume in the series views the character and achievement of a great world figure in three perspectives - through his own words, through the opinions of his contemporaries and through retrospective judgments...'. The editor of this volume is Professor of History and Director of the Institute for Research in the Humanities at the University of Wisconsin, Madison.

337 Marcus Garvey, 1887-1940.

Adolph Edwards. London; Port of Spain, Trinidad: New Beacon Publications, 1972. 45p. bibliog.

A concise, factual account. First published 1967.

338 Garvey: the story of a pioneer black nationalist.

Elton C. Fax, foreword by John Henrik Clarke. New York: Dodd, Mead, 1972. 305p. bibliog.

John Henrik Clarke, the Garvey scholar, states in his foreword that this work 'explores and explains a dimension in the life, mission and legacy of Marcus Garvey that has been neglected by previous writers', namely, 'that there is no way to understand Marcus Garvey without some insight into the history of the West Indies in general and Jamaica in particular.' (p. x). Illustrated with photographs from the James Van Der Zee Institute.

339 Garvey and Garveyism.

Amy Jacques Garvey, introduced by John Henrik Clarke. New York: Collier Books; London: Collier Macmillan, 1970. 336p.

Originally published by the author, without the Epilogue, in 1963. This biographical study was written by the biographee's devoted and valiant wife, compiler, editor and publisher of his thought and writings - realizing, as she states, that when I pass on much of the authentic story of his life will be lost'. It records otherwise unknown details of the personal and family life of Garvey from the later 1920s onwards.

340 **Philosophy and opinions of Marcus Garvey: or, Africa for the Africans.**
Compiled by Amy Jacques Garvey, with a new introduction by E. U. Essien-Udom. London: Frank Cass, 1967. 2nd ed. 2 vols. in 1. (African Modern Library, no. 1).

First edition, 1923-25. A collection of the speeches and writings of Marcus Garvey, edited by his wife, to demonstrate to the world his thoughts on the rehabilitation of the Negro race and the redemption of Africa from colonial exploitation. Marcus Garvey was declared Jamaica's first National Hero. A sup-plementary volume covering the period 1926 to 1940 has been issued as volume three under the following title: *More philosophy and opinions of Marcus Garvey*, selected and edited from previously unpublished material by E. U. Essien-Udom and Amy Jacques Garvey. (Vol. 3, London: Cass, 1977. 248p. Africana Modern Library, no. 20).

341 **Race first: the ideological and organizational struggles of Marcus Garvey and the Universal Negro Improvement Association.**
Tony Martin. Westport, Connecticut; London: Greenwood Press, 1976. 421p. bibliog. (Contributions in Afro-American and African studies, no. 19).

'After a brief biographical introduction, the study examines the major features of Garvey's ideological outlook as they manifested themselves in theory and in prac-tice.' (Preface, p. xi). The work is based on a wide range of published and unpublished sources of which there is an excellent bibliography. Among sources consulted are the UNIA records (including membership files) discovered in 1970 and now in the Schomburg Collection, New York Public Library. At the time of writing the author was Associate Professor of History and Black Studies at Wel-lesley College, Massachusetts.

342 **Trials and triumphs of Marcus Garvey.**
Len S. Nembhard (with a new introduction by the author). Kingston: Gleaner Co., 1940. Reprinted, Millwood, New York: Kraus Reprint Co., 1978. 249, [2]p.

The earliest biographical study of Garvey, written by a countryman, with conside-rable emphasis on his youth, early struggles and his homecoming to Jamaica. Part three (p. 239-51) includes biographical notes on leading local contemporaries.

343 **Black power and the Garvey movement.**
Theodore G. Vincent. Berkeley, California: Ramparts Press, [1975?]. 299p. bibliog.

The author was, at the time of writing, teaching black studies in the Center for Participant Education of the University of California at Berkeley. This study was written with the express intention of presenting a more balanced picture of Garveyism and of rebutting some of Garvey's early critics as well as some of the views presented by later scholars such as David Cronon, in his *Black Moses*.

Social structure and social conditions

344 The working class in the Third World: a study in class consciousness and class action in Jamaica, 1919-1952.

Fitzroy L. Ambursley. St. Augustine, Trinidad & Tobago: Department of Sociology, Faculty of Social Sciences, University of the West Indies, 1978. 65p. bibliog. (Working Papers on Caribbean Society; Series B, no. 1).

This paper, originally presented as an undergraduate dissertation at Birmingham University, 1978, examines the theories upon which a number of recent studies of the social formation of Jamaica are based, rejects the cultural pluralist hypotheses inherent in these studies and attempts to justify the use of class analysis. This study is based on the years during which the author discerned the emergence of a Jamaican working class.

345 Symbolic aspects of land in the Caribbean: the tenure and transmission of land rights among Caribbean peasantries.

Jean Besson. In: *Peasants, plantations and rural communities in the Caribbean.* Edited by Malcolm Cross, Arnaud Marks. Guildford, England: Department of Sociology of the University of Surrey, and Department of Caribbean Studies of the Royal Institute of Linguistics and Anthropology, Leiden, Netherlands, 1979, p. 86-116. bibliog.

An interpretation of the subject, based on the author's work in Jamaica, which complements or suggests alternative approaches to those of the works of a number of well-known students of this subject, e.g. studies by Edith Clarke and M. G. Smith. The author is Lecturer in Sociology, University of Aberdeen.

346 Family structure in Jamaica: the social context of reproduction.

Judith Blake, in collaboration with J. Mayne Stycos, Kingsley Davis. New York: Free Press of Glencoe, 1961. 262p. bibliog.

On the basis of questionnaires and field-work the authors examine attitudes to sexual unions, child rearing, marriage and contraception, with a view to discovering the factors already present in Jamaica which might lead to the voluntary limitation of offspring. The research was carried out with the support of the Conservation Foundation of New York.

347 Color, class, and politics in Jamaica.

Aggrey Brown. New Brunswick, New Jersey: Transaction Books, 1979. 172p. bibliog.

An analysis of Jamaica's social and historical development, with particular reference to the interrelationship between colour, class and politics, based on a dissertation for the degree of Doctor of Philosophy at Princeton University.

Society and Social Conditions. Social structure and social conditions

348 **Land tenure and the family in four selected communities in Jamaica.**

Edith Clarke. *Social and Economic Studies,* vol. 1, no. 4 (Aug. 1953), p. 81-118. bibliog.

An account of land tenure in its relation to family structure and organization. The concept of 'family land' and the resultant principles of inheritance are described. This study is based on original field research in four communities selected as being together representative of rural working-class and small farmer communities. The research was financed by the Colonial Social Science Research Council under the supervision of the London School of Economics.

349 **My mother who fathered me: a study of the family in three selected communities in Jamaica.**

Edith Clarke, with a preface by Sir Hugh Foot (Lord Caradon), and introduced by M. G. Smith. London: Allen & Unwin, 1966. 2nd ed. 227p.

First published in 1957. 'This account of the family in rural Jamaica consists of a comparative study of three communities which reflect the different ways in which the rural population is organized, and attempts to show how these different ways of life affect patterns of family life....' (Foreword, p. 12). Professor Smith describes it as 'one of the fundamental studies of West Indian family and social organization....'.

350 **Urbanization and urban growth in the Caribbean: an essay on social change in dependent societies.**

Malcolm Cross. Cambridge, England: Cambridge University Press, 1979. 174p. map. bibliog. (Urbanization in Developing Countries).

A general view of urbanization as a social process within the context of broader social changes and social problems in the Caribbean. A helpful study from the viewpoint of setting the process of Jamaican urbanization within the context of similar processes in the wider Caribbean region. This study is based on material collected by the author, a lecturer in Sociology at the University of Surrey, during a visit to the Caribbean in 1975.

351 **Report of the Conference on Social Development in Jamaica... July 16-25, 1961.**

Edited by George [E.] Cumper. Kingston: Standing Committee on Social Services, [1961]. 181p.

The background papers provide useful information on the social structure and services and on economic development and population growth in Jamaica immediately prior to independence. The public lectures and addresses inform us of how Jamaican politicians, academics and social workers viewed the society at that crucial point in the country's political development.

352 The social structure of Jamaica.

George [E.] Cumper. [Kingston]: Extra-Mural Department, University College of the West Indies, [1949?]. 90p. (Caribbean Affairs, no. 1).

Based mainly on data of the census of Jamaica and its dependencies taken in 1943, it was intended primarily for the use of study and discussion groups.

353 Role and status of rural Jamaican women: higglering and mothering.

Victoria Durant-Gonzalez. PhD thesis, University of California, Berkeley, California, 1976. 227 leaves. 2 maps. bibliog. (Available from University Microfilms, Ann Arbor, Michigan, 1976).

An anthropological study of the primary roles of older Jamaican women, i.e. the economic and familial roles represented by higglering and mothering, in the Maroon settlement of Scotts Hall, St. Mary, Jamaica. An interesting presentation based on data gathered during sixteen months of field-work in 1972 and 1973.

354 Jamaican higglers: their significance and potential.

Melvin R. Edwards. Norwich, England: Geo Abstracts for the Centre for Development Studies, University College of Swansea, Wales, 1980. 58p. bibliog. (Monograph Series, 7).

An historical and socio-cultural study of the petty trading business called 'higglering' in Jamaica, with particular reference to its effects on popular culture, internal migration, social mobility and the economy.

355 Readings on the sociology of the Caribbean.

Edited by Jerold Heiss. New York: MSS Educational Publishing Co., 1970. 322p.

A work designed to provide West Indian students of introductory sociology with articles relating to their own societies which illustrate the major concepts of the discipline. The following articles relate specifically to Jamaica: 'Character formation and social structure in a Jamaican community' by Yehudi A. Cohen (published originally in *Psychiatry*, vol. 18, 1955, p. 275-96); 'Color and class in a Jamaican market town' by Robert A. Ellis (published originally in *Sociology and Social Research*, vol. 41, 1957. p. 354-60); 'Body image, physical beauty and colour among Jamaican adolescents' by Errol A. Miller (published originally in *Social and Economic Studies*, vol. 18, no. 1, 1969, p. 72-89); 'A family system of Jamaica,' by William Davenport (published originally in *Social and Economic Studies*, vol. 10, 1961, p. 420-35); and 'Functions and dysfunctions of revivalist cults' by George Simpson (published originally in *Social and Economic Studies*, vol. 5, 1965, p. 411-15).

356 Family and colour in Jamaica.
Fernando Henriques, with a preface by Meyer Fortes. Jamaica: reprinted specially for Sangster's Book Stores, in association with Granada Publishing, 1976. 2nd ed. 208p. 2 maps. bibliog.

Although this study, first published in 1953, is somewhat out of date both in respect of its findings and the illustrative material cited, it is still a notable contribution to the study of the aspects of social structure indicated by its title. The style is readable and impressionistic and, in a work of this nature, one could wish for a more complete documentation and analysis of the data on which the author has drawn for many perceptive views on the colour-class system of Jamaica. The final chapter attempts an assessment of the modifications which this relationship has undergone between the date when the study first appeared and that of the publication of the second edition in 1968. The work includes a number of interesting accounts of folk customs relating to birth, marriage and death. The author was Director of the former joint University of the West Indies and University of Sussex Centre for Multi-Racial Studies, Barbados.

357 The Jamaican country higgler.
Margaret Fisher Katzin. *Social and Economic Studies*, vol. 8, no. 4 (Dec. 1959), p. 421-40. bibliog.

The above is an account of the weekly routine of a typical country higgler of Jamaica, including a section on 'Partners': an informal savings institution in Jamaica. In a further paper entitled 'The business of higglering in Jamaica' (*Social and Economic Studies*, vol. 9, no. 3, Sept. 1960, p. 297-331), the author describes the internal distribution system of Jamaica for locally grown food and assesses its efficiency as a marketing device. These papers form part of the writer's doctoral dissertation, entitled 'Higglers of Jamaica', submitted to Yale University in 1959.

358 Sociological report on the Christiana area: a sociologist's contribution to extension work in rural Jamaica.
G. J. Kruijer. [Jamaica]: Agricultural Information Service, Ministry of Agriculture and Fisheries, 1969. 3rd ed. 86p. bibliog.

A sociological report on a farming community in the central rural highlands of Jamaica, undertaken as a UNESCO mission and prepared as part of a general investigation embracing agricultural, geological and social surveys with a view to rehabilitating the area. Based on information gathered in 1956, the report has stood the test of time and has gone into a third edition.

359 Changing Jamaica.
Adam Kuper. Kingston: Kingston Publishers, 1976. 163p. map. bibliog.

An anthropological study of which the aim is 'to sketch a total analysis of contemporary Jamaican society; to suggest the ways in which political, economic and social relationships, and actors' models, are articulated with each other in a changing and dynamic fashion' (p. 4). With the fresh insights of a non-actor the author rejects the simple stratification model of Jamaican society, held by a number of sociologists and anthropologists of West Indian origin, or of long

Society and Social Conditions. Social structure and social conditions

domicile there. While recognizing a number of distinct variables relating to class, colour and culture, he also recognizes a striking cultural uniformity in Jamaica and concludes that such changes as are introduced 'will be contained within the present institutional arrangements'. During 1972-73 the author was attached as planner to the National Planning Agency of Jamaica, where he did the field-work for this book.

360 **Race and ethnic relations in Latin America and the Caribbean: an historical dictionary and bibliography.**
Robert M. Levine. Metuchen, New Jersey; London: Scarecrow Press, 1980. 251p. bibliog.

This dictionary contains a significant number of terms, names or events which relate to Jamaica, or which are described with reference to Jamaica. The bibliography of Jamaica is to be found at p. 175-80.

361 **Black Jamaica: a study in evolution.**
W. P. Livingstone. London: S. Low, Marston, 1900. 2nd ed. 298p.

The author states that the work 'is the outcome of ten years' careful study of the social and economic circumstances of Jamaica'. Given the requisite conditions he is very optimistic of the progressive social evolution of the Blacks of Jamaica. He expressly excludes the large class of people of mixed origin - 'the presence of the alien mixture is not considered' (p. 7) - while he is deeply conscious of the white man's burden. Despite some oddities of judgement, the work was in advance of its time in the strongly sympathetic view held of the character of the Negro.

362 **Consequences of class and color: West Indian perspectives.**
Edited and introduced by David Lowenthal, Lambros Comitas. New York: Anchor Books, 1973. xx, 334p. bibliog.

A conspectus of West Indian cultural, artistic and social development as an expression of class and colour, in a collection of 18 articles contributed by West Indians and others. Each article is prefaced by a brief editorial comment on its salient features and a short biographical note on the contributor. Social and political status and the need to find and express group identity are the principal foci of the study. Most of the material deals with the Commonwealth Caribbean and a preponderant part of this with Jamaica and Trinidad.

363 **West Indian societies.**
David Lowenthal. New York; London; Toronto: Oxford University Press for the Institute of Race Relations, London, in collaboration with the American Geographical Society, New York, 1972. 385p. map. bibliog. (American Geographical Society Research Series, no. 26).

This book aims to explain how the West Indies became what they are, the likenesses and differences of their societies and their relations with one another and with the outside world. Although it is essentially a general study of the area a great deal of the illustrative material relates to Jamaica and as an overall account it has the merit of setting the study of Jamaican society fully in the context of West Indian societal study. It is written by a non-West Indian geographer, not a social anthropologist. The work was in gestation for about ten years and hence its well-documented thoroughness and comprehensiveness suffers from a certain lack of currency due to changes which have taken place during its preparation. There are chapters devoted to 'History'; 'Social structure'; 'East Indians and creoles'; 'Ethnic minorities'; 'Emigration and neo-colonialism'; and 'Racial and national identity'.

364 Warning from the West Indies: a tract for Africa and the empire.

William M. Macmillan. London: Faber & Faber, [1936].
Reprinted, Freeport, New York: Books for Libraries Press,
1971. 213p. map. bibliog.

A survey of economic, social and political conditions in the West Indies, pointing out the failure of British imperial policy and calling for reconstruction to improve the quality of life in these ancient colonies. The work was prophetic of the social discontent which was to manifest itself in less than two years after its original publication. As a study, it draws notably on the Jamaican experience. The author spent most of his early life in South Africa, pioneered social studies of the African peoples and later became Professor of History at the University of the Witwatersrand, Johannesburg.

365 Caribbean transformations.

Sidney W. Mintz. Chicago: Aldine, 1974. 355p. bibliog.

A collection of independent essays written by an American anthropologist. Part two, 'Caribbean peasantries', relates specially to Jamaica, three of the five essays comprising this part being entitled: 'The historical sociology of Jamaican villages'; 'The origins of the Jamaican market system'; and 'The contemporary Jamaican market system'.

366 Persistence, continuity and change in the Jamaican working-class family.

H. Orlando Patterson. *Journal of Family History*, vol. 7,
no. 2 (summer 1982), p. 135-61. bibliog.

A case study of social change in the familial patterns of lower-class Jamaicans. The author focuses on the Jamaican working-class family, on the patterns of mating and familial organization that developed from slavery to modern shanty town. He discusses the various interpretations of the West Indian family to be found in the recent work of sociologists and anthropologists and concludes: 'Slavery has absolutely nothing to do with the present pattern of familial instability among urban, or for that matter rural, lower-class Jamaicans. We are dealing here with a clear case of persistence brought about by intervening congruences.' (p. 155).

367 Women in Jamaica: patterns of reproduction and family.

George W. Roberts, Sonja A. Sinclair, with an introduction
by Vera Rubin. New York: Kto Press, 1978. 346p. ([The
Caribbean – Historical and Cultural Perspectives]).

'This work has been undertaken in order to attain further understanding of the family in Jamaica mainly in the context of union formation and reproduction.'

Society and Social Conditions. Social structure and social conditions

(Preface, p. xv). Demographic, medical and social implications of the subject are brought out in the survey, which was conducted by means of questionnaires, taped interviews and by using census data. The project was supported by the American Association for the Advancement of Science under a grant from the United States Agency for International Development administered by the Research Institute for the Study of Man. The authors carried out the work on behalf of the Census Research Programme of the University of the West Indies.

368 **Welfare & planning in the West Indies.**
T. S. Simey. Oxford, England: Clarendon Press, 1946. 267p. map. bibliog.

This is an investigation of the social forces which have shaped West Indian society and is an attempt to demonstrate the possibility of attacking social problems from newer and non-traditional angles. It is the work of an academic sociologist who gained extensive experience of the West Indies during the first half of the decade of the 1940s when he was Social Welfare Advisor to the Comptroller for Development and Welfare in the West Indies. It is based very largely on his experience of conditions in Jamaica, as is evident from a perusal of the text and, in particular, the author's acknowledgments made in the final paragraph of his preface. It is regarded as a standard work on the subject for the period which it covers.

369 **Race, colour and miscegenation: the free coloured of Jamaica and Barbados.**
Arnold A. Sio. *Caribbean Studies*, vol. 16, no. 1 (April 1976), p. 6-21. bibliog.

A synoptic and comparative account of the evolution and social status of the free coloured in Jamaica and Barbados up to emancipation.

370 **Community organization in rural Jamaica.**
M. G. Smith. *Social and Economic Studies*, vol. 5, no. 3 (Sept. 1956), p. 295-312. bibliog.

The model of community organization which this paper presents is intended for the practical guidance of persons working on development and welfare projects and hence it avoids the discussion of abstract sociological issues. It was derived from field-work in eight districts during a rural labour survey undertaken in 1955 by the author, then an anthropologist attached to the staff of the Institute of Social and Economic Research, University College of the West Indies.

371 **The plural society in the British West Indies.**
M. G. Smith. Kingston: Sangster's Book Stores in association with University of California Press, 1974. 359p. bibliog.

First published, University of California Press, 1964. A collection of essays written between 1952 and 1961, while the author, a Jamaican anthropologist, was attached to the University College of the West Indies. A study of the nature of West Indian society, in which he applies J. S. Furnivall's concept of the plural society 'as a unit of disparate parts which owes its existence to external factors, and lacks a common social will.' Much of the illustrative matter is drawn from his Jamaican experience and three chapters are devoted exclusively to Jamaica. Considered a basic work for the study of West Indian society.

372 **West Indian family structure.**
M. G. Smith. Seattle; London: University of Washington Press, 1962. 311p. bibliog. (American Ethnological Society, Monograph 36).

A comparative study of family structure based on data on Carriacou, Grenada, and Jamaica, collected in 1953 and 1955, from field-work studies of household composition and from Jamaican official statistical samples of households in eight rural districts of Jamaica, as well as in Kingston. The work is furnished with numerous statistical tables and kinship charts which strongly complement the text. This study was done while the author was on the staff of the Institute of Social and Economic Research of the University College of the West Indies.

Social problems

373 **Jamaica: Babylon on a thin wire.**
Adrian Boot, Michael Thomas. London: Thames & Hudson, 1976. 93p. photos.

The eighty-two photographs of urban ghetto scenes and rural dereliction graphically convey some of the social problems and pressures which characterize Jamaica of the 1970s, with an accuracy that exceeds that of the text. The latter is interspersed with extracts from the Jamaican daily press and with lyrics from the Rasta-reggae culture, which is the dominant concern of the work.

374 **Abandonment of children in Jamaica.**
Erna Brodber. Jamaica: Institute of Social and Economic Research, University of the West Indies, 1974. 104p. 2 maps. bibliog. (Law and Society in the Caribbean, no. 3).

A study of the records of the Child Care and Protection Division of the Ministry of Youth and Community Development, Jamaica, intended to document the abandonment of children, to suggest explanations and remedial measures against the wider background of social problems affecting the welfare of children in Jamaica. Data were collected October 1968 to January 1970.

375 **Drug use in Jamaica.**
[A. Barrington] Chevannes. [Jamaica]: [s.n.] 1976. 68p. bibliog.

A report prepared by a research fellow of the Institute of Social and Economic Research of the University of the West Indies in fulfilment of a contract between UNESCO and the Institute. There are chapters on marijuana, alcohol, hard drugs, pharmaceuticals, folk medicines, tobacco and drug education programmes, concluding with recommendations. The preface to the report states that it is anthropological in its approach, is sympathetic to those drugs which are rooted in

Society and Social Conditions. Social problems

the cultural traditions of the working masses, is mindful of the relationships between drug use and the political process evolving from the post-emancipation era and hence the recommendations are based on a strategy which considers drug use primarily from the point of view of the classes of people as users, rather than that of the drugs themselves.

376 **Ganja. (Marijuana.)**
John W. Commissiong. Mona, Jamaica: Department of Extra-Mural Studies, University of the West Indies, 1978. 56p. bibliog.

The contents include an historical synopsis of cannabis in medicine, religion and commerce and chapters on the abuse of cannabis in the Caribbean, chemical and pharmacological aspects of cannabis, the effects of cannabis on man and the legalization of marijuana. This monograph is intended mainly for Caribbean readers and its primary aim is to present to the general public the proven effects of marijuana in man.

377 **Working men and ganja: marihuana use in rural Jamaica.**
Melanie Creagan Dreher. Philadelphia, Pennsylvania: Institute for the Study of Human Issues, 1982. 216p.

A study based on eighteen months of field-work done in Jamaica between July 1970 and January 1973 as part of a multidisciplinary research effort undertaken by the Research Institute for the Study of Man and the University of the West Indies on the effects of chronic smoking of ganja in Jamaica. It focuses on the socio-cultural dimensions of ganja use among the rural working class and is organized around the cultivation, distribution and consumption of ganja. More narrowly it focuses on the relationship of ganja to agricultural work and other aspects of rural life.

378 **Men in prison.**
Henry A. Guy. Jamaica: the author, 1962. 106p.

A journalist's account of the main features of prison life, including a number of factual and historical details which would be difficult to discover elsewhere. The work is concluded by four chapters giving the author's views on aspects of criminal psychology and rehabilitation.

379 **Illegal entrepreneurship and social networks in rural Jamaica.**
Claudia Rogers. PhD thesis, Columbia University, New York, 1976. 188 leaves. bibliog. (Available from University Microfilms, Ann Arbor, Michigan, 1976).

The focus of this study is the recreational use of cannabis (or ganja) among lower-class people in one village and one town in Jamaica, specifically emphasizing the retailing and smoking of ganja and the interpersonal relationships which support this entrepreneurial activity. The field-work was done as part of a multidisciplinary research project on long-term usage of marijuana published as *Ganja in Jamaica*, by Vera Rubin and Lambros Comitas (The Hague: Mouton, 1975).

380 **Cannabis and culture.**

[Edited by] Vera Rubin. The Hague; Paris; Mouton, 1975. 598p. bibliogs. (World Anthropology).

Comprises papers presented at a conference on Cross-Cultural Perspectives on Cannabis during the IXth International Congress of Anthropological and Ethnological Sciences, Chicago, August 1973. Four contributions relate to Jamaica, treating of socio-cultural, economic and medico-pharmacological aspects of cannabis use, as follows: 'The social nexus of ganja in Jamaica', by Lambros Comitas (p. 119-32); 'The significance of marihuana in a small agricultural community in Jamaica', by Joseph Schaeffer (p. 355-88); and 'Cannabis or alcohol: the Jamaican experience', by Michael H. Beaubrun (p. 485-94). Each paper is prefaced by an abstract.

381 **Ganja in Jamaica: a medical anthropological study of chronic marijuana use.**

Vera Rubin, Lambros Comitas. The Hague; Paris; Mouton, 1975. 205p. bibliog. (New Babylon: Studies in the Social Sciences, 26).

'This volume presents the findings of an investigation of the effects of chronic cannabis smoking carried out by the Research Institute for the Study of Man (RISM) in collaboration with the University of the West Indies (UWI), supported by the National Institute of Mental Health (NIMH), US Department of Health, Education and Welfare (Contract No. 42.70-97)' (Preface, p. ix). The sponsors state that it is the first intensive multidisciplinary study of marihuana use and users to be published. 'The study examines the use of ganja as part of the life style of the Jamaican working class where its use in various forms is endemic and delineates the traditions and value systems that control marihuana use and condition expectations and reactions to its use.' (Foreword, p. vi). Administrative and legal problems had to be overcome to enable in-hospital clinical studies on selected subjects. The names and offices of the forty-five professionals who comprised the staff of consultants are listed at p. xvii-xx.

Yards in the city of Kingston.
See item no. 383.

The United States and West Indian unrest, 1918-1939.
See item no. 495.

Periodicals

382 **Social and Economic Studies.**

Mona, Jamaica: Institute of Social and Economic Research, University of the West Indies. Feb. 1953- . quarterly.

This journal reports on work undertaken by, or in association with, the Institute of Social and Economic Research. It is the principal forum of social and economic research in the Commonwealth Caribbean. In addition, a number of special issues dealing with single topics have appeared from time to time. An author

Society and Social Conditions. Periodicals

index to the issues from 1953 to 1977, compiled by F. E. Nunes, has been issued as Working Paper no. 23 of the Institute of Social and Economic Research.

Social Services, Health and Welfare, Benevolent and Friendly Societies

383 **Yards in the city of Kingston.**
Erna Brodber. Jamaica: Institute of Social and Economic Research, University of the West Indies, 1975. 87p. map. bibliog. (University of the West Indies, Institute of Social and Economic Research. Working Paper, no. 9).

An exploration of the meaning of 'yard', an urban residential unit in Jamaica, and the proposition that it is a problem-solving agency in the lives of low-income persons.

384 **Directory of services and resources for the handicapped in the Caribbean.**
Kingston: produced by the Caribbean Institute on Mental Retardation, 1979. 1 vol. (unpaged).

Services and resource persons are listed for each country of the Caribbean separately, under an alphabetical arrangement of countries. The nature of the services are outlined and the names of contact persons for each agency given.

Social Services, Health and Welfare, Benevolent and Friendly Societies

385 Fishermen and cooperation in rural Jamaica.
Lambros Comitas. PhD thesis, Columbia University, New York, 1962. 364 leaves. 2 maps. bibliog. (Available from University Microfilms, Ann Arbor, Michigan, 1962).

An investigation of the socio-cultural factors responsible for differing methods and patterns of fishing in five communities which rely on marine fishing for all or part of their subsistence and of the viability of fishing co-operatives which were introduced relatively recently to the island.

386 A handbook of the social services of Jamaica.
Kingston: compiled and published by the Council of Voluntary Social Services, 1978. 5th ed. 128p.

Provides basic information on some 110 social service organizations, such as historical background, aims and objects, programme, address and name of principal officer(s). The services fall under headings which include services for children, youth services, services for the handicapped, services provided by the churches, specialized health and welfare services, co-operatives, friendly societies, benevolent trusts and associations, service clubs, statutory and government services and a number of voluntary organizations including the Jamaica Red Cross Society, the Jamaica Legion and the Howard League of Jamaica. The first edition of this handbook was published in 1963.

387 Selected cases in Jamaican social welfare.
June Dolly-Besson. Toronto: School of Social Work, University of Toronto, 1969. 136p. bibliog.

A presentation of case records of students in the two-year Certificate Course in Social Work at the University of the West Indies, Mona, Jamaica, by the Tutor in Social Casework of the University's Department of Sociology, undertaken during a year's fellowship leave, with the assistance of the Caribbean Programme of the Canadian International Development Agency. It is not only a valuable contribution to a particular area of social work in Jamaica on which little has been written but the case records themselves provide an insight into the mores and values of the society. The case reports relate to group work and community development, as well as casework, and are concerned with problems of family mental health, foster home placement, institutional foster care, truancy, parental control and adoption.

388 The after-care of discharged prisoners in Jamaica; report of the sub-committee appointed by the Howard League of Jamaica.
Kingston: Farquharson Institute of Public Affairs for the Howard League, 1968. 52p.

This report documents facilities, professional staff and administration of after-care and probation services in Jamaica, briefly evaluates results obtained and makes summary recommendations on aspects of the service.

389 The co-operative movement in Jamaica: an exercise in social control.

E. R. M. LeFranc. *Social and Economic Studies*, vol. 27, no. 1 (March 1978), p. 21-43. bibliog.

A discussion of the Jamaican experience in co-operative organization from 1940 onwards and of the reasons for the failure of many co-operative efforts in Jamaica.

390 The Jamaican Sugar Workers Cooperatives and the severance pay crisis.

Frank Lindenfeld. *Humanity & Society*, vol. 6, no. 2 (May 1982), p. 135-51.

An account of how the co-operatives came into existence and of the organizational and financial problems encountered during the 1970s.

391 Social welfare work in Jamaica: a study of the Jamaica Social Welfare Commission.

Roger Marier. Paris: UNESCO, 1953. 166p. bibliog. (Monographs on Fundamental Education, 7).

A detailed, informative study, basic to an understanding of the development of social welfare work in Jamaica between 1937 to 1953, undertaken for UNESCO by Dr Roger Marier of the Department of Social Work, McGill University, Canada. The work was conceived as a field study on fundamental education addressed to specialists engaged in administration or teaching, in the promotion of welfare work through educational techniques. The field-work was done over a period of three months in 1952.

392 The Salvation Army: 50 years of work with the blind and visually handicapped in Jamaica 1927-1977.

Kingston: Salvation Army, [1977?]. 60p.

A commemorative brochure, including personal reminiscences of those concerned in founding a notable work for the handicapped and short biographies of some persons who benefited from this service.

393 An historical account of Jamaican freemasonry.

F. W. Seal-Coon. Kingston: Golding Printing Service, 1976. 127p. 3 maps. bibliog.

An interesting compilation of biographical and historical information based on extensive research in printed sources and in archival collections, by an English journalist who spent many years in the West Indies where he came into freemasonry in 1948.

Social Services, Health and Welfare, Benevolent and Friendly Societies

394 **Report of the International Seminar on Community Development held at the Social Welfare Training Centre, U.W.I. [University of the West Indies], Jamaica, W.I., January 3rd-13th, 1972.**
Prepared by the Research Unit, Social Development Commission, Jamaica. Kingston, Jamaica: [Social Development Commission?, 1972]. 151p. map.

Seminar sponsored by the Social Development Commission, the University of Missouri, the Sugar Industry Labour Welfare Board and the University of the West Indies. In addition to papers of general background interest there are papers which deal in some detail with the community development infrastructure and programmes of the sponsoring bodies. Edited by Sonia Latibeaudiere, assisted by Marjorie Gammon.

395 **An appraisal of the co-operative process in the Jamaican sugar industry.**
Carl Stone. *Social and Economic Studies*, vol. 27, no: 1 (March 1978), p. 1-20. bibliog.

An appraisal of the Jamaican government's experience in establishing twenty co-operative farms on three of the island's sugar estates during the years 1974-1976. The appraisal is based on on-site surveys and on the author's experience in advisory and educational roles in the co-operative movement.

396 **Caribbean resource book focusing on women in development: collaborative effort on the part of the Women's Bureau of Jamaica, Extra-Mural Dept. of the University of the West Indies, the International Women's Tribune Centre.**
New York: International Women's Tribune Centre, [1977?]. 213p. bibliog.

A loose-leaf compilation of information on projects and organizations, publications and funding sources and possibilities for action. Jamaican organizations are listed at p. 46-72. Information given includes name of organization or project, address and short description.

397 **Jamaica's youth programmes for the seventies.**
Youth Development Agency, Government of Jamaica. In: *Youth and development in the Caribbean: report of the Commonwealth Caribbean Regional Youth seminar*, Port of Spain, Trinidad, Aug. 1970; London: Commonwealth Secretariat, 1970, p. 192-209.

A synopsis of government programmes and plans, some of which have been implemented in part, at least.

Social Services, Health and Welfare, Benevolent and Friendly Societies

A review of the developments in education and social welfare in Jamaica during the period 1944-1954.
See item no. 823.

Caribbean directory of human resources in social development. Directorio caribeño de recursos humanos en areas de desarrollo social.
See item no. 1140.

Politics

General

398 **Jamaica: the demise of 'democratic socialism'.**
Fitzroy [L.] Ambursley. *New Left Review*, no. 128
(July-Aug. 1981), p. 76-87. bibliog.

An account of the People's National Party's experiment in 'democratic socialism' and of its defeat by the opposition Jamaica Labour Party. The author argues that the CIA and its local allies were able to destabilize the government by exploiting the weaknesses in the populist and nationalist politics of its leader.

399 **Jamaica's Michael Manley: messiah, muddler or marionette?**
Christopher Arawak[*pseud.*]. Miami, Florida: Sir Henry
Morgan Press, 1980. 232p.

An admittedly subjective and 'angry' study of Michael Manley's leadership of the government of Jamaica under the People's National Party from 1972 to 1980. It is, nevertheless, a lively indictment which poses many pertinent questions and accurately reflects the concerns of many Jamaicans who opposed the policies which prevailed in the eight years prior to the general elections of October 1980.

400 **Jamaican leaders: political attitudes in a new nation.**
Wendell Bell. Berkeley, California; Los Angeles: University
of California Press, 1964. 229p. map. bibliog.

This study is based on the premise that 'the élites in any society have an importance far exceeding their numbers'. (p. 53). After a general review of Jamaica's social and political development it attempts to identify the leaders and to analyse, especially from a survey of the attitudes of the leaders, the likely directions which Jamaican society might take in matters such as social structure, political system and global alignments. Although the analysis is based very largely on data collected by questionnaires distributed a few years prior to Jamaica achieving independence, and on interviews also prior to that event, the work is of particular interest in so far as it is now possible to recognize how far certain indications or developments have or have not taken place and why.

Politics. General

401 **Mass parties in Jamaica: structure and organisation.**
C. Paul Bradley. *Social and Economic Studies*, vol. 9, no.
4 (Dec. 1960), p. 375-416. bibliog.

A study of the political party system of Jamaica, and, more particularly, of the
political process which began with the rise of mass political parties in the late
1930s. This study was sponsored by a research grant from the University of
Michigan which enabled the author, then Assistant Professor of Political Science
in the University of Michigan, to make two visits to Jamaica in 1957 and 1958
for the purpose of interviewing political leaders and consulting documentary
records.

402 **Some aspects of Jamaica's politics: 1918-1938.**
James [A.] Carnegie, with a preface by Trevor
Munroe. [Kingston]: Institute of Jamaica, 1973. 194p.
bibliog. (Cultural Heritage Series, vol. 4).

An objective account of political life in the years between the First and Second
World Wars, years which saw the emergence of a politically active Black petty
bourgeoisie embracing elected representatives, reformers, journalists and trade
unionists in growing conflict with the colonial official caste, on the threshold of
internal self-rule. The book had its genesis as an MA thesis presented to the
University of the West Indies in 1969. It is liberally illustrated with portrait
photographs of the principal public figures of the period. It is perhaps the only
account of Jamaican politics during this formative period in the development of
modern Jamaica. A list of references (20p) is included.

403 **Detained: 283 days in Jamaica's detention camp, struggling
for freedom, justice and human rights.**
Pearnel Charles. Kingston: Kingston Publishers, 1977.
207p.

Senator Charles, trade unionist and Deputy Leader of the Jamaica Labour Party,
was detained under the regulations which came into force when the Government
of Jamaica declared a state of emergency on the 19th June 1976. His book is not
only a record of life in the camp but is of interest for the account he gives of his
work as a trade unionist and it is significant as an indication of quite new
developments in the political life of the country.

404 **Political growth in Jamaica: 1938-1969 from colony to
nationhood.**
Wesley Walton Daley. PhD thesis, Howard University,
Washington, DC, 1971. 276 leaves. bibliog. (Available from
University Microfilms, Ann Arbor, Michigan, 1972).

A factual and evaluative account of the development of political institutions in
Jamaica throughout the period studied, with some consideration of the socio-
economic structure which is felt to be the corner stone of effective and successful
national development.

405 Jamaican politics, economics and culture: an interview with Edward Seaga.

Stephen Davis. *Caribbean Review*, vol. 10, no. 4 (fall 1981), p. 14-17.

Reflects the new perspectives of the recently elected Jamaican government under Edward Seaga, commenting on the economic fortunes of the country under the People's National Party (PNP) government and the country's prospects in the new economic climate which is 'wedded to investment', with some comments on Jamaican folk culture with particular reference to religious cults and reggae music. This interview is from the author's forthcoming book *Reggae International*.

406 Jamaica.

W. Raymond Duncan. In: *Communism in Central America and the Caribbean*. Edited by Robert Wesson. Stanford, California: Hoover Institution Press, 1982, p. 117-30. bibliog.

Discusses the strength and economic roots of communist ideology in Jamaica and its effects on the country's international relations. The author is Professor and Director of Global Studies at the State University of New York (SUNY), Brockport.

407 The newer Caribbean: decolonization, democracy and development.

[Edited by] Paget Henry, Carl Stone.   Philadelphia, Pennsylvania: Institute for the Study of Human Issues, 1983. 348p. bibliog. (Inter-American Politics Series, vol. 4).

A collection of essays by Caribbean scholars which grew out of two seminars on the title theme held in New York and Jamaica between 1978 and 1980. The essays have been revised and brought up to date and are now presented to a wider public concerned about contemporary affairs in the Caribbean. The following essays relate specifically to Jamaica: 'Decolonization and the Caribbean state system: the case of Jamaica' by Carl Stone; 'The Commonwealth Caribbean and the contemporary world order: the cases of Jamaica and Trinidad' by Paul W. Ashley; and 'Democracy and socialism in Jamaica: 1972-1979' by Carl Stone.

408 The struggle for the settler vote: politics and the franchise in post-emancipation Jamaica.

Gad [J.] Heuman. In: *Peasants, plantations and rural communities in the Caribbean*. Edited by Malcolm Cross, Arnaud Marks. Guildford, England: Department of Sociology of the University of Surrey and Department of Caribbean Studies of the Royal Institute of Linguistics and Anthropology, Leiden, Netherlands, 1979, p. 1-28. map. bibliog.

This article throws new light on the political role of peasants and small farmers in post-emancipation Jamaica. The author is a lecturer in history at the University of Warwick and has been engaged in making a special study of the social and political life of Jamaica between emancipation and the Morant Bay Rebellion.

409 **Legitimacy and change in Jamaica.**
Richard S. Hillman. *Journal of Developing Areas*, vol. 13, no. 4 (July, 1979), p. 395-414. bibliog.

'This paper analyzes Jamaican perceptions of contemporary politics and assesses how development in Jamaica has been conditioned by people's attitudes toward their government.' It is based on research conducted in Jamaica from January to May 1978 by the author, who is Associate Professor and Chairman, Department of Political Science, St. John Fisher College, Rochester, New York.

410 **Appeals by Jamaican political parties: a study of newspaper advertisements in the 1972 Jamaican general election campaign.**
W. Richard Jacobs. *Caribbean Studies*, vol. 13, no. 2 (July 1973), p. 19-50. bibliog.

A study of newspaper advertisements as projections of party images in what was to prove an election of great consequence to Jamaica.

411 **The origins and development of political parties in the British West Indies.**
Charles Henry Kunsman. PhD thesis, University of California, Berkeley, California, 1963. 832 leaves. 6 maps. bibliog. (Available from University Microfilms, Ann Arbor, Michigan, 1963).

A factual account, of which part two (p. 128-280) is devoted to Jamaica. The author makes extensive use of contemporary sources such as newspapers, periodicals and party pamphlets as well as information gathered in the course of personal interviews with West Indian government and political leaders in 1954, 1955 and 1960. The work is of particular interest in that it is possible to review developments in Jamaica alongside those elsewhere in the West Indies in the period before these countries gained independence.

412 **Violence and politics in Jamaica, 1960-70: internal security in a developing country.**
Terry Lacey. Manchester, England: Manchester University Press, 1977. 184p. bibliog.

The author, an official of the European Economic Community Development Commission, provides an outsider's pioneering 'case study of the problems related to the maintenance of internal security in a developing country... based on events in Jamaica between 1960 and 1970...' (p. 1). He concludes that in many ways Jamaican society is a frustrated one and that 'economic and social conflicts have shaped the Jamaican political system'. His analysis of these conflicts suggests that their resolution is a necessary condition to solving the problems of political violence (cf. p. 161-62).

413 **The fall of Michael Manley: a case study of the failure of reform socialism.**
Arthur Lewin. *Monthly Review: an independent Socialist magazine*, vol. 33, no. 9 (Feb. 1982), p. 49-60. bibliog.

The author attributes the failure of Michael Manley and the People's National Party government's socialist policies to the Jamaican political system, to the development programme pursued by the government and to the fact that 'Manley was really only a rhetorical socialist.' (p. 58). The author teaches in the Department of Black and Hispanic Studies at Baruch College, New York.

414 **The emergence of national society: Jamaica.**
Gordon K. Lewis. In: *The growth of the modern West Indies.* Gordon K. Lewis. London: Macgibbon & Kee, 1968, p. 167-96.

A succinct account of the growth of national awareness and the emergence of Jamaica as an independent country from Crown Colony status. Though many of the views stated are controversial the account covers all the salient influences, movements and persons and, within its short compass, helps one to appreciate the convergence and role of these factors in the creation of a nation.

415 **The myth of independence: middle class politics and non-mobilization in Jamaica.**
Louis Lindsay. Mona, Jamaica: Institute of Social and Economic Research, University of the West Indies, 1975. 73p. bibliog. (University of the West Indies, Institute of Social and Economic Research. Working Paper, no. 6).

'My purpose is to develop... a framework for a theory of symbolic manipulation in Jamaican political life.' (Preface, p. i). The author's main contention is that as Jamaica achieved independence without direct struggle against colonial rule no real nationalist movement was generated, in which middle-class political leaders could involve 'the broad masses of Jamaican people in a quest for real self-determination and political economy'. (cf. p. 48-49). This is a reprint of the first edition of 1975 with additional pages.

416 **The birth of self-government in Jamaica, 1937 to 1944.**
Walter G. McFarlane. Brooklyn, New York; Kingston: Gleaner Co. [for the author?], 1957. 25p.

A critical view of the roles of Alexander Bustamante and Norman Manley in the early movement of Jamaica towards self-government. The author was organiser and former secretary of the Jamaica Progressive League of Kingston, founded in Jamaica in 1936, as a branch of the parent league of the same name, which had been founded in New York earlier in that year to promote the economic and political advancement of the Jamaican people.

Politics. General

417 Jamaica: struggle in the periphery.
Michael Manley. London: Third World Media in
association with Writers and Readers Publishing Cooperative
Society, [1982]. 259p. bibliog.

The author's reflections on the Jamaican experience during the eight and a half
years of People's National Party government, 1972-80, during which he was
prime minister and during which his government strove in the periphery of the
Third World to explore another path to that pursued by either Puerto Rico or
Cuba, described by the author as 'a third path, a Jamaican way rooted in our
political experience and values, capable of providing an economic base to our
political independence and capable of some measure of social justice for the
people'. (p. 38). He writes at some length in defending the policies, both domestic
and foreign, of his government whose defeat in the 1980 general elections he
attributes to a programme of destabilization, as well as to the protracted economic crisis of the country.

418 The politics of change: a Jamaican testament.
Michael Manley. London: Andre Deutsch, 1974. 223p.

The author became Prime Minister of Jamaica as a result of the general elections
held in February 1972. The work is a personal testament of the author's hopes
and intentions for a reform and restructuring of Jamaican society on principles of
equality, social justice and democracy, summoning 'the whole nation to rally to
new challenges and new opportunities' (p. 216). Part two, which concerns the
strategy of change, deals with politics, the economy, foreign policy, education,
basic institutions and the initial steps taken by his government to bring about
change.

**419 The search for solutions: selections from the speeches and
writings of Michael Manley.**
Edited with notes and an introduction by John
Hearne. Oshawa, Canada: Maple House Publishing Co.,
1976. 322p.

A selection which helps to define the thought of Michael Manley, trade unionist
and politician, on a wide range of subjects, spanning the years 1952 to 1976. The
book is intended for the busy layman interested in the politics of Jamaica and not
as a definitive work of reference.

420 Electoral reform in Jamaica.
G. E. Mills. *The Parliamentarian: Journal of the
Parliaments of the Commonwealth*, vol. 42, no. 2 (April
1981), p. 97-104. bibliog.

An account of electoral reform in Jamaica preceding the general elections of
1980, by the Chairman of the Electoral Advisory Committee, Professor of Public
Administration and Dean of the Faculty of Social Sciences, University of the
West Indies.

421 The Marxist 'Left' in Jamaica, 1940-1950.

Trevor Munroe. Mona, Jamaica: Institute of Social and Economic Research, University of the West Indies, 1977. 76p. bibliog. (University of the West Indies, Institute of Social and Economic Research. Working Paper, no. 15).

'This article is a preliminary contribution to deepening our understanding of the "left-wing", the communist elements in the Jamaican national movement at a crucial stage of its development between 1940 and 1950... the years in which the goal of national self-determination gained ground amongst different social classes and, in particular, the years in which substantial sections of the working people were brought organisationally into the movement against colonialism.' Thereby the author hopes 'to lay the foundation for understanding both the developments in the two decades after 1950 as well as the reappearance after 1972 of socialist trends long dormant in national politics.' (cf. Introduction, p. 3-4).

422 The politics of constitutional decolonization: Jamaica 1944-62.

Trevor Munroe. Jamaica: Institute of Social and Economic Research, University of the West Indies, 1972. 239p. bibliog.

'This book, originally a doctoral thesis presented to the University of Oxford and researched and written in the United Kingdom 1966 and 1968, deals with the political and constitutional aspects of the final decades of British colonial rule which lasted from 1655 to 1962.' (Preface, p. vii). Much attention is given to the development of party politics and the process whereby independence was achieved. The work concludes by suggesting likely political developments in the post-independence period based on contemporary socio-economic tendencies.

423 Readings in government and politics of the West Indies.

Edited by Trevor Munroe, Rupert Lewis. [Kingston]: Department of Government, University of the West Indies, 1971. rev. ed. 270p. bibliog.

This revised edition of an earlier work with the same title, compiled by A. W. Singham and published in 1967, is in fact a different work, in that it includes but a small fraction of the readings included in the edition of 1967. New material was selected 'to reflect the interest of the working classes' as manifested in 'the post-1968 mass upsplurge in the region' (cf. Introduction, p. vii).

424 Struggles of the Jamaican people.

Trevor Munroe, Don Robotham. London: Workers' Liberation League, 1978. 2nd ed. 174p. (Popular Political Education Series, no. 1).

First published in Kingston in 1977, the second edition has been published in co-operation with Caribbean Labour Solidarity (CLS), London. A practical tool for political education and ideological instruction, prepared and published by the Workers' Liberation League, whose 'fundamental organisational aim... is the building of a genuine Jamaican Communist Party...' (cf. inside front cover). An anti-imperialist interpretation of working-class struggles since the end of slavery. Illustrated with drawings by Clinton Hutton and photographs.

425 The Workers Party: what it is, why it is necessary.
Trevor Munroe. Kingston: WLL [Workers Liberation League], December 1978. 25p.

This booklet sets out to explain how the Workers Party differs from the other two major political parties in Jamaica. It is made up of articles written by the General Secretary of the Workers Liberation League, just prior to the transformation of the League into the Workers Party, a communist party based on the principles of Marxism-Leninism, and which were first published in *Struggle* newspaper from July to October 1978.

426 Political dissidence in post-independence Jamaica and Trinidad: 1962-1972.
Canute Nicholas Parris. PhD thesis, New School for Social Research, New York, 1976. 301 leaves, bibliog. (Available from University Microfilms, Ann Arbor, Michigan, 1976).

A study of the political behaviour of dissident groups drawn principally from the unemployed and the underemployed, including the Ras Tafari brethren, the 'Rudies' (or Rude Boys), the Unemployed Workers' Council, the Independent Trade Union Advisory Council, and the Young Socialist League, all of Jamaica.

427 From Michael with love: the nature of socialism in Jamaica.
Anthony Payne. *Journal of Commonwealth & Comparative Politics*, vol. 14, no. 1 (March 1976), p. 82-100. bibliog.

An interpretation of the nature of socialism in Jamaica against a background view of the nature of the political system itself. The focus of the article is the programme of the People's National Party from September 1974 when the government announced that Jamaica was to be considered one of the socialist countries of the world. The author is of the view that Jamaican socialism is 'indeed a tepid brew'.

428 Seaga's Jamaica after one year.
Anthony Payne. *World Today*, vol. 37, no. 11 (Nov. 1981), p. 434-40.

Reviews the revival of the Jamaican economy and the transformation of the Jamaican government under the Jamaica Labour Party and its leader Edward Seaga, who was voted into power on 31 October 1980. Discusses the problems which the new government might be expected to encounter and the extent to which renewed economic growth can solve the more intractable problems of the Jamaican economy such as unemployment, unequal distribution of income and inadequate social welfare. The author is Senior Lecturer in Politics at Huddersfield Polytechnic.

429 Democratic socialism: the Jamaican model.
People's National Party. [Kingston]: People's National Party, [1976?]. [50]p.

An official statement of the fundamental beliefs of the People's National Party and of the principles of democratic socialism that were laid down for the guidance of the government during the term of office of the PNP from 1977 to 1980.

430 **Principles and objectives.**
People's National Party. Kingston: People's National Party,
1979. 68p.

This document was the outcome of two years of intense discussion at all levels of the party. 'In the tradition of the PNP, we have sought to develop a modern interpretation of our socialist philosophy in the context of today's world and the accumulated experience of the Jamaican people, particularly in the last forty years.' (Foreword by the President, Michael Manley). The document sets forth party policies in the ideological, economic, social and international orders.

431 **A climate for expansion.**
Edward Seaga. Kingston: Agency for Public Information,
1980. 20p.

Edward Seaga's first speech to Parliament as Prime Minister of Jamaica, 18 November 1980, in which he reported on the historic general elections which were held on 30 October 1980 and indicated in broad outline the policies which his government would pursue.

432 **The message is change: a perspective of the 1972 general elections.**
Olive Senior. Kingston: Kingston Publishers, 1972. 98p.

A record of an historic election.

433 **Quotes from the Rt. Hon. Hugh Lawson Shearer, the Prime Minister of Jamaica.**
Hugh Lawson Shearer. [Kingston]: Jamaica Information
Service, [1971?]. [32]p.

Excerpts from addresses and speeches, primarily on the implications of independence and the demands of nationhood. They provide an insight into the thought of one of the important figures associated with laying the foundations of Jamaica as an independent nation.

434 **The political élite of Jamaica: recruitment patterns, 1962-1972.**
Keith Cecil Simmonds. PhD thesis, University of Illinois,
Urbana-Champaign, Illinois, 1977. 274 leaves. bibliog.
(Available from University Microfilms, Ann Arbor,
Michigan, 1977).

A study of the social composition, recruitment process and political attitudes of the political élite of Jamaica, in the decade after independence. The author discovers a number of changes and developments in this field since Wendell Bell published his study, *Jamaican leaders* in 1964. He concludes that the Jamaican élite not only reflects the on-going social change but is itself an instrument of that change.

435 Readings in government and politics of the West Indies.
Compiled by A. W. Singham [and others]. [Kingston:
Department of Government, University of the West Indies,
1967]. 518p. bibliog.

'This reader is intended primarily for students in government at the University of
the West Indies' (Introduction, p. i) and was published for private circulation
only. The readings relate variously to the Commonwealth Caribbean as a whole,
or to specific territories or countries such as Jamaica. It is one of two works
which attempts to introduce West Indian readers to political science through
writings which relate to the political experience of the area. The contents include:
'Approaches to the study of government and politics of the West Indies'; 'Political
institutions'; 'Political socialization'; 'Race, culture and personality'; 'Bureaucracy'; 'Parties, elections and pressure groups'; 'Trade unions and politics'; 'Elites
and power'; and 'Political unification' Appendices include: polemics; party
manifestoes; extracts from independence constitutions and a bibliography (p.
477-518).

436 Class, race and political behaviour in urban Jamaica.
Carl Stone. Jamaica: Institute of Social and Economic
Research, University of the West Indies, 1973. 188p. bibliog.

An analytical study of the relations between social stratification and political
behaviour, focusing on the degree of mass support for the political institutions
which have evolved since the achievement of independence in 1962. The author, a
Jamaican, is Reader in Political Sociology in the University of the West Indies,
Mona, Jamaica.

437 Democracy and clientelism in Jamaica.
Carl Stone. New Brunswick, New Jersey: Transaction
Books, 1980. 262p. bibliog.

A study of Jamaican society with particular reference to class and classes and the
way in which class structure and social attitudes have influenced the country's
political life and behaviour. The work assembles a considerable body of opinion
and social profile data gathered in a series of national polls between 1976 and
1978. The author was closely associated with a number of government boards and
agencies and the work is particularly valuable as a study of Jamaican politics
during the 1970s.

438 Democracy and socialism in Jamaica, 1962-1979.
Carl Stone. *Journal of Commonwealth & Comparative
Politics*, vol. 19, no. 2 (July 1981), p. 115-33.

An analysis of the inter-related factors which have influenced the process of
democratization in Jamaica, more particularly during the period 1972 to 1979,
under the socialist government of the People's National Party.

439 Electoral behaviour and public opinion in Jamaica.
Carl Stone. Jamaica: Institute of Social and Economic
Research, University of the West Indies, 1974. 107p. bibliog.

A survey and analysis of the electoral process, with particular reference to the
general elections of 1972, designed to illuminate the attitudes and issues which
determine voting behaviour and the functioning of the competitive party system in

Jamaica. The sociological analysis has been simplified to render the work amenable to readers outside the disciplines of the Social Sciences.

440 **Jamaica's 1980 elections: what Manley did do; what Seaga need do.**
Carl Stone. *Caribbean Review*, vol. 10, no. 2 (spring 1981), p. 4-7, 40-43.

An analysis of a crucial Jamaican election by a political sociologist and foremost political pollster in Jamaica.

441 **The 1976 parliamentary election in Jamaica.**
Carl Stone. *Journal of Commonwealth & Comparative Politics*, vol. 15, no. 3 (Nov. 1977), p. 250-65. bibliog.

An examination of the People's National Party's electoral victory with regard to the campaign issues, voting patterns and the responses of the electorate, based in part on public opinion polls conducted by the author.

442 **The political opinions of the Jamaican people (1976-81).**
Carl Stone. Kingston: Blackett Publishers, 1982. 78p.

A collection of the more important polls done by the author in the period August 1976 to December 1981 grouped in six main categories as follows: the polls, parties, leaders and ideology, the media, foreign policy, social issues, economic issues.

443 **Jamaica: problems of Manley's politics of change, 1972-1980.**
Winston Van Horne. *Journal of Caribbean Studies*, vol. 2, nos. 2 & 3 (autumn/winter 1981), p. 210-26. bibliog.

This essay is full of acute insights into the political, social and economic changes which Jamaica experienced during the years of People's National Party government under the leadership of Michael Manley. The author is chairman of Afro-American Studies at the University of Wisconsin, Milwaukee.

444 **Jamaica: why Manley lost.**
Winston A. Van Horne. *World Today*, vol. 37, no. 11 (Nov. 1981), p. 428-33.

A brief and highly critical comment on the reasons why, in the opinion of the author, the People's National Party under the leadership of Michael Manley lost the general elections of October 1980. The author, who is Associate Professor in the Department of Afro-American Studies at the University of Wisconsin, Milwaukee, was born in Jamaica where he spent his first 20 years. He has revisited the island in 1973, 1977, 1980 and 1981.

445 **The British Caribbean from the decline of colonialism to the end of Federation.**
Elisabeth Wallace. Toronto; Buffalo, New York: University of Toronto Press, 1977. 274p. bibliog.

A study of political developments in the Commonwealth Caribbean territories from the beginning of the 20th century to the collapse of West Indian Federation

Politics. Sir William Alexander Bustamante

in 1962. It presents an objective outsider's comparative view of the political, constitutional and trade union history of Jamaica and the eleven other territories studied. The study was commissioned by the Canadian Institute of International Affairs and written by a member of the Department of Political Economy, University of Toronto.

The dynamics of change in a slave society: a sociopolitical history of the free coloreds of Jamaica, 1800-1865.
See item no. 139.

Between black and white: race, politics and the free coloreds in Jamaica, 1792-1865.
See item no. 155.

Color, class, and politics in Jamaica.
See item no. 347.

The role of statutory boards in the political process in Jamaica.
See item no. 482.

Royal government and political conflict in Jamaica, 1729-1783.
See item no. 484.

Caribbean conflict: Jamaica & the US.
See item no. 502.

Communication and politics in Jamaica.
See item no. 119.

Some observations on the role of mass media in the recent socio-political development in Jamaica.
See item no. 1122.

Caribbean Insight.
See item no. 1131.

Sir William Alexander Bustamante

446 Alexander Bustamante and modern Jamaica.
George E. Eaton. Kingston: Kingston Publishers in association with McGraw Hill FEP, 1975. 276p. bibliog.

A detailed, factual and highly readable account of Bustamante's life and of his role as a politician in the decolonization and modernization of independent Jamaica.

447 Bustamante: anthology of a hero.
B. St. J. Hamilton. Kingston: Publications & Productions, [1978]. 162p.

A biographical study, constructed mainly from anecdotes and information gleaned in conversation with Bustamante and his contemporaries, interspersed with a generous selection of his letters.

448 **Bustamante and his letters.**

Frank Hill. Kingston: Kingston Publishers, in association with the Matalon Group of Companies and Radio Jamaica, 1976. 126p.

A sympathetic and deftly executed biographical sketch of Bustamante and of Jamaican society as it was prior to the social upheaval of 1938. The texts of Bustamante's letters, reproduced *in extenso*, are a solid documentary basis for the portrait of the man and his times.

449 **The Bustamante letters 1935.**

Trevor Munroe. *Jamaica Journal*, vol. 8, no. 1 (March 1974), p. 3-15. bibliog.

The letters are reproduced in facsimile from the columns of the *Daily Gleaner* and are accompanied by a detailed commentary on the political, economic and cultural ideas of Bustamante, when he emerged into public life, as evinced by the letters. With the exception of a couple letters all are reproduced in *Bustamante and his letters* by Frank Hill (1976); however, the commentaries of these two works are different in perspective and purpose.

450 **The best of Bustamante: selected quotations 1935-74.**

[Researched and compiled by] Jackie Ranston, [edited by] Ken Jones. Jamaica: Twin Guinep, 1977. 111p.

A selection from Bustamante's letters and speeches, on a wide range of topics, arranged alphabetically, without comment, designed not only to illustrate his wit and wisdom but to give an insight into his character. The selections are nearly all brief and pithy and are identified by the year and, in some instances, the occasion on which they were delivered. Includes a few illustrations.

451 **Alexander Bustamante: portrait of a hero.**

Hugh Lawson Shearer. Kingston: Kingston Publishers for the Bustamante Industrial Trade Union, 1978. 126p.

The text of the remembrance by the Rt. Hon. Hugh Lawson Shearer, on the occasion of the state funeral of the Rt. Hon Sir William Alexander Bustamante, 14 August 1977, amplified with many excellent and unusual photographs of Bustamante in his public and private life.

Norman Washington Manley

452 **The autobiography of Norman Washington Manley.**

Jamaica Journal, vol. 7, no. 1-2 (March-June 1973), p. 2-19, 92.

Includes the texts of two unfinished autobiographical accounts which differ considerably in wording (though not in substance) from the fragment of autobiography contained in *Norman Washington Manley and the new Jamaica*, edited by Rex Nettleford (1971).

453 Norman Manley.
Therese Mills. Arima, Trinidad: Giuseppi Publications, 1976. 91p. (Little Biographies of Great West Indians Series).

A biography written in clear simple language, the authenticity of which is attested by the fact that the manuscript was read and commented upon by the biographee's widow and eldest son (cf. Acknowledgments, p. 3).

454 Manley and the politics of Jamaica; towards an analysis of political change in Jamaica, 1938-1968.
Rex Nettleford. [Mona, Jamaica]: Institute of Social and Economic Research, University of the West Indies, 1971. 72p. (Supplement to *Social and Economic Studies*, vol. 20, no. 3, Sept. 1971).

An assessment of the impact of the personality of N. W. Manley on the political development of Jamaica. The author concludes that Manley's tutelage of the electorate in 'the need to conduct the nation's public affairs on principled foundations rather than on the whims and caprice of unprincipled self-indulgence' may very well be a lasting contribution of the period 1938 to 1968 (cf. p. 71).

455 Norman Washington Manley and the new Jamaica: selected speeches and writings 1938-68.
Edited with notes and introduction by Rex Nettleford. Jamaica: Longman Caribbean, 1971. 393p.

'... this volume of selections tries to present to the reader the thought and plans for action by Norman Manley; political leader, in his role as thinker and practical politician.' (General introduction, p. xi).

456 Norman Manley.
Philip [Manderson] Sherlock. London: Macmillan, 1980. 223p. bibliog.

A readable and vivid account of Manley the patriot, statesman and politician, written by a contemporary and a friend and drawn from contemporary sources, including Manley's unpublished papers and from Colonial Office despatches. It is an equally interesting account of contemporary events and personalities most closely associated with him during the thirty years, 1938 to 1968, when he was actively engaged in politics.

Constitution, Legal and Judicial System

General

457 The constitutional law of Jamaica.
Lloyd G. Barnett. Oxford, England: Oxford University Press for the London School of Economic and Political Science, 1977. 468p.

'This book is an attempt to study the evolution and adaptation of the principles of responsible cabinet government and constitutionalism in Jamaica' (Preface, p. xi). The Jamaican Independence Constitution is examined in detail against its historical background. The book is likely to be of interest to students, politicians, government administrators and lawyers. Based on a thesis submitted in 1965 for the degree of PhD of the University of London, the text has been revised up to 1975, and, where possible, later developments of particular importance have been included. The author is a former President of the Jamaican Bar Association.

458 Jamaica and the West Indies Federation: a case study on the problems of political integration.
Noel Joseph Brown. PhD thesis, Yale University, New Haven, Connecticut, 1963. 460p. map. bibliog. (Available from University Microfilms, Ann Arbor, Michigan, 1964).

Perhaps the most detailed study of Jamaica's involvement in the West Indies Federation and of the operative factors in the referendum of 1961 which led to the dissolution of the Federation. The study is divided into three parts. The first is a general description of the West Indies and of the influences which led to the establishment of the Federation. The second examines the factors affecting political integration and the third analyses Jamaica's referendum as the crucial test of West Indian integration.

Constitution, Legal and Judicial System. General

459 A brief history of the post of Master of the Supreme Court Jamaica, his appointment and functions.
Hugh V. T. Chambers. Kingston: printed by Metro Press, [1972]. 38p.

A contribution to the sparsely documented subject of the law courts of Jamaica, by the first Master to be appointed to the Supreme Court of Jamaica in 1967 since the office was abolished in 1871.

460 Family law in the Commonwealth Caribbean.
Gloria Cumper, Stephanie Daly. Mona, Jamaica: Department of Extra-Mural Studies, University of the West Indies, 1979. 256p.

A series of surveys of family laws undertaken as part of a project of the Regional Pre-School Child Development Project of the University of the West Indies, sponsored jointly by UNICEF, with the aim of making understandable to the non-specialist laws relating to children and their families. The surveys were used as background papers for two workshops held in 1975 and 1976, of which the resolutions and recommendations are also included. The Jamaica survey (p. 93-129) has been rewritten from the relevant sections of Cumper's *Survey of social legislation in Jamaica* (1972) and brought up to date.

461 Planning and implementing the Family Court project, Jamaica.
Gloria Cumper. Kingston: Institute of Social and Economic Research, University of the West Indies, 1981. 75p. (Working Paper no. 27).

The author was chairman of the committee whose report recommended the establishment of a family court, and was appointed co-ordinator for the establishment of the first such court in Kingston and St. Andrew in 1974. In principle, the family court superseded the former juvenile court system. The paper attempts a critical look at the family court, with emphasis on the areas of difficulty in planning and implementation.

462 Survey of social legislation in Jamaica.
Gloria Cumper. Jamaica: Institute of Social and Economic Research, University of the West Indies, 1972. 122p. (Law and Society in the Caribbean, no. 1).

An overall view of the subject written for those engaged in social services, with the secondary purpose of indicating areas where legislation may stand in need of change.

463 The Jamaican Independence Constitution of 1962.
James B. Kelly. *Caribbean Studies*, vol. 3, no. 1 (April 1963), p. 18-83.

A critical analysis of the principles involved and of the procedures followed in drafting and ratifying the constitution. The author was at the time of publication a Research Associate at the Institute of Caribbean Studies and had formerly been with the Institute of Social and Economic Research in the University of the West Indies.

464 Criminal law and its administration - a Jamaican view.
J. S. Kerr. In: *Law in the West Indies: some recent trends.* London: British Institute of International and Comparative Law, 1966, p. 101-16. bibliog.

An outline of the system of criminal law in Jamaica, with the author's perception of the direction in which it is heading. The author was a resident magistrate in Jamaica, who, at the time of the conference organized by the British Institute, at which this paper was presented, held the office of Acting Passport Officer and Legal Attaché to the Jamaican High Commission in London.

465 The West Indies: the federal negotiations.
John Mordecai, epilogue by W. Arthur Lewis. London: Allen & Unwin, 1968. 484p. bibliog.

A particularly knowledgeable account of the West Indies Federation and especially useful in understanding Jamaica's role in the federal experiment, written by the former deputy governor-general, who was, prior to that, secretary of the Federation and of its forerunner, the Regional Economic Committee of the West Indies. At the end is a 'Who's Who' of the former West Indies Federation.

466 Some notes on the law and land settlement in Jamaica, 1661-1736.
C. Dennis Morrison. *West Indian Law Journal,* vol. 6, no. 2 (Oct. 1982), p. 219-31. bibliog.

Discusses the legal framework which regulated the distribution and settlement of land in the first seventy-five years after the English conquest of Jamaica had been completed. The author is an attorney-at-law, Jamaica.

467 Freedom in the Caribbean: a study in constitutional change.
Sir Fred Phillips, with a foreword by the Hon. Mr. E. V. Luckhoo. Dobbs Ferry, New York: Oceana Publications, 1977. 737p. bibliog.

This work attempts 'to bring into focus the manifold lines of constitutional development in the whole region', i.e. in the Commonwealth Caribbean, (Preface p. ix), and is intended for research workers, students of law and for the general public interested in constitutional law. In the author's text, as well as in the substantial appendix of legal documents and instruments, constitutional developments in Jamaica and the other territories of the Caribbean are outlined, with particular reference to the experiment of West Indian Federation, judicial review in the Caribbean (referring to the Gun Court cases in Jamaica), constitutionalism by closer economic association (e.g. CARICOM, the Caribbean Development Bank), training of lawyers in the Caribbean, etc. The author is a barrister-at-law and a former Governor of St. Kitts, Nevis, Anguilla.

468 **Constitutional development of the West Indies 1922-1968: a selection from the major documents.**
Ann Spackman. Barbados: Caribbean Universities Press in association with the Bowker Publishing Company, 1975. xxxxiv, 619p. bibliog.

Includes the Jamaica constitution of 1944 with documents leading to its adoption and extracts from the Jamaica constitution of 1962. A long preface and introduction provide a useful outline of constitutional development in the region and of the social and political background against which this development took place.

469 **Public opinion, lawyers and the legal system in Jamaica.**
Carl Stone. *West Indian Law Journal*, vol. 6, no. 1 (May 1982), p. 99-115.

A report on the findings of a survey of public attitudes to and opinions on the impact of law and lawyers on Jamaican society. This national survey of public opinion was carried out in November 1980 and was financed by the Council of Legal Education from funds provided by the Canadian International Development Research Centre.

470 **Latin America and the development of the law of the sea: regional documents and national legislation.**
[Edited by] Alberto Szekely. Dobbs Ferry, New York: Oceana Publications, 1976-78. 2 vols. bibliog.

A loose-leaf collection comprising, volume one, the editor's study of the contribution of Latin American states to the development of the international law of the sea since 1945 and volume two, a collection of national legislation on the subject. 'Jamaica, booklet 13' (9p.) reproduces extracts from three legislative documents, 1948-71, including its Territorial Sea Act No. 14, 29 April 1971.

471 **The constitutional development of Jamaica, 1660 to 1729.**
Agnes M. Whitson. Manchester, England: Manchester University Press, 1929. 182p. bibliog.

A standard work on the early constitutional history of Jamaica.

472 **Land transactions in Jamaica.**
Ashton G. Wright. Kingston: Rightart Printers, 1976. 26p. (Layman's Legal Series, no. 1).

A guide to vendors and purchasers on legal matters relating to land transactions, written in simple language, free of legal terminology, by a Jamaican attorney-at-law.

Periodicals

473 **Bulletin on Current Legal Developments.**
Jamaica: Ministry of National Security and Justice, Legal Reform Division, 1975-76. six issues only.

Contains summaries of the more important judgments of the higher courts and other important or interesting developments in law in Jamaica and elsewhere in the common-law world.

474 **West Indian Law Journal.**
Kingston: Council of Legal Education, 1977- . biannual.

Supersedes the *Jamaica Law Journal*, 1970-75. Includes editorials, signed articles and speeches, commentaries on legislation, case notes and book reviews. Illustrated.

Administration and Local Government, Civics

General

475 **Public sector issues in the Commonwealth Caribbean. (Studies in Caribbean public enterprise).**
Edited by Adlith Brown. *Social and Economic Studies,* special issue, vol. 30, no. 1 (March 1981). 252p. bibliog.

The essays in this issue were abstracted from a set of studies on the title theme and were produced under the aegis of the Institute of Social and Economic Research, University of the West Indies and the Institute of Development Studies, University of Guyana. The project was financed by the International Development Research Centre of Canada and was carried out between 1976 and 1979, under the direction of Adlith Brown, Senior Research Fellow of the Institute. The essays focus attention on some of the issues involved in state economic activity in the Caribbean region and the following are particularly relevant to the study of Jamaican public enterprise: 'Issues of public enterprise' by Adlith Brown; 'Role of the state in public enterprise' by Edwin Jones; 'The administration of public enterprise: Jamaica and Trinidad-Tobago' by G. E. Mills; 'The rationale for state ownership of public utilities in Jamaica' by Raphael A. Swaby; 'External financing of the Water Commission of Jamaica' by Helen McBain; and 'Issues of public financial enterprise in Jamaica: the case of the Jamaica Development Bank' by Compton Bourne.

Administration and Local Government, Civics. General

476 The political process, and attitudes and opinions in a Jamaican parish council.
Neville C. Duncan. *Social and Economic Studies*, vol. 19, no. 1 (March 1970), p. 89-113.

This article gives the background to local government, outlines the political process of a parish council, namely, that of the Manchester Parish Council, and attempts a critical explanation of the process. The article results from the author's study *The political process in the Manchester Parish Council, Jamaica*, presented as an MSc thesis to the Department of Government of the University of the West Indies, 1969.

477 The Jamaican civil service: an exploratory analysis of higher civil servants in four ministries.
Walter Glen Ellis. PhD thesis, University of Washington, 1971. 192 leaves. bibliog. (Available from University Microfilms, Ann Arbor, Michigan, 1971).

A systematic study of the Jamaican civil service based on data gathered during a year's stay in Jamaica, including data gathered from interviews.

478 The ecology of development administration in Jamaica, Trinidad and Tobago, and Barbados.
Jean-Claude Garcia-Zamor. [s.l.]: Organization of American States, 1977. 122p. bibliog.

A study of national development in the three countries mentioned, in which the author formulates a typology of Caribbean bureaucracy and reviews the problem areas of Caribbean administration and development planning. The author draws on his experience as an officer in the Division of Development Administration in the OAS.

479 Government of Jamaica.
Kingston: Agency for Public Information, 1977. 16p.
A simple outline of the system and structure of the government of Jamaica.

480 Public office and private gain: a note on administration in Jamaica in the later 18th century.
Neville A. T. Hall. *Caribbean Studies*, vol. 12, no. 3 (Oct. 1972), p. [5]-20.

A study of the corrupt practices associated with the major public offices in Jamaica which were patentable and in the gift of the crown since the settlement of Jamaica in the 17th century. The author is Senior Lecturer in History at the University of the West Indies.

481 Problems of administration in an emergent nation: a case study of Jamaica.

B. L. St. John Hamilton. New York; London: Frederick A. Praeger, 1964. 218p. map. bibliog. (Praeger Special Studies in International Economics and Development).

A study of the problems arising from the adaptation of a colonial civil service to meet the needs of an emerging independent country. The work is based on a thesis written in 1959 in partial fulfilment of the degree of Master of Public Administration by the Faculty of the Graduate School of Public Administration of New York University. A chapter was added in 1964 to bring the study up to date with Jamaica achieving independence in 1962. The author spent a life-time in the civil service, rising to the level of Permanent Secretary in the Office of the Prime Minister.

482 The role of statutory boards in the political process in Jamaica.

Edwin Jones. *Social and Economic Studies*, vol. 19, no. 1 (March 1970), p. 114-34.

This article focuses on the political role of these public bodies established by law to exercise official or governmental functions, yet possessing varying degrees of independence from the departments or ministries of state under which they fall.

483 Sir John Peter Grant: Governor of Jamaica, 1866-1874: an administrative history.

Vincent John Marsala. [Kingston]: Institute of Jamaica, 1972. 125p. bibliog. (Cultural Heritage Series, vol. 3).

A factual work, filling a long-felt need for a study of the initiator of the crown colony system of government in Jamaica.

484 Royal government and political conflict in Jamaica, 1729-1783.

George Metcalf. London: Longman for the Royal Commonwealth Society, 1965. 256p. bibliog. (Imperial Studies, no. 27).

A study in imperial administration elaborated from the political history of Jamaica. The book is based on a doctoral thesis completed at King's College, University of London, 1963.

485 Issues of public policy and public administration in the Commonwealth Caribbean.

Edited by G. E. Mills. Mona, Jamaica: Institute of Social and Economic Research, University of the West Indies, 1974. 145-360p. bibliog. (*Social and Economic Studies*, vol. 23, no. 2, June 1974; special number).

Includes the following: 'Political aspects of postwar agricultural policies in Jamaica (1945-1970)', by Carl Stone; 'Some problems of public utility regulation by statutory board in Jamaica: the Jamaica Omnibus Services case' by Raphael

Administration and Local Government, Civics. General

A. Swaby; 'Administrative institution-building in Jamaica - an interpretation' by Edwin Jones; 'The attitudes and behaviour of the senior civil service in Jamaica' by G. E. Mills and Paul D. Robertson; and 'The declining status of the Jamaican civil service' by F. E. Nunes.

486 **Public enterprise in the Commonwealth Caribbean (with special reference to Jamaica and Trinidad and Tobago).**
G. E. Mills. In: *The role and management of public enterprises*: report of a seminar organized by the Commonwealth Secretariat, the Government of Jamaica and the University of the West Indies, Kingston, Jamaica, 25-29 October 1976. London: Commonwealth Secretariat, Marlborough House, 1977, p. 37-62. bibliog.

Reviews the increasing trend of Commonwealth Caribbean governments to become involved in entrepreneurial enterprises hitherto regarded as falling within the domain of the private sector and the issues and problems of that experience. The study is particularly topical in the light of recent controversies in Jamaica on the development of public enterprise under socialist policies.

487 **Report of the commission of enquiry into the award of contracts, the grant of work permits and licences and other matters.**
Kingston: Government Printer, 1973. 162p.

A thorough investigation by a commission of enquiry under the chairmanship of H. L. DaCosta, into the distribution and use of scarce benefits under the control of government. The Commission made recommendations relating to the award of contracts, allotment of land under land settlement schemes, housing schemes, licences under the Trade Law, work permits, jobs in public projects, land acquisition by government, disposal of government-owned land, purchase, sale and hireage of equipment by government and rental of property from or to government.

488 **Report on the reform of local government in Jamaica.**
Kingston: [s.n.], 21 May 1974. 116p. bibliog.

The report was prepared for and submitted to the Hon. Minister of Local Government by a committee under the chairmanship of Professor G. E. Mills. The committee examined the structure, organization and functions of local government, proposals made in earlier relevant reports and submitted recommendations for reform of local government institutions.

489 **Issues and problems in Caribbean public administration: a reader.**
Edited by Selwyn Ryan. St. Augustine, Trinidad: Department of Government, University of the West Indies, 1977. 2 vols.

A selection of some of the principal documents on public administration in the Caribbean required for students of the subject. The reader draws heavily on material from Trinidad and Jamaica.

490 Local democracy in the Commonwealth Caribbean: a study of adaptation and growth.
Paul G. Singh. Trinidad, Jamaica: Longman Caribbean, 1972. 146p. bibliog.

A comparative study of the process of transplantation of the British idea of local government to the Commonwealth Caribbean (Barbados, Guyana, Jamaica and Trinidad) and of its subsequent development there, with particular reference to the structure and functions of local government, problems of local finance, relations with central government and the attitudes of mass political parties to local government. The study is a revised version of a doctoral thesis accepted by the University of London in 1964. The author was a lecturer on the staff of the Department of Government, University of Guyana.

491 Early West Indian government showing the progress of government in Barbados, Jamaica and the Leeward Islands, 1660-1783.
Frederick G. Spurdle. Palmerston North, New Zealand: the author, [1962?]. 275p. bibliog.

This work covers a wider span of administrative and constitutional history of the early colonial period of development than any other existing work.

Civics

492 Introduction to civics for Jamaican schools.
Vivien Carrington. Trinidad, Jamaica: Longman Caribbean, 1971. 138p.

An introduction in clear, simple English, with well-chosen illustrations and diagrams, the latter by Dennis Ranston.

493 A manual for Jamaicans: how your government works.
Jamaica. Ministry of Housing and Social Welfare. Kingston: Government Public Relations Department, 1959. 135p.

A factual account of government services, intended particularly for people living in rural areas.

494 Civics for young Jamaicans.
L. C. Ruddock. London, Glasgow: Collins, 1967. 191p. bibliog.

An illustrated textbook of the rights and responsibilities of Jamaican citizens with particular reference to the workings of government and democratic practice, written for schools by a former Principal Education Officer in the Ministry of Education, Jamaica.

Foreign Relations

General

495 The United States and West Indian unrest, 1918-1939.
Fitz A. Baptiste. Kingston, Jamaica: Institute of Social and Economic Research, University of the West Indies, 1978. 60p. bibliog. (Working Paper no. 18).

A study of United States-British Caribbean relations, based mainly on US Department of State records in the National Archives, Washington, DC. Specific references are mostly to Trinidad and Jamaica. The author, who is a member of the Department of History of the University of the West Indies, discusses the growing interest of the United States in the British Caribbean in the inter-war period, a period during which tighter US immigration policies and economic depression in the United States contributed to West Indian unrest.

496 Independent Jamaica enters world politics: foreign policy in a new state.
Wendell Bell. *Political Science Quarterly*, vol. 92 (winter 1977-78), p. 683-703. bibliog.

A descriptive case study of the foreign policy of Jamaica from the time it entered world politics as an independent state in 1962 up to 1976, with special attention to the ways in which domestic and foreign policy interrelate. This is part of a larger re-study of Jamaican leaders originally undertaken in 1958 and published under the title *Jamaican leaders* (1964) and taken up again in 1974, by a professor of sociology at Yale University.

497 EEC - Jamaica cooperation.
Roger Booth. *The Courier: Africa-the Caribbean-Pacific-European Community*, no. 72 (March-April 1982), p. 23-24. map.

The relationship was established in 1976 with the ratification of the Lomé I Convention by the Government of Jamaica. The author of this short report is the European Economic Community delegate in Jamaica.

498 The Caribbean connection.
Robert Chodos. Toronto: James Lorimer, 1977. 269p. map. bibliog.

Presents a profile of Canadian-West Indian relations up to early 1975. Includes much on political, economic and cultural relations between Canada and Jamaica.

499 The United States Navy and the Jamaica earthquake.
Francis A. Coghlan. *Prologue: the Journal of the National Archives*, vol. 8, no. 3 (fall 1976), p. 163-73.

An account of Anglo-American relations as they were affected by an incident following the earthquake which destroyed Kingston on 14 January 1907. This account, based on documents in the National Archives, Washington, relates the circumstances of the conflict which arose between Sir Alexander Swettenham, the Governor of Jamaica, and Rear-Admiral Charles Davis, who led the American naval relief mission to Kingston. Apart from the diplomatic significance of the incident this article helps us to form an impression of the devastation wrought by the earthquake and of the mood which prevailed in Kingston immediately after. The author is professor of American History at the University of New Brunswick, Canada. An account of the same incident, based on contemporary printed sources, was published as 'Caribbean catastrophe: the earthquake and fire at Kingston, Jamaica, BWI, 17-19 January 1907', by Roger Willock in *American Neptune*, vol. 29, no. 2 (April 1969), p. 118-32. Roger Willock is a former US naval attaché in South America and the Caribbean and is a writer on naval history.

500 Jamaica assumes treaty rights and obligations: some aspects of foreign policy.
L. B. Francis. *International and Comparative Law Quarterly*, vol. 14 (April 1965), p. 612-27.

This article is mainly concerned with Jamaica's approach to treaty inheritance and to the role of the International Court of Justice on Jamaica's becoming an independent state. The author was then a barrister on the staff of the Attorney General's Department and a delegate of Jamaica to the United Nations General Assembly.

501 Contemporary international relations of the Caribbean.
Edited by Basil A. Ince. St. Augustine, Trinidad & Tobago: Institute of International Relations, University of the West Indies, 1979. 367p. bibliog.

Jamaica's foreign policy is examined as part of a regional study of Caribbean international relations, in essays by scholars indigenous to the region. Among the key issues treated are: nationalization of multinationals, regional economic integration, non-alignment and other aspects of relations with the Third World and the metropolitan countries.

502 Caribbean conflict: Jamaica & the US.

Sherry Keith, Robert [K.] Girling. *NACLA Report on the Americas*, vol. 12, no. 3 (May-June 1978), p. 1-36. map. bibliog.

As a background to the article's main thesis, namely, that United States imperialism and international capital pursued a campaign of destabilization against the left-wing government of Michael Manley, the authors examine the development of the island's bauxite industry under the control of North American aluminium companies, its influences on the country's social structure, and the attempts of Michael Manley's People's National Party government to assert control over the bauxite industry, and they conclude by outlining their understanding of the events whereby the local Jamaican capitalists are said to have 'entered into a tacit alliance with the aluminium companies and the US government with the objective of ousting the PNP from office to halt a further drift to the left.' (p. 29). The authors formerly lived in Jamaica and taught at the University of the West Indies. The latter author was also Deputy Director of the National Planning Agency under the government of Michael Manley.

503 Canada-West Indies economic relations.

Kari Levitt, Alister McIntyre. [Montreal, Canada]: Canadian Trade Committee, Private Planning Association of Canada; Centre for Developing-Area Studies, McGill University, 1967. 181p.

This work, jointly sponsored by the publishers and undertaken by professors from McGill University and the University of the West Indies, is concerned with trade, migration and aid up to the time of the Commonwealth Caribbean-Canada Conference held in Ottawa in July 1966. It includes a substantial body of information and discussion on Canada-Jamaica relations.

504 Cuba and the Commonwealth Caribbean: playing the Cuban card.

Anthony P. Maingot. *Caribbean Review*, vol. 9, no. 1 (winter 1980), p. 7-10, 44-49.

A perceptive and articulate statement of recent Cuban involvement in the Commonwealth Caribbean by the Head of the Department of Sociology and Anthropology at Florida International University.

505 Overcoming insularity in Jamaica.

Michael Manley. *Foreign Affairs: an American quarterly review*, vol. 49, no. 1 (Oct. 1970), p. 100-10.

Discusses Jamaica's foreign relations with regard to Commonwealth Caribbean regionalism and 'the necessity for the developing world as a whole to evolve a common strategy with regard to its economic dealings with the metropolitan nations.'.

132

506 The restless Caribbean: changing patterns of international relations.
Edited by Richard Millett, W. Marvin Will. New York: Praeger, 1979. 295p. map. bibliog.

In addition to being part of this general study of Caribbean international relations, Jamaica's role in these relationships is the subject of a separate chapter, no. 13, entitled 'Foreign policy and attitudes of élites in Jamaica: the first twelve years of nationhood' by Wendell Bell (p. 149-65). The major features of independent Jamaica's foreign policy are outlined with particular reference to cold war issues, non-aligned and Third World politics, socialism and foreign ownership.

507 Handbook of the Ministry of Foreign Affairs, Jamaica.
Kingston: printed by the Government Printer, 1982. 14th ed. 165p.

This, the latest edition of the *Handbook*, has been issued in a loose-leaf format to facilitate keeping the volume up to date by supplementary material promised for publication in the months of June and November each year. The publication has been prepared by the Protocol and Consular Division of the Ministry and provides directory type information on Jamaican diplomatic and consular corps of foreign governments and international organizations in Jamaica.

508 Canada's role in West Indian trade before 1912.
Peter K. Newman. *Inter-American Economic Affairs*, vol. 14, no. 1 (summer 1960), p. 25-49. bibliog.

Surveys the development of trade relations between Canada and Jamaica and other countries of the West Indies from the 1770s up to the West Indies Trade Agreement of 1912. The author states that he carried his survey no further, as the period after 1912 is well covered in the literature, citing the following references among others: C. M. Isbister's 'Canada-West Indies trade - the general pattern' in *Canada and the West Indies* (Sackville, New Brunswick 1957, p. 57-68) and H. P. Jacob's 'Canada's bonds with the West Indies' in *West Indian Review*, (vol. 4, no. 1 (Jan. 1959), p. 37-44). The author was Senior Lecturer in Economics, University College of the West Indies, Mona, Jamaica.

509 The business sector and Jamaican foreign relations: a study of national capitalist orientations to Third World relations.
Peter Phillips. *Social and Economic Studies*, vol. 26, no. 2 (June 1977), p. 146-68. bibliog.

'This essay is focused on an examination of the extent and form of domestic socio-political supports for Jamaica's Third World-centred foreign policy initiatives especially in so far as these relate to the attitudinal orientations of national capitalists.' (p. 146).

510 **Jamaican foreign relations and national capitalism: some research notes and perspectives.**
Peter Phillips. In: *Caribbean Yearbook of International Relations*, 1975. Edited by Leslie F. Manigat. Leiden, Netherlands: A. W. Sijthoff; St. Augustine, Trinidad: IIR-UWI, 1976, p. 503-17. bibliog.

A brief résumé of Jamaican foreign relations and a stimulating hypothesis concerning those relations.

511 **Manual [of the] United Nations Association of Jamaica.**
[Leo A. Pinnock]. Mandeville, Jamaica: Litho-College Press, [1979]. 80p.

Provides information, especially current information, on the work of the Association and also guidelines for establishing chapters and preparing programmes. Includes much biographical information, with several individual and group portraits of founders and officials of the Association. Parts two and three provide general information on the World Federation of United Nations Associations (WFUNA) and the United Nations and on Jamaica's involvement with these bodies. Reproduces text of addresses by Prime Minister Michael Manley to a special meeting of the General Assembly, held on 11 October 1978 to observe International Anti-Apartheid Year and by Jamaica's Ambassador to the United Nations, Donald Mills, to the first annual general assembly of the reconstituted Association on 29 March 1979.

512 **Documents on international relations in the Caribbean.**
Edited by Roy Preiswerk, foreword by Jacques Freymond. Rio Piedras, Puerto Rico: Institute of Caribbean Studies, University of Puerto Rico, 1970. 853p. bibliog.

Part one defines the main themes of the foreign policy of the newly independent English-speaking Caribbean states; part two includes documents which deal with extra-regional economic relations - more particularly, economic relationships with the Commonwealth, the United States, the European Economic Community, Latin America and the Communist countries; part three deals with regional co-operation and integration; part four deals with the status of dependent territories; part five with defence and part six with conflicts and disputes. This collection of source material is intended primarily for the use of students of history and for those engaged in diplomatic work. Among the documents which relate specifically to Jamaica are a statement by Prime Minister Hugh Shearer to the General Assembly of the United Nations on South-West Africa and on self-determination of small countries, 10 October 1967; general agreement for economic, technical and related assistance between the United States and Jamaica, 24 October 1963; Jamaica and the European Economic Community: excerpts from a statement by Prime Minister Hugh Shearer, November 1967; speech by the Hon. Edward Seaga, Minister of Finance and Planning in Jamaica, at the meeting of Ministers, Guyana, presenting an ultimatum on the location of the Caribbean Development Bank, March 1968; agreement between Jamaica and the United Kingdom concerning the provision of personnel to assist in the staffing, administration and training of the armed forces, 20 February 1964.

513 **The President's trip to Jamaica and Barbados - Jamaica.** *Weekly Compilation of Presidential Documents*, vol. 18, no. 15 (April 1982), p. 457-63.

Includes text of President Reagan's remarks on arrival, 7 April 1982; the White House statement on the meeting of the President and Prime Minister Seaga, 7 April 1982; and the text of toasts at a working dinner, 7 April 1982.

514 **Canadian-West Indian union, 1884-1885.** Alice R. Stewart. *Canadian Historical Review*, vol. 31, no. 4 (Dec. 1950), p. 369-89. bibliog.

A study of the movement in the 19th century for political union between Canada and the West Indies, in the debate concerning which Jamaica played a leading part. Although the effort failed, it presaged and ushered in a series of trade agreements between Canada and the British West Indies.

515 **The United States and the Caribbean.** [Edited by] Tad Szulc. Englewood Cliffs, New Jersey: Prentice-Hall, American Assembly, Columbia University, 1971. 212p. map.

A collection of essays by specialists on the Caribbean, edited by the foreign affairs correspondent for the *New York Times*, intended to reassess the new Caribbean reality and the issues and problems facing the area. Flowing from this is an examination of the present status of relations between the Caribbean and the United States and their likely development in the future. The essays deal both collectively and separately with the countries and groupings of countries in the Caribbean.

516 **Jamaica and the US civil war.** Mary Elizabeth Thomas. *Américas*, vol. 24, no. 1 (Jan. 1972), p. 25-32.

Discusses the tensions produced in Jamaica by the fear of possible involvement through military conflict between Great Britain and the United States arising from the latter's blockade of the Confederacy, or from Confederate ships seeking refuge in Jamaican ports.

517 **UNDP technical co-operation in Jamaica.** New York: United Nations Development Programme, [1977?]. 5p. (Global - 1; Changing Factors in World Development. Background Brief, 15).

A concise statement of the programme of assistance with which UNDP expected to provide Jamaica during the years 1977-81. The following themes were identified for UNDP technical co-operation: human resource development; agricultural development; industrial development; and health.

518 **Jamaica: time of changes.**
V. Ulasevich. *International Affairs* (Moscow), Dec. 1979,
p. 100-06.

A Soviet journalist's view of the domestic and foreign policies of the Government
of Jamaica since the People's National Party came to power in February 1972.

519 **Visit of Prime Minister Edward Philip George Seaga of
Jamaica [to the President of the United States] January 28,
1918.**
Weekly Compilation of Presidential Documents, vol. 17, no.
5 (2 Feb. 1981), p. 54-58.

Includes remarks of President Reagan and Prime Minister Seaga at the luncheon
honouring the Prime Minister and at the departure of the Prime Minister.

520 **The Caribbean people of color and the Cuban independence
movement.**
Donna Marie Wolf. PhD thesis, University of Pittsburgh,
Pennsylvania, 1973. 464 leaves. bibliog. (Available from
University Microfilms, Ann Arbor, Michigan, 1973).

In chapter eight, 'A case apart - Jamaica and the Cuban independence movement' (leaves 362-421) the author discusses the continuous and extensive interaction between Jamaica and Cuba during the years 1868-98. Based in part on
official correspondence in the Jamaica Archives, on the 19th-century newspapers
in the National Library of Jamaica and on manuscript material in the Archives
of the Roman Catholic Church, Jamaica, the work treats knowledgeably of the
following topics - Jamaican sympathy with the Cuban revolutionary movement,
the sale of arms to the revolutionaries, the official British colonial government
attitude, Cuban refugees and revolutionaries in Jamaica and the effect of Cuban
refugees on the Jamaican tobacco industry. 'People of color' is a translation of
the Spanish 'gente de color' and in this study it is used to designate all those of
African descent whether mulatto or black.

**The effects of the population explosion on Jamaica's international
relations.**
See item no. 243.

Jamaica.
See item no. 406.

Jamaica: struggle in the periphery.
See item no. 417.

**Trade union foreign policy: a study of British and American trade union
activities in Jamaica.**
See item no. 753.

Spanish American independence in the Jamaican press, 1808-25: a survey.
See item no. 1126.

Ideology, public opinion and the media in Jamaica.
See item no. 1127.

Periodicals

521 **Caribbean Yearbook of International Relations.**
Leiden, Netherlands: A. W. Sijthoff; St. Augustine, Trinidad
& Tobago: Institute of International Relations, University of
the West Indies, 1975- . annual.

The 'Chronology and Documentary Supplement', published separately from 1977
(the last issue examined) is a particularly useful record of events concerned with
the foreign relations of Jamaica and other Caribbean countries, as well as of
foreign policy documents such as: Joint Communiqué between Prime Minister
Manley of Jamaica and President Pérez of Venezuela, 18 April 1975; Extracts
from the Speech of Prime Minister Manley at Alpart, dealing with the Caribbean
Smelter Project and Venezuela; Joint Communiqué of Cuba and Jamaica, 1975;
Agreement between the Prime Ministers of Barbados, Guyana, Jamaica, Trinidad
& Tobago, 9 June 1976; Statement by the Minister of Foreign Affairs of
Jamaica in relation to Import Restrictions, 31 October 1977. In addition, the
yearbook includes studies and reviews of books on international relations.

Economics, Economic Conditions and Economic History

General

522 Small garden... bitter weed: the political economy of struggle and change in Jamaica.

George Beckford, Michael Witter. Morant Bay, Jamaica: Maroon Publishing House; London: Zed Press, 1982. 2nd ed. 167p. bibliog.

The intention of the book as set out initially in the 'limited student and electoral edition' which appeared in October 1980, is 'to provide the reader with a deep understanding of the political economy of underdevelopment in Jamaica... and to provide the kind of educational ammunition to launch a final assault to eradicate the bitter weed of capitalism/imperialism, once and for all'. (cf. Preface p. ix-x). It is concerned primarily with social and economic history from 1938 onwards. The revised and extended edition of 1982 has an additional chapter which analyses the consequences of the defeat of the People's National Party government in the 1980 general elections.

523 Inflation in the Caribbean.

Edited by Compton Bourne. Mona, Jamaica: Institute of Social and Economic Research, University of the West Indies, 1977. 166p. bibliog.

A selection of papers from the Seventh Annual Conference of the Regional Programme of Monetary Studies, Georgetown, Guyana, 13-15 October 1975. Includes the following papers which relate specifically to Jamaica: 'The price determination process in a small open economy - the Jamaican experience' by Huntley G. Manhertz, General Manager of the National Savings Committee,

Jamaica; 'Inflation, inflationary expectations and monetary behaviour in Jamaica' by Wallace Joefield-Napier, Research Fellow, Institute of Social and Economic Research (ISER), UWI, St. Augustine Campus, Trinidad; 'Financial variables in the inflationary process: two Caribbean cases (Jamaica, Trinidad & Tobago)', by Compton Bourne, Co-ordinator of the Regional Programme of Monetary Studies, ISER, UWI, Mona Campus, and Wilberne Persaud, Research Fellow, ISER, Mona Campus; 'The effect of inflation on Caribbean economies (with special reference to Barbados, Dominica, Jamaica)' by Owen Jefferson, Director, Economics and Projects Analysis Division, Caribbean Development Bank and Darcy Boyce, Economist, Caribbean Development Bank, Barbados.

524 **Development in Jamaica: year of progress, 1954.**
Esther Chapman. Kingston: Arawak Press, [1954]. 209p.

A survey of economic development based on a series of articles which appeared originally in *West Indian Review*.

525 **The Commonwealth Caribbean: the integration experience. Report of a mission sent to the Commonwealth Caribbean by the World Bank.**
Sidney E. Chernick. Baltimore, Maryland; London: Johns Hopkins University Press for the World Bank, 1978. 521p. map. (World Bank Country Economic Report, [no. 16]).

A study of the problems and prospects of economic integration in the group of twelve Commonwealth Caribbean countries, including Jamaica. There are separate chapters, supported by a detailed statistical appendix, on trade and monetary arrangements; population, manpower and employment; transport; agriculture; tourism; industry. Proves useful insights from a regional viewpoint. The author was the chief of mission.

526 **Spotlight on the Caribbean: a microcosm of the third world.**
Edmund H. Dale. Regina, Canada: Department of Geography, University of Regina, 1977. 95p. maps. (Regina Geographical Studies, no. 2, 1977).

The contents include: 'The New International Economic Order: Caribbean small and middle states'; and 'Political intervention, a third world strategy in agricultural renaissance: the Jamaican case'. Part two of this study is an examination of the attempts of the Government of Jamaica to promote greater self-sufficiency through agricultural production within a framework of democratic socialism. The author concludes that Jamaica 'is beginning to show small gains won by intelligent, courageous, political action' (p. 93). This study is based largely on field and questionnaire surveys, official documents and speeches by government members and officials and interviews with officials and other informed persons.

527 **Consumer price indices: percentage movements, January 1970-December 1980.**
Department of Statistics. Kingston: Department of Statistics, 1981. 259p.

'The Consumer Price Indices, published monthly by the Department of Statistics, provide the parameters within which the limits of movements in the wage rates under the Government's Wage Guidelines are set. This report presents monthly and cumulative percentage movements for the period... in an attempt to simplify

Economics, Economic Conditions and Economic History. General

the calculation of these movements over any given time segment during the overall span covered.' (Preface). The Department of Statistics also issues *Consumer Prices Indices (Annual Review)*.

528 Jamaica: Caribbean challenge.
Ecumenical Program for Interamerican Communication and Action (EPICA) Task Force. Washington, DC: EPICA Task Force, 1979. 119p. 4 maps. illus. bibliog.

This study, which is sub-titled 'a people's primer', was prepared by the task force of an organization which describes itself as 'a non profit education/action project focusing on socio-economic problems and political struggles in Central America and the Caribbean.' The work comprises a brief history of Jamaica followed by chapters on Jamaica's foreign economic relations (foreign investment, the IMF, etc.) and the social reform measures of Jamaica's government since 1972. The illustrations include photographs, line drawings and cartoons.

529 Jamaica, 1830-1930: a study in economic growth.
Gisela Eisner. Manchester, England: Manchester University Press, 1961. Reprinted, Westport, Connecticut: Greenwood Press, 1974. 399p. bibliog.

'The purpose of this book is to see how far national income accounting can help us to understand long-term historical change' (p. v). Based on various statistical sources the national income of Jamaica has been computed at roughly twenty-year intervals and used to give a long-term statistical account of Jamaican development. Professor Sir W. Arthur Lewis, who wrote the foreword to this work, says that 'of its kind, this is a model study. It is also a pioneer' (p. xvi). The work for the study was done while the author was a member of the Economic Research Section of the University of Manchester, 1951-56, during which period she visited Jamaica for the winter of 1953-54.

530 Understanding the Jamaican economy.
[Mark Figueroa]. [Jamaica]: National Savings Committee in co-operation with the Ministry of Finance, [1980?]. 28p.

An outline of the basic features of the Jamaican economy, its problems and developments which have taken place in transforming the economy. The booklet was prepared by an economist and lecturer at the University of the West Indies, as part of the programme of the National Savings Movement to promote a lively public awareness of economic issues affecting national development.

531 Foreign capital and economic underdevelopment in Jamaica.
Norman Girvan. Jamaica: Institute of Social and Economic Research, University of the West Indies, 1971. 282p. bibliog.

A modified version of the author's doctoral thesis for the London School of Economics completed in 1965 but revised to cover the period 1946 to 1968. It is an analysis of the Jamaican economy with particular reference to the bauxite industry, the public sector and the financial system. The author concludes that large-scale capital inflows have not solved Jamaica's problems of material poverty and dependence and suggests policy implications for the future.

532 The IMF and the Third World: the case of Jamaica, 1974-80.
Norman Girvan, Richard Bernal, Wesley Hughes. Uppsala, Sweden: reprint from *Development Dialogue*, 1980: 2, published by the Dag Hammarskjöld Foundation, with the support of the Swedish International Development Agency (SIDA), p. 113-55, bibliog.

A study by three Jamaican economists attached to the Jamaican government's National Planning Agency, of Jamaica's relations with the International Monetary Fund (IMF) during a period of intensifying economic and political crisis in Jamaica. It is a critical commentary on the economic, social and political consequences of the IMF experience in Jamaica. Presented at the South-North Conference on the International Monetary System and the New International order, Arusha, Tanzania, 30 June-3 July 1980. A summary and update of this paper by Norman Girvan and Richard Bernal has appeared as 'The IMF and the foreclosure of development options: the case of Jamaica', *Monthly Review*, vol. 33, no. 9 (Feb. 1982), p. 34-48.

533 Five year independence plan, 1963-1968.
Government of Jamaica. Jamaica: Government of Jamaica, 1963. 240p.

This plan was the first phase of a long-term development programme whereby the government proposed to deal with the main social and economic problems of Jamaica in the years immediately after the country gained independence. It was the third such plan since 1947.

534 Free Jamaica, 1838-1865: an economic history.
Douglas Hall. New Haven, Connecticut: Yale University Press, 1959. Reprinted, [Barbados]: Caribbean Universities Press, 1969. 290p. fold. map. (Caribbean History Reprint Series).

The work is based largely on the author's doctoral dissertation presented to the London School of Economics in 1954. It is one of the very few detailed contemporary studies of the early formative period of free Jamaica. 'I have, in the final assessment, posed questions rather than offered definite opinions. This is because I think that the time is not yet ripe for firm opinion' (Preface, p. vii-viii). It is a work characterized by objectivity and by freedom from ideological partisanship.

535 The changing face of the Caribbean.
Irene Hawkins. Barbados: Cedar Press, 1976. 271p. map. bibliog.

An outside freelance writer on economic subjects attempts to provide a non-technical introduction to the economies of the Caribbean suitable for general readers. The treatment is comparative rather than based on individual case studies, but contains much on the Jamaican economy seen in relation to the wider regional economic picture.

Economics, Economic Conditions and Economic History. General

536 The economic development of Jamaica: report by a mission.
International Bank for Reconstruction and Development. Baltimore, Maryland: Johns Hopkins University Press, 1952. 288p. 5 maps.

A study by a mission, headed by John C. DeWilde, of the development requirements of Jamaica undertaken by a team of experts at the invitation of the Government of the United Kingdom. Surveys agriculture, mining, manufacturing industry, the tourist industry, transport, electric power, the social services (education, health, housing) and the financing of development, making recommendations for development over a ten-year period. The second part of this work includes detailed factual and statistical appendices on certain aspects of the subjects surveyed.

537 The post-war economic development of Jamaica.
Owen Jefferson. Jamaica: Institute of Social and Economic Research, University of the West Indies, 1972. 302p. 3 maps. bibliog.

The contents include: the economic background and the approach to planning; population, labour force and employment; the growth of national income and expenditure; agriculture; manufacturing industry; mining; the tourist industry; external trade and payments; the financing of economic development; public expenditure and the development process; and a conclusion. The development of the Jamaican economy is judged by the following criteria: a sustained increase in per capita income; the internal generation of sufficient domestic savings to maintain the growth rate and the transformation of the structure of production. The author concludes that development of the economy satisfied the first two criteria but far less so the third and he ends with the following work of warning: 'If, within a scheme of economic integration, the old strategies continue to inform economic policy, structural transformation and the benefits which flow from it will continue to be elusive' (p. 286). The study grew out of a PhD thesis entitled *The economic development of Jamaica 1950-61*, submitted to Oxford University in 1964.

538 Blueprint island: a survey of Jamaica.
Janet Morgan. *The Economist*, vol. 286, no. 7,276 (Feb. 1983). 18p. 3 maps.

This survey article reviews current economic, social and political conditions in Jamaica and outlines the policies and programmes of the government to solve Jamaica's problems.

539 Five year development plan 1978-82.
National Planning Agency, Ministry of Finance and Planning. Kingston: printed by API Press, April 1979. 150p. 3 maps.

The main document of the fourth and latest in a series of ten-and five-year development plans, the first of which was prepared in 1947. This is a relatively short and compact document outlining the main objectives and strategies for human-resource development, the macro-economy, the main economic and social sectors and foreign economic policy to be followed over the five-year period, within the context of the philosophy of democratic socialism.

141

540 **Caribbean dependence on the United States economy.**
Ransford W. Palmer. New York: Praeger, 1979. 173p.
bibliog. (Praeger Special Studies).

A study of the nature of the economic and financial dependence of Jamaica,
Trinidad and Tobago, Guyana and Barbados, upon the economy of the United
States, with considerable attention to the Jamaican economy. Includes several
detailed tables and figures relating to the foreign economic relations and eco-
nomic conditions of the area. The author is Professor of Economics at Howard
University, Washington, DC.

541 **The Jamaican economy.**
Ransford W. Palmer. New York; Washington, DC;
London: Frederick A. Praeger, 1968. 185p. bibliog. (Praeger
Special Studies in International Economics and
Development).

The first comprehensive study of the modern Jamaican economy since the World
Bank published its report on *The economic development of Jamaica* in 1952, this
work concentrates on development since 1950.

542 **Jamaica: 'Out of many, one people'.**
Ian Piper. *The Courier: Africa-the
Caribbean-Pacific-European Community*, no. 72
(March-April 1982), p. 7-22.

A feature article which covers the main sectors of the Jamaican economy -
agriculture, tourism, bauxite - and includes an interview with Prime Minister
Edward Seaga in which he explains his government's policies during the first
fifteen months of office and the prospects for Jamaica's economic recovery.

543 **The Jamaican economy and its portrayal and analysis
through appropriate systems of sector and national accounts.**
Alfred P. Thorne. PhD thesis, Columbia University, New
York, 1959. 310 leaves. bibliog. (Available from University
Microfilms, Ann Arbor, Michigan, 1973).

This study is addressed primarily to students of economics and to policy makers
rather than to the general reader. It analyses the structure and historical trends
of the Jamaican economy and designs specific sector and national systems of
economic accounts for Jamaica.

544 **Size, structure and growth of the economy of Jamaica: a
national economic accounts study.**
Alfred P. Thorne. [Mona, Jamaica]: Institute of Social and
Economic Research, University College of the West Indies,
[1955]. 112p. bibliog. (*Social and Economic Studies*;
supplement to vol. 4, no. 4).

The author, an economist, was Director of a Jamaica National Income and Eco-
nomic Accounts Study, undertaken by the Institute of Social and Economic
Research of the University College of the West Indies from December 1953 to
January 1955. The study was concentrated on economic data for the year 1952.

Economics, Economic Conditions and Economic History. Local and special aspects

British slave emancipation: the sugar colonies and the great experiment 1830-1865.
See item no. 151.

'The notorious riot'. The socio-economic and political base of Paul Bogle's revolt.
See item no. 167.

Central banking in a dependent economy: the Jamaican experience, 1961-1967.
See item no. 567.

The IDB in Jamaica.
See item no. 574.

Caribbean investment handbook.
See item no. 575.

Balance of Payments of Jamaica.
See item no. 587.

Bank of Jamaica Report and Statement of Accounts.
See item no. 588.

Technology and dependent development in Jamaica: a case study.
See item no. 856.

Local and special aspects

545 **Bananas from Jamaica: the story of the Jamaica Banana Producers' Group.**
Fruit Trades' Journal (Aug. 1964), p. 37-50.
An unsigned account of the formation of the first Jamaican company for the co-operative shipping and marketing of Jamaican bananas.

546 **A modern Jamaican sugar estate.**
G[eorge] E. Cumper. *Social and Economic Studies*, vol. 3, no. 2 (Sept. 1954), p. 119-60. 4 maps. bibliog.
An exploration of the history and the social and economic features of Frome estate in the parish of Westmoreland. The author explores the relationship between the estate and the surrounding rural area and its effect on the patterns of settlement in that area.

547 **Salt fish and ackee; an historical sketch of the introduction of food crops into Jamaica.**
J. H. Parry. *Caribbean Quarterly*, vol. 2, no. 4 [1954?], p. 29-35.
The author, who was formerly Professor of History at the University College of the West Indies, observes that the story of crops grown to feed West Indians has still to be written. This article is a brief but informed sketch of the subject.

Economics, Economic Conditions and Economic History. Local and special aspects

144

548 Fe wi land a come: choice and change on a Jamaican sugar plantation.
James J. Phillips. PhD thesis, Brown University, Providence, Rhode Island, 1976. 2 vols. 608 leaves. 9 maps. bibliog. (Available from University Microfilms, Ann Arbor, Michigan).

An anthropological study of the rural community of the Monymusk sugar plantation and its environs in the district of Vere, parish of Clarendon, with implications for land tenure, land reform, agricultural policy and community development. Against a background study of the history of land and labour in the area, the author analyses decision-making among sugar workers with regard to migration, population pressures, consumption, production, land capture and membership and involvement in the Sugar Workers' Cooperative Council. The study is based on extensive periods of observation and field-work during the summer of 1971, in 1972 and from August 1973-December 1974.

549 Bananas: an outline of the economic history of production and trade with special reference to Jamaica.
D. W. Rodriguez. Kingston: printed by the Government Printer, 1955. 69p. 2 maps. bibliog. (Jamaica. Department of Agriculture. Commodity Bulletin, no. 1).

A useful source of historical data and of banana production statistics prior to the date of publication. The author was an agricultural economist on the staff of the Department of Agriculture.

550 Coffee: a short economic history with special reference to Jamaica.
D. W. Rodriguez. Kingston: printed by the Government Printer, 1961. 77p. map. bibliog. (Jamaica. Ministry of Agriculture and Lands. Commodity Bulletin, no. 2).

A readable account of the coffee industry supported by several statistical tables pertaining to the cultivation, production and sale of coffee since its introduction into Jamaica during the early years of the 18th century.

551 Ginger: a short economic history.
D. W. Rodriguez. Jamaica: Agricultural Information Service, Ministry of Agriculture and Fisheries, 1971. 35p. bibliog. (Jamaica. Ministry of Agriculture and Fisheries. Commodity Bulletin, no. 4).

After brief introductory sections on the botany, history and propagation of ginger, the second half of this publication consists mainly of tables showing the amounts and prices of Jamaican ginger exported, with comparable statistics for other ginger-producing countries of the world.

Economics, Economic Conditions and Economic History. Local and special aspects

552 **Pimento: a short economic history.**
D. W. Rodriguez. Kingston: Agricultural Information Service, [1969]. 52p. bibliog. (Jamaica. Ministry of Agriculture and Fisheries. Commodity Bulletin, no. 3).

This is one of a series 'intended to bring together in one compact publication for easy reference all the relevant bits and pieces of information about a particular commodity which are contained in numerous unrelated documents and accounts...' (Preface, p. [37]).

553 **The wealth of Jamaica in the eighteenth century.**
R. B. Sheridan. *Economic History Review*, 2nd ser., vol. 18, no. 2 (Aug. 1965), p. [292]-311. bibliog.

A penetrating short study on the wealth of Jamaica, and, more particularly, on that of the Jamaican sugar planters of the 18th century, based in part upon hitherto little-used source materials in Jamaica. The subject is further elaborated in the author's rejoinder to a critique of his article, which rejoinder appeared in *Economic History Review*, 2nd ser., vol. 21, no. 1 (April 1968), p. 46-61. A fuller treatment of the subject may be found in the author's extended study *Sugar and slavery: an economic history of the British West Indies 1623-1775* (Baltimore, Maryland: Johns Hopkins University Press, 1973. 529p. bibliog.).

554 **A sugar plantation in Jamaica.**
Phyllis Thornton, Moya Cozens. [London]: Oxford University Press, 1960. 31p. (People of the World, 14).

A simple, clear description of the operations of sugar-cane cultivation and the manufacture of sugar, with brief attention to the history of these processes and their contemporary milieu. Written for juveniles, it is nevertheless suitable for the general reader not requiring technical details.

555 **Food in the Jamaican economy, 1900-1950.**
Arthur William Wood. PhD thesis, Stanford University, Stanford, California, 1956. 294 leaves. 3 maps. bibliog. (Available from University Microfilms, Ann Arbor, Michigan, 1961).

A contribution to the economic history of Jamaica in a little-studied area. Against a background study of the Jamaican land and people, their political and economic structures, agricultural production and food processing industries, the author attempts to estimate the composition of the Jamaican diet in the post-Second World War period and to determine whether the level of living of the Jamaican people rose, fell or changed but little during the first half of the 20th century. Includes lengthy statistical appendices.

The Jamaican Sugar Workers Cooperatives and the severance pay crisis.
See item no. 390.

Periodicals

556 Economic Activity in Caribbean Countries.
Economic Commission for Latin America, Office for the
Caribbean. [Port-of-Spain?]: Economic Commission for
Latin America, Office for the Caribbean, [1971?-]. annual.

This publication provides a summary of economic and financial information for
the Caribbean, indicating regional trends and outlining major regional developments towards Caribbean regional integration. In addition to the opening sub-
regional summary there are notes on individual countries. They analyse and disseminate information on current economic trends and developments, highlighting
major sectors of the various economies. The 'Jamaica country notes' comprising
41 pages of a recent issue, that for 1979 published 8 October 1980
(CEPAL/CARIB 80/5) has sections on: investment, production and employment;
inflation; the external sector; economic policy; with relevant statistical tables.
Sources of information for Jamaica are the Department of Statistics, the National
Planning Agency, the Bank of Jamaica and the Jamaica Tourist Board. The
country notes are revisions of the texts prepared for inclusion in the annual
Economic Survey of Latin America. The revisions incorporate revised data for
earlier years and additional data for 1979.

557 Economic and Social Progress in Latin America.
Inter-American Development Bank. Washington, DC:
Inter-American Development Bank, 1961- . annual.

This report, originally published under the title *Socio-Economic Progress in Latin
America*, and since the issue for 1972 under the present title, sets out to give a
detailed review of economic and social developments of the Bank's developing
member countries in the Western hemisphere. Part one comprises a regional
description of general and sectoral trends and part two consists of such an analysis on a country-by-country basis with a statistical summary for each country. In
the 1979 report the chapter on Jamaica occupies p. 301-08 and deals with general
socio-economic trends and outlook: sectoral development; fiscal situation; money,
credit and prices; balance of payments and international trade; development planning; and, statistical profile. Sources of information are international and regional
organizations such as the United Nations, the Organization of American States,
Pan American Health Organization, the International Development Bank, the
International Monetary Fund and Jamaican institutions such as the Bank of
Jamaica, the Department of Statistics and the Ministry of Finance. A statistical
appendix provides 71 tables of economic indicators on the countries of the region.

558 Economic and Social Survey Jamaica.
Prepared by the National Planning Agency. Kingston:
Government Printer, 1973- . annual. bi-annual since 1981.

Supersedes *Economic Survey of Jamaica*, published by the Central Planning Unit
annually, 1957-71. The survey provides an evaluation of economic performance in
Jamaica and a record of the country's achievements in the main areas of economic and social life during the year under review. The issue for 1979 introduced
two new chapters on energy and on the environment, and also included a special
report on the effects of the June flood rains in Jamaica in 1979. The issue for
January to June 1981 contains chapters on the economy, sectoral performance,
manpower and industrial relations and the social situation.

Economics, Economic Conditions and Economic History. Periodicals

559 Monthly Review.
Bank of Jamaica. Kingston: Bank of Jamaica, 1972- . monthly.

A continuation of the Bank of Jamaica's *Review of Economic Conditions*, 1968-71. Reviews economic conditions, banking, money and credit, non-bank financial institutions, capital markets, public finance, external assets, external trade, tourism and remittances, consumer prices, production, the labour market, international currency and related developments.

560 National Income and Product.
Department of Statistics. [Kingston]: Department of Statistics, 1959/63- . annual.

This report presents a view on the operation of the Jamaican economy as it experienced and reacted to seven years of consecutive "negative growth", and seeks to identify those mechanisms which might have some bearing on future policy action. The method employed is through disaggregation of the main basic parameters, relating the changes being experienced within the system of their consequent effects.' (Preface to issue for 1980). The latest issue for 1980 comprises a descriptive review of economic activity in Jamaica during 1980 (xvip.) followed by accounts and tables of gross domestic product and consumption expenditure.

561 Quarterly Economic Review of the West Indies, Belize, Bahamas, Bermuda, Guyana.
London: Economist Intelligence Unit, 1952- . quarterly + annual supplement.

Provides a current, up-to-date synthesis of economic and related events and activities, without excessive statistical data, pitched at the level of the undergraduate or informed general reader, but also useful for the specialist who requires a concise, current account. The annual supplement provides basic statistical data on population, national accounts, agriculture, forestry and fishing, mining, fuel and power, transport and communication, tourism, manufacturing, finance and foreign trade. All statistics are based on official national and international sources unless otherwise stated.

562 Social and Economic Studies.
Kingston: Institute of Social and Economic Research, University of the West Indies, Jamaica, Feb. 1953- . quarterly.

This journal contains reports on the work undertaken by, or in association with, the Institute of Social and Economic Research, as well as, from time to time, contributions on the social and economic problems of underdeveloped countries outside the West Indies.

Caribbean Insight.
See item no. 1131.

Finance and Banking

General

563 The role of the life insurance dollar in the Jamaican economy.
Asgar Ally. [Kingston]: Research Department, Bank of Jamaica, 1972. 59p.

A summarized version of a more comprehensive study in preparation on the insurance industry in Jamaica, presented at one of the Interdisciplinary Seminars for the 1972-73 academic year in the Faculty of Social Sciences, University of the West Indies, Jamaica.

564 Central banking in Jamaica.
Bank of Jamaica, Research Department. Kingston: Bank of Jamaica, [1976]. 23p.

This work, prepared by the Research Department of the Bank of Jamaica, is designed for the general public and senior students in schools but may be useful to more advanced students. There are appendices relating to the Jamaican Stock Exchange and the Students' Loan Bureau.

565 Kingston stock market.
Bank of Jamaica, Research Department. Kingston: Bank of Jamaica, 1966.

First edition published 1964. Provides basic information on government securities and company stocks and shares, such as names of companies, registered addresses, directors, bankers, share and loan capital, accounts and dividends, transfers and market prices, concluding with some general information on stamp duties and exchange control.

566 The banks of Canada in the Commonwealth Caribbean: economic nationalism and multinational enterprises of a medium power.
Daniel Jay Baum. New York, London: Praeger, 1974. 158p. (Praeger Special Studies in International Economics and Development).

The author, Professor of Law and Administrative Studies, York University, Toronto, examines the function and role of Canadian banks in the Caribbean and how they are viewed by the governments and people of the region. The treatment is general but there are substantial data on the operations of Canadian banks in Jamaica.

567 Central banking in a dependent economy: the Jamaican experience, 1961-1967.
Courtney Newlands McLaurin Blackman. PhD thesis, Columbia University, New York, 1969. 202 leaves. bibliog. (Available from University Microfilms, Ann Arbor, Michigan, 1972).

A review of central banking policy in Jamaica since the establishment of the Bank of Jamaica in 1961, with particular reference to economic growth and economic stability, with a descriptive analysis of the Jamaican economy.

568 Jamaica - tax profile of an island in the sun.
Ian Brown. *Tax Executive*, vol. 26, no. 2 (Jan. 1974), p. 117-32.

A summary account of information on company taxation, double taxation treaties, provisions affecting company distributions and payments of other amounts to non-residents, exchange control, personal taxation, incentive legislation and general points on taxation by a chartered accountant and a partner in an international firm of chartered accountants in Jamaica.

569 The coinage of Jamaica.
Ray Byrne, Jerome Remick. San Antonio, Texas: Almanazar's, 1966. 106p. bibliog.

A monograph on a subject upon which little has been written.

570 The development of the capital market institutions of Jamaica.
Charles Victor Callender. Jamaica: Institute of Social and Economic Research, University of the West Indies, 1965. 174p. bibliog. (*Social and Economic Studies*, supplement to vol. 14, no. 3).

An historical review of Jamaica's monetary and financial system for the period 1834 to 1961, with suggestions for its improvement.

Finance and Banking. General

571 Caribbean Capital Markets Symposium, Kingston, Jamaica, 22nd-27th May, 1972: summary report.
[Kingston: Bank of Jamaica?, 1973?]. 91p.

This symposium was held under the auspices of the Government of Jamaica and the Organisation of American States, the Bank of Jamaica acting as host to 84 participants drawn from Jamaica, the United States and international financial institutions, the United States and international financial institutions. There are summarized reports and discussions on the following topics: structure of capital markets, savings and capital formation, banking and financial institutions, savings and loan institutions, insurance and investment companies, government incentives and the regulation of capital markets, the securities market, financing of corporate enterprises, integration of Caribbean capital markets. The recommendations as they pertain to each country are set out separately.

572 Public finance and economic development: spotlight on Jamaica.
Hugh N. Dawes. Washington, DC: University Press of America, 1982. 147p. bibliog.

Starting with an analysis of the declining Jamaican economy since 1965, this work focuses on public finance and the extent to which it may be used to restore economic growth. The author attempts to project capital needs over a ten-year period from 1975 and suggests certain conditions for the restoration of the economy, such as import substitution of some consumer goods and the attraction of a higher level of foreign exchange from abroad. The book is aimed at a wide variety of audiences - graduate and undergraduate students in public finance and economic development, policy makers and planners and those seeking general information on the subject. The author is currently a professor of economics at the City University of New York.

573 Report on finance and taxation in Jamaica.
J. R. Hicks, U. K. Hicks. Kingston: Government Printer; London: Crown Agents for Overseas Governments and Administrations, 1955. 171p.

An official report to the Government of Jamaica on its system of finance, with recommendations for the most efficient use of revenue, made on the basis of a visit to Jamaica from 2 March to 13 April 1954. Against the background of a general economic survey the report examines budgetary problems, the sources of revenue, the control of expenditure and local finance (i.e. the financial relations between central government and the parochial boards and the finance of the boards themselves).

574 The IDB in Jamaica.
Inter-American Development Bank. Washington, DC: Inter-American Development Bank, March 1983. 14p.

An account of the Bank's activities in Jamaica going back over thirteen years to Jamaica's entry into the IDB in 1969, describing its part in projects in the fields of agriculture, industry, tourism, energy, transportation, education, water supply and regional integration.

575 **Caribbean investment handbook.**
Claude M. Jonnard. Park Ridge, New Jersey; London:
Noyes Data Corporation, 1974. 306p. maps. (Corporate
Investor's Review, no. 1).

A reference manual of business conditions and procedures for the guidance of
investors, evaluating potential investments in the area. Each country is treated
separately, Jamaica occupying p. 52-71, with sections on background information,
establishing a business, taxes, incentive legislation, investment opportunities, real
estate, tourism, economic and financial conditions, transfer of funds, foreign trade
regulations and political conditions.

576 **Labour banks in Latin America and the Caribbean.**
Jurgen Lewerenz. Frankfurt; Cologne, GFR: Europäische
Verlagsanstalt, 1979. 60p. (Series Commonweal Economy
no. 21).

A publication which seeks to explain the political and social background permit-
ting the establishment of these credit institutions. It also deals with the savings
and credit co-operatives of workers to the extent that they act as labour banks.
The Workers' Savings and Loan Bank, Jamaica, is one of this kind of institution.
The author is a banking expert who has studied and advised in Latin America
and the Caribbean, including Jamaica.

577 **The incidence of Jamaican taxes, 1971-1972.**
Charles E. McLure. Mona, Jamaica: Institute of Social
and Economic Research, University of the West Indies,
1977. 103p. bibliog. (University of the West Indies, Institute
of Social and Economic Research. Working Paper, no. 16).

This study uses data from the household budget survey made in 1971-72, and
from other sources, to gain an idea of the distribution of income among Jamaican
households and of the incidence of Jamaican taxes among households in various
income classes. The comparison of the resulting sets of figures may be used 'to
determine the effective rate of incidence of each tax and of the tax system as a
whole.' (Introduction, p. 1). The Department of Statistics of the Government of
Jamaica provided the tabulations of income and expenditure patterns which form
the basis of the study. The contents include: an introduction; 'Perspectives of the
study'; 'The distribution of income'; 'Tax incidence'; 'Summary and policy
implications'.

578 **The accountancy profession in Jamaica.**
M. J. Mepham. *Charter: the Official Journal of the*
Institute of Chartered Accountants (Oct. 1979). p. 4-5, 9.

A brief account of the historical background, the size, training and practice of the
profession in Jamaica.

Finance and Banking. General

579 Building societies in Jamaica: some aspects of their development.
National Savings Committee. Jamaica: National Savings Committee, 1976. 95p. (Working Paper no. 17, 2nd issue).

Presents information on the extent of use of building societies by savers, demographic features of savers, the structure of such societies and developments in their assets and liabilities, and general recommendations arising from the study. Mr Joseph Bailey, a Research Officer at the National Savings Committee, was responsible for the design and development of this study.

580 Methods and techniques to mobilise savings in Jamaica: papers and proceedings [of a symposium, October 21-22, 1976].
Kingston: National Savings Committee, [1977?]. 214p.

This seminar was a sequel to one held in 1973, the emphasis on this occasion being on saving facilities and instruments available, embracing the following topics - credit, money management, investment, savings allocation and economic growth and savings education.

581 Proceedings of the Seminar on Savings in Jamaica, September 1973.
[Kingston]: National Savings Committee, 1974. 171p.

Opening addresses and the texts of six papers, with commentaries, presented at a seminar whose primary objective was to provide a forum for evaluating the activities and programmes of the National Savings Committee. The central theme was the mobilization and allocation of savings in Jamaica in the 1970s.

582 The significance of non-bank financial intermediaries in the Caribbean: an analysis of patterns of financial structure and development.
Maurice A. Odle. [Kingston]: Institute of Social and Economic Research, University of the West Indies, 1972. 212p. bibliog.

An analysis of the operations and policies of insurance companies, building societies and government savings banks of Guyana, Trinidad and Jamaica, under the programme of Regional Monetary Studies financed by the central banks of the three countries concerned and undertaken on a collaborative basis by the Institute of Social and Economic Research, University of the West Indies and the Department of Economics, University of Guyana. The author was a former Visiting Research Fellow at the University of the West Indies.

583 Shares in Jamaica: an introduction to securities ownership.
Cal. A. Parsons-Taylor. [Kingston]: produced with the approval of the Jamaica Stock Exchange, [1971?]. 48p.

A useful introduction to the Jamaica Stock Exchange and the stock market during a period of economic growth in Jamaica.

584 The fiscal structure of Jamaica.
H. W. T. Pepper. *Bulletin for International Fiscal Documentation*: official organ of the International Fiscal Association - IFA, vol. 36, no. 2 (Feb. 1982), p. 51-57. map.

Discusses major aspects of income tax both corporate and individual, double tax relief, indirect taxation, property tax and tax incentives.

585 Public finance in Jamaica 1971-76.
E[xcly] S. Taylor. *Social and Economic Studies*, vol. 26, no. 4 (Dec. 1977), p. 500-13.

Discusses the performance of public finance, and more specifically the budget, in Jamaica, in the light of resource mobilization and use, as well as against the background of government's economic and social objectives and the implications of the operations of the government sector for the rest of the economy. The author is Assistant Director of Research, Bank of Jamaica.

586 The structure, performance and prospects of central banking in the Caribbean.
Clive Y. Thomas. [Kingston]: Institute of Social and Economic Research, University of the West Indies, 1972. 77p. bibliog.

An analysis of the institutional and legal structures and of the experience of the central banks of Guyana, Jamaica and Trinidad & Tobago, with suggestions for their reorganization. The author was Professor and Head of the Department of Economics, University of Guyana.

Periodicals

587 Balance of Payments of Jamaica.
Bank of Jamaica, Research Department, Balance of Payments Division. Kingston: Bank of Jamaica, 1971- . annual.

This publication is a revival of an earlier publication by the Bank of Jamaica for the years 1964-70, which in turn superseded earlier publications by the Department of Statistics for the years 1959-65 and by the Central Bureau of Statistics for the years 1952-64. It reviews balance of payments against the background of the international economy, international trade negotiations and developments in the Jamaican economy.

588 Bank of Jamaica Report and Statement of Accounts.
Kingston: Bank of Jamaica, 1961- . annual.

Reviews the economy, operations of the bank, financial legislation and gives an audited statement of account for the year ended 31 December.

Finance and Banking. Periodicals

589 **Charter: the Official Journal of the Institute of Chartered Accountants.**
Kingston: Institute of Chartered Accountants, 1979- . biannual.

Official journal of the Institute.

590 **Current Account: Official Newsletter of the Jamaica Bankers Association.**
Kingston: Jamaica Bankers Association, 1978- . bimonthly.

Current information, for the most part unsigned, on banking and finance in Jamaica.

591 **Monetary Statistics.**
Department of Statistics. [Kingston]: Department of Statistics, 1952- . annual. 1957- . quarterly.

The coverage of this report extends to the major financial institutions operating in Jamaica. Five sections are covered: banking, non-banking, money and the capital market, government financing and a miscellaneous section. A descriptive chapter introduces the relevant statistics.

592 **Statistical Digest.**
Bank of Jamaica, Research Department. Kingston: Bank of Jamaica, 1969- . monthly.

Statistics of money and banking, public finance, foreign trade, international payments and consumer price indices.

Trade

General works, internal and external trade

593 **Lorenzo Dow Baker and the development of the banana trade between Jamaica and the United States, 1881-1890.** Wilson Randolph Bartlett. PhD thesis, American University, Washington, DC, 1977. 265 leaves. bibliog. (Available from University Microfilms, Ann Arbor, Michigan, 1977).

The sole detailed study of the life and work of this New England entrepreneur, during the years when he resided in Jamaica and may be said to have been the architect of the banana trade and the banana industry of Jamaica. Based on hitherto unused primary sources.

594 **The competitive position of Jamaica's agricultural exports.** S. St. A. Clarke. [Kingston]: Institute of Social and Economic Research, University of the West Indies, [1962]. 156p.

An analysis of Jamaica's agricultural exports and markets for the period 1926-56, with some general conclusions as to the future of these markets.

595 **Trade-patterns in early English Jamaica.** W. A. Claypole, David Buisseret. *Journal of Caribbean History*, vol. 5 (Nov. 1972), p. 1-19.

An attempt to reconstitute in outline the trade figures for 17th-century Jamaica, based on contemporary sources. 'In view both of the scarcity of figures for the years before 1696, and of the later importance of the Jamaican trade, this effort of reconstitution seems worthwhile.' (p. 1).

596 Trends and patterns of Commonwealth Caribbean trade, 1954-1970.
John Gafar, W[allace] Joefield-Napier. [Kingston]: Institute of Social and Economic Research, University of the West Indies, 1978. 179p. bibliog.

This study pertains to the foreign trade of the four more developed countries of CARICOM - Barbados, Guyana, Jamaica and Trinidad and Tobago. The Jamaican aspect of the work was originally undertaken by John Gafar as part of his PhD thesis *The structure of Jamaica's foreign trade: an econometric analysis*, which formed the basis of this study. A short introductory chapter deals with the value, composition, direction, quantity and terms of trade of each country, followed by detailed statistics of trade.

597 The banana in Jamaica: export trade.
Ansell Hart. *Social and Economic Studies*, vol. 3, no. 2 (Sept. 1954), p. 212-29.

A readable and informed sketch of the growth of the Jamaica banana trade from its beginnings, by a Jamaican solicitor and local historian who was long acquainted with the industry and many of its pioneers.

598 The West Indian trade of an English furniture firm in the eighteenth century.
K. E. Ingram. *Jamaican Historical Review*, vol. 3, no. 3 (March 1962), p. 22-37. bibliog.

A contribution on a little-studied aspect of West Indian history, based on the records of the furniture firm, Waring & Gillow of Lancaster, England, with some sidelights on domestic furniture and life in the planter houses of the period.

599 Trade and underdevelopment: a study of the small Caribbean countries and large multinational corporations.
Iserdeo Jainarain. Guyana: Institute of Development Studies, University of Guyana, 1976. 390p. bibliog.

A study of the more widely accepted theories of international trade and economic development with particular reference to case studies of the economies of Jamaica, Trinidad and Tobago, Guyana and Barbados. The presentation is suitable for specialist and non-specialist readers. The author is Senior Lecturer and Head of the Department of Economics, University of Guyana.

600 Directory of exporters.
Jamaica National Export Corporation. Kingston: Jamaica National Export Corporation, 1977. 45p.

The directory is based upon information by individual companies and upon research done by officers of the Corporation, November 1976-January 1977. It contains lists of Jamaican missions (embassies, high commissions, consulates, trade missions), goods, firms and special services (e.g. management consultants, chartered accountants, etc.) and an alphabetical index. 'Addendum' (4p) included.

601 **The bi-centennial handbook, 1779-1979 [of the Jamaica Chamber of Commerce].**
Edited by Jacqueline A. King. Kingston: Jamaica Chamber of Commerce, 1979. 210p.

The first section of this work is an historical account of the Chamber. The second section comprises accounts of major areas of commerce affecting the Jamaican economy, embracing historical details as well as the current state of several business concerns falling within the areas of bauxite mining, banking, transportation, building societies, tourism, export and insurance. The photographic illustrations are a notable feature of the work.

602 **The economic role of the Chinese in Jamaica: the grocery retail trade.**
Jacqueline Levy. [Kingston]: Department of History, University of the West Indies, 1967. 28p.

A paper produced for the Department of History's Postgraduate Seminars. A contribution to a little-studied area of the Jamaican economy, based on interviews as well as on printed sources.

603 **The Jamaican internal marketing pattern: some notes and hypotheses.**
Sidney W. Mintz. *Social and Economic Studies*, vol. 4, no. 1 (March 1955), p. 95-103. bibliog.

Briefly sketches the historical and cultural foundations of the system and discusses some of its features with reference to other aspects of Jamaican life such as land tenure and mode of agriculture. Data for the paper were collected during the summers of 1952 and 1954, while the writer was serving as field director of Yale University's Inter-Disciplinary Training Programme.

604 **The internal marketing systems of Jamaica.**
Ann Norton, Richard Symanski. *Geographical Review*, vol. 65, no. 4 (Oct. 1975), p. 461-75. 3 maps. bibliog.

This article presents very complete data relating to Jamaican marketing systems together with related historical and geographical material in the wider context of Jamaican agricultural practices and marketing reform. The authors are respectively, Lecturer of Geography at the University of the West Indies and Assistant Professor of and Latin American Studies at the University of Texas, Austin.

Jamaican higglers: their significance and potential.
See item no. 354.

Canada-West Indies economic relations.
See item no. 503.

Canada's role in West Indian trade before 1912.
See item no. 508.

Periodicals

605 External Trade: provisional.
Department of Statistics. [Kingston]: Department of Statistics, 1947- . annual.

Presents provisional statistics for the year January to December, with some comparative data for earlier years.

606 Indices of External Trade.
Department of Statistics. [Kingston]: Department of Statistics, 1965- . annual.

'Indices of External Trade provide, in an easily assimilable form, the movements occurring in imports and exports of goods to and from Jamaica and the international markets. They provide indicators of movements in volume, in price and in value. In addition, they identify the purchasing power of exports expressed as the income terms of trade... The indices are presented in both US and Jamaican dollar values.' (Preface to volume for years 1969-78). The latest issue examined, with base year 1974, covers the period 1969-78 and also presents the indices based on the old series with base year 1965 and extending over the period 1955-69.

607 Jamaica Exports: a guide to trade and investment opportunities.
Kingston: Gleaner Co. in co-operation with Jamaica National Export Corporation, Jamaica Exporters Association, Jamaica Manufacturers Association, 1979- . bimonthly.

A publication designed to promote exports. Includes articles, advertisements, directory information.

608 The Jamaican Exporter.
Kingston: Jamaica Exporters' Association, 1967- . annual.

Begun as an official journal in 1967 it has become a yearbook and membership directory.

Industry

General and non-farm industry

609 Gypsum operations in Jamaica.
Locksley Allen. *Journal of the Geological Society of Jamaica.* Special issue: Proceedings of Industrial Minerals Symposium, Sept. 1981, p. 17-30. bibliog.

An account of the distribution, mining and processing of gypsum in Jamaica with recommendations for the future exploitation of the island's gypsum and anhydrite resources.

610 Made in Jamaica: the development of the manufacturing sector.
Mahmood Ali Ayub. Baltimore, Maryland; London: Johns Hopkins University Press for the World Bank, 1981. 128p. bibliog. (World Bank Staff Occasional Papers, no. 31).

An account of the development of the manufacturing sector in Jamaica and an assessment of various factors which determine its structure, with an examination of the prospects for future growth. The study is based on macro-economic data derived from government and private sector organizations as well as from micro-economic data gathered by a questionnaire sent out in 1979 to about 100 large- and medium-scale manufacturing firms, 71 of which replied. The author is an economist formerly attached to the Latin American and Caribbean Regional Office of the World Bank.

611 Capacity utilization and export potential in the manufacturing sector.
Paul Chen-Young & Associates. Kingston: [Jamaica Manufacturers' Association], 1978. 134p.

An evaluation of the manufacturing sector in order to identify enterprises capable of generating more production and to estimate their export potential with particular reference to alleviating Jamaica's balance of payment problems. The study

Industry. General and non-farm industry

was commissioned by the Jamaica Manufacturers' Association, the Bank of Jamaica and the Jamaica Development Bank.

612 Investors guide to Jamaica.
Paul Chen-Young & Associates. Kingston: Jamaica National Investment Co., 1981. 182p.

This work deals with the following topics: introduction to the economic and political sectors of Jamaica, the investment environment, industrial services for investors, the labour force, public utilities and infrastructure, the investment opportunities, industry profiles. A comprehensive guide by well-known economic and financial consultants.

613 An economic evaluation of the tax incentive program in Jamaica.
Paul [Louis] Chen-Young. PhD thesis, University of Pittsburgh, Pennsylvania, 1966. 674 leaves. bibliog. (Available from University Microfilms, Ann Arbor, Michigan, 1967).

An empirical study on the subject of industrialization in Jamaica which fills a gap in the literature of the subject.

614 Report on private investment in the Caribbean.
Paul L[ouis] Chen-Young. Kingston: Caribbean Association of Industry and Commerce, 1973. 86p. map.

The author, a consultant economist, undertook this study for the publisher, a regional body representing the private sector throughout the Caribbean, in order to appraise the role of foreign private investment in the development of the Caribbean and, also, government policies affecting the private sector. The treatment is regional though the author comments that only in the case of Jamaica was there any significant response to the questionnaires sent out relative to ownership and policy issues regarding foreign investment and the Caribbean Free Trade Area (CARIFTA).

615 A study of tax incentives in Jamaica.
Paul Louis Chen-Young. *National Tax Journal*, vol. 20, no. 3 (Sept. 1967), p. 292-308.

An appraisal of Jamaica's experience including a discussion of the general nature of the tax incentive programme, the importance of tax incentives in investment decisions and of the cost benefits to the economy. The author was at the time on the staff of the International Bank for Reconstruction and Development. The study was based on an unpublished dissertation completed in 1966 at the University of Pittsburgh, with the research done under the auspices of the Central Planning Unit, Kingston, Jamaica.

616 **Small-scale, non-farm enterprises in Jamaica: initial survey results.**

Omar Davies, Yacob Fisseha, Claremont Kirton. Kingston: Institute of Social and Economic Research, University of the West Indies; East Lansing, Michigan: Michigan State University, Department of Agricultural Economics, 1979. 56p. bibliog. (MSU Rural Development Series: Working Paper no. 8).

This paper is one of a series of reports produced by Michigan State University's Off-Farm Employment Project designed to generate new knowledge relating to rural non-farm activities and to disseminate existing knowledge of such activities. The basic purpose is to identify and implement programmes and policies that will generate these activities, thereby benefiting the rural poor. It is a survey and a descriptive profile of non-agricultural small industries in Jamaica, made by the Institute of Social and Economic Research, UWI, in collaboration with MSU.

617 **Taxing the transnationals in the struggle over bauxite.**

A. A. Francis. The Hague: Institute of Social Studies in association with Heinemann Educational Books, Caribbean, Jamaica, 1981. 104p. bibliog. (Research Report Series, no. 9).

Chapter one studies the historical background to the penetration of the Jamaican economy by the aluminium transnational corporations and criticizes the Jamaican government's efforts in taxing the transnationals. Chapter seven studies the actual experience of bauxite host countries, Jamaica in particular, with regard to production, pricing and taxation. Chapter eight discusses in detail the Jamaican Bauxite Production Levy and the bauxite agreements between the Jamaican government and the individual companies. The study is intended for students, scholars and policy makers, especially in the Third World. The author is Professor of Economics at the University of the West Indies, Jamaica.

618 **An analysis of import substitution in a developing economy: the case of Jamaica.**

John Gafar. *Caribbean Studies*, vol. 18, nos. 3 & 4 (Oct. 1978-Jan. 1979), p. 139-56. bibliog.

A presentation of some quantitative evidence to evaluate the performance of import substitution in Jamaica during the period 1954-72, with the hope that this study would also provide a basis for evaluating similar policies within the Caribbean Community (CARICOM). The author is a lecturer in the Department of Economics, University of the West Indies, Mona, Jamaica.

619 **The Caribbean bauxite industry.**

Norman Girvan. [Mona], Jamaica: Institute of Social and Economic Research, University of the West Indies, 1967. 45p.

This study examines the scope for rationalization and regional collaboration of the bauxite industry in Jamaica, Guyana, the Dominican Republic, Haiti and Surinam.

620 Aluminium in changing communities.

H. D. Huggins. London: Andre Deutsch in association with Institute of Social & Economic Research, University of the West Indies, 1965. 309p. bibliog.

A survey of the development of the aluminium industry and of the interplay of export-oriented policies controlling the industry, on changing circumstances of western economic developments. Much of the study is based on the bauxite-alumina industry in Jamaica and a chapter is devoted to these enterprises and the Jamaican economy. The author was a former Director of the Institute of Social and Economic Research.

621 JNIP makes it easy.

Sky Writings, no. 32 (April 1982), special supplement. 16p.

An illustrated overview of the aims and objectives, structure and functions of Jamaica National Investment Promotion Limited (JNIP), a government agency to assist and guide those who decide to invest in Jamaica.

622 Handbook of industry and commerce in Jamaica.

Compiled and published by the Jamaica Industrial Development Corporation. Kingston: Jamaica Industrial Development Corporation, [1967?]. 1 vol. (loose leaf).

A compendium of information on a variety of subjects relevant to the operation of industry and commerce in Jamaica, with particular reference to legislation and taxation. The work was brought up to date by *Amendments and Supplements* issued annually for 1967 to 1970. It was intended to facilitate prospective investors and developers and provide information on the following subjects: government and public utilities, industrial incentives legislation, legislation affecting employment of labour, taxation and other laws affecting manufacturing industry, customs laws and regulation, transportation and shipping services, currency, exchange control and financial institutions, immigration law and procedure for the landing of immigrants in Jamaica. Publisher's address: 4 Winchester Rd., Kingston 10.

623 A review of industrial development in Jamaica, W.I.

Prepared by Jamaica Industrial Development Corporation, Office of Economic Research. Kingston: Jamaica Industrial Development Corporation, 1962. rev. ed. 29, [22]p.

An historical review of industrial development, supported by several appendices with useful historical and statistical information.

624 Jamaica trade and investment survey.

Journal of Commerce (New York), (Oct. 1981). 31p.

A survey of various aspects of the economy as they pertain to trade and investment. It touches on bauxite, the hotel industry, agriculture, dependence on foreign oil, air and sea transportation, Kingston as a duty-free zone, export plans and investment opportunities in Jamaica.

625 **Transnational corporations in the bauxite industry of Caribbean countries: recent development in Jamaica.** [Prepared by J. Kñakal]. Santiago de Chile: CEPAL, 1979. 40, [16]p. (E/CEPAL/L.201).

This document complements the study E/CEPAL/L.199: *Transnational corporations in the bauxite industry of Caribbean countries* (1979. 181p.) and both were presented at the Interregional Expert Group Meeting on Bargaining Capacity and Distribution of Gains in Primary Export Commodities, Bangkok, 8-13 October 1979. The first study describes the change produced by the new fiscal policies of the Government of Jamaica in 1974 and the most recent commercial agreements with ALCOA Minerals of Jamaica Inc., Kaiser Bauxite Company, Reynolds Jamaica Mines Ltd. and ALCAN Jamaica Company, with tables of statistics. The second study describes the activities of the principal transnational corporations of the aluminium and bauxite industries of the Caribbean, commercial negotiations and governmental policies of Jamaica and Guyana in the 1970s with statistical tables. This work contains the results of research work conducted by the Joint CEPAL/CTC (Comisión Económica Para América Latina/Centre for Transnational Corporations) Unit concerning the activities of transnational corporations in the bauxite industry of the Caribbean and is edited by J. Kñakal, Regional Adviser to the Unit. This latter title is furnished with a bibliography.

626 **The partial nationalization of the Jamaican bauxite industry: state-corporate relations after the fact.** Joan Ava Lipton. PhD thesis, University of Texas, Austin, Texas, 1978. 2 vols. 693p. bibliog. (Available from University Microfilms, Ann Arbor, Michigan, 1979).

A survey of the bauxite industry in Jamaica against the background of the world bauxite and aluminium industry and a more detailed study of the relationship between the Jamaican government and the aluminium companies arising from policies relating to control, ownership and diversification, especially since 1972. The author is an economist at the American Paper Institute.

627 **Towards a rational management of Jamaica's bauxite resources.** Parris A. Lyew-Ayee. *Natural Resources Forum*, vol. 5, no. 2 (April 1981), p. 129-39.

Discusses Jamaica's experience in the management of its bauxite resources from the early pre-1970 period through the decade of the 1970s to the approach for the 1980s. This article is written by the Director of the Bauxite Reserves Division of the Jamaica Bauxite Institute and is based on a paper presented at the Fourth Bauxite-Alumina Symposium organized by the Geological Society of Jamaica, Kingston, in 1980.

628 **Industrial development in Jamaica, Trinidad, Barbados and British Guiana: report of..** Mission of United Kingdom Industrialists, October to November 1952. London: HM Stationery Office, 1953. 51p. (Great Britain, Colonial Office. Colonial no. 294).

The mission, appointed by the Secretary of State for the Colonies and led by J. L. S. Steel, Director, Imperial Chemical Industries Ltd., was charged with looking into the possibilities of further industrial development in the territories named, to suggest the direction which such development might take and to indicate what industries or types of industry appeared suitable for establishment in the light of local conditions.

629 **Trends in the industrialization of Jamaica.**
Vernon C. Mulchansingh. Kingston: Department of Geography, University of the West Indies, 1970. 77p. 4 maps. bibliog. (University of the West Indies. Department of Geography. Occasional Papers, no. 6).

After discussing the general problems of industrial development there are chapters on the Jamaican institutional framework, fiscal institutions, achievements of Jamaican industrialization, classification of industry in Jamaica, the location of industries and the contribution of industry to the Jamaican economy.

630 **Jamaica: a national export plan 1981-1983.**
Prepared by the National Export Committee, under the chairmanship of the Hon. S. Carlton Alexander, O. J. [s.l.]: National Export Committee, 1981. 2nd ed. 218p.

This report, prepared by the Jamaican National Export Committee Secretariat on behalf of the Committee, includes profiles of industries concerned with non-traditional products and makes recommendations for their development.

631 **The P. A. Benjamin centenary book.**
Kingston: ICD Group of Companies, 1979. 33p. map.
A publication to commemorate the centenary of a Jamaican firm of manufacturing chemists, 1879 to 1979. An interesting mixture of historical writing, personal reminiscence and current photography to record an example of Jamaican entrepreneurship.

632 **Doing business in Jamaica.**
Price Waterhouse. United States: Price Waterhouse Center for Transnational Taxation, April 1981. 111p. (Information Guides).

This guide, prepared for the assistance of those interested in doing business in Jamaica, is based on material assembled in November 1980. Although it does not deal exhaustively with the subjects it treats, it provides a considerable number of items of specific information within the broad subject fields of the investment climate, doing business with regard to legal and financial requirements and to labour relations, accounting and taxation. It is one of a series of such guides on business conditions in the countries in which Price Waterhouse firms have offices and is based on the latest available information from these offices. This 1981 edition supersedes an earlier guide dated January 1974.

164

633 **Juridical aspects of the New International Economic Order: the Jamaican experience in the case of bauxite.**

K. O. Rattray. *Journal of the Geological Society of Jamaica.* Special issue: Proceedings of Bauxite Symposium IV, June 1980, p. 301-24.

After discussing the legal basis for nation states to exercise effective control over the exploitation of their natural resources, Jamaica's Solicitor General describes the country's experience with the Bauxite (Production Levy) Act of 1974 and afterwards, with particular reference to the attitudes of multinational corporations. In the same volume of proceedings Roy K. Anderson's 'The legislative framework of the bauxite/alumina industry in Jamaica after 1974' (p. 325-34) provides complementary information.

634 **Strategy of resource bargaining: a case study of the Jamaican bauxite-alumina industry since 1974.**

Stanley Reid. Mona, Jamaica: Institute of Social and Economic Research, University of the West Indies, 1978. 111p. map. (University of the West Indies, Institute of Social and Economic Research. Working Paper, no. 20).

'The work is divided into four parts: chapter one looks at the role of bauxite in the national economy prior to the levy; chapter two examines the international dimensions and the other factors involved in the conflict between Jamaica and the aluminium multinational corporations; chapter three places the aluminium industry in perspective and observes some tentative directions and trends which have implications for the future direction of Jamaican bauxite policy; chapter four critically examines the results of the levy, reviews some of the issues which are still outstanding and suggests some policy alternatives.' (Preface, p. i-ii). A shorter and more specialized treatment of this subject by the author is his 'The politics of resource negotiation: the transnational corporation and the Jamaican Bauxite Levy' (*Natural Resources Forum*, vol. 5, no. 2 (April 1981), p. 115-27. bibliog.). The author is an Assistant Professor in International Marketing and Marketing Management at Syracuse University.

635 **Reynolds in Jamaica: the activities of Reynolds Jamaica Mines and of its associated companies and how these activities affect Jamaica.**

[Jamaica]: Reynolds Jamaica Mines, 1971. 85p. map.

An illustrated, summary, historical account bringing up to date the published record of the activities of the Reynolds group of companies in Jamaica, in the fields of bauxite mining, farm operations, processing and marketing, with a concluding chapter on industrial relations and Reynolds' contribution to Jamaica's economy and ecology. The publishers acknowledge their indebtedness to Irving Lipkowitz, Director of Economic Affairs for Reynolds Metals Company, for his assistance in the preparation of this book.

636 Jamaica Wicker Works: a case study of a small industry in the development of rural Jamaica.
Dennis William Sinclair. PhD thesis, University of Michigan, Ann Arbor, Michigan, 1975. 250 leaves. bibliog. (Available from University Microfilms, Ann Arbor, Michigan, 1976).

A narrative of the establishment of Jamaica Wicker Works, setting forth a theoretical rationale for the introduction of cottage industries in rural Jamaica and an analysis of the particular industry under study as a means of stabilization between rural and urban development.

637 Jamaica: government partnerships and recent declines shape industry's profile.
Richard A. Thomas. *Engineering and Mining Journal*, vol. 178, no. 11 (Nov. 1977), p. 98-122. 3 maps.

This entire issue of the journal is devoted to 'The Caribbean: new faces in a mixed mining scene.' The article on Jamaica is written by the Associate Editor and is based in part on an interview with the Acting Executive Director and the Chairman of the Jamaica Bauxite Institute, summarizing their views on government policy. It also provides factual information on the bauxite geology of Jamaica and on the operations of the five companies - four US and one Canadian - which have mined Jamaican bauxite. The closure of Revere Jamaica Alumina Ltd. and the effects of Jamaica's 1974 Bauxite Production Levy are also discussed.

638 Mineral industry health and safety 1981.
Prepared by David Thompson, Clinvern Case. Jamaica: Mines and Quarries Division, Ministry of Mining and Energy, May 1982. 36, 28p. (Safety Report no. 8).

A report on safety records and achievements in Jamaican industry, to which is appended a substantial body of relevant statistics.

639 Jamaica tax incentives.
Prepared by Touche Ross, Ogle & Co., Touche Ross, Thorburn & Co. [Jamaica?]: Touche Ross International, May 1981. 11p.

'The aim of this booklet is to provide an overview for those persons who are directing investments from seven countries (Canada, Denmark, the GFR, Norway, Sweden, the UK and the US) into Jamaica. This overview enables the prospective investor to direct enquiries for information which relates more specifically to the contemplated investment. Part one of the booklet describes the tax incentives which are offered in Jamaica, while Part two explains how the Double Taxation Agreements between Jamaica and each of those seven countries recognizes Jamaican tax incentive benefits as credits against, or exemptions from, the taxes of those countries in respect of the tax-relieved income earned in Jamaica.' (Foreword).

640 **Multinationals in Third World development: the case of Jamaica's bauxite industry.**
Madaleine Lorch Tramm. *Caribbean Quarterly*, vol. 23, no. 4 (Dec. 1977), p. 1-16. bibliog.

This paper weighs the effects of multinationals, and the bauxite-alumina industry, on economic growth and social mobility in Jamaica and concludes that, on the basis of research done in Jamaica in 1972 and 1973, their influence is more negative than positive.

641 **Survey of industry in the West Indies.**
Walter D. Voelker. [Mona], Jamaica: Institute of Social and Economic Research, University College of the West Indies, [1960?]. 28p. (Studies in Federal Economics, no. 1).

Although this study by an independent industrial engineer from the United States was concerned with the effects of customs union on manufacturing industries of the West Indies - a union not then realized through the break-up of the West Indian Federation - many of its observations on industry in Jamaica and Trinidad, the principal objects of its concern, are still relevant and it provides useful statistical data on the state of industry at that time.

642 **Caribbean cases in small business.**
George Wadinambiaratchi. Mona, Jamaica: Institute of Social and Economic Research, University of the West Indies, 1981. 448p.

A collection of 46 cases meant for the use of undergraduates, practising managers and aspirants to management positions. Each set of cases has a brief textual introduction which is meant to focus attention on some important aspect of the problem in a functional area. Several of the cases relate to small businesses in Jamaica though most of the companies referred to have been disguised by changing one or more variables: name, location product(s), sales, assets, dates and the names of individuals. The author is a member of staff of the Management Studies Department, University of the West Indies, Jamaica.

643 **The performance of industrial development corporations: the case of Jamaica.**
Stacey H. Widdicombe. New York; Washington, DC; London: Praeger, 1972. 418p. bibliog. (Praeger Special Studies in International Economics and Development).

Beginning with a general survey of industrial development corporations the author examines the factors leading to the establishment of the Jamaica Industrial Development Corporation, the economic and sociopolitical environment of the JIDC, 1952-71, its place in Jamaica's development strategy, its general operations and its performance. In the final chapter, he extrapolates the performance criteria used, in a more general form, which may be applied to assess the performance of industrial development corporations in other developing countries. The author was Associate Director of the Latin American Caribbean Program of the Ford Foundation.

Industry. General and non-farm industry

644 **The Yearbook of Industry and Agriculture in Jamaica 1960.** Kingston: compiled and published by City Printery, [1961?]. 160p.

In addition to a lengthy and authoritative review of agriculture and a briefer review of industry this publication provides alphabetical listings of agricultural organizations and of factories and organizations contributing directly to industry.

Periodicals

645 **Abstract of Building and Construction Statistics.** Department of Statistics. [Kingston]: Department of Statistics, 1976- . annual.

A descriptive survey of building and construction activity during the year prefaces statistics of production, employment, earnings and hours worked, supplemented by information collected from administrative records of the Ministry of Housing and the National Housing Corporation. Statistics of the construction sector are presented as indicators of output and input.

646 **Business Latin America: Weekly Report to Managers of Latin American Operations.** New York: Business International Corporation, 1966- . weekly.

Provides current information on topics such as the economy, business climate, business incentives, investment regulations and treaties of the countries of Latin America. The geographical index allows information on Jamaica to be readily located. Information on Jamaica can also be located in the parallel weekly publications, *Business International* and *Business International Money Report*.

647 **The J. B. I. Journal: Journal of the Jamaica Bauxite Institute.** Kingston: Jamaica Bauxite Institute, 1980- . semi-annual.

The first issue, vol. 1, no. 1, appeared in November 1980 and contains four articles basic to an understanding of the current state of the bauxite industry in Jamaica. They are: 'Jamaica in the world aluminium industry: 1. The discovery and commercialization of aluminium' by Carlton E. Davis; 'The evolution of the bauxite mining laws in Jamaica' by W. Gillett Chambers; 'The development of the Jamaica Bauxite Institute' by Hu Gentles; and 'Energy and mineral resource development in the bauxite aluminium industry: a Jamaican case study' by Owen Arthur.

Tourism and the tourist industry

648 Corner stones of Jamaica's tourism future.
Tony Abrahams. *Jamaica Architect*, issue 5 (vol. 2, no. 2)
(1969), p. 21-22.

Briefly outlines the advantages of Jamaica for the tourist industry and mentions
some problems, such as those which revolve around the sociology of the industry.
The author was Assistant Director of Tourism.

**649 The role of the airlines in the development of Jamaica's
tourism.**
M. C. Arner. *Jamaica Architect*, issue 5 (vol 2, no. 2)
(1969), p. 35-38.

A director of Pan-American Airlines for Jamaica outlines the development of
scheduled airline services to Jamaica since December 1930, with special reference
to the development of the Jamaican tourist industry.

650 Tourist expenditure in Jamaica, 1958.
G[eorge] E. Cumper. *Social and Economic Studies*, vol. 8,
no. 3 (Sept. 1959), p. 287-310.

Presents the substance of an investigation carried out in the winter tourist season
of 1957-58 by Professor S. Sargant Florence and during that period and the
summer of 1958 by the Institute of Social and Economic Research, University of
the West Indies, on behalf of the Jamaica Tourist Board.

651 Jamaica's economy and the contribution of tourism.
Ainsley Elliot. *Jamaica Architect*, issue 11 (1974-75), p.
34.

A brief account of the economic benefits, real and projected, of the tourist trade,
by a member of the Jamaica Tourist Board.

**652 Caribbean tourism policies and impacts: selected speeches and
papers.**
Compiled by Jean S. Holder. [Barbados]: Caribbean
Tourism Research and Development Centre, 1979. 325p.

A compilation of important statements on tourism made between 1975 and 1978.
The third chapter, entitled 'The importance of tourism to Jamaica' (p. 24-29),
consists of a report of a speech by the Prime Minister of Jamaica and extracts of
a speech by the Hon. P. J. Patterson, minister responsible for tourism, excerpted
from *Jamaica Vacation Travel News*, vol. 1, no. 1, March 1977. Both extracts
are concerned with government policy towards tourism. The compiler is the executive director of the Caribbean Tourism Research and Development Centre, an
international organization with its headquarters in Barbados, founded in September 1974 with the broad objective of channelling Caribbean tourism into the
economic and social development patterns appropriate for the area.

653 **Survey and report on the potentialities of the tourist industry of Jamaica, with recommendations for post-war development.**
Jamaica Tourist Trade Development Board, Tourist Trade Convention Committee. Kingston: Government Printer, 1945. 70p. 4 maps.

An evaluation of the potential of tourist trade development and its benefits with a programme for its development and financing. Two recommendations of particular interest in the light of later developments were those for the establishment of the National Trust of Jamaica and for checking land speculation in resort areas.

654 **Tourism as a tool for economic development with specific reference to the countries of Jamaica, Trinidad and Guyana.**
John Fremon Jones. PhD thesis, University of Florida, Gainesville, Florida, 1970. 308 leaves. bibliog. (Available from University Microfilms, Ann Arbor, Michigan, 1971).

This study seeks to demonstrate that industrialization is not the only method of economic growth and development. It includes a detailed investigation of Jamaica's tourist market and the impact of tourism on the Jamaican economy.

655 **Tourism in Latin America and the Caribbean in the 1970's.**
Thomas Riegert. *Statistical Bulletin of the OAS,* vol. 1, no. 1. (Jan.-March 1979), p. 1-8.

Includes statistical data for sub-regions and individual countries of the Organization of American States, including Jamaica, of tourist arrivals, foreign exchange earnings from tourism and average expenditure per tourist for the years 1970, 1974, 1975, 1976 and 1977. The author is an economist attached to the Program of Tourism Development of the OAS General Secretariat.

656 **Jamaica - the welcoming society: myths and reality.**
Frank Taylor. [Kingston]: Institute of Social and Economic Research, University of the West Indies, 1975. 48p. bibliog. (Working Paper no. 8).

Traces the growth of the idea of Jamaica as a welcoming society and of the tourist industry and their socio-economic and political inter-relations.

657 **The tourist industry in Jamaica 1919-1939.**
Frank Taylor. *Social and Economic Studies,* vol. 22, no. 2 (June 1973), p. 205-28. bibliog.

A review of the growth of the tourist industry in the interwar years with some observations on the social and economic effects and implications of this industry. The study was conducted for and on behalf of the Institute of Social and Economic Research, University of the West Indies, Mona, Jamaica.

658 **Tourism impact. Volume 1. The economic impact of tourism with reference to the Caribbean.**
Barbados: Caribbean Tourism Research Centre, [1975?]. 91p. bibliog.

Selected papers from a regional Commonwealth Caribbean Seminar on tourism and its effects, held in November 1975, with the support of the Government of the Bahamas. The following are included in this volume: 'Tourism as a vehicle for Caribbean economic development' by Edwin Carrington and Byron Blake; 'Some economic aspects of tourism' by Owen Jefferson; and 'Tourism as a tool of development' by George Doxey. The authors are all economists, those of the first two papers being at the time employed by the CARICOM Secretariat and the Caribbean Development Bank.

659 **The tourist industry in Jamaica.**
Kingston: Agency for Public Information, 1975. 20p.

A slender publication produced by a Government Agency, with some handy statistics of the industry.

Jamaica Architect: a review of architecture in the tropics.
See item no. 992.

Periodicals

660 **Travel Statistics, Jamaica.**
Compiled by the Ministry of Tourism. Kingston: Ministry of Tourism, 1980- . monthly and annual.

An introductory review of the year touches on the volume of tourist arrivals, factors affecting the tourist trade, and comments on the various types of tourists - stop-over arrivals, cruise passengers and the armed forces - also other aspects of the industry such as number of available hotel rooms and beds, levels of occupancy, employment generated, visitor expenditure. There follow detailed tables of statistics on which the above review is based. The annual volume is a consolidation of information given in the monthly issues.

Agricultural industry

661 **The sugar industry of Jamaica.**
Produced by the Agency for Public Information (Government of Jamaica). Kingston: Agency for Public Information, March 1975. 16p. map.

A simple and popular outline of the history and organization of the sugar industry and of international agreements affecting the marketing of sugar.

662 The West Indian banana industry.
George Beckford. [Mona], Jamaica: Institute of Social and Economic Research, University of the West Indies, 1967. 33p.

This study examines the scope for regional co-operation in the production and external marketing of bananas in the Commonwealth Caribbean and makes recommendations for improving the competitive position of the regional industry. Much of the study is devoted to the state of the industry in Jamaica, for which it provides summary statistical data on yields, amounts exported, acreages under production, production and marketing costs and sales realization. The author is a Jamaican economist.

663 Two studies in Jamaican productivity.
G[eorge] E. Cumper. *Social and Economic Studies*, vol. 1, no. 1, (Feb. 1953), p. 3-83.

'Essentially this study is an attempt to explore the motivation of the Jamaican unskilled agricultural worker....' (p. 64), with particular reference to the Jamaican sugar industry. It was carried out with the co-operation of the Central Bureau of Statistics, Jamaica, the Sugar Manufacturers' Association of Jamaica and the managements of Frome and Caymanas estates.

664 Jamaica's sugar industry.
Carol Record. *Jamaica Journal*, vol. 3, no. 4 (Dec. 1969), p. 27-33.

An outline of sugar growing and manufacture for the layman, with illustrations of the industry as it was in the days of slavery and as it is today.

665 Report of the Sugar Industry Enquiry Commission (1966) Jamaica.
Jamaica: Government Printer, 1967. 233p. map.

The Commission, headed by Sir John Stanley Mordecai, enquired into and reported on all aspects of the sugar industry in Jamaica, including land use, mechanization and management-labour relations and also made recommendations towards ensuring the viability of the industry.

666 Sugar and Jamaica.
Ian Sangster. London: Nelson, 1973. [60]p. 3 maps.

Provides historical and current information on the sugar industry. The book is planned for use in secondary and junior secondary schools but will also be of interest to the general reader. Illustrated.

667 The coffee industry of Jamaica: growth, structure and performance.
R. L. Williams. Kingston: Institute of Social and Economic Research, University of the West Indies, 1975. 82p. bibliog.

This study evaluates the performance of the industry under public management since 1950 and how far the social objectives identified have been achieved. The author is professor of Accounting at the University of the West Indies, Jamaica.

Industry. Agricultural industry

668 **A report on the Jamaican citrus industry.**
Working Party on the Citrus Industry. Kingston: Working
Party on the Citrus Industry, 1978. 96p.

Outlines the history, the performance and the problems of the citrus industry and
makes recommendations for its improvement.

669 **Agro-industry development in Jamaica.**
Workshops on Science and Technology, Jamaica, 1978,
sponsored by the Organization of American
States. Kingston: Scientific Research Council/National
Planning Agency, 1978. 174 leaves.

The second of the series of such workshops aimed at assessing technological
capabilities and requirements. Includes papers by experts on agro-industries in
respect of a number of agricultural crops, animal and forest products, also a
review of the Jamaican fishing industry, a discussion of research and development
of Jamaica's indigenous drugs and policy and financing of agro-industrial projects.

Agriculture, Forestry and Horticulture

Agriculture

670 Background to the formulation of a national plan for agriculture and rural reconstruction in Jamaica.
Kingston: Jamaica Agricultural Society, 1972. (vol. 1 only published to date). 126p.

Extracts from basic documents such as: 'Decisions of a seminar on planning agricultural development, July 11-13, 1969'; 'Annual report of the Jamaican Agricultural Society, 1967-68'; 'A national physical plan for Jamaica, 1970-1990'; and from papers presented by agricultural and economic experts.

671 Institutions in the agricultural sector of Jamaica (a catalogue): preliminary version.
Samuel B. Bandara. Jamaica: IICA/Jamaica, 1982. 126p.

Lists in 453 directory entries particulars concerning agricultural organizations, including name, address, telephone and, in some instances, date of foundation and services/functions performed. The compilation is based on information gathered by questionnaires sent to the organizations and that given in published reports, prospectuses and press notices.

672 Sectoral task force on agriculture and agro-industry for the Caribbean sub-region: Jamaica.
Edward R. St. J. Cumberbatch. [Washington, DC]: OAS Regional Scientific and Technological Development Programme, Sectoral Task Force, October, 1976. 63p.

This report reviews agricultural performance, referring specifically to 'Operation Grow', 'Rural development project', 'Sugar workers co-operative farms', the role and performance of agricultural institutions such as the Ministry of Agriculture, the Commodity Boards, the Agricultural Marketing Corporation and the Jamaica Agricultural Society. The role of agro-industries is also examined. Recommendations for OAS action are offered. The Appendix comprises 48 statistical tables relating to the subject of the report. The author was General Manager of the Barbados Agricultural Development Corporation.

673 **Census of agriculture, 1968-69, Jamaica: final report.**
Agricultural Census Unit, Department of
Statistics. Kingston: Department of Statistics, 1973-74. 4
vols. in 8. (World Agricultural Census Programme).

The census of agriculture was undertaken by the Department of Statistics in collaboration with the former Ministry of Agriculture and Lands and was carried out during December 1968 to August 1969, under the World Agricultural Census Programme sponsored by the Food and Agriculture Organization of the United Nations. This was the initial step in a programme of research into the agricultural sector of Jamaica which the government agreed upon in 1966. The preliminary report presents a brief summary of the planning and organization of the census together with some preliminary results. The final report, a comprehensive statement of the findings, is presented in two parts, one classified on a land authority basis and the other on a parish basis. The first part provides information which may be used to identify the structural and other characteristics of the new agricultural divisions; the second provides the basis for comparative analysis. (cf. Prefaces).

674 **Report on an economic study of small farming in Jamaica.**
David Edwards. [Kingston]: Institute of Social and
Economic Research, University College of the West Indies,
1961. 370p. 2 maps. bibliog.

Based on a number of case studies, this report examines the economic problems of small farming from the perspectives of geography, human resources, labour and management, capital investment and financing, production, income and level of living and discusses the farmers' attitudes to change and the possibilities of improving farming systems. Several useful tables and statistical appendices are included. This report is similar to a thesis approved for the degree of Doctor of Philosophy in the University of London.

675 **Incorporating nutrition policy in agricultural planning,
Jamaica.**
M. El Moghazi. In: *Protein Foods For the Caribbean:
proceedings of a conference held at Georgetown, Guyana,
July 29-August 1, 1968.* Edited by John I. McKigney,
Robert Cook. Kingston: Caribbean Food and Nutrition
Institute, [1968?], p. 13-17. bibliog.

Includes statistics of Jamaica's imports of crops, crop products, livestock and livestock products and of Jamaica's local meat production. The author was chief agricultural planner in the Ministry of Agriculture and Lands.

676 Agricultural innovation in Jamaica: the Yallahs Valley Land Authority.

Barry Floyd. *Economic Geography*, vol. 46, no. 1 (Jan. 1970), p. 63-77. bibliog.

A short account followed by an evaluation of the work of the Yallahs Valley Land Authority, which was inspired by the Tennessee Valley Authority and established in 1951 to improve and rehabilitate the distressed and eroded Yallahs Valley. The author was Head of the Geography Department, University of the West Indies, Kingston, Jamaica.

677 Agriculture in Jamaica.

Barry Floyd. *Geography*, vol. 57, pt. 1, no. 254 (Jan. 1972), p. 32-36. 2 maps.

A brief account, based on the Jamaican census of agriculture, 1968-69, with particular reference to the number and sizes of farms.

678 The structure of plantation agriculture in Jamaica.

Phillips Foster, Peter Creyke. Maryland: Agricultural Experiment Station, University of Maryland, May 1968. 102p. 10 maps. bibliog. (Miscellaneous Publication, 623).

Surveys management, land, labour, capital, suppliers and buyers as elements in the system of resource organization in plantation agriculture, with particular reference to Innswood Estate Ltd., Jamaica. Dr Phillips W. Foster acted as chairman of the author's MS Graduate Committee.

679 Local organizations and participation in integrated rural development in Jamaica.

Arthur A. Goldsmith, Harvey S. Blustain. Ithaca, New York: Rural Development Committee, Center for International Studies, Cornell University, February 1980. 144p. (Special Series in Rural Local Organization).

This study is based on research conducted between January and June 1979. It was initiated principally to generate information on local organizations in the rural sector as part of the Cornell University Rural Development Committee's project as well as to provide a detailed portrait of Jamaican small farmer organizations for the Second Integrated Rural Development Project jointly undertaken by the Government of Jamaica and the US Agency for International Development with a view to revitalizing the country's farming areas.

680 Green paper on agricultural development policy.

[Jamaica: Ministry of Agriculture], 1974. 15p.

Sets out the government's policies and goals in the light of the earlier *Green paper on agricultural development, strategy* and the comments on that paper received from private persons and private and public organizations. Signed at end: K. A. Munn, Minister of Agriculture, 27 March 1974.

681 **Green paper on agricultural development strategy.**
[Jamaica: Ministry of Agriculture], 1973. 42p.

The green paper on agricultural development strategy, signed at end: K. A.
Munn, Minister of Agriculture, 21 November 1973.

682 **Forestry development and watershed management in the
upland regions, Jamaica. Economic study of the small hillside
farmers in the Lucea/Cabaritta watershed complex.**
Based on the work of C. Helman. Rome: Food and
Agriculture Organization of the United Nations, 1972. 74p.
2 maps.

An agro-economic survey of farms within the watershed area, covering pattern of
land tenure, present land use and the physical conditions of the land, employment
and unemployment and farmers' incomes, agricultural credit. Recommendations
are made for improving farm incomes and employment practices.

683 **Agricultural extension service in Jamaica.**
D. Daniel Henry, I. E. Johnson. Kingston: Instituto
Interamericano de Ciencias Agrícolas, Jamaica Office, 1979.
40p.

A concise historical account of an aspect of agriculture upon which little has been
written on a structured basis. It brings together salient information from scattered
sources relative to the roles played by the Jamaica Agricultural Society, the
commodity associations, the 4-H clubs and various government agencies in this
area of agriculture.

684 **The life and times of Willie Henry.**
Clyde Hoyte. Kingston: Institute of Jamaica, 1975. 74p.
(Jamaicans of Distinction).

'Few men in Jamaica today have given longer and larger service in every field of
agriculture than Mr. Henry has done...' said N. W. Manley in 1964 (cf. p.[v]).

685 **JAS/UWI Seminar No. 1 on current problems of Jamaican
agriculture held at Casa Blanca Hotel, Montego Bay, June
9-11, 1967. Report on proceedings.**
Kingston: Extra-Mural Department of the University of the
West Indies, Jamaica Agricultural Society, [1967?]. 107p.

The principal topics, of which papers and discussions are recorded, were: the
implications for Jamaica of Britain's possible entry into the European Economic
Community; and the case for regional economic collaboration in the Caribbean.

177

686 Agricultural research in Jamaica: proceedings of a seminar held at the University of the West Indies [Mona, Jamaica], June 19th, 1965.
Jointly sponsored by the Jamaica Agricultural Society, Botany Department, University of the West Indies. [Kingston]: Extra-Mural Department of the University of the West Indies, [1965?]. 40p. (Caribbean Affairs).

The contents include: an opening address by the Vice-Chancellor of the University Dr. P. M. Sherlock; 'The potential significance of the University in relation to agricultural research' by A. D. Skelding; 'Research priorities in Jamaican agriculture' by Winston Stuart; 'First steps in the development of a university research programme' by G. P. Chapman; 'The commodity boards and research sponsorship by R. F. Innes; 'A strategy for agricultural research in Jamaica' by D. T. Edwards; 'Regional Research Council in relation to Jamaica's agricultural needs' by J. Lamb; and both a list of organizations represented and a list of participants. This pamphlet consists of abstracts of papers and accounts of the discussions.

687 The farmer's guide.
Prepared and published with the help and collaboration of the Ministry of Agriculture, by the Jamaica Agricultural Society, Kingston, Jamaica. Glasgow, Scotland: Glasgow University Press, 1962. rev. enl. ed. 1,053p. 34 maps. bibliog.

An authoritative and comprehensive companion for the farmer, covering topics such as soils, cultivation methods, farm management, field crops, horticulture, livestock, pests and pesticides. It is well printed and illustrated with numerous black-and-white and coloured illustrations and with maps illustrating soils, production areas and geological and physical features.

688 The farmer's handbook.
[Prepared and published by the] Jamaica Agricultural Society. Kingston: Jamaica Agricultural Society, [1960]. rev. ed. 297p.

This is a compendium of various services and programmes of assistance available to farmers through the Jamaica Agricultural Society, government departments and related organizations. Although out-of-date in many respects it still provides useful information, e.g. on the working of the various commodity boards.

689 Jamaica.

I. E. Johnson, A. M. Morgan Rees. In: *World Atlas of Agriculture*, under the aegis of the International Association of Agricultural Economists. Edited by the Committee for the World Atlas of Agriculture. Vol. 3: Americas. Novara, Italy: Istituto Geografico di Agostini, 1970, p. 307-16. 7 maps in text + 2 maps of Caribbean (including Jamaica) in accompanying portfolio.

A concise and authoritative summary of the agricultural economy of Jamaica. There are sections captioned: regional environment and communication; population; exploitation of land; ownership and land tenure; land utilization; crops and animal husbandry; agricultural economy. The text includes much statistical data.

690 Small-farm financing in Jamaica.

C. S. McMorris. [Kingston]: Institute of Social and Economic Research, University College of the West Indies, 1957. 128p. map. bibliog. (*Social and Economic Studies*, supplement to vol. 6, no. 3).

This work is supplementary to and was undertaken in conjunction with a wider investigation of the economics of small-scale farming in Jamaica conducted by David T. Edwards, published in 1961 under the title *Report on an economic study of small farming in Jamaica.*

691 Diseases of plants in Jamaica.

A. G. Naylor. Kingston: Agricultural Information Service, Ministry of Agriculture, 1974. 129p.

An account of plant diseases by a plant pathologist in the service of the government.

692 Report on seminar on an action programme for agriculture, at the Golden Head Beach Hotel [Jamaica], 7-9 December 1973.

Kingston: printed by the Herald, [1973?]. 204p.

The seminar was sponsored by the Ministry of Agriculture and the Ministry of Industry, Commerce and Tourism of the Jamaican government, the University of the West Indies, Grace Kennedy & Co. Ltd, and the Jamaica Agricultural Society, the last being also the convenor. This publication includes, in summary form and then as a verbatim report, the addresses and discussions at the seminar, which was concerned with national policy, plans and goals for agriculture and included workshops on specialized aspects of agriculture such as extension work, livestock, crop development, credit and marketing.

693 Political aspects of postwar agricultural policies in Jamaica (1945-1970).

Carl Stone. *Social and Economic Studies*, vol. 23, no. 2 (June 1974), p. 145-75. bibliog.

'This paper develops the thesis advanced by Beckford that in plantation economies such as Jamaica, the primary obstacles to agricultural development in the period since World War II are political in character and that the administrative and economic failures are mere symptoms of these underlying political factors.' (p. 145).

694 Socialism and agricultural policies in Jamaica in the 1970s.

Carl Stone. *Inter-American Economic Affairs*, vol. 35, no. 4 (spring 1982), p. 3-29. bibliog.

'This paper, therefore, tries to identify the major policy goals defined by the socialist thinking of the People's National Party government in Jamaica in the 1970's and to evaluate the policies and policy results that are evident from what actually happend over the period.' (p. 5).

695 A national programme for the development of hillside farming in Jamaica.

Marie Strachan. Kingston: Instituto Interamericano de Ciencias Agricolas, Zona de las Antillas, 1978. [67] leaves. 4 maps. bibliog. (IICA Series, Agriculture in Jamaica, no. 11).

An outline of projects which could bring about an increase in domestic food production and improve the general well-being of people in rural areas, keeping in view the fact that traditionally hillside farmers have produced the bulk of local foodstuffs. The outline also serves as an inventory of projects which may attract assistance from international agencies desirous of helping with the development of agriculture in Jamaica. Includes a number of statistical tables relating to farm acreages, costs of food imports, and production of domestic food crops, yields and prices of crops and soil conservation measures. The author is an agricultural economist attached to the Planning, Policy and Review Division of the Ministry of Agriculture, Government of Jamaica.

696 Agricultural reorganization and the economic development of the working class in Jamaica.

Allan Nathaniel Williams. PhD thesis, Cornell University, Ithaca, New York, 1976. 289p. bibliog. (Available from University Microfilms, Ann Arbor, Michigan, 1976).

Based on information gathered in Jamaica on two visits, in 1973 as a private researcher, and in 1974 as a member of an FAO/UNDP Mission to advise on agrarian reorganization and rural development. In addition to theoretical considerations for social reform - 'we are concerned with a reorganization of agriculture that will contribute to the economic development of the working class...' (p.2) - the work contains much current information on the crisis in the Jamaican economy and society and on state policies and programmes for a reorganization of

Agriculture, Forestry and Horticulture. Forestry

agriculture 'that enhances the economic development of the working class... [as] the only way to a new social formation which will inevitably arise.' (p.229).

The competitive position of Jamaica's agricultural exports.
See item no. 594.

Periodicals

697 **The Farmer: Journal of the Jamaica Agricultural Society.**
Kingston: Jamaica Agricultural Society, Jan. 1897- .
bi-monthly.

An official organ of the Society, formerly monthly, now bi-monthly, this journal is largely concerned with news and events in the farming world of Jamaica. Short articles provide an elementary presentation of technical subjects such as plant disease, food crops research, etc.

698 **Investigations 1964/1970-** . Kingston: Agricultural
Ministry of Agriculture.
Information Service, 1973- . (Bulletin, no. 63, n.s.-).

This series predated the initial issue mentioned above. Bulletin no. 63 covered research carried out by most of the agricultural agencies of the Ministry of Agriculture but not including the statutory bodies. Published in 1973 after a lapse of many years this updated publication was designed to maintain an annual presentation.

Forestry

699 **Forestry development and watershed management in the upland regions, Jamaica. Watershed management and soil conservation activities in Jamaica: an evaluation report.**
Prepared for the Government of Jamaica by the Food and Agriculture Organization of the United Nations, acting as executing agency for the United Nations Development Programme, based on the work of T. C. Sheng, Watershed Management Officer. Kingston: United Nations Development Programme, Food and Agriculture Organization of the United Nations, 1973. 121p. 3 maps. bibliog.

This report evaluates the present activities in Jamaica in the fields of watershed management and soil conservation. Reviews extensively the background, watershed problems, policy, legislation, institutions and past activities and evaluates technical aspects as well as the results of the present programme.

700 Forestry development and watershed management in the upland regions, Jamaica. Project for the rehabilitation and development of the Pindars River and Two Meetings Watersheds.

Rome: United Nations Development Programme, Food and Agriculture Organization of the United Nations, 1977. 281p. 35 maps (in separate box).

This project was proposed for the treatment of two pilot sub-watershed areas with a view to applying the experience gained to some 400,000 acres of cultivated lands which have been estimated as requiring soil conservation.

701 Afforestation planning in relation to national economy.
K. C. Hall. *Journal of the Scientific Research Council of Jamaica*, vol. 1, no. 1 (April 1970), p. 35-40.

A summary account of Jamaica's afforestation plans and programmes in relation to industries using forest products, by the Conservator of Forests, Jamaica.

702 Forestry in Jamaica.
Christopher Swabey. Kingston: Government Printer, 1945. 44p. bibliog. (Forest Department, Jamaica. Forestry Bulletin no. 1).

This bulletin was prepared by the Conservator of Forests eight years after the creation of the Forest Department, during a formative period. It attempted to present the basic data on which sound forest management in Jamaica should be founded.

703 The Jamaica forests.
Guy A. Symes. *Jamaica Journal*, vol. 5, no. 4 (Dec. 1971), p. 32-36. 2 maps.

A short, popular description, illustrated with excellent aerial photographs, written by the Senior Assistant Conservator of Forests.

Horticulture

704 The botanic gardens of Jamaica.
L. Alan Eyre. London: Andre Deutsch, 1966. 96p.

A guide to the layout and plants, with plans of the grounds and brief historical notes on each of the gardens.

705 The flower gardener: a survey of the flowering trees, shrubs and plants suitable for the gardens of Jamaica and how to grow them.

Kingston: Jamaica Agricultural Society, 1964. 207p. 2 maps.

A well-produced work of enduring value, written through the joint efforts of several persons long experienced in the fields of horticulture, agriculture, botany, entomology, natural history, archives and history. Principal among these was the late Mrs Kathleen Pomeroy, who, after having become familiar with tropical flora through living in West Africa, spent nearly two decades living among the hill farmers of the Port Royal mountains of Jamaica. During this period she taught them to grow flowers and laid the foundations of a local industry. The work treats authoritatively general subjects such as soils, planning a garden, propagation, as well as of the culture of more specialized types of trees, shrubs and plants. It is practically oriented towards Jamaican conditions and other tropical countries with similar flora. The introduction includes historical data on plant introduction to Jamaica. There are several illustrations, of which the majority are in colour.

706 The Botanic Garden, Liguanea (with a revision of *Hortus Eastensis*).

Dulcie Powell. Kingston: Institute of Jamaica, 1972. 94p. 4 maps. bibliog. (Bulletin of the Institute of Jamaica. Science Series, no. 15, pt. 1).

An historical account of the 18th-century garden of Hinton East, subsequently acquired as a public garden in 1793, and of plant introductions up to 1804.

707 Directory of horticultural workers in the Caribbean 1975.

Edited by Egbert A. Tai. [Puerto Rico]: Association of Caribbean Universities and Research Institutes/UNICA, 1975. 93p.

This directory is divided into two parts: Part one lists the horticultural centres according to country, including three from Jamaica, and gives the number of horticultural workers at each; Part two provides details of the names and particular interests of the horticultural workers according to the crops and institutions. There followed indexes of personal names and of crop names. The editor is Chairman of UNICA's Technical Committee on Horticultural Development in the Caribbean, a professor in the Department of Crop Science, University of the West Indies, and was responsible for a previous issue of this directory which appeared in 1974.

708 Caribbean gardening with special reference to Jamaica: a complete guide to growing the Tropic's best-loved trees, shrubs, annuals and pot plants, laying out the garden, maintaining lawns and hedges, propagating, controlling pests and diseases.

Aimee Webster. London: printed by Spottiswoode, Ballantyne, [1964]. 138p. bibliog.

The author, who is a Fellow of the Royal Horticultural Society and garden editor of Jamaica's *Sunday Gleaner*, acknowledges the help of many botanists and practical gardeners in the preparation of this comprehensive guide. Part two consists of a glossary of popular and botanic plant names with directions as to culture and propagation. The work is liberally illustrated with black-and-white and coloured plates. The volume is distributed by Edward A. Menninger, Florida and Sangster, Kingston, Jamaica. A later edition of this work appeared as *Caribbean gardening and flower arranging; with special reference to Jamaica* (London: 1968. 160p.).

Animal husbandry

709 **Fifty years of cattle breeding and development.**
Kingston: Government Public Relations Office for the Animal Husbandry Division of the Ministry of Agriculture and Lands, 1960. 16p.

A commemorative illustrated booklet comprising short pieces on various aspects of livestock breeding in Jamaica from 1910 to 1960 by local experts.

710 **Goat rearing in Jamaica.**
Kingston: Agricultural Information Service, 1970. 55p. bibliog.

Goats have been reared by the small farmers of Jamaica for very many years. This booklet, which is based largely on the knowledge and experience of members of the staff of the Ministry of Agriculture and the Agricultural Development Corporation, has been prepared to acquaint present and prospective goat farmers with desirable methods for developing and maintaining their herds.

711 **Jamaica breeds fine livestock.**
Jamaica Livestock Association.   [Kingston]: Jamaica Livestock Association, 1979. 23p.

'By using the finest of the British breeds of cattle on descendants of the original Spanish (creole) cattle and latterly on Brahman stock there have been developed the hardy, clean-skinned disease-resistant and yet highly productive breeds described in the few pages of this booklet.' (Introduction, p. 1). Appended is a directory of cattle-breeding societies in Jamaica.

712 **The development of the Jamaica Hope breed of dairy cattle.**
Dairy Cattle Research Branch, Division of Livestock Research, [Ministry of Agriculture]. Kingston: Agricultural Information Service, Ministry of Agriculture, 1972. 78p. bibliog. (Jamaica. Ministry of Agriculture. Animal Husbandry Bulletin no. 2).

'This bulletin is designed to bring together and make widely available a number of scientific contributions on the Jamaica Hope breed of dairy cattle. It will also serve to draw attention to three learned treatises in which data on the breeding work of the Jamaica Hope have been extensively used.' (Preface p. 5). The Jamaica Hope is derived from the Jersey and other strains and represents the greatest single story of success in dairy cattle breeding in the tropics and has

Agriculture, Forestry and Horticulture. Animal husbandry

gained worldwide recognition. The publication consists of a number of papers by experts in livestock breeding, summarizing the earlier work of H. H. Cousins and T. P. Lecky and of work in developing the breed since 1962, especially work by K. E. Wellington, L. E. McLaren, K. L. Roache and O. G. McCorkle. Publisher's address: Bodles, Old Harbour, Jamaica.

Communications and Transport

Postal service

713 Jamaica: its postal history, postage stamps and postmarks.
Jointly edited by G. W. Collett, W. Buckland Edwards, C. S. Norton, L. C. C. Nicholson. London: Stanley Gibbons, 1928. 248p. map. bibliog.

A comprehensive handbook prepared on the basis of extensive research in historical records held in public repositories.

714 The postal history of Jamaica 1662-1860.
Thomas Foster. London: Robson Lowe, 1968. 180p. 3 maps. bibliog.

'The aim of the author was not one of originality, but was to compile and collate all available information relevant to the subject under one cover and present it in an easily digestible manner.' The contents include: Part one, 'The history of the Jamaica Post Office 1662-1860'; Part two, 'The early handstamps of Jamaica'; and Part three, 'British postage stamps used in Jamaica'.

715 Three hundred years of postal service in Jamaica.
Stephen Hopwood. *Jamaica Journal*, vol. 5, nos. 2-3 (June-Sept. 1971), p. 11-16.

A brief historical outline, with illustrations, written by the Secretary of the Jamaica Philatelic Society, to commemorate the opening of the first post office in Jamaica on 31 October 1671.

Communications and Transport. Air, road, rail and sea traffic

716 **Jamaica: a review of the nation's postal history and postage.**
Alfred N. Johnson. Pennsylvania: American Philatelic
Society, 1964. 62p. 2 maps. bibliog.

The author was editor of the *British Caribbean Philatelic Journal* and was commissioned to do this study for *American Philatelist*, in which it was first
published, to mark the independence of Jamaica in August 1962. It was, at that
time, the most complete postal history of Jamaica and an authoritative work of
reference.

717 **Jamaica.**
Fred J. Melville. London: Melville Stamp Books, 1910.
89p. bibliog.

Includes the postal history of Jamaica with a description of the issues of Jamaican stamps up to 1910. A handbook issued to mark fifty years of the Jamaican
Post Office, established in 1860.

Air, road, rail and sea traffic

718 **Urban transportation study, Kingston, Jamaica, 1964.**
[Caribbean Road Traffic and Planning Research
Unit]. Great Britain: Road Research Laboratory, Ministry
of Transport, [1964 or after]. 99p. 38 maps. incl. fold. map
of Jamaica (scale 1:250,000).

A report based on studies of the urban area of Kingston and St. Andrew and its
outer suburbs, undertaken between 1962 and 1964, at the invitation of the
Government of Jamaica, by the Caribbean Road Traffic and Planning Research
Unit, set up in Kingston for the purpose by the Road Research Laboratory of
Great Britain. Detailed surveys of traffic flows, vehicular use and population
distribution, copiously documented with statistical tables and plans, attempt to
determine the existing pattern and to forecast growth and development over a
twenty-year period. A similar study of rural Jamaica was published as *A study of
road needs in rural Jamaica* [1964 or after] (121p. 11 maps).

719 **Report on West Indian shipping services.**
Commonwealth Shipping Committee. London: HM
Stationery Office, 1948. 46p. map.

The committee was charged with surveying the shipping needs of the British
colonies in the Caribbean area and making recommendations for their improvement. There are chapters on cargoes and cargo services; sea passenger facilities;
mail services; inter-island communications; air services; ports and port facilities;
and recommendations.

Communications and Transport. Air, road, rail and sea traffic

720 **Problems of the Caribbean air transport industry.**
S. De Castro. [Kingston], Jamaica: Institute of Social and
Economic Research, University of the West Indies, 1967.
25p.

The problems of the region's air industry are treated from a Caribbean-wide
perspective though examples were chosen and solutions discussed only in terms of
the Commonwealth Caribbean territories, focusing at times on the setting up of a
new airline, Air Jamaica Ltd., by the Jamaican government in 1963.

721 **Public transport in Kingston, Jamaica and its relation to low
income households.**
Margaret J. Heraty. Crowthorne, England: Overseas Unit,
Transport and Road Research Laboratory, 1980. 26p. 2
maps. bibliog. (Supplementary Report 546).

This report, by a transport consultant, examines the operation and organisation of
the public transport system in the city of Kingston. This embraces the Jamaica
Omnibus Services Ltd., the minibuses and taxis. An analysis of the attitudes of
passengers, with particular reference to low-income households, helps in formulating ways in which bus services may be improved. The report is based on a study
undertaken in March 1978 under the sponsorship of the Government of Jamaica. This
Research Laboratory with the co-operation of the Government of Jamaica. This
report is an abbreviated version of a fuller report which was made available to
the Jamaican authorities and which contained specific recommendations for
improvements relative to Kingston.

722 **A note on factors influencing the present distribution of the
Jamaican road network.**
Raymond Hubbard. *Caribbean Studies*, vol. 12, no. 4 (Jan.
1973), p. 36-43. 5 maps.

A short study of the geography and socio-economic factors affecting the develop-
ment of roads, intended as an extension of an earlier work by W. F. Maunder,
'Notes on the development of internal transport in Jamaica', *Social and Economic
Studies*, vol. 3, no. 2 (1954). The author was a member of the Department of
Geography, University of Nebraska, who has also done a study on the earlier
spread of roads in Jamaica entitled: 'The development of the Jamaican road
network by 1846', which appeared in *Journal of Tropical Geography*, vol. 38
(June 1974), p. [31]-36. 2 maps. bibliog.

723 **Jamaica gets set for jets.**
Engineering News-Record, vol. 161, no. 19 (Nov. 1958), p.
22.

A brief note on the construction of two international airports at Kingston and
Montego Bay with runways designed to accommodate jet-planes. Notes estimated
costs, a few design features and the names of two companies responsible for
design and construction.

Communications and Transport. Air, road, rail and sea traffic

724 The railway in Jamaica 1845-1970: a short history.
[Jamaica Railway Corporation]. Kingston: printed by Golding Printing Service [197-?]. 19p. map. bibliog.

A short account of the railway from its beginnings, illustrated with photographs of old prints and portraits.

725 Notes on the development of internal transport in Jamaica.
W. F. Maunder. *Social and Economic Studies*, vol. 3, no. 2 (Sept. 1954), p. 161-85. map. bibliog.

A brief historical review of railway and competitive road transport developments in Jamaica leading to an assessment of their situation at the time of writing.

726 The significance of transport in the Jamaican economy: an estimate of gross expenditure on internal transport.
W. F. Maunder. *Social and Economic Studies*, vol. 3, no. 1 (June 1954), p. 39-63. bibliog.

This study is based on gross totals for expenditure on the main categories of internal transport for the financial year 1 April 1950-31 March 1951 and is intended to provide some quantitative knowledge of the overall importance of transport in the economy.

727 The railway in Jamaica, 1845-1978.
Jamaica Inter Com, vol. 4, no. 3 (autumn 1978), p. 24-26.

A very brief historical sketch illustrated with some interesting photographs.

728 Air Jamaica.
Tony Scott. *Jamaica Architect*, vol. 2, issue no. 5, no. 2 (1969), p. 39.

A brief note on the emergence of Jamaica's national airline, by an official of the company.

729 Some problems of public utility regulation by a statutory board in Jamaica: the Jamaica Omnibus Services case.
Raphael A. Swaby. *Social and Economic Studies*, vol. 23, no. 2 (June 1974), p. 242-63. bibliog.

An analysis of the effectiveness of the public control of the Public Passenger Transport Board in regulating the Jamaica Omnibus Service in the public interest. Reviews the development of urban transportation over a period of some twenty years.

730 **Transportation for Jamaica.**
Workshops on Science and Technology, Jamaica, 1978, sponsored by the Organization of American States. Kingston, Jamaica: Scientific Research Council, National Planning Agency, 1978. 50 leaves.

The workshops were intended to examine the role of science and technology in the improved use of resources in high priority areas defined by government, to recommend policies and measures to help increase resource utilization and to identify gaps in local research. The papers submitted to this workshop, which are reproduced in this volume, indicate developments in the transport sector since 1970, and the lines along which further developments in training, service, maintenance of equipment and roads, alternative fuel sources and environmental protection might proceed.

Periodicals

731 **Port of Kingston Handbook, including outports.**
Kingston: Shipping Association of Jamaica and the Port Authority of Jamaica, 1975/76-. annual.

Includes information on navigation, harbour fees, shipping services, coast guard, commercial facilities, security, bunkering facilities and on various agencies directly or indirectly connected with shipping and port services.

Employment and Manpower

General

732 **Profile of the impact worker in Kingston, Jamaica.**
Sylvan Alleyne, Scarlet Gillings, Lebert Lawrence. In: *Contemporary Caribbean: a sociological reader*. Edited by Susan Craig. [s.l.]: published by Susan Craig (Maracas, Trinidad and Tobago: printed by College Press), 1982, vol. 2, p. 111-25.

This paper discusses the Special Works Programme introduced in 1974 as one means of coping with some of the unemployment problems in Jamaica and, in particular, the Impact Programme which operates within Kingston and St. Andrew. It is based on data collected by two social work students as part of their course at the University of the West Indies, on library research and on interviews with government officials.

733 **Growth, development and unemployment in the Caribbean.**
John Atkins, Shaffique Khan, Vernon Pindar. [s.l.]: Caribbean Labour Economics Research Training Program, joint project of the Caribbean Congress of Labour and the American Institute for Free Labor Development, 1977. 71p. bibliog. (Caribbean Congress of Labour Research Studies, Monograph 4).

Discusses economic and population growth in relation to unemployment. Section five (p. 43-69) gives a picture of the Jamaican situation which is supported by several statistical tables. The authors, who are attached to workers' unions in Jamaica and Guyana, are graduates of the Labour Economics Programme at Georgetown University, Washington, DC.

734 **Work attitude in Jamaica: a critical sidelight on the 'human resources' approach.**
G[eorge] E. Cumper. In: *Human resources in the Commonwealth Caribbean:* report of the Human Resources Seminar, UWI, Mona, Jamaica, August 1970. Edited by Jack Harewood. St. Augustine, Trinidad: Institute of Social and Economic Research, University of the West Indies, [1970?], p. 8-1 - 8-14. (i.e. 14p).

A brief stimulating analysis of work attitudes looked at as aspects of the whole individual in the social context within which he operates, rather than as those limited aspects of his situation most accessible to the economist, demographer and statistician.

735 **Labour shortage and productivity in the Jamaican sugar industry.**
R. B. Davison. [Kingston]: Institute of Social and Economic Research, University of the West Indies, [1966]. 39, [6]p. map.

An investigation, made in 1965, at the request of the Sugar Manufacturers Association of Jamaica, based on interviews with the managers of 16 sugar estates. The investigation answered few of the questions posed but is a concise statement of the factors affecting manpower and productivity in the industry.

736 **Unemployment and underemployment in Jamaica, 1972-78.**
John Gafar. *International Labour Review,* vol. 119, no. 6 (Nov.-Dec. 1980), p. 773-85. bibliog.

An outline of the magnitude of the problem with some explanations and some policy proposals for combating unemployment. The author was Lecturer, Department of Economics, University of the West Indies, Jamaica.

737 **Employment in an underdeveloped area: a sample survey of Kingston, Jamaica.**
W. F. Maunder. New Haven, Connecticut: Yale University Press, 1960. 215p. bibliog. (Caribbean Series, 3).

A much-quoted study, by an economist, of urban employment and manpower in Jamaica, based on data gathered during the academic year 1953-54 when the author held a research fellowship at the Institute of Social and Economic Research, University College of the West Indies, Jamaica. As a quantitative assessment, the work is amply provided with tables of statistical data. In carrying out the research for this work the author joined forces with R. G. Goodman, United Nations statistical consultant who was engaged in an island-wide population survey sample.

738 **Women and the division of labor: a Jamaican example.**
Nancy J. Pollock. *American Anthropologist,* vol. 74, no. 3 (June 1972), p. 689-92. bibliog.

An account of how women may do field-work while caring for a family of small children until a male partner can be found to help share the burden of raising a family. Based on field data collected in rural Jamaica during three months in 1964.

739 Guidelines for action in the informal sector of central Kingston.

Programa Regional del Empleo para América Latina y el Caribe (PREALC). [Santiago de Chile]: Organizacion Internacional del Trabajo, 1976. 56p. (Programa Mundial del Empleo. Working Paper... PREALC 101).

An exploratory report on the informal sector (i.e. small or unskilled economic enterprises, or similar activities of self-employed persons) with a view to assisting government in formulating policies relating to production of goods and services and to providing urban employment in the face of migratory pressures from rural areas and growing capital restraints on conventional employment openings. The appendices include useful data and case studies on some of these informal economic activities, e.g. handicrafts, tailoring, street vending, etc. The report was a joint undertaking of the National Planning Agency of Jamaica and the Regional Employment Programme for Latin America and the Caribbean (PREALC).

740 The ordeal of free labour in the British West Indies.

William G. Sewell. London: Sampson Low, 1862. 2nd ed. Reprinted, Frank Cass, 1968. 325p.

Letters originally written for the *New York Times* and subsequently revised and published in book form. Approximately half the volume deals with Jamaica between emancipation and 1860 and in particular, the advantages of free labour, the effects of labour shortages and mismanagement on the plantation economy and the author's advocacy of immigration.

741 A report on labour supply in rural Jamaica.

M. G. Smith. Kingston: Government Printer, 1956. 167p.

A systematic documentation of working conditions in the peasant areas of Jamaica. The author concluded that the 'labour shortage' problem was not a problem of labour shortage at all but a problem of labour recruitment and administration. This investigation of labour shortages was undertaken at the request of the Government of Jamaica by the author, who was then Senior Research Fellow in the Institute of Social and Economic Research, University College of the West Indies.

742 Unemployment and female labour: a study of labour supply in Kingston, Jamaica.

Guy Standing. New York: St. Martin's Press, 1981. 364p. bibliog.

A study of female labour force participation in the context of rapid industrialization and, more specifically, in the urban labour market of Kingston. A study prepared for the International Labour Office within the framework of the World Employment Programme with the financial support of the United Nations Fund for Population Activities. The author is a senior economist in the International Labour Office.

Emigration of high-level manpower and national development: a case study of Jamaica.
See item no. 237.

Periodicals

743 **Employment, Earnings and Hours in Large Establishments.** Department of Statistics. [Kingston]: Department of Statistics, 1976- . annual.

This serial was preceded by three earlier reports for the years 1957-62, 1963-64, and 1965, entitled *Employment and earnings in large establishments.* It consists mainly of statistical tables relative to the subject of the title in the mining, manufacturing, private construction, electricity, distribution, transportation and other selected services.

744 **JEF Newsletter.** Jamaica Employers' Federation. Kingston: Jamaica Employers' Federation, 1962- . monthly.

Includes unsigned articles, extracts of legislation, awards, speeches, statistics relating to business, employment and industrial relations.

745 **The Labour Force.** Department of Statistics. [Kingston]: Department of Statistics, 1968- . annual.

A statistical survey of the population, the total labour force, the employed labour force and the unemployed labour force.

Labour Movement and Trade Unions

746 **Trends in labour legislation in the Caribbean.**
J. Burns Bonadie. Barbados: Caribbean Labour Economics Research Training Program, 1977. 585p. bibliog. (Caribbean Congress of Labour Research Studies. Monograph 3).

The section on Jamaica (p. 356-409) gives a summary description of labour legislation since 1919, lists the ILO conventions ratified by Jamaica since being admitted to membership of that organisation in 1962, reproduces the text of the Employment (Termination and Redundancy Payments) Act and Regulations, 1974, gives a summary of the Labour Relations and Industrial Disputes Bill, 1975 and the text of the Labour Relations Code. The author/compiler is Secretary/Treasurer of the Caribbean Congress of Labour.

747 **Labour relations in the Caribbean region: record of proceedings of, and documents submitted to a**
Caribbean Regional Seminar on Labour Relations, Port-of-Spain, March 1973. Geneva: International Labour Office, 1974. 205p. (Labour-Management Relations Series, no. 43).

Contains two papers on 'Industrial relations in Jamaica' (p. 132-52) by E. M. Parchment, Director of Industrial Relations, Ministry of Labour and Employment and by Audley Gayle, Education Officer, National Workers' Union of Jamaica, outlining the main features of industrial relations policy, collective bargaining procedures and agreements and labour disputes settlement procedures.

748 **Studies in Caribbean labour relations law.**
Roop L. Chaudhary. Barbados: Coles Printery, 1977. 234p.

Includes an appraisal of the Jamaica Labour Relations and Industrial Disputes Act, 1975. Among the appendices is a table of statutes arranged by country and a table of cases arranged alphabetically by first name mentioned in each case.

749 Osmond Dyce - labour leader: a life and its times, 1918-1970.

George E. Eaton. *Caribbean Quarterly*, vol. 20, no. 3 & 4 (Sept.-Dec. 1974), p. 59-73.

A biographical sketch of a radical working-class activist and an outline of the influence of Marxist-Socialist ideology on the post-World War II development of trade unionism in Jamaica.

750 Proceedings of industrial relations conference on the theory and practice of arbitration, held November 11-12, 1962, under the auspices of the Institute of Social and Economic Research, University of the West Indies, Mona.

[Edited] with an extended introduction by G[eorge] E. Eaton. [Jamaica]: Feb. 1963. 102p. bibliog.

Includes much useful information on trade union, arbitration and conciliation practices and trends in Jamaica.

751 Trade union development in Jamaica.

G[eorge] E. Eaton. *Caribbean Quarterly*, vol. 8, no. 1 & 2 (March, June 1962). p. 43-53, 69-75.

A survey of the early attempts at trade union organization in Jamaica from 1898 to 1920.

752 Compulsory arbitration in Jamaica, 1952-1969.

Walter J. Gershenfeld. [Mona], Jamaica: Institute of Social and Economic Research, University of the West Indies, 1974. 187p. (Law and Society in the Caribbean, no. 4).

A study based on the case records of 79 arbitration cases, interviews with employers, union officials and arbitration panel members and on observation of actual hearings of the arbitration tribunals, with the co-operation of the Ministry of Labour and National Insurance. The cases are summarized in a substantial appendix at p. 91-170. The author was, at the time of this study, Ford Visiting Professor of Management Studies at the University of the West Indies, from his substantive post of Professor of Management and Director of the Center for Labor and Manpower Studies at Temple University, United States.

753 Trade union foreign policy: a study of British and American trade union activities in Jamaica.

Jeffrey Harrod. London: Macmillan, 1972. 485p. bibliog. (Publications of the International Institute for Labour Studies, Industrial Relations: Contemporary Issues).

This study in international relations is made against a background of the Jamaican society, economy and culture and in relation to the Jamaican and Caribbean trade union movement. It concludes with an analysis of foreign union objectives in Jamaica and some general considerations on foreign trade union participation in policy-making and the achievement of a national social policy. It is an unrevised thesis as accepted by the University of Geneva for the degree of PhD through the Graduate Institute of International Studies.

754 An introduction to industrial relations and labour law in Jamaica.

S. G. Kirkaldy. Mona, Jamaica: Trade Union Education Institute, Department of Extra-Mural Studies, University of the West Indies, 1979. 97p.

A concise account of a rapidly changing field. 'There are four parts to the book - Part I gives a picture of the organizations of employers and employees, and the negotiating machinery in the public and private sectors; Part II touches on the contents of collective agreements including the grievance procedure; Part III sets out the statutory requirements in the field of industrial relations (in particular the provisions of the Labour Relations and Industrial Disputes Act [1975]....) and the Labour Relations Code; Part IV deals with such miscellaneous matters of interest as the International Labour Organization (ILO), the Labour Advisory Council, and includes a summary of more topical labour legislation such as the Employment (Termination and Redundancy Payments) Act. Also described is the Government's Wage Guidelines for 1975 and 1976.' (Foreword, p. viii). Includes information up to 1978. The author has spent twenty-three years as a public service employee and latterly as a private consultant and special adviser in the field of industrial relations.

755 Labor law and practice in Jamaica.

[Report prepared in the Branch of Foreign Labor Monographs by Elizabeth K. Kirkpatrick, under the direction of Harriet Micocci]. [Washington, DC]: United States Department of Labor. Bureau of Labor Statistics, 1967. 57p. map. bibliog. (BLS Report no. 320).

This report is one of a series intended to provide background information for US businessmen employing local workers abroad, trade union and labour specialists, consulting economists and students. There are chapters on legislation affecting labour, labour and management, industrial relations, conditions of employment, health, safety, workmen's compensation and social insurance. It is based in part on publications by the Government of Jamaica and on information obtained in Jamaica through interviews with representatives of government, labour and management and through personal observations of the author. The research was completed in May 1967.

756 Labour in the West Indies: the birth of a workers' movement.

W. Arthur Lewis, with an afterword by Susan Craig. London; Port-of-Spain: New Beacon Books, 1977. 104p. bibliog.

Lewis's pamphlet, first published in London (Fabian Society, 1938), is a seminal and succinct account of the birth of West Indian trade unionism. It sets the developments in Jamaica within the context of West Indian social conditions and of the labour movement as it emerged in the rest of the West Indies. Susan Craig, in her afterword, 'Germs of an idea', comments on Lewis's ideas in the light of post-1939 developments in the West Indies.

757 **A voice at the workplace: reflections on colonialism and the Jamaican worker.**
Michael Manley. London: Andre Deutsch, 1975. 239p.

A portrayal of class attitudes in Jamaica, the growth of the trade union movement in Jamaica and the author's involvement in it, as perceived by a committed socialist, a trade unionist for two decades and subsequently a politician and Prime Minister of Jamaica.

758 **The development and impact of collective bargaining in the bauxite and alumina industry in Jamaica, 1952-1968.**
Keith St. Elmo Panton. PhD thesis, Washington State University, Pullman, Washington, 1970. 308p. bibliog. (Available from University Microfilms, Ann Arbor, Michigan, 1971).

An historical, legal and structural view of the collective bargaining process in the Jamaican bauxite and alumina industry with an exploration of the effects of that process on industrial relations in other industries and of North American influences on the evolving patterns of collective bargaining and industrial relations in the Jamaican industry.

759 **Papers & findings from seminar on 'Worker Participation' held at Trade Union Education Institute, University of the West Indies, Mona, Kingston, Jamaica, July 12-23, 1976.**
Jamaica: co-sponsored by the Trade Union Education Institute (TUEI), the ILO/DANIDA Caribbean Project on Worker's Education, the Caribbean Congress of Labour (CCL) and the Friedrich-Ebert-Stiftung (FES), [1976?]. 1 vol. (variously paged).

The seminar examined the Worker Participation Report of the Nettleford Committee which was presented to the Government of Jamaica in November 1975, against the study and understanding of various worker participation models existing in several countries.

760 **The rise of the labour movement in Jamaica.**
O. W. Phelps. *Social and Economic Studies*, vol. 9, no. 4 (Dec. 1960), p. 417-68. bibliog.

Traces the rise of the labour movement in Jamaica from 1919 to 1934, and, more especially from the disturbances of 1938 up to the time of writing, with particular reference to the Bustamante Industrial Trade Union, the Trade Union Council and the relation of trade unionism to politics. This study was done in 1957-58 when the author, then Professor of Industrial Relations at Claremont Men's College, California, spent nine months as a Fulbright Research Scholar at the Institute of Social and Economic Research, University of the West Indies, Jamaica.

761 **Arise ye starvelings: the Jamaican labour rebellion of 1938 and its aftermath.**
Ken Post. The Hague; Boston, Massachusetts; London: Martinus Nijhoff, 1978. 502p. map. bibliog. (Institute of Social Studies, the Hague. Series on the Development of Societies, vol. 3).

The most detailed study of the subject, based on research done in 1967-69 when the author was attached to the University of the West Indies and during six weeks in October to November, 1972, when he revisited the island. 'It will soon be apparent to the reader that this work is intended to be an analysis in the Marxist theoretical tradition... What I have attempted to do, therefore, is to take an episode of British colonial history which is, more importantly, an essential conjunction in the development of modern Jamaica... and to master the available historical material as far as I could by sifting it critically through a frame of Marxist theory.' (Foreword, p. vii-viii). The contents include: Part one, 'Some questions of theory'; part two, 'Social classes: the makers of history'; and part three, 'Making history'. A continuation was issued by the author as *Strike the iron: a colony at war: Jamaica, 1939-1945* (Atlantic Highlands, New Jersey: Humanities Press; the Hague: Institute of Social Sciences, 1981. 2 vols. map.) The author is on the staff of the Institute of Social Studies, the Hague.

762 **Report of the Advisory Committee on Worker Participation.**
[Jamaica: 1975]. 2 vols.

The Committee, under the chairmanship of the Hon. Rex Nettleford, O. M., was charged with examining and making recommendations on the necessary laws and strategies to implement a system of worker participation in Jamaica at the earliest possible time. Part two includes memoranda submitted to the Committee and 'Workers participation in industry (a survey of workers' opinion)' by Dr Carl Stone, Vice-Chairman of the Committee.

763 **Industrial relations in Jamaica and Trinidad.**
Deryck H. F. Stone. Kingston: [the author?], 1969. 490p.

The author, a solicitor of the Supreme Courts of Jamaica and England and a lecturer in labour relations in the University of the West Indies, wrote this book to supply the need for an outline of the position in Jamaica and Trinidad, intended primarily for use amongst students, personnel officers and junior trade union officers. Lengthy appendices, comprising more than half the volume, include the texts of relevant statutes.

764 **The system of industrial relations in Jamaica.**
Deryck H. F. Stone. Kingston: [the author?], 20 Duke Street, 1972. 174p.

The work covers in five chapters the following topics: the sociology of labour relations, the legal position of unions and their members, the system of labour relations in Jamaica from its origins in 1938 up to 1971, fair labour code and collective agreement and termination of employment and compensation for injury. It is factual and the presentation suggests that it was prepared as a manual for those pursuing university-level courses in industrial relations or for those engaged in industrial relations work.

765 **Wage determination in English-speaking Caribbean countries: record of proceedings of, and documents submitted to, ILO/DANIDA Regional Seminar (Kingston, Jamaica, 1–7 March 1978).**

Geneva: International Labour Office, 1979. 121p.
(Labour-Management Relations Series, 57).

Although the approach of the seminar was regional this selection of papers includes the opening address by the then Parliamentary Secretary in the Ministry of Labour, Jamaica, indicating factors which were reflected in the Jamaican government's approach to the subject of the seminar, e.g. self reliance and worker participation, and a paper entitled 'Prices and incomes policy in Jamaica' by Headley Brown, Trade Administrator, Jamaica. The seminar was the first of its kind in the Caribbean and was organized by the ILO, on the invitation of the Government of Jamaica and with the assistance of the Danish International Development Agency (DANIDA).

Struggles of the Jamaican people.
See item no. 424.

Statistics

General

766 **Statistics America: sources for social, economic and market research (North, Central & South America).**
Joan M. Harvey.   Beckenham, England: CBD Research; Detroit, Michigan: Gale Research, 1980. 385p. 2nd ed. rev. and enl.

Gives directory information on the central statistical offices of countries included, other important organizations that collect and publish statistical material, libraries and information services, the principal bibliographies of statistics and the major statistical publications. The section on Jamaica comprises p. 212-20. Lists 36 statistical publications.

Consumer price indices: percentage movements, January 1970–December 1980.
See item no. 527.

National primary socio-economic data structures. IX: Barbados, Jamaica, Trinidad and Tobago.
See item no. 1093.

Periodicals

767 **CARICOM Statistics Yearbook.**
Trade, Economics and Statistics Division, Caribbean Community Secretariat.   Georgetown, Jamaica: Caribbean Community Secretariat, 1978- . annual.

The first edition of the 1978 yearbook appeared 6 May 1980. Gives in one volume the most recent economic and social statistical data available on CARICOM countries. The statistical data have been divided into the following twelve

Statistics. Periodicals

sections: Population and Vital Statistics, Labour and Employment, Migration, Tourism, Trade, Production, Prices, National Accounts, Balance of Payments, Finance, Transportation, Education. While the data reflect the institutions and practices of each country, a common system of definitions and classifications allows for comparisons with other countries.

768 **Pocketbook of Statistics, Jamaica.** Department of Statistics. [Kingston]: Department of Statistics, 1976- . annual.

A handy reference book giving statistical information on the main areas of social and economic interest to the general public.

769 **Production Statistics.** Department of Statistics. [Kingston]: Department of Statistics, 1972- . annual.

This report provides information on the volume and value of output in the major productive areas, specifically, in agriculture, mining, manufacturing and electricity. Sources of data are mainly the surveys of establishments conducted by the Department of Statistics, supplemented by data on agricultural production supplied by the Ministry of Agriculture, commodity boards and other organizations. The statistical tables are prefaced by an introductory chapter.

Economic Activity in Caribbean Countries.
See item no. 556.

Economic and Social Progress in Latin America.
See item no. 557.

National Income and Product.
See item no. 560.

Monetary Statistics.
See item no. 591.

Statistical Digest.
See item no. 592.

External Trade: provisional.
See item no. 605.

Indices of External Trade.
See item no. 606.

Abstract of Building and Construction Statistics.
See item no. 645.

Employment, Earnings and Hours in Large Establishments.
See item no. 743.

The Labour Force.
See item no. 745.

770 **Statistical Bulletin of the OAS.**
Washington, DC: General Secretariat, Organization of American States, 1979- . quarterly.

This bulletin, which is concerned with the Latin American and Caribbean member states of the OAS, contains three sections. The first is devoted to one or more articles on selected relevant subjects, the second and third are permanent features - regional statistical tables and selected indicators for individual countries. The statistics are obtained from official sources as well as from other sources such as the International Monetary Fund, the Inter-American Development Bank, the United Nations Statistical Office and the OAS offices in member states. Vol. 1, no. 1, January-March 1979, includes statistical tables on the following subjects for the individual member countries, through various periods from 1959 to 1978: regional economic and demographic trends; foreign trade and international reserves; domestic prices, interest and exchange rates; employment, unemployment and salaries; production indicators, and the following selected country tables for Jamaica: Jamaica national accounts and balance of payments, 1950-77 and Jamaica: short term economic indicators, 1975-78.

771 **Statistical Review.**
[Produced by the] Department of Statistics. Kingston: Department of Statistics, August 1981- . monthly.

'A new monthly series of statistical reviews designed to provide up-to-date information on the Jamaican economy. Statistics presented in this series will be summary in form, complementing the more detailed monthly reports now being published in such areas as External Trade and the Consumer Price Indices... Basic coverage relates to data on population including employment and travel statistics, importation, exportation and production of goods as well as aspects of financial statistics... Data included in this review have been derived from surveys of persons and private sector activities... [and] tabulation of administrative records derived from a wide cross section of government agencies.' (Preface, p. [3]).

772 **Statistical Yearbook of Jamaica.** [Kingston]: Department of Department of Statistics. Statistics, 1973- . annual.

Data are presented in summary form. More recent information may be obtained from current publications, *Statistical Abstracts*, *Statistical Review* and other relevant publications of the Department of Statistics.

Environment, Conservation and Planning

Environment and conservation

773 A study of cultural determinants of soil erosion and conservation in the Blue Mountains of Jamaica: progress report.

James M. Blaut, Ruth P. Blaut, Nan Harman, Michael Moerman. *Social and Economic Studies*, vol. 8, no. 4 (Dec. 1959), p. 403-20.

A pilot study, by a geographer and three graduate student assistants of Yale University, of the cultural determinants of bad soil management and lack of conservation measures on the part of peasant farmers in an area which the authors describe as 'some of the most erosive and highly eroded farming land in the world.'

774 Preservation of national monuments in Jamaica.

T. A. L. Concannon. *Caribbean Quarterly*, vol. 9, no. 3 (Sept. 1963), p. 3-9.

A factual account of the legal basis and programme of work of the Jamaica National Trust Commission, of which the author was Technical Director.

Environment, Conservation and Planning. Environment and conservation

775 Conservation in Jamaica: a symposium.

Edited by Brian Hudson. [Kingston: Jamaican Geographical Society, 1974]. 47p.

In seven papers an archaeologist, an architect, an agriculturalist, two geographers, a public relations officer and a water planner discuss some of the environmental problems facing Jamaica.

776 Proceedings of the Symposium on Environmental Studies in Jamaica, Chemistry Department, UWI, Mona, May 25 & 26, 1979.

Kingston: Scientific Research Council Press, 1980. 274p.

Includes the texts of addresses relating to current programmes on subjects such as air quality, water quality, meteorology, pesticidal residues in soils and crops, chemical control of pests, effluent control and related subjects, by participants in the academic, public and private sectors.

777 Kingston harbour study.

Stanley Consultants. Muscatine, Iowa: Stanley Consultants, 1968. 4 vols.

This report, prepared for the Government of Jamaica by the consultants under contract to the United States Agency for International Development of the Department of State, 'examines all those elements which contribute to the Kingston harbour regimen' - its hydrology, physiography, oceanography, watershed characteristics - 'the effect of present and contemplated projects upon the balance of natural forces', and makes recommendations for future action and guidelines for the development of Kingston harbour and its environs. The contents include: 'Kingston harbour study (text)'; an appendix; synopsis, conclusions and recommendations; and historic maps of Kingston harbour (reproduces 33 historic maps from the 17th century to date).

778 Final report - environmental feasibility study of the Jamaica Peat Resources Utilization Project.

Submitted by the Traverse Group, Ann Arbor, Michigan, and the Natural Resources Conservation Department, Ministry of Mining and Energy, Kingston, Jamaica to the Energy Division, Ministry of Mining and Energy. Kingston: Ministry of Mining and Energy, 30 Sept. 1981. 3 vols. maps.

Incorporates studies in the disciplines of hydrology, water chemistry, oceanography, ecology, sociology and economics in respect of the Black River Morass and the Negril Morass, by a team of scientists and technologists. The team studied the environmental effects of various alternatives for mining peat in two large wetlands of Jamaica. The existence of substantial deposits of peat in Jamaica presents an opportunity for decreasing Jamaica's dependence on foreign purchased fuel.

206

779 **Jamaica: conservation and development of sites and monuments. [Final report of UNESCO Mission to Jamaica] September 1968-April 1969.**
C. Tunnard, J. C. Pollaco. Paris: UNESCO, 1969. 121p. 7 maps.

The terms of reference of the mission were to survey artistically or historically important buildings or historic sites, to recommend a programme for their conservation and development as tourist centres and to prepare recommendations for the development of tourism with reference to the conservation programme proposed. In addition to its recommendations with regard to particular sites and to government policy the report gives useful information on the development of interest in conservation and of programmes of conservation in Jamaica, as well as regards tourism in Jamaica up to the time of the mission's visit. Christopher Tunnard was Professor of City Planning, Yale University, New Haven and John C. Pollaco was Chairman, Malta Government Tourist Board.

780 **Coastal water pollution in Jamaica with special reference to Kingston harbour.**
Barry Wade. *Jamaica Journal*, vol. 6, no. 2 (June 1972), p. 14-19. maps. bibliog.

An account of the causes of pollution and of the relevant legislation, with some recommendations as to the urgent steps which are essential to save Kingston Harbour from ecological destruction. The author was a lecturer in the Department of Zoology, University of the West Indies.

781 **The pollution ecology of Kingston harbour, Jamaica: scientific report of the UWI/ODM Kingston Harbour Research Project 1972-1975.**
Barry Wade. Mona, Jamaica: Zoology Department, University of the West Indies, 1976. 3 vols. maps. bibliog. (Research Report no. 5).

This report is the result of work made possible by a grant from the United Kingdom Ministry of Overseas Development. It concerns water quality, oxygen balance, benthic ecology, pollution abatement and harbour improvement. The author was formerly a senior lecturer in the Department of Zoology, University of the West Indies.

Hellshire Hills Scientific Survey, 1970.
See item no. 872.

Planning, general studies, urban and rural planning

782 **Report of the Second Meeting of Planning Officials in the Caribbean, Kingston, Jamaica, 29 May-2 June 1980.**
CEPAL/Economic Commission for Latin America. [Port-of-Spain, Trinidad?]: United Nations Economic and Social Council, 1980. 55p. (E/CEPAL/CDCC/66/Rev.1).

This report relates to the state of planning in the Caribbean with particular reference to agriculture, energy, transport, environment, population, information, training and women, and reproduces in full the address delivered by the Hon. Hugh Small, Minister of Finance and Planning of the Government of Jamaica, outlining his government's policy in planning for the above-mentioned sectors. Annex III: 'Lists of documents' lists the following relating to Jamaica: 'The relationship between physical, regional and national planning: the Jamaican situation', by O. Davies (C DCC/PO/WP/80/9); 'Some aspects of manpower planning in Jamaica: issues and problems' by M. G. Ssemanda (CDCC/PO/WP/80/17); 'Statement' by Dr. T. E. Aldridge (Jamaica delegation) on 'Dimensions and status of environmental planning in the Caribbean-Latin American region' (CDCC/PO/WP/80/2). The meeting was organized by the Economic Commission for Latin America through its Office for the Caribbean and was held within the framework of activities of the Caribbean Development and Co-operation Committee, with the collaboration of the Latin American Institute for Economic and Social Planning.

783 **Uncontrolled urbanization in the developing world: a Jamaican case study.**
Klaus De Albuquerque, Wesley Van Riel, J. Mark Taylor. *Journal of Developing Areas*, vol. 14, no. 3 (April 1980), p. 361-86. map. bibliog.

Reviews research on uncontrolled urbanization arising from the march of rural migrants to major metropolitan areas and compares some of the substantive findings with results of a study conducted in a stabilized slum of West Kingston, Jamaica, during 1972. The authors were respectively, Associate Professor, Department of Sociology and Anthropology, College of Charleston; a teacher of economics, University of the West Indies, Mona, Jamaica (who was also associated with the National Planning Agency in Jamaica); and a member of the Divinity School, Harvard University.

784 **Housing for Jamaica.**
Kingston: Scientific Research Council, National Planning Agency, 1978. 99p. (Workshops on Science and Technology, Jamaica, 1978, sponsored by the Organization of American States).

The texts of papers and summaries of discussions by government administrators and technologists in a workshop organized by the Scientific Research Council and

785 **The Jamaica Urban Development Corporation.**
Gloria Knight. *Ekistics: the problems and science of human settlements*, vol. 41, no. 244 (March 1976), p. 144-47. map.

Gives the background to the creation of the Urban Development Corporation in 1968 and briefly outlines its functions and some of the projects undertaken by it. The author is the general manager of the Corporation and this article is based on a paper presented at the 1975 Town and Country Planning Summer School, University College of Wales at Aberystwyth, supplemented by more recent illustrations and information.

786 **Urban planning in Jamaica.**
Gloria Knight. In: *Urban and regional planning in the Caribbean*: proceedings of the UNICA workshops on Caribbean Urbanism. [Edited and translated by] Gustavo A. Antonini. Florida: Association of Caribbean Universities and Research Institutes, 1976, p. 6-20. map. bibliog.

An authoritative synopsis of urban planning and public policy by the general manager of the Urban Development Corporation of Jamaica.

787 **Bauxite land-use policy and resettlement programmes in Jamaica.**
Parris A. Lyew-Ayee. *Natural Resources Forum*, vol. 5, no. 1 (Jan. 1981), p. 69-75.

Briefly discusses new agreements, effective 1 February 1980, between the Government of Jamaica and four of the bauxite and alumina companies operating in Jamaica, for the acquisition of all company-owned bauxite lands by the government and the rationalization of bauxite reserves. Describes some of the problems associated with resettlement of people and relocation of roads. The author is Director of the Bauxite Reserves Division of the Jamaica Bauxite Institute, which is responsible for the overall management of the country's bauxite resources.

788 **The planning process in Jamaica.**
Prepared by the National Planning Agency. In: *Documents submitted to the first meeting of planning officials in the Caribbean* (25-31 January 1979, Havana, Cuba). Vol. 2: [Chile?]: United Nations, 1979, p. 13-24. (CEPAL/CARIB 79/10, 16 July 1979).

An official outline of the planning process in Jamaica, including a statement of the government's objectives for the economy with particular reference to the public and private sectors.

the National Planning Agency to help to identify areas in which further research is necessary in order to make local materials adaptable to Jamaica's building needs and acceptable to its public. Includes factual information on subjects such as building regulations, environmental control, development programmes and raw materials.

Environment, Conservation and Planning. Planning, general studies, urban and rural planning

789 The free village system in Jamaica.

Hugh Paget. *Jamaican Historical Review*, vol. 1, no. 1 (June 1945), p. 31-48.

A contribution towards an understanding of the transformation of an amorphous collection of ex-slaves freed in 1838 into communities of self-respecting peasantry by 1865, thus laying the foundations of a free society.

790 Land development patterns in Jamaica.

Neil O. Richards. *Jamaica Journal*, vol. 6, no. 4 (Dec. 1972), p. 4-11. map.

An account of the patterns of total land development for urban purposes in Jamaica, with reference to land subdivision, infrastructure, buildings and community services for residential, industrial and commercial purposes. The author is an architect-planner.

791 Kingston waterfront redevelopment: a report commissioned by the Ministry of Overseas Development, United Kingdom, on behalf of the Government of Jamaica.

Shankland Cox & Associates. Kingston: November 1968. 43p.

A report on a major urban redevelopment by government, conceived as part of a 15 to 20 year national plan of development, amply illustrated with diagrams and architect's models. The Kingston Redevelopment Plan has since become a reality. The technical details upon which this report is based were published separately as a *Technical Report* (November 1968. 58p.) and a *Landscape Design Manual* (May 1971. 24p.).

792 Low cost housing in Jamaica: study and proposals for the redevelopment of a squatter area in Trench Town, Kingston, Jamaica.

Prepared by Shankland Cox. London: Shankland Cox, 1971. 104p. fold. plan. bibliog.

This report was prepared in the Kingston and London offices of Shankland Cox. It records work carried out for the Jamaican Ministry of Public Utilities and Housing in 1969 and 1970. Section one: 'Trench Town today', describes how the community came into being and its pattern of communications and services. Section two: 'Trench Town tomorrow', describes the social objectives of the plan and details of housing and other services planned. Section three is entitled 'A closer look at people and their homes', Section four discusses 'General housing policy... It has been a basic consideration in this study that proposals for Trench Town should have a relevance for the island as a whole and should be seen as part of a potential nationwide housing programme.' (Summary, p. 8). A carefully illustrated development plan and an interesting study of local people and their homes. Publisher's address: 16 Bedford Square, London WC1.

Environment, Conservation and Planning. Planning, general studies, urban and rural planning

793 **Experiment in low income housing in Jamaica: an evaluation.** Edited by Carl Stone, Marie Sutherland. Kingston: Institute of Social and Economic Research, University of the West Indies, 1978. 275p.

A collection of research papers and evaluation reports on self-help low-income housing projects undertaken by the World Bank and the Government of Jamaica. The evaluation research was carried out over the period 1975 to 1978 by the Sites and Services Unit in the University of the West Indies' Institute of Social and Economic Research. The evaluation reflects a wide range of perspectives including those of architecture, building, sociology, political science and economics and is concerned with details of project development as well as wider issues of public and social policy. The principal contributors were the editors and Lascelles Dixon, Peter Phillips, Errol Boyd and Wilberne Persaud.

794 **Kingston metropolitan regional plan.** Town Planning Department, Ministry of Finance and Planning. Kingston: Town Planning Department, 1978. 2 vols. 36 maps.

A development plan for Kingston and its environs up to 1995, including a number of detailed studies of the demography, social amenities, recreational facilities, infrastructure, housing, employment, transportation and land use of the area.

795 **May Pen development plan.** Town Planning Division, Ministry of Mining and Natural Resources. Kingston: Town Planning Division, 1978. 72p. 16 maps.

A development plan for a rapidly growing urban area, prepared in 1975.

796 **Montego Bay development plan.** Town Planning Department, Ministry of Finance and Planning. Kingston: Town Planning Department, 1978. 200p. 16 maps.

A development plan for Jamaica's second largest urban centre and only other city than Kingston, the capital, embracing studies on the demography, social and recreational facilities, infrastructure, environment and transportation of the area.

797 **Morant Bay development plan.** Town Planning Department, Ministry of Finance and Planning. Kingston: Town Planning Department, 1980. 1 vol. (variously paged). 8 maps.

A development plan for a historic town long linked with the production and shipping of sugar.

Environment, Conservation and Planning. Planning, general studies, urban and rural planning

798 A national physical plan for Jamaica, 1970-1990.
Town Planning Department, Ministry of Finance and Planning. Kingston: Town Planning Department, Oct. 1971. 116p. 28 maps.

Guidelines for the use of land resources based on studies and detailed surveys carried out from 1968 by the Government of Jamaica with the assistance of the United Nations Development Programme. The studies embrace agriculture, mining, tourism, manufacturing, population, urbanization, housing, utilities, social health and recreational facilities. This, the main document of the plan, is complemented by a second volume consisting of the National Atlas.

799 Ocho Rios development plan.
Town Planning Department, Ministry of Finance and Planning. Kingston: Town Planning Department, Nov. 1979. 1 vol. (variously paged). 9 maps.

This preliminary plan for the second tourist town in Jamaica includes chapters on demography, social amenities and recreation, housing, infrastructure, economy and employment, land use, action areas, administration and implementation. The maps are a noteworthy feature of the publication.

800 St. Ann's Bay development plan.
Town Planning Department, Ministry of Finance and Planning. Kingston: Town Planning Department, April 1979. 1 vol. (variously paged). 10 maps.

Plan for a historic town located near the site of Columbus's landing place on his fourth voyage to America.

801 Urbanization in Jamaica.
James W. Trowbridge. New York: Ford Foundation, [1972]. 30p. map. bibliog.

A working paper on urban growth, urban conditions, planning, research and training needs, prepared as supportive material for an International Survey of Urbanization in developing countries, by a former assistant representative of the Ford Foundation for the Caribbean based in Kingston, Jamaica.

Five year independence plan, 1963-1968.
See item no. 533.

Education

General and historical studies

802 The educational system and nation building in Jamaica (1944-70).
Douglas Kentish Archer. PhD thesis, Northwestern University, Illinois, 1973. 150 leaves. bibliog. (Available from University Microfilms, Ann Arbor, Michigan, 1973).

A descriptive account of the educational system in the quarter century following the introduction of universal adult suffrage in 1944. The system is viewed in the light of its contribution to nation building and the growth of national identity. Unfortunately, the text is marred by the frequent misspelling of the names of prominent persons mentioned.

803 An analytical and developmental study of the educational programs and plans for Jamaica.
Wanda Lea Bickel. PhD thesis, St. Louis University, St. Louis, Missouri, 1972. 276 leaves. 3 maps. bibliog. (Available from University Microfilms, Ann Arbor, Michigan, 1972).

A descriptive account of the Jamaican educational system and programmes in the ten years following political independence, with a critical chapter on Jamaican educational development in relation to national identity problems. The study embraces education at all levels and is refreshingly free of jargon.

804 Social and economic obstacles to the development of popular education in post-emancipation Jamaica, 1834-1865.
C. Campbell. *Journal of Caribbean History*, vol. 1 (Nov. 1970), p. 57-88.

The attitudes of various groups and interests in the country to the development of popular education are outlined and the author concludes that the obstacles were not merely financial but social and philosophical, comprising considerations of race, colour and class arising from the materialistic nature of the society.

805 Education in Jamaica.

Mary Manning Carley. [Kingston]: Institute of Jamaica with the assistance of Jamaica Welfare, 1942. 30p. (Social Survey Series, no. 1).

A brief, factual survey of education at a time when many changes were taking place in the structure of Jamaican life.

806 Education and development in the English-speaking Caribbean: a contemporary survey.

Laurence D. Carrington, [introduced by] Germán W. Rama. [s.l.]: UNESCO; ECLA; UNDP, 1978. 127p. bibliog. (Project Development and Education in Latin America and the Caribbean).

An informed and readable summary of the state of education in the English-speaking countries of the Caribbean with special emphasis on Barbados, Guyana, Jamaica and Trinidad and Tobago, within the frame of reference constituted by the economic conditions and social prospects of each country. The study embraces all levels of education and includes a chapter on multilingualism and educational development.

807 The Mico College, Jamaica: some account of the Mico family, the story of the Mico fund, its diversion to the West Indies and its latest developments in Jamaica, with a brief history of the College.

Frank Cundall. Kingston: printed by the Gleaner Co. for the Directors of the Mico College, 1914. 98p.

The early history of a training college for primary teachers, which has been a formative educational influence in Jamaican life and from whose ranks have emerged several prominent educators.

808 Development and disillusion in Third World education, emphasis on Jamaica.

Edited by Vincent D'Oyley, R. N. Murray. Toronto: Ontario Institute for Studies in Education, 1979. 185p. bibliog. (Symposium Series - Ontario Institute for Studies in Education, 10).

Traces the historical development of teacher training, skill training, secondary education and management of the school system in Jamaica. Jamaica is used as an example of a Third World country for purposes of comparison with Guyana and Ghana. The historical process is linked with an inquiry into the factors which account for the system not always having realized its expectations in Jamaica.

809 **Society, schools and progress in the West Indies.**
John J. Figueroa. Oxford, England: Pergamon Press, 1971.
208p. 2 maps. bibliog.

A comparative study which draws extensively on the author's experience of the
subject in the Jamaican context. The author was Professor of Education in the
University of the West Indies.

810 **Sociology of education: a Caribbean reader.**
Edited by Peter M. E. Figueroa, Ganga Persaud. London:
Oxford University Press, 1976. 284p. bibliog.

A collection of papers, written mostly by West Indian-born scholars, aimed
largely at university students, student-teachers or anyone interested in the development of the region and designed to fill a gap in the literature on Caribbean
education. The following papers relate specifically to Jamaica: 'Education and
society in Jamaica' by Errol Miller; 'School authority pattern and students' social
development in Jamaican primary schools' by Ganga Persaud; 'Socialization in
the Jamaican primary school: a study of teacher evaluation and student participation' by Sherry Keith; 'Values and academic achievement among high school boys
in Kingston, Jamaica' by Peter M. E. Figueroa; 'School and environmental factors
in Jamaica' by L. H. E. Reid; and 'Parent teacher relationships in a Jamaican village'
by Edward P. G. Seaga.

811 **The Commonwealth Caribbean: a study of the educational
system of the Commonwealth Caribbean and a guide to the
academic placement of students in educational institutions of
the United States.**
Stephen H. Fisher. Washington, DC: International
Education Activities Group of the American Association of
Collegiate Registrars and Admissions Officers, 1979. 238p.
map. (World Education Series).

Includes sections on secondary education system, certificates and examinations,
teacher education programmes in Jamaica and also on the programmes of the
University of the West Indies, institutions of further education (e.g. College of
Arts, Science and Technology) and on training in the allied health professions.

812 **Status and power in rural Jamaica: a study of educational
and political change.**
Nancy Foner. New York: Teachers College Press, 1973.
172p. map. bibliog.

A study of the effects of the educational system on the status and aspirations of
rural Jamaica and the extent to which these are being modified by recent
national and political developments. An anthropological study based on field-work
in Jamaica from July 1968 to September 1969.

813 Reports and repercussions in West Indian education, 1835-1933.

Shirley C. Gordon. Kingston: Caribbean Universities Press, 1968. 190p.

The author introduces eight of the most important reports on West Indian education during the period of colonial administration, discusses their main common features and presents edited texts of the reports, including those of the following two which relate to Jamaica: *The report upon the condition of the juvenile population* (1879) and *The Lumb report* (1898). Invaluable for the study of the early history of education.

814 Educational trends in the Caribbean: European affiliated areas.

Charles C. Hauch. Washington, DC: US Government Printing Office, 1960. 153p. map. bibliog. (US Department of Health, Education and Welfare. Bulletin 1960 no. 26).

Information in this bulletin is based in considerable part on direct observation by the author, a specialist in comparative education, of educational institutions and practices and on discussions with educational and other specialists in certain of the Caribbean areas during the latter part of 1958. From the point of view of educational trends in Jamaica the chapters on technical education and the University College of the West Indies were particularly relevant at the time.

815 Educational change in postcolonial Jamaica.

Wills S. Jervier. New York: Vantage Press, 1977. 163p. map. bibliog.

A summary examination of new educational policies and trends in Jamaica viewed as changes from a colonial model to meet the expectations of a developing country. The organizational pattern, with particular reference to the development of junior high schools and curricula, is considered against the historical and social background to the system.

816 An historical overview of the state and educational policy in Jamaica.

Sherry Keith. *Latin American Perspectives*, vol. 5, no. 2 (spring 1978), p. 37-52. bibliog.

This paper approaches the subject from a Marxist perspective and attempts to show 'how the educational system itself was and continues to be an institution in maintaining and perpetuating the colonial and neo-colonial class system in Jamaica'. (p. 37). It covers educational developments up to the end of 1974. The author, was, at the time of publication, Program Co-ordinator at the Center for Latin American Studies, Stanford University and formerly was Lecturer in Sociology of Education, University of the West Indies, Mona, Jamaica.

817 Research conference report: studies in Jamaican education. Report of the First Conference on Educational Research of the Ministry of Education held at the Education Development and Demonstration Centre, Caenwood Centre, February 2-5, 1982.

[Edited by] Yvonne C. Mahy. [Kingston]: Ministry of Education, Research Section, Caenwood, May 1982. 78 leaves.

The main objective of the conference was to disseminate the finding of educational research studies carried out in Jamaica from 1978 to 1981 under the Rural Education Sector Loan Programme, by the Government of Jamaica and the United States Agency for International Development. Another objective of the conference was to invite critical reviews of the research from other researchers and educational practitioners as a means of learning and teaching. Among subjects researched and discussed were the effects of school feeding on school attendance, training in human resources technique in school management, the development of diagnostic tests, the shift system, vocational training, career aspirations of Jamaican college students and expectations of parents, students and teachers in respect of schooling.

818 Education and society in Jamaica.

Errol Miller. *Savacou*, no. 5 (June 1971), p. 51-70. bibliog.

An examination of the relationship between the social order and the educational system in which the latter is viewed as an agent of the social structure.

819 From research to action: language policy in Jamaica.

Errol Miller. *Prospects: Quarterly Review of Education*, vol. 11, no. 3 (1981), p. 372-80.

The central concern of this article is to examine ways in which language and language-teaching research carried out in the School of Education, University of the West Indies, have influenced policies in the Ministry of Education, Jamaica, in the areas of curriculum and textbook selection. It reviews three projects for improving the learning and teaching of standard English to creole-speaking children in Jamaican schools. The author is Professor of Teacher Education, University of the West Indies, Mona, Jamaica.

820 Directory of educational institutions 77-78.

Ministry of Education. [Kingston: the Ministry, 1979 or later]. 75p. annual.

This is the fourth edition of a work which previously appeared under the title of *School Directory*. This edition for the first time includes information on tertiary institutions, as well as on all categories of schools. Under each parish there is a listing of schools by type, giving the name and address of each school and its owner, grade, capacity, enrolment and attendance. Tertiary institutions included are teachers training colleges, technical and agricultural colleges and community colleges.

Education. General and historical studies

821 New deal for education in independent Jamaica.
Ministry of Education. Jamaica: Ministry of Education,
1966. 40p. (Ministry Paper no. 73).

A memorandum to Parliament setting out the education extension programme,
educational policy and proposed reforms of the Minister of Education. The programme involved the expenditure of $8 million in development over three years.
Issued also by the Ministry's Publication Branch in a more popular format,
illustrated, 107p.

822 Five-year education plan, 1978-1983.
Prepared in the Planning Division, Ministry of
Education. Jamaica: Ministry of Education, 1977. 224p.

This document was a final draft distributed for public examination and comment
before the final document was prepared for Parliament. Section one outlines the
social goals and their educational implications. Section two deals with strategies
and activities and with quantitative analysis involving demographic and enrolment
forecasts. The plan does not deal with the development of tertiary education.

**823 A review of the developments in education and social welfare
in Jamaica during the period 1944-1954.**
Ministry of Education and Social Welfare. Kingston:
Government Printer, 1954. 39p.

A brief and concise report for the general public on the more important developments which took place in these fields since the grant of a new constitution in
1944.

824 J. J. Mills: his own account of his life and times.
Edited by R. N. Murray. [Kingston]: William Collins &
Sangster (Jamaica), 1969. 192p.

Memoirs of John James Mills (1888-1966), widely known educator and public
servant. A straightforward, unpretentious and informal account of early schooling
in rural Jamaica, teacher training at Mico College, later association with educational organizations and of public life and persons including a series of biographical sketches of teacher legislators, together with personal observations on aspects
of cultural and social life. The memoir is prefaced by a perceptive memorial
address on the subject of the autobiography by the editor of the memoirs.

**825 New horizons in teacher education: report of the Conference
of the Institute Board of Teacher Education, Mona, Jamaica,
6th-10th September, 1971.**
Mona, Jamaica: University of the West Indies, Institute of
Education, 1972. 79p.

A distillation of the proceedings of the principal Caribbean regional body concerned with teacher education, in which the salient features of the state of
teacher education are analysed and proposals made for new approaches which it
was thought would provide a new kind of experience and would promote professional growth and maturity.

826 **An analytical study of the development of teacher preparation in Jamaica from its inception to the present.**
Kenneth Alexander Paddyfote. PhD thesis, Central Connecticut State College, New Britain, Connecticut, 1975. 279 leaves. bibliog. (Available from University Microfilms, Ann Arbor, Michigan, 1981).

An historical and descriptive account of the institutions providing teacher training and of the internal tasks and external forces affecting teacher preparation in Jamaica up to 1974, based on interviews with Jamaican educators, questionnaires and documentary research.

827 **Adolescence in Jamaica.**
A. S. Phillips. Kingston: Jamaica Publishing House, 1973. 148p. bibliog.

A study of adolescent behaviour in the Jamaican setting, with particular reference to cultural, racial, social and vocational factors which characterize the environment. The work is derived from several studies, done for the most part in the School of Education of the University of the West Indies.

828 **A teacher's guide to Jamaica.**
Kingston: Ministry of Education, Jamaica, 1971. 105p. map.

Though much of the information is outdated this is still a useful illustrated directory of educational institutions, the locations of which are shown on the accompanying map.

829 **A short history of education in Jamaica.**
Millicent Whyte. London: Hodder & Stoughton, 1977. 128p.

A very condensed account specially written for students in teacher training colleges. R. N. Murray, former Dean and Professor of Education, University of the West Indies, who writes the foreword, opines that 'it will form a springboard for deeper excursions into particular periods and aspects of the history'.

830 **Teacher internship as an adventure: can it be a replanning strategy in Jamaica?**
Sybil Wilson, Vincent D'Oyley. Toronto: Department of Educational Planing, Ontario Institute for Studies in Education, 1973. 132p. bibliog.

The report of an investigation, with recommendations, of a programme of teacher training, involving a one-year school internship, introduced in 1967 to help expedite the training of teachers in Jamaica in order to meet the acute shortage of trained personnel.

School system

831 Early childhood education in Jamaica: a project monograph.
Bernard van Leer Foundation. The Hague: Bernard van Leer Foundation, 1972. 47p.

After a concise account of the beginnings of early childhood education (basic schools) in Jamaica this monograph presents a factual account of the objectives and accomplishments to the date of writing of the Project For Early Childhood Education (PECE) in Jamaica, jointly launched in 1966 by the University of the West Indies Institute of Education and the Bernard van Leer Foundation. The Project aims at improving the quality of early childhood education by improving teaching skills, the school curriculum, the physical facilities of the school and by stimulating public interest in pre-primary education.

832 Accessibility and teacher utilization of the newer media in Jamaican junior secondary classrooms.
Ardis Daphne Kamra. EdD dissertation, University of Washington, 1977. 212 leaves. bibliog. (Available from University Microfilms, Ann Arbor, Michigan, 1978).

A study of the use of audio-visual instructional media in junior secondary schools, which 'were selected for study since they had been developed as a model upon which reform in secondary and primary education would be based'.

833 Technical and vocational education in Jamaica.
Produced by the Ministry of Education, Technical and Vocational Education Exhibition Committee. Kingston: Ministry of Education, [1970?]. 40p.

An illustrated informational booklet briefly describing types of schools with regard to curricula, admission, examinations and extra-curricular activities, with other general information.

834 Report in depth of primary education in Jamaica.
Kingston: Ministry of Education, 1974. 128, [130]p.

Report of a committee under the chairmanship of Professor R. N. Murray, appointed in 1972 by the Minister of Education to make a study of the primary school system and to recommend improvements in the system. In addition to discussing educational content and strategy, the committee gave prior consideration to concepts and notions out of which 'a philosophy of Jamaican education may evolve'. The appendices, which constitute the unpaged half of the volume, comprise supplementary papers relating to persons submitting memoranda, recommendations received, questionnaires and an analysis of data collected.

Jamaican interlude.
See item no. 26.

Higher education

835 The development of higher education in the British West Indies.

Lloyd Braithwaite. *Social and Economic Studies*, vol. 7, no. 1 (March 1958), p. 1-64. bibliog.

This paper outlines the history of the various attempts to establish higher education within the area and relates the failure of these attempts to the nature of the social structure in the West Indies. Among these attempts were James Mursell Phillipo's plan for a college in Jamaica and the attempts to establish Queen's College at Spanish Town, Jamaica and to develop a programme of higher education at Jamaica College.

836 The student and the university's civilising role.

Lucille Mathurin-Mair. *Caribbean Quarterly*, vol. 15, no. 2 & 3 (June-Sept. 1969), p. 8-19.

A perceptive review of student interaction with the changing social and intellectual climate of the University of the West Indies during its first twenty-one years of existence, with particular reference to the Mona campus, Jamaica.

837 UWI School of Education Mona, Jamaica: report of staff retreat 1979.

Kingston: School of Education, 1979. 63p.

The theme of the retreat was: 'Relevant educational policy and practice for a developing Jamaica: role of the School of Education in the teaching profession in Jamaica.' The papers presented reviewed the courses offered by the School leading to various qualifications conferred by the University, with recommendations regarding these courses.

838 The university in the Caribbean.

Eric Williams. In: *Universities for a changing world: the role of the university in the later twentieth century.* Edited by Michael D. Stephens, Gordon W. Roderick. Newton Abbot, England: David & Charles, 1975, p. 83-113. bibliog. (p. 206-08).

Although this contribution is based on a wide-ranging survey of Caribbean universities it contains much that is relevant to the specific role of the University of the West Indies, with its three campuses in Jamaica, Barbados and Trinidad. It was written by an academic and politician who had had considerable influence on recent developments in the University of the West Indies.

839 **The university – symbol of freedom: address to the graduating class at the University of the West Indies, Jamaica, February 16, 1963.**
Eric Williams. Trinidad and Tobago: Government Printing Office, 1963. 10p.

This address by the former Prime Minister of Trinidad and Tobago and Pro-Chancellor of the University was given at the first graduation after the University became independent and in the year after the two largest territories serviced by the University, Jamaica and Trinidad & Tobago, became independent. At that time, the University was embarking on a vast programme of expansion and re-appraising its role in West Indian society. The address expressed the noble aspira-tion that 'the goal of the University... should be a university symbolic of the democratic freedoms in the entire Caribbean area, serving therefore as an inspira-tion to those countries of the area where universities are not free, the suppression of academic freedom being merely a part of this suppression of freedom in general.' (p. 2).

Jamaica: its past and present state.
See item no. 37.

Adult education and literacy programmes

840 **Evaluation of the adult literacy programme: a report to the Literacy Evaluation and Planning Committee [of the Jamaica Social Welfare Commission].**
Erna Brodber. [Kingston]: Department of Sociology, University of the West Indies, 1971. 64 leaves. map.

The literacy programme was conducted by the Jamaica Social Welfare Commis-sion from 1951 to 1970.

841 **Literacy in the English-speaking Caribbean.**
Lawrence D. Carrington. Paris: UNESCO, March 1981. 214p. bibliog.

A study undertaken by a senior research fellow of the School of Education, University of the West Indies, St. Augustine, Trinidad, to describe and analyse the state of illiteracy in the region, with particular attention to 'those demo-graphic characteristics of the region that appear to relate to literacy, as well as the conditions within the educational systems that influence progress towards full literacy.' Includes information on the Jamaica Movement for the Advancement of Literacy's (JAMAL) programme.

842 **Building Jamaica by educating adults.**

Hopeton [L. A.] Gordon. *Caribbean Quarterly*, vol. 23, no. 4 (Dec. 1977), p. 22-32. bibliog.

A brief survey of recent adult education programmes being implemented by the government and non-governmental bodies to meet the changing cultural, educational and social needs of Jamaica.

843 **University adult education in Jamaica: origins and characteristics.**

Hopeton L. A. Gordon. *Caribbean Educational Review*, vol. 6, no. 2 (May 1979), p. 15-49.

A comprehensive survey of the origins, organization, development and programmes of the Department of Extra-Mural Studies of the University of the West Indies, with particular attention to its special character and philosophy as dynamic elements in nation-building in Jamaica and elsewhere in the Commonwealth Caribbean.

844 **JAMAL Foundation (formerly National Literacy Board) 5 year plan (1978-1983).**

[Kingston: JAMAL Foundation, 1978]. 77p.

The Jamaica Movement for the Advancement of Literacy was established in November 1974 and is the organization currently responsible for Jamaica's basic adult education programme, originally started as the National Literacy Programme in September 1972. After recapitulating developments from 1972 to 1977 this development plan covers subjects such as recruitment of students and staff, instructional programmes, evaluation and research, finance and fund raising. A complementary publication by way of a public relations effort is entitled *JAMAL* ([Kingston: JAMAL, in collaboration with Media Skills Ltd., 1978?]. 60p.).

845 **Literacy programmes and the public library service in Jamaica.**

Prepared by the JAMAL Foundation. *Unesco Journal of Information Science, Librarianship and Archives*, vol. 3, no. 4 (Oct.-Dec. 1981), p. 235-40.

The objective, operations and achievements of the Jamaica Movement for the Advancement of Literacy (JAMAL) are outlined and its collaboration with the Jamaica Library Service in providing non-formal continuing education for new literates is described.

846 **Educational deficits in the Caribbean/Los deficits educativos en el Caribe. Atlas of illiteracy and population without instruction of the Caribbean countries/Atlas de analfabetismo y de la población sin instrucción de los países del Caribe.**
Organization of American States, Department of Educational Affairs, Unit of Planning, Research and Studies of Education. Washington, DC: OAS, 1979. 128p. maps. tables. (Collection of Monographs and Studies of Education).

Contains data concerning illiteracy as well as the population on a precarious level, broken down by politico-territorial divisions in each country and by age groups. The section on Jamaica (p. 67-75) includes 2 maps and tables.

847 **A survey of adult education in Jamaica.**
Margaret Taylor, Hopeton [L. A.] Gordon. [Jamaica]: sponsored by Ministry of Youth & Community Development, National Council of Jamaican Organisations and Department of Extra-Mural Studies, University of the West Indies, (Dec. 1971). 27p.

An attempt 'to put on record in one place a comprehensive survey of such activity... and to reveal the areas of inadequacy.' (p. 1).

Periodicals

848 **Report of the Secretary-General.**
Jamaica National Commission for UNESCO. [Kingston: Jamaica National Commission], 1979/80- . irregular.

During the biennium 1979-80, the Jamaica National Commission for UNESCO was re-structured by the Cabinet to become a ministerial body. The report summarizes the main activities of the Commission in the fields of education, science and culture, during the period. This report incorporates the news features of the *Bulletin of the Jamaica National Commission for UNESCO* which appeared irregularly for the years 1968 to 1978 and which also included articles and speeches.

849 **Torch: journal of the Ministry of Education, Jamaica.**
Kingston: Publications Branch, Ministry of Education, Jamaica, 1947- . biannual.

The last issue was vol. 27, no. 1 (1980), but the publishers had hoped to resume publication in 1983. The articles cover 'a wide range of ideas and trends in education, from developments in the school system at large, to interesting innovations in the classroom.'.

Science, Technology and Medicine

Science and technology

850 **Jamaica - a case study of energy planning.**
Trevor A. Byer. *Natural Resources Forum*, vol. 3, no. 2 (Jan. 1979), p. 117-32.

Discusses the impact of the 'New International Energy Order' on Jamaica, the historical energy supply/demand situation in Jamaica, the import dependency of the Jamaican energy system, indigenous energy resources, the national energy plan. The author is a nuclear physicist who was Energy Adviser to the Government of Jamaica from 1973 to 1977 and subsequently was Consultant to the World Bank, conducting an Energy Survey of the Caribbean.

851 **Proceedings of the eighth annual conference of Caribbean water engineers. September 19-22, 1977, New Kingston, Jamaica.**
Sponsored by the Caribbean Council of Engineering Organizations, hosted by the Institution of Engineers, Jamaica, the National Water Authority, the Water Commission. [Jamaica: 1977?]. 326p. 10 maps.

Included are a number of papers on the water resources of Jamaica and the administration and control of these resources, by administrative and technical staff of the Government of Jamaica.

852 **Human resources for the development and management of land -the role of the surveying and land economy professions - theme [of the...].**

Commonwealth Association of Surveying and Land Economy Atlantic Regional Meeting, held at the Pegasus Hotel, Kingston, Jamaica 24-28 September, 1979. [Kingston?: the Association?], 1979?. 1 vol. (variously paged).

Includes papers on the development and management of land resources in Jamaica, quantity surveying (Jamaica standard form of contract), education for surveying and land economy in Jamaica by government, academic and private sector experts.

853 **The development and use of Jamaica's water resources: MAL./UWI/JAS Seminar no. 4, Golden Beach Hotel, Sept. 13-15, 1968, Oracabessa, Jamaica.**

Kingston: printed for the University of the West Indies and the Jamaica Agricultural Society, [1968?]. 211p. 4 maps.

The contents include: 'Some considerations involved in development and use of water resources' by Don Mills and A. S. Johnson; 'Some problems facing us in water supplies in Jamaica' by Harold Miller; 'Meteorological aspects' by D. O. Vickers; 'A review of the water resources in Jamaica' by John Williams; 'Influence of climate on crop selection' by C. M. Hewitt; 'Hydrological role of forests' by Keats Hall; 'Some watershed management problems of Taiwan and Jamaica', by Ted Sheng; 'Irrigation and water economy' by L. G. Campbell; 'Water needs of crops' by George Smith; 'Costs and benefits of irrigation in a development area of Jamaica' by R. N. S. Harris; 'Observation of agricultural water management in Jamaica' by J. M. Myers; 'The water supply of the Corporate Area of Kingston and St. Andrew' by E. E. Fraser; 'Domestic water supplies' by Neville Glegg; 'Domestic water supplies' by Clinton Davis; 'Water situation in relation to agricultural needs in Jamaica' by J. E. Pusey; 'Organisation, administration and methods with respect to the rational use of water on a national basis, as is done in Israel' by Keith Martin; and 'A water balance sheet for Jamaica' by G. P. Chapman. Includes text of papers and discussion.

854 **Directory of Caribbean marine research centres/Directorio de los centros de investigaciones marines del Caribe/Répertoire des centres caraïbes de recherche marine.**

Geneva: United Nations Environment Programme; Paris: Intergovernmental Oceanographic Commission, 1980. 1 vol. (unpaged loose-leaf work).

An unofficial compilation jointly prepared and published by UNEP (UN Environment Programme) and IOC (Intergovernmental Oceanographic Commission) of UNESCO to facilitate communication between scientists. The section on Jamaica (14p. of text) gives full directory particulars, including some lists of publications, for the following organizations: Discovery Bay Marine Laboratory; Division of Environmental Control of the Ministry of Health and Environmental Control; Fisheries Division of the Ministry of Agriculture; Geology Department of the University of the West Indies; Natural Resources Conservation Department of the Government of Jamaica; and Port Royal Marine Laboratory of the University of the West Indies.

855 Energy resources in the CDCC member countries.
[Port-of-Spain?]: United Nations, Economic Commission for
Latin America, Caribbean Development and Co-operation
Committee, 1980. 67p. bibliog.

A document presented at the fifth session of the Committee held in Kingston,
Jamaica, 4-10 June 1980, based on information provided in answer to questionnaires first sent out in 1978. Includes brief documentation on oil refinery production, hydropower and other sources of energy, non-conventional or potential,
which pertain to Jamaica as one of the CDCC countries covered.

**856 Technology and dependent development in Jamaica: a case
study.**
R[obert] K. Girling. *Social and Economic Studies*, vol. 26,
no. 2 (June 1977), p. 169-89. bibliog.

'This is a study of the ways in which the development of technology in the setting
of dependent capitalist development in Jamaica has served to retard not promote
socio-economic development. In the following sections I discuss theories of technology and development. I then present some data from a study of the food
processing industry in Jamaica. Those findings are analysed and their implications
assessed for the future development of Jamaica as well as other underdeveloped
countries.' (p. 169).

857 Essays on science and technology policy in the Caribbean.
Edited by Norman Girvan. Kingston: Institute of Social
and Economic Research, University of the West Indies,
1979. 336p. bibliog. (*Social and Economic Studies*, vol. 28,
no. 1, March 1979. Special number).

The essays are abstracted from a set of studies on this theme produced under the
aegis of the Institute of Social and Economic Research, University of the West
Indies and the Institute of Development Studies, University of Guyana. The
project was undertaken between 1975 and 1978 and was financially supported by
the International Development Research Centre of Canada. The papers, in so far
as they relate specifically to Jamaica, discuss the activities of the Scientific
Research Council of Jamaica and national and regional bodies concerned with
agricultural research and development.

858 Marine lab at Port Royal.
Ivan Goodbody. *Jamaica Journal*, vol. 2, no. 1 (March
1968), p. 31-35.

A brief description of marine biological work done in Jamaica since 1891 and of
the marine biological laboratory completed in 1960 as a research adjunct to the
Department of Zoology, University of the West Indies.

859 The work of the University's marine laboratories.
Ivan Goodbody. *Journal of the Geological Society of
Jamaica*, vol. 21 (1982), p. 58-62.

An account of the Discovery Bay Laboratory and the Port Royal Laboratory,
their programmes and their role in teaching and training.

226

Science, Technology and Medicine. Science and technology

860 **The oil and gas potential of Jamaica.**
Hugo R. Greiner. Kingston: Geological Survey
Department, Jamaica, 1965. 24p. 7 maps. bibliog. (Bulletin
no. 5).

This report was done under a contract between the Canadian External Aid Office
and the Government of Jamaica, by a geologist versed in petroleum prospecting
who was a member of staff of the University of New Brunswick. The work was
carried out during a three-month period of assignment and the report constitutes
a digest of information available to the government at that time on the island's
oil and gas potential as well as of Dr Greiner's geological examinations and the
recommendations made by him in relation to an exploration programme.

861 **Prefeasibility report – the Blue Mountain Water Supply
Project.**
Prepared by Harza Engineering Company, Chicago, Hue
Lyew Chin, Kingston, for the Government of Jamaica and
the Water Commission. Chicago: Harza Engineering Co.;
Kingston: Hue Lyew Chin, 1971. 1 vol. (variously paged). 7
maps.

A plan for systematic expansion of the public water supply facilities serving
Kingston and the surrounding urban area. The report describes the studies conducted to identify the most favourable project for using the Blue Mountain rivers
to supply public needs through the year 2000.

862 **Caribbean Commonwealth fisheries: some developmental
problems and developmental strategies.**
Julian S. Kenny. St. Augustine, Trinidad: Department of
Zoology, University of the West Indies, April 1981. 21p.
bibliog.

A concise overall view of fisheries development in the Commonwealth Caribbean
which focuses on the major problems which have arisen in Barbados, Jamaica, the
Windward and Leeward Islands, Trinidad and Tobago and Guyana.

863 **The biology, ecology, exploitation and management of
Caribbean reef fishes: scientific report of the ODA/UWI
Fisheries Ecology Research Project, Port Royal Marine
Laboratory, Jamaica, 1969-1973.**
Edited by J. L. Munro, R. Thompson. Kingston: Zoology
Department, University of the West Indies, 1973-78. 7 vols.
in 20 parts. (Research Report no. 3).

The investigations by the Overseas Development Administration and the University of the West Indies were conducted from the Port Royal Marine Laboratory
of the University of the West Indies and several of the volumes relate to the
Jamaican fishing industry, the composition of catches and the assessment of its
potential productivity.

864 The sea fisheries of Jamaica, past, present and future.
J. L. Munro. *Jamaica Journal*, vol. 3, no. 3 (Sept. 1969),
p. 16-22. map.

One of a series of articles entitled 'Science for the layman', with illustrations of
species of fish found in Jamaican waters, by a member of the Fisheries Ecology
Research Project of the University of the West Indies.

**865 Survey of Jamaican science and technology research
institutions and preliminary outline of development needs.**
National Planning Agency, Science and Technology
Section. [Kingston]: National Planning Agency, [1975?].
86p.

An exploratory evaluation of the setting within which science and technology are
conducted in Jamaica, the financial, manpower and infrastructural resources
employed in the conduct of these activities, the nature of scientific investigation
and the probable areas of local research findings (cf. 'Summary, conclusions and
recommendations', p. 79).

866 Jamaica's energy resources.
E[dward] Robinson. *Jamaica Journal*, vol. 8, no. 4
([1974?]), p. 22-27.

A short popular account of potential and known energy resources of Jamaica in
respect of petroleum, coal, nuclear fuels and geothermal energy, by a geologist on
the staff of the University of the West Indies.

**867 Technological adaptations to solar and aeolian energy
utilization, two case studies in rural Jamaica.**
Herbert Robert Anton Schaeper. [Gainesville, Florida]:
University of Florida, 1969. 331p. 11 maps. bibliog.

Perhaps the only such detailed investigation of the possibility of modifying and
adapting modern technology to mobilizing the local resources of non-industrialized
rural communities in Jamaica. The purpose of this study is to analyse cultural,
technical and economic aspects of solar and aeolian energy utilization as a
regional power source base for the economic growth and expansion of selected
developing regions. Two independent projects were designed and completed in
Jamaica: one in the field of solar energy and the other in wind power utilization.
An analysis is made of Jamaica with regard to its physical background, its
agriculture and industry and its electric power grid. The installation of solar
dryers on farms and of wind turbines is discussed and a short chapter on solar
and aeolian energy utilizations in other Antillean islands is given by way of
comparison. The author is an American engineer, who carried out one year of
field-work in the West Indies. The work was submitted as a dissertation for the
degree of doctor of philosophy at the University of Florida.

Science, Technology and Medicine. Science and technology

868 **Jamaican national paper [for submission to] United Nations Conference on Science and Technology Development, 1979.** Scientific Research Council. Kingston: Scientific Research Council, 1978. 35p.

The paper was a joint effort representing a wide spectrum of interests. Contents include: summary; introduction; objectives of the conference; the Jamaican situation (science and technology organizations, resources and education); foreign implications (North-South negotiations, regional co-operation in technology, transfer of technology); appendix: general information (statistics).

869 **The fisheries of Jamaica: report.** Ernest F. Thompson. Barbados: (printed by) Advocate Co., [1945]. 103p. (Development and Welfare in the West Indies. Bulletin no. 18).

This report summarizes the results of a survey carried out from 1 April 1943 to October 1944 covering a wide spectrum of concerns to the fisheries industry of Jamaica, including importation and consumption of fish, fishing methods, distribution and marketing, fisheries laws, tourist possibilities of Jamaican fishing, organization among fishermen and recommendation for the control of Jamaican fisheries.

870 **Science in the 70's: observations on science education in Jamaica.** D. A. Turner. *Caribbean Quarterly*, vol. 20, no. 2 (June 1974), p. 15-22. bibliog.

A brief survey of the organizations providing science education and some considerations on the influence of each of these organizations - the Association of Science Teachers of Jamaica, the Ministry of Education and the University of the West Indies.

871 **The development of a low-technology oysterculture industry in Jamaica.** Barry Wade, Robert Brown, Carl Hanson, Lawrence Alexander, Richard Hubbard, Bertie Lopez. *Proceedings of the Thirty-Third Annual Gulf and Fisheries Institute, San José, Costa Rica, November 1980.* Edited by James B. Higman. Miami, Florida: University of Miami Rosenstiel School of Marine and Atmospheric Science, June 1981, p. 6-18. map. bibliog.

An account of techniques used since 1977 by the Oysterculture (Jamaica) Project, sponsored by the International Development Research Centre of Canada (IDRC), the Government of Jamaica (Ministry of Agriculture) and the University of the West Indies (Department of Zoology) to determine what is feasible for establishing an oyster industry in Jamaica. The techniques stress the use of local resources in all stages and are designed to benefit low-income coastal communities generally within relatively close access to a mangrove system.

872 **Hellshire Hills Scientific Survey, 1970.**
Edited by J[eremy] D. Woodley. [Kingston]: Department
of Zoology, University of the West Indies, June 1971. 168p.
maps. bibliog.

This report describes a scientific survey of the Hellshire Hills, St. Catherine,
Jamaica, carried out by members of the University of the West Indies and the
Institute of Jamaica in anticipation of the proposed development of that area. The
site was one of the largest areas of almost virgin country and natural wilderness
left in Jamaica prior to its development. This study of its vegetation, geology,
surface water, climate and environment was made in order to gain knowledge of
what might be destroyed and to make recommendations for conserving the environment.

Periodicals

873 **The Journal of the Scientific Research Council of Jamaica.**
Kingston: Scientific Research Council of Jamaica, 1970- .
bi-annual.

This publication replaced an earlier quarterly bulletin entitled *Information* which
first appeared in June 1960. Its purpose is to present papers dealing either with
research work in progress in Jamaica or with the application of scientific method
to problems in the Jamaican context.

Medicine

874 **Mary Seacole.**
Ziggi Alexander, Audrey Dewjee. *History Today*, vol. 31
(Sept. 1981), p. 45.

A brief sketch of the life of Mary Seacole (d. May 1881) and of the esteem in
which her medical and nursing skills were held during the Crimean War.
Although Mary Seacole has been remembered in Jamaica by the naming of two
public buildings in her honour, she has become elsewhere a forgotten figure of a
period with which the name of Florence Nightingale is still widely remembered
and respected.

875 **Nutrition in Jamaica - 1969-70.**
Ann Ashworth, J. C. Waterlow. [Mona, Jamaica]:
Extra-Mural Department, University of the West Indies,
[1974]. 102p. bibliog.

The aim of this report is to give a comprehensive picture of conditions in 1969
and it remains the most current baseline account of the state of nutrition in
Jamaica, superseding the McCulloch report of 1945, which was the last previous
attempt to cover all aspects of nutrition. The material for the report was originally collected by the Nutrition Advisory Committee of the Scientific Research
Council under the chairmanship of the second of the two joint authors and is here

Science, Technology and Medicine. Medicine

published under the auspices of the Tropical Metabolism Research Unit, University of the West Indies, on whose staff both joint authors served.

876 Clinical undernutrition in the Kingston/St. Andrew metropolitan area: 1967-1976.
Wilma Bailey. *Social Science & Medicine*, vol. 15D, no. 4 (Nov. 1981), p. 471-77. bibliog.

This study examines the spatial distribution of clinical undernutrition in the Kingston/St. Andrew metropolitan area during the ten year period 1967-1976, based on data obtained from the patients' dockets at the two hospitals admitting such cases, and also the relationship between the incidence and certain social and economic indices. The study showed that unemployment of mothers was the most important variable factor explaining the distribution of malnutrition and concludes that 'there must be positive attempts to ensure that increased income filters down to the poor'. The author was associated with the Harvard School of Public Health and the Department of Geography, University of the West Indies, Kingston, Jamaica.

877 The unripe akee - forbidden fruit.
Rubin Bressler. *Nutrition Reviews*, vol. 34, no. 11 (Nov. 1976), p. 349-50.

A brief account of the medical history of 'vomiting sickness', a disease geographically localized to Jamaica and brought on by eating unripe ackee, and of the biochemical investigation of two cases. The account refers to K. R. Hill's earlier review 'The vomiting sickness of Jamaica: a review', *West Indian Medical Journal*, vol. 1 (1952), p. 243-64, which summarizes knowledge on the subject up to 1952, enriched by his personal observations of many patients, and to C. H. Hassall's and K. Reyle's review of the literature from 1952 to 1955, in their article 'The toxicity of the ackee (*Blighia sapida*) and its relationship to the vomiting sickness of Jamaica: a review', *West Indian Medical Journal*, vol. 4 (1955), p. 83-90.

878 Medical services in Jamaica.
Mary Manning Carley. Kingston: Institute of Jamaica, with the assistance of Jamaica Welfare, 1943. 19p. (Institute of Jamaica, Kingston. Social Survey Series, no. 2).

A factual survey of the development of medical services in Jamaica for the use of students or of the general public wishing to examine this aspect of Jamaica's social life.

879 The University College Hospital of the West Indies.
E. K. Cruickshank. *West Indian Medical Journal*, vol. 1, no. 3 (Oct. 1952), p. 274-80.

An account of the buildings, administration and staffing of the teaching hospital of the University of the West Indies, which was occupied early in 1953, written by the first Dean of the Medical Faculty.

880 Epidemiology and community health in warm climate countries.

[Edited by] Robert Cruickshank, Kenneth L. Standard, Hugh B. L. Russell, foreword by E. K. Cruickshank. Edinburgh, London, New York: Churchill Livingstone, 1976. 492p. bibliog. (Medicine in the Tropics).

Includes a number of contributions by health care specialists in Jamaica. The first and second authors named have successively held the Chair of Social and Preventive Medicine at the University of the West Indies, Mona, Jamaica and the writer of the foreword was formerly Professor of Medicine and Dean of the Faculty of Medicine, University of the West Indies, Mona, Jamaica.

881 Socio-economic and cultural influences on child growth in rural Jamaica.

Patricia Desai, K[enneth] L. Standard, W[illiam] E. Miall. *Journal of Biosocial Science*, vol. 2, no. 2 (April 1970), p. 133-43. bibliog.

Describes an investigation into the relationship between growth and a number of socio-economic factors such as family structure, parental characteristics, housing and income. A strong relationship between growth and these variables was found.

882 Training primary health care workers for the Caribbean.

Olive N. Ennevor, Kenneth L. Standard. *World Health Forum: an international journal of health development*, vol. 3, no. 2, 1982, p. 156-58.

Discusses a programme inaugurated in Jamaica whereby community aides have been trained to act as primary health workers. The idea has spread to other Caribbean countries and is helping to solve the problem of manpower to meet health service needs. The authors are, respectively, Research Assistant and Professor/Head of the Department of Social and Preventive Medicine, University of the West Indies, Kingston, Jamaica.

883 The Caribbean Food & Nutrition Institute.

Derrick B. Jelliffe. *West Indian Medical Journal*, vol. 20 (1971), p. 51-59. bibliog.

Account of the objectives and programmes of the Caribbean Food and Nutrition Institute (CFNI) which began its activities early in 1967 as a collaborative undertaking of Pan-American Health Organization (PAHO), the World Health Organization (WHO, FAO, the Williams-Waterman Fund (Research Corporation), the University of the West Indies and the Governments of Jamaica and Trinidad and Tobago, with centres in Jamaica and Trinidad. The author was the first Director of the Institute.

884 List of resource persons in food, nutrition and related fields for use by mass media in the CARICOM region.

Kingston: Caribbean Food and Nutrition Institute, with the Pan-American Health Organization, Pan-American Sanitary Bureau, Regional Office of the World Health Organization, 1978. 17p.

A list of nutritionists, dietitians and others from fields related to food and nutrition (with their addresses), who have volunteered to co-operate in the preparation and presentation of radio and television programmes, including 41 names from Jamaica.

885 Jamaican medicine: choices between folk healing and modern medicine.

Joseph K. Long. PhD thesis, University of North Carolina, 1973. 278 leaves. 2 maps. bibliog. (Available from University Microfilms, Ann Arbor, Michigan, 1974).

A hypothetical study concerning the prediction of the choices made by Jamaicans between folk healing and modern medicine in the face of cultural change. Chapter five (leaves 73-133) is of particular interest for its account of balmyards and the balm system of folk medicine.

886 Jamaican folk medicine.

H. I. C. Lowe. *Jamaica Journal*, vol. 6, no. 2 (June 1972), p. 20-24.

A brief account of medicinal plants and other therapeutic materials and procedures used by practitioners of Jamaican folk medicine, by a scientist on the staff of the College of Arts, Science and Technology.

887 Child mortality in Jamaica.

Herman I. McKenzie, Howard G. Lovell, Kenneth L. Standard, William E. Miall. *Milbank Memorial Fund Quarterly*, vol. 45, no. 3 (July 1967), p. 303-20. bibliog.

This paper reports on a survey designed to compare the circumstances of Jamaican children who die with those of their fellows who survive. Early childhood mortality in Jamaica is briefly reviewed. The survey and its findings suggest that malnutrition and poor socio-economic circumstances were major contributory factors to child mortality. The investigators were a sociologist, a medical statistician, a specialist in preventive medicine and an epidemiologist, respectively, attached to the University of the West Indies, Mona, Jamaica.

888 **The ecology of malnutrition in the Caribbean: the Bahamas, Cuba, Jamaica, Hispaniola (Haiti and the Dominican Republic), Puerto Rico, the Lesser Antilles and Trinidad and Tobago.**
Jacques M. May, Donna L. McLellan. New York: Hafner Press, 1973. 490p. maps. bibliog. (Studies in Medical Geography, vol. 12).

The chapter which deals with Jamaica (p. 87-144, including 4 maps) gives background information on the country and reviews food resources, diets and nutritional disease patterns. This study was sponsored by the Office, Chief of Research and Development, United States Army and acknowledges as one of its sources the nutrition surveys carried out by the Caribbean Food and Nutrition Institute, Mona, Jamaica.

889 **The Medical Faculty U.W.I. - a brief review of twenty-five years of activity, 1949-1974.**
M. M. S. Ragbeer. *West Indian Medical Journal*, vol. 23 (1974), p. 113-28.

The author was a former Dean of the School of Medicine of the University of the West Indies (UWI).

890 **Jamaican herbs: nutritional and medicinal values.**
Diane Robertson. Kingston: Jamaican Herbs, 1982. 34p. bibliog.

A compendium of useful information on Jamaican fruit, vegetables and herbs, with particular reference to their uses in folk medicine. The author is a pharmacist by profession. The volume is furnished with an index of botanical names.

891 **Four decades of advances in health in the Commonwealth Caribbean: proceedings of a symposium.**
[Coordinated by] Kenneth L. Standard, José R. Teruel. Washington, DC: Pan-American Health Organization, 1979. 159p. (Scientific Publication no. 383).

The symposium was jointly sponsored by the Department of Social and Preventive Medicine, University of the West Indies, the Barbados Association of Medical Practitioners and the Ministry of Health of the Government of Barbados, at Bridgetown, Barbados, 14-16 September 1977. Among the papers are the following: 'Present and future areas of research in the Commonwealth Caribbean' by Kenneth L. Standard; 'The development of public health in Jamaica' by C. C. Wedderburn; 'The community health aide in the Commonwealth Caribbean with special reference to Jamaica' by Kenneth L. Standard and O. Ennevor.

892 **The Department of Medicine - the University of the West Indies, 1948-1973.**
K. L. Stuart. *West Indian Medical Journal*, vol. 23 (1974), p. 129-36.

An historical account by a former Professor of Medicine at the University of the West Indies. It was written to commemorate the twenty-fifth anniversary of the founding of the Faculty of Medicine, with other historical articles on the Departments of Paediatrics and Orthopaedic Surgery and the Tropical Metabolism Unit which appeared in the same volume (p. 137-59).

893 **Vomiting sickness of Jamaica.**
K. L. Stuart. In: *Hypoglycin:* proceedings of a symposium, Kingston, Jamaica... Edited by E. A. Kean. New York: Academic Press, 1975, p. 39-44. bibliog.

An account of the experiences of the medical staff of the University Hospital of the West Indies in 1952 when they first had to deal with cases of the condition known locally as 'vomiting sickness' and later termed acute toxic hypoglycaemia. The clinical features of this disease which occurred in inadequately nourished Jamaicans are described and possible aetiological agents are considered, including poisoning by immature or damaged ackee fruit.

894 **A discourse of the state of health in the island of Jamaica. With a provision therefore calculated from the air, the place and the water: the customs and manners of living, &c.**
Thomas Trapham. London: R. Boulter, 1679. 149p.

The earliest treatise on the medical state of Jamaica and the first book in English to be published on medicine in the tropics. For an account of this book and of other important historical writings on medicine in Jamaica see M. T. Ashcroft, 'Tercentary of a Jamaican medical book', *West Indian Medical Journal*, vol. 28 (1979), p. 133-34.

895 **An assessment of the Community Health Aide Programme in Jamaica, 1978-79.**
Department of Social and Preventive Medicine, University of the West Indies, Mona, in collaboration with the Ministry of Health and Environmental Control, Jamaica, supported by the International Development Research Centre, Ottawa, Canada. [Kingston]: Department of Social and Preventive Medicine, UWI, 1979. [123]p.

'The Community Health Aide Training Programme was developed in the late sixties through the Department of Social & Preventive Medicine, University of the West Indies, Mona... The usefulness of the aide having been demonstrated, this new category of worker has been fully incorporated as a member of the health team in Jamaica.' (Foreword, p. ii).

896 **A general report on environmental health in Jamaica.**
John R. T. Williams. *Environmental Health*, vol. 84, no. 8 (Aug. 1976), p. 196-99. bibliog.

The author, a public health inspector of Birmingham, England, spent six weeks in Jamaica in 1974 on a University of Aston travel scholarship, making an official tour of the island observing and lecturing on environmental health with particular attention to his own special fields of interest, namely housing and food control. He reports on food control and on the official bodies responsible, on the control of markets, on shanty towns and on government schemes for rehousing their dwellers, on water supplies, on certifying food handlers, on the *Aedes aegypti* and

Science, Technology and Medicine. Medicine

Anopheles control programmes, on occupational health measures, noise control and the Hansen Home for leprosy in Spanish Town.

A voyage to the islands Madera, Barbados, Nieves, S. Christophers and Jamaica, with the natural history of the herbs and trees, four-footed beasts, fishes, birds, insects, reptiles, &c. of the last of those islands; to which is prefix'd an introduction, wherein is an account of the inhabitants, air, waters, diseases, trade, &c. of that place, with some relations concerning the neighbouring continent and islands of America. Illustrated with the figures of the things describ'd, which have not been heretofore engraved; in large copper-plates as big as the life. *See* item no. 118.

Periodicals

897 **Cajanus: the Caribbean Food and Nutrition Institute Quarterly.**
Kingston: Caribbean Food and Nutrition Institute, 1968- . quarterly.

This serves as a newsletter of the Institute as well as a vehicle for articles on nutrition in the Caribbean.

898 **Jamaican Nurse.**
Kingston: Nurses' Association of Jamaica, 1961- . four-monthly.

The official organ of the Nurses' Association of Jamaica, it carries news of meetings, addresses etc., in addition to articles on nursing.

899 **West Indian Medical Journal.**
Mona, Jamaica: Faculty of Medicine, University of the West Indies, 1951- . quarterly.

This publication was the child of the short-lived *Jamaica Medical Review* which it superseded, being the product of the establishment of the University College of the West Indies (later, the University of the West Indies) and of its Faculty of Medicine. It is a journal of established repute, reporting developments in treatment and research in the Faculty of Medicine and elsewhere in the West Indies. It is indexed in four of the major scientific and medical abstracting journals.

Literature

Literary history and criticism

900 Critics on Caribbean literature: readings in literary criticism.
Edited by Edward Baugh. London: Allen & Unwin, 1978.
164p. bibliog. (Readings in Literary Criticism, 19).

This volume fills a special need for critical material on West Indian literature. The selection has been made 'with a view to introducing the literature' as well as to 'showing off the critics' (cf. Introduction, p. 12). Among the individual critiques are the following relating to Jamaican authors: Kenneth Ramchand on Claude McKay's *Banana Bottom*, Edward Brathwaite on Roger Mais's *Brother Man* and Mervyn Morris on the dialect poetry of Louise Bennett.

901 West Indian poetry 1900-1970: a study in cultural decolonisation.
Edward Baugh. Jamaica: Savacou Publications, [1977?].
20p. (Pamphlet no. 1).

A brief but penetrating study of West Indian poetry of the 20th century in which the strand of Jamaican poetry is clearly delineated.

902 'Escapism' in the novels of John Hearne.
Frank M. Birbalsingh. *Caribbean Quarterly*, vol. 16, no. 1
(March 1970), p. 28-38.

A scathing critique of Hearne's five novels and, in particular, of his handling of the theme of race and colour consciousness in Jamaican middle- and upper-class society. His criticism is well argued and is often illuminating.

Literature. Literary history and criticism

903 The novels of H. G. De Lisser.
F[rank] M. Birbalsingh. *International Fiction Review*, vol.
9, no. 1 (winter 1982), p. 41-46. bibliog.

A criticism of the novels of Herbert George DeLisser (1878-1944) which are
conveniently discussed in two groups labelled 'historical' and 'regional'. The author
is critical of the novelist's sensationalism and finds his characters lacking in
conviction, 'reacting puppetlike to mechanical stimuli'. For all that, however, he
considers that DeLisser's novels reveal 'a thorough understanding of the prevailing
social, economic and political issues of his time' - an understanding evinced in
those novels which illustrate the social stratification of Jamaica. The 'regional'
novels are characterized by a vivid sense of authentic local colour. This is a
perceptive assessment of DeLisser's achievement which places him in the context
of the dominant British imperial culture of his time.

904 The novels of John Hearne.
Wilfred Cartey. *Journal of Commonwealth Literature*, no.
7 (July 1969), p. 45-58.

A generally favourable critique, focusing on Hearne's handling of personal relationships, social classes, physical environment, landscape and characterization.

905 Roger Mais.
Jean D'Costa. London: Longman, 1978. 74p. bibliog.
(Critical Studies of Caribbean Writers).

A perceptive study of Mais's two novels, *The hills were joyful together* and
Brother Man, with particular reference to them as experiments in form and to
their literary style and world view. The author was formerly Senior Lecturer in
English at the University of the West Indies.

906 Mr Salkey's truth and illusion.
C. R. Gray. *Jamaica Journal*, vol. 2, no. 2 (June 1968), p.
46-54.

An evaluation of Andrew Salkey's four books *Hurricane* (1964), *Earthquake*
(1965), *Drought* (1966) and *Riot* (1967) as literature for young Jamaican readers.

**907 Caribbean writers: a bio-bibliographical critical
encyclopaedia.**
[Edited by] Donald E. Herdeck, associate editors Maurice A.
Lubin, John Figueroa, Dorothy Alexander Figueroa, José
Alcántara Almánazar, general editor Margaret
Lanick-Herdeck. Washington, DC: Three Continents Press,
1979. 943p. bibliog.

A comprehensive work containing biographical information on some 2,000
creative writers, bibliographic details on some 15,000 works and brief introductory
essays on the major authors, themes and developments. One hundred and
seventy-four authors' names are listed in the section on Jamaica which forms part
of the volume on *Anglophone literature from the Caribbean*, edited by the associate editors John and Dorothy Alexander Figueroa. Other parts of the work are
devoted to the Francophone literature of the Caribbean, the literatures of the

Literature. Literary history and criticism

Netherlands Antilles and Suriname and Spanish-language literature from the Caribbean, with Maurice A. Lubin and José Alcántara Almánazar as associate editors.

908 **A companion to West Indian literature.**
Michael Hughes. [London]: Collins, 1979. 135p.

An introduction, intended for the general reader, to the works of the major West Indian writers in English. Each entry consists of a biographical sketch, a select bibliography of works by the writer and of critical writings on these works. Also included is information on important literary journals.

909 **The islands in between: essays on West Indian literature.**
Edited with an introduction by Louis James. London; Ibadan, Nigeria; Nairobi: Oxford University Press, 1968. 166p. bibliog.

A concise account in which diverse views are represented. The following contributions relate specifically to Jamaican literature: 'A prophet armed: the novels of Roger Mais' by Jean Creary; 'Of redcoats and leopards: two novels by V. S. Reid' by Louis James; 'A complex fate: the novels of Andrew Salkey' by Bill Carr; 'The seekers: the novels of John Hearne' by Barrie Davies.

910 **Authors and areas of the West Indies.**
Joseph Jones, Johanna Jones. Austin, Texas: Steck-Vaughn, 1970. 82p. (People and Places in World-English Literature, no. 2).

A bio-bibliography. More than half of the 35 sketches relate to authors associated with Jamaica.

911 **West Indian literature.**
Edited by Bruce King. London: Macmillan, 1979. 247p. bibliog. (Macmillan New Literature Handbooks).

A concise historical and critical survey, each chapter written by a different contributor, intended for students and the general reader. The first six chapters are a useful comprehensive survey of West Indian literature in English. The final eight chapters are devoted to individual writers, none of whom, with the exception of Jean Rhys and Edward Brathwaite, draw significantly upon experience of Jamaican life. The author is a professor at the University of Canterbury, New Zealand.

912 **My green hills of Jamaica and five Jamaican short stories.**
Claude McKay. Kingston: Heinemann Educational Books (Caribbean), 1979. 162p.

The first part, a draft autobiography, of which the typescript is preserved in the Schomburg Collection of Negro Literature and History in the New York Public Library, has been edited, with an introduction by Mervyn Morris, who describes it 'as a document of Jamaican history, particularly social history.' (Introduction, p. vi). The five stories first appeared in *Gingertown*, New York: Harper Brothers, 1932).

913 Contending values: the prose fiction of Claude McKay.
Mervyn Morris. *Jamaica Journal*, vol. 9, nos. 2 & 3 (1975), p. 36-42, 52. bibliog.

Of particular interest is the author's treatment of McKay's stories of Jamaican life, *Gingertown* and *Banana Bottom*.

914 Literature: some trends.
Mervyn Morris. *Jamaica Journal*, special issue, Jamaica's 20th anniversary of independence (1982), p. 37-42. illus.

A knowledgeable and brief survey of literary trends since 1960, with photographic portraits of several of the authors mentioned. The author is himself a poet and Senior Lecturer in the Department of English, University of the West Indies, Mona, Jamaica.

915 The West Indian novel and its background.
Kenneth Ramchand. London: Faber & Faber, 1972. 295p. bibliog.

Although it treats of the West Indian novel under broad generic headings rather than geographic ones, considerable attention has been given to the work of Jamaican novelists T. H. MacDermot, H. G. DeLisser, Roger Mais, Claude McKay and others. A scholarly study and the best one of its kind. It is a version of a thesis presented at the University of Edinburgh.

Anthologies

916 North of Jamaica.
Louis Simpson. New York: Harper & Row, 1972. 285p.

Published in England by London Magazine Editions under the title *Air with armed men*, 'The sadness of the tropics is the thought of life vanishing without a mark. You are cut off from the world, and nothing you do will ever be noticed.' (p. 78). In the first eighty pages of this autobiography of a recognized American poet, he has forestalled this prediction with regard to his early life in Jamaica, where he was born. With deft strokes he captures the fleeting image of a colonial society in the 1920s and 1930s - its social life and its snobberies, its aspirations and its pursuits - as experienced at home and in school by a sensitive and awakening mind.

917 New poets from Jamaica: an anthology.
Edited with an introduction by Edward Kamau Brathwaite. Kingston: Savacou Publications, 1979. 134p. (Poets Series, 5).

The editor, in his introduction, presents this collection as a conscious choice of 'a highly expressive society: a "partial plantation", very much aware of the history of conflict between Prospero and Caliban planter and maroon: weaving a "creole" synthesis out of these contentions which constantly challenge our very sense of cultural definition...'. The contributors are Pam Hickling, Pam Mordecai, Christine Craig, Jean Goulbourne, Opal Palmer, Brian Meeks, Oku Onuora, Michael Smith, Noel Walcott, Lorna Goodison, Bob Stewart, Beverley Brown, Lloyd Richardson. Biographical sketches of the contributors are included.

918 **New planet: anthology of modern Caribbean writing.**
Compiled and edited by Sebastian Clarke, illustrations by William Timothy. London: Karnak House, Caribbean Cultural International, 1978. 93p.

An anthology of prose and poetry, recent and old, of innovative writers with a commitment to change. Illustrations by William Timothy. 'Biographical notes' (p. 91-93) indicate that the following contributors were born or lived in Jamaica: George Campbell, Damx, Eseoghene (Lindsay Barrett) and Basil Hanson Smith.

919 **Caribbean verse: an anthology.**
Edited and introduced by O. R. Dathorne. London: Heinemann Educational Books, 1967. 132p.

Includes selections from the following Jamaican poets: Vera Bell, George Campbell, John Figueroa, A. L. Hendricks, Basil McFarlane, J. E. Clare McFarlane, Roger Mais, Una Marson, W. Adolphe Roberts, Philip M. Sherlock, M. G. Smith. A useful feature of the book, intended for the use of students of Caribbean literature, is the extensive critical notes on individual poems and the biographical notes on the poets.

920 **The independence anthology of Jamaican literature.**
Selected by A. L. Hendricks, Cedric Lindo, with an introduction by Peter Abrahams. Jamaica: Arts Celebration Committee of the Ministry of Development and Welfare, 1962. 227p.

Published to commemorate the achievement of Jamaica's independence, 6 August 1962. The anthology covers the whole range of Jamaican prose and poetry from the writers of the early 20th century to those at the time of publication. The introduction is a succinct and useful review of the development of Jamaican literature from its beginnings in the early years of this century, noting the principal landmarks on the way.

921 **Caribbean rhythms: the emerging English literature of the West Indies.**
Edited with an introduction by James T. Livingston. New York: Washington Square Press, 1974. 379p. map.

This selection covers a variety of literary forms - short stories, poetry, essays, drama - in which Jamaican writing is well represented. Bio-bibliographical notes are included for each of the writers.

Literature. Anthologies

922 A treasury of Jamaican poetry.
Selected and edited by J. E. Clare McFarlane, with an introduction by B. H. Easter. London: University of London Press, 1949. 159p.

An anthology for schools selected and edited by the President of the Poetry League of Jamaica, with an introduction by B. H. Easter, formerly Director of Education, with an introduction by B. H. Easter, formerly Director of Education, Jamaica. The anthology includes poetry of the pre-1938 period which 'adhered to the established traditions of English verse' and that of the post-1938 decade representing 'the revolt against accepted forms and customs...concomitant of the social and political upheavals of recent times.' (cf. Preface, p. 7).

923 Focus, Jamaica, 1943.
Edited by Edna Manley. [Kingston: printed by the City Printery, 1944]; New York: Kraus Reprint Co., 1976. 130p.

An anthology, which brought together for the first time poems, short stories, one-act plays, other short prose pieces and three linocuts giving expression to the creative surge which accompanied the awakening of national sentiment and social awareness, following the civil disturbances in the late 1930s. L. A. G. Strong, commenting on the work in a BBC 'Calling the West Indies' programme in June 1944, recognized its uneven quality but also recognized immediately 'that it is inspired by a proud and fervent national spirit. This spirit has great strength and great vitality, and it is seeking for a national means of expression.' This work was followed by three similar anthologies bearing the same title and under the same editorship, in 1948, 1956 and 1960, but none of these later collections were characterized by the almost rhapsodical national fervour which emanated from the first work. The four volumes were reprinted by Kraus Reprint and reissued in two volumes in 1976.

924 Caribbean stories: fifteen short stories by writers from the Caribbean.
Edited by Michael Marland (with a sequence of photographs). London: Longman, 1978. 152p. 2 maps. photos. (Longman Imprint Books).

The stories selected reflect the tensions between generations and races in the West Indies during the period from the end of the Second World War to the accomplishment of independence for the larger Commonwealth Caribbean countries by the mid-1960s. Three of the stories relate to Jamaica and well illustrate some of the tensions in Jamaican society. They are: A village tragedy by John Hearne; Blackout by Roger Mais; and The visitor by H. Orlando Patterson. The volume is intended for student readers at secondary school level and is furnished with points for discussion, suggestions for writing, short biographies of the authors, a brief historical note on the West Indies and suggestions for further reading. The editor is headmaster of a London school.

Literature. Anthologies

925 Jamaica woman: an anthology of poems.
Edited by Pamela Mordecai, Mervyn Morris. Kingston; Port of Spain: Heinemann Educational (Caribbean), 1980. 110p.

New Jamaican poems by fifteen women, concerned with a wide variety of situations and attitudes expressed in language demonstrating the continuum of Jamaican English. Includes notes on contributors and an index of first lines.

926 Focus 1983: an anthology of contemporary Jamaican writing.
Edited by Mervyn Morris. Kingston: Caribbean Authors Publishing Co., 1983. 294p.

An anthology of previously unpublished prose fiction and poetry by Jamaicans and people who have experienced Jamaica, as a contribution to the process of self-definition and in revival of the earlier idea of the original volumes published under the same title in 1943, 1948, 1956 and 1960. The editor is a member of the Department of English, University of the West Indies, Mona, Jamaica.

927 Seven Jamaican poets: an anthology of recent poetry.
Edited by Mervyn Morris, illustrated by Anne Weinholt. Jamaica: Bolivar Press, 1971. 58p.

This collection offers a sample of poems by seven Jamaicans who have contributed to leading West Indian newspapers and journals and most of whom have published also in reputable journals outside the West Indies. There are eight full-page illustrations. Biographical notes are included.

928 West Indian stories.
Edited by Andrew Salkey. London; Boston, Massachusetts: Faber & Faber, 1960. 224p.

Of the 25 short stories included, eight are by Jamaican authors - John Hearne, A. L. Hendricks, Roy Henry, Roger Mais, Stuart Hall, V. S. Reid and John Figueroa. The Jamaican stories can be seen within the wider context of West Indian short story writing while they illustrate some of the predominant characteristics and concerns of Jamaican life. The editor generalizes about the latter as 'the Jamaican's restlessness, class consciousness and intolerable arrogance.' (Introduction, p. 11). A later compilation by the same editor entitled *Stories from the Caribbean: an anthology* (London: Paul Elek Books, 1972. 2nd ed. 257p.) includes stories of Jamaican life and character by some of the above writers as well as by the following Jamaicans: R. O. Robinson, Donald Hinds and Claude Thompson.

929 West Indian plays for schools.
[Introduced with] production notes by Jeanne Wilson. [Kingston]: Jamaica Publishing House, 1979. 2 vols.

A collection of seven plays by West Indian playwrights - six of whom are Jamaican and the other a St. Lucian, compiled for classroom use in Caribbean secondary schools, with introductions and production notes by the editor. Contents include: Volume one, *One dollar for dog*, by W. G. Ogilvie; *Drums of revolt*, by Derek Walcott; *Heavens above*, by Mitzie Townshend; *A question of loyalty*, by Jean Wilson; and in volume two *Tarshan lace and velvet*, by Easton Lee;

243

Selected works of individual authors

Maskarade by Sylvia Wynter; *The vision* by Enid Chevannes. Each volume is supplied with a glossary.

930 **The arrivants: a New World trilogy.**
Edward Kamau Brathwaite. London: Oxford University Press, 1973. 275p.

These poems were first published by Oxford University Press in three separate volumes: *Rights of passage* (1967), *Masks* (1968) and *Islands* (1969). Issued as a single work in 1973, they are an incantatory evocation of the experience of the New World Negro, but more especially of the denizens of the Caribbean islands, through which their African past moves like a procession of ceremonial masks and which gives expression to their violent entrapment in the cage of islands, their adaptation and their values - 'claxons, screams, flags over Kingston' (p. 236) -ending with the dawn of a new day 'now waking/making/making/with their/rhythms some -/thing torn/and new.' (p. 270-71). A glossary of Afro-Caribbean religious terms is included (p. 271-75). The author was born in Barbados in 1930, taught in Ghana and is Reader in History at the University of the West Indies, Mona (Jamaica) campus, where he has resided since 1962.

931 **Jane and Louisa will soon come home.**
Erna Brodber. London; Port of Spain: New Beacon Books, 1980. 147p.

In a series of short poetical prose sketches, using a variety of techniques including flash-back and stream of consciousness writing and interwoven with folk tales (anansi stories), the author presents a kaleidoscope of experience as perceived by one bred and fostered in the heart of the Jamaican countryside.

932 **First poems: a new edition with additional poems.**
George Campbell, [with an] introductory poem by Derek Walcott. New York, London: Garland Publishing, 1981. 116p. (Critical Studies on Black Life and Culture, vol. 10).

First published 1945. Campbell led the way in the literary flowering which marked the growth of a national spirit and deepened social consciousness towards the end of the 1930s. He was probably the first Jamaican poet to handle free verse successfully.

933 **The rag doll and other stories.**
Hazel D. Campbell. Mona, Jamaica: Savacou Cooperative, 1978. 56p.

Vignettes of Jamaican character and life which illustrate and explore the perennial concerns of human relationships simultaneously as they comment on aspects of contemporary social life. Two of these stories won awards in annual Jamaica Festivals, in which the author has won prizes on four successive occasions.

Literature. Selected works of individual authors

934 Wages paid.

James [A.] Carnegie. Havana: Casa de las Américas, 1976. 104p.

Within the unity of a single day on a Jamaican plantation during the time of slavery, the *dramatis personae* who are the embodiment of the depravity of the system, move with dramatic speed to a destructive climax. The excessive use of four-letter expletives neither enhances the artistry nor the verisimilitude of an otherwise gripping tale. The novel won the Casa de Las Américas Prize for 1976.

935 Escape to Last Man Peak.

Jean D'Costa, illustrated by Imre Hofbauer. Trinidad: Longman Caribbean, 1975. 179p. map. (Blue Mountain Library).

An account of the adventures of a party of children on trek from an orphanage in Spanish Town to a refuge in the Cockpit Country, during a period when the adult population had been largely decimated by an epidemic. The novel describes the geography of the Jamaican countryside and the simple pursuits of country life as seen and experienced by the children. The illustrations are notably sensitive.

936 Interim.

Neville Dawes. Kingston: Institute of Jamaica, 1978. 216p.

This tale by a skilful raconteur opens with an authentic and refreshing account of country life in Jamaica from which the youthful characters emerge into adult life and the political and private intrigues of the city of Kingston, culminating in their involvement in a revolution which failed. Its readable and amusing exploration of Jamaican social mores is not without its ideological burden, though the author is too accomplished a writer to let his message encumber his narrative. That message is probably best summed up in the apprehension of defeat of the chief protagonist Lucien - 'the expression of his eyes shifted from understanding to resignation as if he knew he could not escape destruction from the historical triad of great house, mulatto and house-slave' (p. 192).

937 Jane's career: a story of Jamaica.

Herbert G. DeLisser, introduced by Kenneth Ramchand. London: Heinemann, 1972. 207p. (Caribbean Writers Series, 5).

First published 1914. This edition has an introduction by Kenneth Ramchand of the Department of English, University of the West Indies. An engagingly written novel exploring the thoughts, sentiments and vicissitudes of a Jamaican peasant girl who migrates to Kingston - the big city - to make her way in life. Ramchand remarks that this is the first West Indian novel in which the central character, whose feelings are explored in depth, is a Negro. It is a social document as well as a work of literature.

938 Under the sun: a Jamaica comedy.

Herbert G. DeLisser. London: Ernest Benn, 1937. 269p.

An entertaining exposé of middle- and upper-class foibles and prejudices, with some pointed shafts aimed at colonial Jamaican attitudes to the metropolis.

939 **The white witch of Rosehall.**
Herbert G. DeLisser. London: Ernest Benn, c.1958. 3rd ed. 255p.

First published in 1929. An immensely popular and readable novel, based on an historic legend of a Mrs Palmer, cruel slave-owner of Rose Hall, murderer and necromancer. DeLisser evokes the climate of tension and fear mixed with seeming familiarity and acceptance which characterized plantation life and weaves into his story elements of Jamaican folklore and superstition.

940 **Between sea and sky.**
Enid D'Oyley, illustrated by Albert Huie. Toronto, Canada: Williams-Wallace Productions International, [1979]. 144p.

A story for children in which two girls on a holiday discover some of Jamaica's history and its traditions - old sugar mills, crab hunting at night, Jonkonnu dancing etc., with illustrations by the doyen of Jamaican painters, Albert Huie.

941 **Obi, or, the history of Threefingered Jack.**
Compiled by William Earle. Worcester, Massachusetts: 1804. Reprinted, Freeport, New York: Books for Libraries Press, 1972. 168p. (Black Heritage Library Collection).

First published at London in 1800. A sympathetic account of the celebrated runaway slave who terrorized the plantations in the neighbourhood of his cave near Mount Lebanus in the Blue Mountains, in and prior to 1780. Cast in the form of a series of letters from a resident in Jamaica to his friend in England, this fictionalized account hails the historic figure of Three Fingered Jack (who was the terror of Blacks also by virtue of his reputedly potent 'Obi' or witchdoctor's charm) as a hero and freedom fighter, as he has come to be regarded by the contemporary generation of Jamaicans. It presents an unfavourable picture of plantation society during the period of slavery.

942 **The fair green weed.**
Elisabeth Hargreaves. London: Hutchinson, 1972. 189p.

A novel - a thriller - about the ganja racket, set in Jamaica, though the latter is not named. Perceptively written in respect of the credibly drawn characters and their relationships against the background of a decayed plantocracy and a brash hotel set.

943 **The faces of love.**
John Hearne. London: Faber & Faber, 1957. 267p.

This novel is based on the lives of urban print-medium people and entrepreneurs on the make, but with roots in the plantation system, on an imaginary island of Cayuna, which is a thin disguise for Jamaica. In addition to the social interest attached to the interplay of personalities drawn from a stratum of contemporary Jamaican society the novel is notable for its descriptions of the Jamaican landscape in all its forms and moods.

Literature. Selected works of individual authors

944 Land of the living.

John Hearne. London: Faber & Faber, 1961. 280p.

A novel in the first person, told by an expatriate Jewish refugee lecturer in Zoology at the University of Cayuna (the island of Cayuna is Jamaica thinly disguised). It is principally an exploration of the narrator's personal relationships and his sensibilities, with much emphasis on sexuality and on love, and his view of the politics of Cayuna and the excursions of a back-to-Africa cult, the Sons of Sheba (Rastafari), into politics and then revolution.

945 Voices under the window.

John Hearne. London: Faber & Faber, 1973. 163p.

First published in 1955. Mark Lattimer, coloured lawyer and politician, is chopped while trying to rescue a child being trampled in a Kingston riot. The story unfolds itself in the thoughts of the dying man as he recaptures the highlights of his life as a youth, as an airforce trainee in Canada and subsequently as an airman in action over Europe during the Second World War, and as a student in England. As he reflects on parental, sexual, political, social and patriotic relationships and sentiments his life ebbs away to the echoes of riotous voices outside. The struggle to retain individuality while serving political causes, especially for persons like the dying protagonist 'who carry both... worlds within [them], in [their] blood', and the awareness of irrational racial antipathies run like thin, strong threads through what would otherwise appear to be a very individual and cathartic musing on life and dying.

946 Banana Bottom.

Claude McKay. Chatham, New Jersey: Chatham Bookseller [1970, c.1933]. 317p.

First published, New York: Harper, 1933. A genial and idyllic vision of Jamaican peasant life in the first decade of this century, recollected at a distance in time and place. In the character of the heroine, Bita Plant, of peasant origin, and her quest for identification with the more natural life-style of her people after having been educated in England for several years, the author explores the black man's search for identity in a strongly European-oriented world, and, more particularly, in the colonial milieu of Jamaica at that time, as he had experienced it, and as it has been interpreted to him by his early patron Walter Jekyll, who is the prototype of Squire Gensir in the novel. Ramchand considers this novel 'the first classic of West Indian prose'.

947 The three novels of Roger Mais.

Roger Mais, with an introduction by the Honourable Norman W. Manley. London: Cape, 1966. 288, 191, 222p.

Contains *The Hills were joyful together* (first published 1953), *Brother Man* (first published 1954) and *Black lightning* (first published 1955). The first two novels are based on slum life in pre-independence Jamaica. Their social realism and intrinsic demand for social reform are invested with a poetic quality and a sense of tragedy which stamp them as artistic creations as well as being social documents. The third novel is a tragic study of interpersonal relationships, devoid of social protest and set in rural surroundings. These novels have been published separately in Heinemann's *Caribbean Writers Series*, the first with an introduction by Daphne Morris, in 1981, the second with an introduction by Edward Brathwaite in 1974, the third with an introduction by Jean DaCosta in 1982.

Literature. Selected works of individual authors

948 Marly; or, a planter's life in Jamaica.
Glasgow: Richard Griffin; London: Hunt & Clarke, 1828.
363p.

A comprehensive and objective account of slavery, plantation life and the mores of Jamaican society on the eve of emancipation, set within the framework of a fictitious narrative but based upon the actual experience of the anonymous narrator who describes himself as a 'slave driver', having been a book-keeper on a sugar estate.

949 The moth and the star.
Una Marson, introduced by Philip M[anderson]
Sherlock. Kingston: Gleaner Co. for the author, 1937.
103p.

Una Marson was one of the first Jamaican writers, and certainly the first Jamaican woman writer, to be seriously concerned about fashioning an authentic West Indian culture. Her poetry reflected a deep love of the Jamaican scene and of the common man and a strong pride in her racial origins.

950 The ghost bank.
W. G. Ogilvie. Kingston: Pioneer Press, 1953. 124p. map.

A well-told tale of the lives and ruthless rivalries of tough, resourceful fishermen and boatbuilders on the coasts of the parish of St. Thomas. The story centres on the search by the Predly family for a 'ghost bank' seen fleetingly by Nathaniel Predly in the early stages of the novel and finally discovered just before the end of the long life of the stern patriarch, familiarly called Nappy. This work has also been adapted by Margery Green and published by the Jamaica Publishing House, Kingston, in 1974, in the *Mahoe Adventure Series.*

951 My father, Sun-Sun Johnson.
C. Everard Palmer. London: Andre Deutsch, 1974. 111p.

A lively narrative, centred on the relationship between father and son, in a rural setting in Jamaica. The author is the recipient of a Certificate of Merit by the Jamaica Reading Association for his contribution to Jamaican children's literature. Based on the book a 28-minute motion picture (1 reel) and videorecording (1 cassette) have been made by BBC-TV in association with the Ontario Educational Communications Authority and the Learning Corporation of America.

952 Jason Whyte, Jamaican.
Terry Parris, illustrated by Trevor Stubley. London:
Oxford University Press, 1973. 48p. map.

A true story, with imaginary dialogue, of a Jamaican boy who drifted for about three weeks in a canoe, after the outboard motor failed and his father had died in the boat from hunger and weakness, until he was picked up by a German freighter the *Eibe Oldendorff*, nearly 300 miles west of Jamaica. A simple story of a boy's courage and of the quiet unsung heroism of Jamaican fishermen, written for juveniles.

Literature. Selected works of individual authors

953 An absence of ruins.
H. Orlando Patterson.   London: Hutchinson, 1967. 160p.

This novel well illustrates the passage from Derek Walcott's *The royal palms* which introduces it and from which its title derives. Particularly evocative of its quality are Walcott's lines: 'If art is where the greatest ruins are,/Our art is in those ruins we became...' It is a chronicle of the thoughts and actions of one Alexander Blackman, introspective and disillusioned, a graduate in social sciences of the University of the West Indies and later a member of its academic staff. It represents the moral vacuum within which the vocal coterie of intelligentsia which he depicts live and move, exemplified in the 'hero's' observation 'that at the heart of the hurricane there is only a vacuum.' (cf. p. 93). An unusual literary presentation of this aspect of the Jamaican *persona*.

954 The children of Sisyphus.
H. Orlando Patterson.   Jamaica: Bolivar Press, 1974. 206p.

First published by New Authors, 1964 (recently issued: London: Longman Drumbeat, 1982). A grimly realistic novel of the sisyphean struggle of the dwellers of a Kingston slum to escape from their environment, depicting the violence, the suffering, the frustration and the resentment of their lives. An influential social document as well as a novel. Winner of the first prize for fiction at the Dakar Festival of Negro Arts, 1966.

955 Orange Valley and other poems.
Tom Redcam (Thomas Henry MacDermot).   Kingston: Pioneer Press, 1951. 143p.

This introduction, by J. E. Clare McFarlane, President of the Poetry League of Jamaica, includes a biographical sketch of the author, who was declared the first Poet Laureate of Jamaica by the Poetry League in 1933. This work is the first publication of his collected verse in book form.

956 The Jamaicans.
Victor Stafford Reid.   Kingston: Institute of Jamaica, 1978. 2nd ed. 266p.

First edition, 1976. A tale woven around the part played by the former Spanish slaves, under their leader Juan de Bolas, in the conflict which followed the English conquest of Jamaica. A novel presentation, both thematically and stylistically, in which the theme of national identity, as conveyed by the title, is elaborated from an early and less well-known episode in Jamaican history. The author is a Jamaican novelist of international repute and the recipient of a number of notable literary awards.

957 New day.
V[ictor] S[tafford] Reid, [introduced by] Mervyn Morris.   New York: Alfred A. Knopf, 1949; London: Heinemann, 1973. 2nd ed. (Caribbean Writers Series, 4).

This is a seminal work in the emergence of the Jamaican, indeed, the West Indian novel. Reid tells the story of the Jamaican people and attempts to capture and express the essence of their experience and feeling in fictional characters which span the period from the Morant Bay Rebellion to the achievement of universal adult suffrage and a new constitution in 1944. He uses and adapts the

Literature. Selected works of individual authors

958 Peter of Mount Ephraim: the Daddy Sharpe rebellion.
V[ictor] S[tafford] Reid. Kingston: Jamaica Publishing House, c.1971. 140p. (Mahoe Adventure Series).

A fictional recreation, for juveniles, of the Daddy Sharpe rebellion, bringing to life the conditions of plantation slavery and the character of Samuel Sharpe the slave leader. It is both a gripping story of adventure and also a tale intended to inculcate a sense of history and tradition among the present descendants of those who rebelled against slavery and helped to destroy the system. Effectively illustrated by Dennis Ranston.

959 Wide Sargasso Sea.
Jean Rhys, [introduced by] Francis Wyndham. London: Deutsch, 1966. 2nd ed. [Harmondsworth, England]: Penguin Books, 1968. 155p.

Winner of the 1967 W. H. Smith & Son Annual Literary Award and the Royal Society of Literature Award. An imaginative and poignant novel, set in post-emancipation Jamaica and Dominica, exploring the alienation of white creole West Indians from the newly emerging West Indian societies and from their English roots. The narrative vehicle of this exploration is the imaginary construction of the lives of Edward Rochester and his mad wife prior to their introduction as characters in Charlotte Bronte's *Jane Eyre.*

960 Earthquake.
Andrew Salkey, illustrated by William Papas. London: Oxford University Press, 1965. 123p.

Includes a vivid account of the earthquake which destroyed Kingston in January 1907. Juvenile fiction.

961 Hurricane.
Andrew Salkey, illustrated by William Papas. London: Oxford University Press, 1964. 118p.

A detailed fictional account of a hurricane's passage over Kingston, written for juveniles.

962 The late emancipation of Jerry Stover.
Andrew Salkey. London: Hutchinson, 1968. 245p.

Jerry Stover, junior civil servant, and his friends of like calling are depicted in their gregarious pursuit of the Bohemian life, rebelling against the *status quo,* espousing the Rastafarian cause in the face of political indifference and ending in disillusionment for the chief protagonist and sudden death for the rest of the group, known as the 'Termites'.

963 Uncle time: poems.

Dennis Scott. [s.l.]: University of Pittsburgh Press, 1973. 53p. (Pitt Poetry Series).

An International Poetry Forum selection. The preface by Edna Manley and the introduction by Mervyn Morris provide valuable insights into the poetical traditions of Jamaica against which background the poet writes, as well as into the language which he uses and the themes with which he is concerned.

964 Tom Cringle's log.

Michael Scott. London: J. M. Dent. 1915. 526p. (Everyman's Library, no. 10).

Begun as a series of sketches in *Blackwood's Magazine*, Sept. 1829-Aug. 1833, it was first published in book form (Edinburgh: William Blackwood: London: T. Cadell, 1833. 2 vols.). The author went to Jamaica in 1806 and served in various capacities, on an estate, in commerce and at sea. He remained in the West Indies until 1817 when he returned to Scotland. The novel recounts in a rambling anecdotal style the uproarious life and 'high jinks' experienced and observed by the author during his stay in the West Indies and is considered a classic of its kind.

965 Shout for freedom: a tribute to Sam Sharpe.

Philip M[anderson] Sherlock. London: Macmillan Caribbean, 1976. 67p. map.

A tribute in the form of a poetic dialogue between the principal characters in the slave rebellion of 1831-32. Sam Sharpe, slave and Baptist preacher, was the most outstanding of the rebel leaders and was later named a National Hero. The work celebrates the blow struck by Sharpe in defence of freedom as the inalienable right of men, rather than as a favour to be accepted by them. The dialogue and characterization are the author's but he has drawn freely from a number of publications contemporary with the events portrayed.

966 Three Finger Jack's treasure.

Philip M[anderson] Sherlock, illustrated by William Reeves. [Kingston]: Jamaica Publishing House, 1961. 176p. (Mahoe Adventure Series).

A juveniles' tale of the Jamaican countryside and country life as a party of children go in quest of the treasure cave of the folk-hero and legendary slave rebel Three Finger Jack.

967 The capture of Jamaica: a historical novel.

S. A. G. Taylor. Kingston: Pioneer Press, 1951. 164p. fold. map.

An account of the English conquest of Jamaica in 1655 'from the point of view of a humble soldier who took part in it' (Preface, p. ix).

Literature

968 Pages from our past.
  S. A. G. Taylor. Kingston: Pioneer Press, 1954. 183p.

Episodes in the early history of Jamaica, reconstructed from contemporary accounts and presented within the fictitious framework of tales told by pictures in a picture gallery.

969 The harder they come: a novel.
  Michael Thelwell. New York: Grove Press; London: Pluto Press, 1980. 399p.

Inspired by the film of the same title, the author has tried 'to write if not the novelistic equivalent of the movie then at least the novel from which the film might have been derived were the process reversed as is more usually the case.' (Preface, p. 8). The novel depicts the experience and struggles of the Jamaican poor and is based on the exploits of an almost legendary gunman in Kingston in the early 1950s. Includes a glossary of Jamaican terms and idioms, p. 393-99.

970 The hills of Hebron.
  Sylvia Wynter. London: Cape, 1962. 283p.

The achievement and settlement of Hebron - the earthly kingdom of a religious cult - is the axis around which the characters and events rotate. The story is woven out of the aspirations, disappointments and frustrations of the Jamaican peasantry with their Messianic yearnings which find expression in religious practices such as Revivalism and Bedwardism, and the central character Moses Barton bears many similarities to the religious leader Bedward. The minor characters and marginal events, such as Moses' contact with Dr O'Malley, alcoholic Superintendent of the Mental Hospital, and the Reverend and Mrs Brooke of the Anglican mission at Cockpit Centre, are vehicles for the author's polemics against the hypocrisies and injustices of the colonial past and the society which evolved therefrom.

Literature in dialect

971 Jamaica labrish.
  Louise Bennett, with notes and introduction by Rex Nettleford. [Kingston]: Sangster's Book Stores Jamaica, c.1966. 224p.

The introduction informs us that this collection of dialect poems is 'designed to give an overview of her art and artistry over the past twenty-five years' and to reveal her in 'her multiple role as entertainer, as a valid literary figure and as a documenter of aspects of Jamaican life, thought and feeling' (p. 10). It is the most representative collection of her poems and the introduction is a perceptive commentary on her artistic achievement.

972 **Selected poems.**

Louise Bennett, edited with an introduction notes and teaching questions by Mervyn Morris. Kingston: Sangster's Book Stores, 1982. 175p.

A useful introduction, both for its biographical information as well as for its commentary on the art of Louise Bennett. The very full notes and a glossary of non-standard words further enhance the quality of the volume. The editor is Senior Lecturer in English, University of the West Indies, Mona, Jamaica.

973 **The dialect poetry of Claude McKay.**

With a preface to this edition by Wayne Cooper. Plainview, New York: Books for Libraries Press, 1972. 2 vols. in 1. (Black Heritage Library Collection).

Contents include: volume one, 'Songs of Jamaica'; volume two, 'Constab ballads'. Both these titles were first published individually in 1912. Claude McKay, of peasant origin, was the first Jamaican poet to write in dialect, describing the life and thought of the peasantry. These two volumes were the first products of his creativity, before he left Jamaica, never to return. They are not only of literary interest as some of the earliest published works of Jamaican literature, but also are of linguistic and sociological interest.

974 **Quashie's reflections in Jamaican creole.**

Inez K. Sibley. Jamaica: Bolivar Press, 1968. 2nd ed. 61p.

First edition, published by the author, 1939; second edition reset, with introduction and glossary by Joan McLaughlin; illustrations by Carl Abrahams. Thirty 'dramatic monologues' presenting Jamaican attitudes to life; also, of historical and linguistic interest.

The Arts

General

975 The arts of an island: the development of the culture and of the folk and creative arts in Jamaica, 1494-1962 (Independence).
Ivy Baxter. Metuchen, New Jersey: Scarecrow Press, 1970. 407p. bibliog.

This is an historical as well as an interpretative work, the emphasis being on folk culture and on visual and performing arts rather than literary culture. The book is packed with obscure but interesting details on the subject, which would be difficult to ascertain otherwise.

976 Edna Manley: the private years: 1900-1938.
Wayne Brown. London: Andre Deutsch, 1975. 264p. bibliog.

An authentic and vivid portrait of the artist and wife of one of Jamaica's national heroes, based on the biographee's personal collection of letters and diaries, other contemporary records and on interviews with Mrs Manley and her friends and acquaintances. With admirable literary style the author delineates Mrs Manley's seminal role in the development of Jamaican art and culture and how this role was played out in the intimate circle of the artist's domestic life. The author was born in Trinidad and is both a literary critic and poet.

977 The Jamaica School of Art and Crafts: discussed by..
Milton Harley, Eugene Hyde, Norma Segree. *Caribbean Quarterly*, vol. 14, no. 1 & 2 (March-June 1968), p. 83-90.

The discussion touched on the history, function, entry requirements of the school and the need of the society for the school. The participants were, respectively, the Director of the School (a painter), a commercial artist (a painter) and a librarian.

978 **National culture and the artist. (A speech delivered 20 January, 1939).**
N[orman] W[ashington] Manley. In: *Caribbean essays: an anthology*. Edited and introduced by Andrew Salkey.
London: Evans, 1973, p. 72-73.

A statement by the leading figure in the modern political awakening of Jamaica on the relationship between national consciousness and artistic and intellectual life.

979 **Prime Minister Hon. Michael Manley's speech at the opening of the Mexican Exhibition, Olympia International Art Centre, on Monday, 13th January, 1975.**
Jamaica Journal, vol. 9, no. 1 (March 1975), p. 12-13.

Reflections on 'the intimate connection between artistic expression and the historical experience' with particular reference to Mexico and Jamaica.

Architecture

980 **Treasure in the Caribbean: a first study of Georgian buildings in the British West Indies.**
A. W. Acworth. London: Pleiades Books, 1949. 36p. ([Georgian Handbooks]).

Pages 5-12 and 13 plates relate to Jamaica.

981 **The changing physical environment.**
Text by Cherry Brady, aerial photography by J. S. [i.e. Jack] Tyndale-Biscoe. *Jamaica Journal*, special issue, Jamaica's 20th anniversary of independence (1982), p. 55-62.

A bird's-eye view of urban buildings and development which have taken place during the last twenty years.

982 **Buildings in Jamaica.**
[Kingston]: Jamaica Information Service, [1970?]. 68p. (chiefly illus.). (Face of Jamaica, no. 9).

Exceptionally fine photographs of public and private buildings, both old and new, preserved and in ruins. Photography by Quito Bryan, Errol Harvey, Neville Hylton, Garth Morgan, Amador Packer; script by Vic Reid.

983 **Historic architecture of the Caribbean.**
David Buisseret. London: Heinemann, 1980. 93p. map.
bibliog.

A survey, in which the illustrations are of equal importance as the text. Jamaica is heavily represented both in the text and illustrations. Buildings are grouped according to use or original function.

984 **Our architectural heritage: houses of the 18th and 19th century with special reference to Spanish Town.**
T. A. L. Concannon. *Jamaica Journal*, vol. 4, no. 2 (June 1970), p. 23-28.

A plea for preservation, with illustrations of the 'Jamaican vernacular' or Jamaican Georgian structures, brief descriptions of architectural features and a short account of the social life which took place within. The author was a notable architect and a member of the Georgian Society.

985 **The discovery of the Spanish carvings at Seville.**
C. S. Cotter. *Jamaican Historical Review* [vol. 1, no. 3], 1947, p. 227-33.

A brief account of the circumstances of their discovery and of the earliest historical references to Spanish buildings in Jamaica. Accompanying the text are three plates, with notes, which describe the figures in detail and give their overall measurements. Cotter refers in the notes to an earlier study by Diego Angulo Iñiguez, *El Gótico y el Renacimiento en las Antillas: arquitectura, escultura, pintura, azulejos, orfebrería* (Gothic and Renaissance in the Antilles... Seville: Escuela de Estudios Hispano-Americanos, 1947), which discusses the historical background to these architectural remains of the earliest Spanish capital in Jamaica, Sevilla Nueva, and comments on the style and date of the carved remains of the abbatial church, preserved in the Institute of Jamaica. They are the most important tangible relics of the Spanish occupation of Jamaica.

986 **Falmouth 1793-1970.**
Georgian Society of Jamaica. Kingston: Georgian Society, [1970]. 28p.

Photographs, sketches and reproductions of old prints illustrating the Georgian vernacular of this town which still preserves some of the spirit of 18th-century Jamaica, with historical and architectural notes and street plans. The book was produced by a team of enthusiasts with a view to stimulating interest in restoring and preserving buildings and artifacts of aesthetic value from Jamaica's past. From the general interest created thereby the Georgian Society of Jamaica was established.

987 **Caribbean Georgian: the great and small houses of the West Indies.**
Pamela Gosner. Washington, DC: Three Continents Press, 1982. 296p. bibliog.

The first 8 chapters discuss in a general and comparative way the architecture of the West Indies from a functional and social perspective, treating of plantations, military, urban, religious and folk architecture. Chapters 9-20 treat of the architecture of individual islands, chapter 11 (p. 115-48) treating of Jamaica. The work is copiously illustrated throughout with excellent line-drawings.

988 **The deceit of motive: looking back on the Georgian age in Jamaica.**
Alex Gradussov. *Jamaica Journal*, vol. 5, no. 1 (March 1971), p. 44-52.

A discussion of the cultural and social considerations involved in the preservation of Jamaica's heritage of Georgian architecture and furniture, as determined by historical and other antecedents such as slavery, colonialism, race, class and prejudice. Includes some interesting photographs of Georgian buildings.

989 **Jamaica fares well.**
Progressive Architecture, vol. 47 (Aug. 1966), p. 192-93.

A short account of the Cornwall Regional Hospital building, St. James, Jamaica.

990 **University College of the West Indies, Jamaica.**
Norman & Dawbarn, Architects & Consulting Engineers. London: reprinted from *Journal of the Royal Institute of British Architects*, May 1953. 11p.

A description of the buildings, their functional planning and floor areas, illustrated with scale diagrams and photographs, presenting a remarkably compact view of the university in its beginnings and of the buildings which remain the central core of the present institution.

991 **Jamaican houses, a vanishing legacy.**
Drawings by Anghelen Arrington Phillips, text by Geoffrey de Sola Pinto. Kingston: printed by Stephenson's Litho Press, 1982. [78]p. including maps & line-drawings.

Fine, accurate drawings of notable examples of Jamaican architecture represented in buildings for domestic and public use, built from the late 17th century to the early 20th century. The accompanying text gives a brief historical account of each house and draws attention to remarkable details of construction.

Periodicals

992 **Jamaica Architect: a review of architecture in the tropics.**
Kingston: Jamaican Society of Architects, 1967-77. quarterly. 1968- . annual.

A journal 'directed at the people of Jamaica and abroad who are interested in what is happening here in the field of architecture.' The publication included feature articles by local and international writers as well as sections on residential, commercial and industrial architecture and society news. Some issues were devoted to a special subject, e.g. vol. 1, no. 3, 1967-68, 'Greater Kingston redevelopment'; vol. 2, no. 2, (issue no. 5) 1969 and issue 11, 1974-75, 'Tourism' including the relationship between Jamaican architecture and tourism; issue no. 7,

1970, 'Designing for health' (hospital designs); issues no. 8, 1971 and 13, 1977, 'Housing'; issue no. 9, 1972, 'Environment'.

Visual arts

993 **Albert Huie illustrates poems by popular poets.**
Kingston: Institute of Jamaica, [1972?]. [8] leaves (illus).

Seven reproductions of linocuts by Albert Huie, the doyen of Jamaican painters, with a complementary verse from seven poems by the following Jamaican poets: George Campbell, M. G. Smith, H. D. Carberry, P. M. Sherlock, K. E. Ingram.

994 **The intuitive eye: a heritage recalled.**
David Boxer [in an interview with Shirley M. Burke, editor of the *Jamaica Journal*]. *Jamaica Journal*, no. 44 ([June 1980]), p. 17-25.

An interesting discussion of the African heritage in Jamaican art, as exemplified by an exhibition of some 165 pieces of Jamaican art by intuitive or self-taught artists. The discussant is himself a painter, art historian and Director of the National Gallery of Jamaica which mounted the exhibition. A slightly abridged version of this interview was published later in the *Journal of African Civilisations*, vol. 3, no. 2 (Nov. 1981) p. 105-19.

995 **Carl Abrahams illustrates prose by: Roger Mais, H. D. Carberry, Victor S. Reid, A. E. T. Henry, John Hearne, Charles Mills.**
[Kingston]: Institute of Jamaica, [1972?]. 7 leaves (illus).

Carl Abrahams started his career as a cartoonist in 1938 and later took up painting. The seven passages which he illustrates here allow him to display his talent for the humorous as well as the macabre.

996 **Interview with a Jamaican master: Albert Huie discusses his life and art with Basil McFarlane.**
Jamaica Journal, vol. 8, no. 1 (March 1974), p. 42-47.

Albert Huie, one of the pioneers of the modern Jamaican art movement, is interviewed by a poet and journalist concerning his early life and his subsequent experiences and views as a painter. Accompanied by three illustrations in colour of his paintings.

997 **Jamaican folkart.**
[Kingston]: Institute of Jamaica, [1970?]. 12p.

Includes illustrations in black-and-white and colour of folk art and paintings of an exhibition by Jamaican self-taught artists, with two articles, the first on oral traditions, entitled 'An old man dies... a book is lost' by Olive Lewin and the second 'Art and society: Kapo, a context' by Edward Brathwaite.

998 The landscape medium. Is there a message? Extrapolations on a conversation with Albert Huie on painting the Jamaican landscape.

Arts Jamaica: a Visual Arts Quarterly, vol. 1, no. 1 (April 1982), p. 4-5.

A look at the Jamaican tradition in landscape painting based on a conversation with Albert Huie, who is one of the foremost painters of the Jamaican landscape.

999 English commemorative sculpture in Jamaica.

Lesley Lewis. London: *Commemorative Art*, Nov. 1965-Feb. 1967. 1 vol. (various pagings).

Work published with separate title-page in *Commemorative Art*, vols. 32, no. 11-12; 33, no. 1-12; 34, no. 1-2. Published also as a single issue of *The Jamaican Historical Review*, vol. 9, 1972 (140p). A comprehensive account, well illustrated.

1000 Selected editorial cartoons.

Livingston McLaren. Kingston: Daily News, 1979. 1 vol. (unpaged).

Graphic pictorial comments on various aspects of Jamaican life by the national and internationally recognized cartoonist of the *Jamaica Daily News*. Commercial art used as a vehicle of humour, political analysis and social criticism.

1001 Development of Jamaican art: five perspectives.

Edna Manley, David Boxer, Andrew Hope, Jean Smith, Rosalie Smith McCrea. *Jamaica Journal*, special issue, Jamaica's 20th anniversary of independence (1982), p. 44-54. bibliog.

In five separate sections the historical beginnings, the thematic and stylistic development, and the social and administrative context of Jamaican art since about 1938 are outlined by a sculptor (who is also a painter), a curator (who is also an art historian and painter), an art critic (who is also a graphic artist and teacher), an administrator (and consultant) with long experience in cultural development and an art historian (who is also an artist and assistant curator).

1002 Five centuries of art in Jamaica.

Exhibition compiled by the National Gallery of Jamaica. Kingston: National Gallery of Jamaica, 1976. 36p.

An illustrated catalogue, with descriptive and historical notes on 186 pieces of visual art produced for or in Jamaica during the period 1530 to date. The exhibition, which coincided with the Caribbean Festival of Arts held in Jamaica during that year, attempted to provide 'an opportunity to study contemporary Jamaican art against the varied background of past art produced in Jamaica or under Jamaican patronage.' (Preface, p. 1).

1003 Ten Jamaican sculptors.

Sir Philip [Manderson] Sherlock. *Jamaica Journal*, vol. 10, nos. 2, 3 & 4 ([1977]), p. 3-7.

A brief account of the first exhibition of a representative collection of sculpture by Jamaican artists to be held overseas. The exhibition, held at the Common-wealth Institute, London, was opened by Sir Philip Sherlock, 4 September 1976. This short account is amplified by several fine photographs.

1004 Jamaican art since the thirties. [Catalogue of an exhibition presented by...].

Spelman College of Atlanta University Center, in association with the Contemporary Jamaican Artists' Association. Atlanta, Georgia: [Spelman College], 1969. [34]p. bibliog.

A catalogue of the exhibition of Jamaican art since the 1930s held 9 November-10 December 1969 by the Spelman College, Atlanta University in Association with the Contemporary Jamaican Artists Association.

Periodicals

1005 Arts Jamaica: a Quarterly Magazine of the Visual Arts.

[Jamaica]: Arts Jamaica, 1982- . quarterly.

The magazine aims to analyse and celebrate those things and persons already recognized as having greatness while remaining open to new ideas. In addition to articles this periodical includes news on the National Gallery, the Jamaica School of Art and exhibitions planned during the next quarter.

Music and dance

1006 Notes on contemporary dance-theatre in Jamaica 1930-1982.

Sheila Barnett. *Jamaica Journal*, special issue, Jamaica's 20th anniversary of independence (1982), p. 80-93. bibliog.

An informative outline and chronicle of the development of dance-theatre in Jamaica, with particular reference to themes, music and choreography, with seve-ral photographs of dancers, choreographers, teachers, producers and dance com-panies, by a founder member of the National Dance Theatre Company and Director of the Jamaica School of Dance.

1007 **Bob Marley: soul rebel - natural mystic.**
Adriaan Boot, Vivien Goldman. London: Eel Pie
Publishing; Hutchinson, 1981. [96]p.

An outline of the musical career and development of Bob Marley who achieved
international star status as a Rasta reggae singer. The text is complemented by a
remarkable collection of photographs which constitutes three-quarters of the
volume. At the end is a three-page discography, which, regrettably, lacks publication dates.

1008 **Notes on the history of jazz and its role in Jamaica.**
James [A.] Carnegie. *Jamaica Journal,* vol. 4, no. 1
(March 1970), p. 20-29.

Mentions some 40 names of Jamaicans involved in jazz and includes some individual and group photographs of Jamaican jazz musicians.

1009 **Jah music: the evolution of the popular Jamaican song.**
Sebastian Clarke. London: Heinemann Educational Books,
1980. 216p. bibliog.

An historical outline of the rise and development of reggae music, with particular
reference to the social and political aspects of its evolution, including much biographical and illustrative material on reggae musicians and their associates.
Includes 'Selected discography' (p. 182-86) and 'Selected artists and musicians
directory' (p. 187-210). The author, a musical journalist, born in Trinidad in
1948, has written scenarios for two TV documentaries on reggae and Jamaican
music, produced in Britain in 1970 and 1976.

1010 **Reggae bloodlines: in search of the music and culture of
Jamaica.**
Text by Stephen Davis, photographs by Peter Simon. [s.l.]:
Anchor Press, Doubleday, 1977. 216p.

'Photographer Peter Simon and I spent most of the winter of 1976 in Jamaica,
visiting and talking with some of these reggae master musicians as well as the
producers, ganja traders, Rastafarian brethren and elders, and even a politician or
two; we were trying to get a line on the force that sets the reggae cosmology into
motion and keeps it spinning. We tried to penetrate Jamaican life to the roots...
rather than a history we present a portrait of reggae and Jamaica at what many
feel is a turning point.' (Introduction, p. 4-5). 'Jamaica discography, compiled by
Don Williams': p. 211-16.

1011 **Jamaica, land we love: a collection of patriotic, national and
folk songs of Jamaica for schools and colleges.**
Compiled by Lloyd Hall. London: Macmillan Caribbean,
1980. 72p.

Words and music of 12 national and patriotic songs and of 23 folk songs, compiled by a Senior Education Officer in the Ministry of Education, Jamaica,
responsible for the encouragement and development of music education in schools
and colleges.

1012 A word with Rex Nettleford Jamaica's dancemaster.
Text by E. Patrick Healy, photographs by Maria La Yacona. *Américas*, vol. 33, no. 8 (Aug. 1981), p. 21-25.

The Director of the Organization of American States' General Secretariat Office in Jamaica interviews the co-founder and artistic director of the National Dance Theatre Company of Jamaica on the achievements of the company on the eve of its 20th birthday.

1013 Celebration: collected liturgical and folk songs.
Richard Ho Lung, SJ, with chords and vocal arrangements by Bart Hopkin (and others), copied and illustrated by Bart Hopkin. Kingston: Jesuit Music, 1978. 112p.

Father Richard Ho Lung's liturgical compositions express religious sentiment using a Jamaican idiom and imagery. They are widely used in Jamaican churches. The words and melodies are his.

1014 [Jamaican folk & traditional dance].
Jamaica Journal, vol. 10, no. 1 (March 1976), 8p. + 33⅓rpm disc.

This special issue records seven traditional dances, collected by Olive Lewin, with a descriptive comment on each, followed by an article titled as above, by D. Joyce Campbell, Dance Co-ordinator with the Jamaica Festival Commission.

1015 Brown gal in de ring: 12 Jamaican folk-songs.
Collected and arranged for schools by Olive Lewin. London: Oxford University Press, 1974. 16p.

A collection of twelve Jamaican folk songs.

1016 Dandy shandy: 12 Jamaican folk-songs for children.
Collected and arranged for schools by Olive Lewin. London: Oxford University Press, 1975. 20p.

A collection of twelve Jamaican folk songs for children.

1017 Forty folk songs of Jamaica.
Collected and transcribed by Olive Lewin. Washington, DC: General Secretariat of the Organization of American States, 1973. 107p. map.

Includes the words and music of songs collected, transcribed and annotated by Olive Lewin, Folk Music Research Officer of the Jamaica School of Music. The text is prefaced by the author's illustrated comments on Jamaican folk music as an important element in Jamaica's search for identity and a short outline of the main types of musical instruments in use. The volume is the seventh in a series of Organization of American States' publications of folk music teaching materials designed to encourage music education as a basis for the people's general culture in the countries of the Americas.

1018 **Jamaican folk music.**
Olive Lewin. *Caribbean Quarterly*, vol. 14, nos. 1 & 2 (March-June 1968), p. 49-56.

An outline of the development of Jamaican folk music in its various forms for work, entertainment and worship, by Jamaica's foremost musicologist in the field of folk music.

1019 **Some Jamaican folk songs.**
Collected and compiled by Olive Lewin. Kingston: Oxford Group Publishers, 1970. 36p.

'Vol. 1' only published. Music, words and commentary for 36 folk songs.

1020 **Some aspects of religious cult music in Jamaica - a conversation with Marjorie Whylie.**
Wendell Logan. *Black Perspective in Music*, vol. 10, no. 1 (spring 1982), p. 85-94.

The interview took place at the Jamaica School of Music, Kingston, Jamaica, on 30 January 1980 and ranged over the various cults, the musical styles associated with them, the dance movements for these styles, the role of the music in cultic possession and its relation to popular Jamaican music. The person interviewed is Head of the Division of Folk Music Research at the Jamaica School of Music and the interviewer is Professor of Music at Oberlin College.

1021 **Bob Marley and the roots of reggae.**
Cathy McKnight, John Tobler. London: W. H. Allen, 1977. 160p. (A Star Book).

A sketch of Marley's life and musical output set against a brief historical and cultural background to reggae. Includes a list of available LPs by Marley and the Wailers.

1022 **George Davis Goode: the man and his work.**
Ethel Marson. Kingston: the author, 1964. 120p.

This work was published as a tribute to George Goode (1882-1962) and is included here because, as Philip M. Sherlock who writes the 'Foreword' says: 'It is so easy to forget these men who enriched today because yesterday they expressed their great loyalties through small fidelities.' He was the pioneer in the development of choral music in Jamaica and was the founder of the Diocesan Festival Choir in 1925. His contribution to the musical life of Jamaica was recognized by the award of the Gold Musgrave Medal by the Institute of Jamaica in 1951. This biography is a factual ungarnished account.

1023 **Folk songs of Jamaica.**
Edited and arranged by Tom Murray. London: Oxford University Press, 1952. 59p.

Thirty songs, edited and arranged from transcripts made by Barbara Ferland of the words as sung by Louise Bennett, with musical accompaniment.

1024 **The dance as an art form - its place in the West Indies.**
Rex Nettleford. *Caribbean Quarterly*, vol. 14, no. 1 & 2 (March-June 1968), p. 127-35.

Discusses the nature, purpose and scope of the art of dance, dance as a folk art, the Jamaican experience of dance as a national art form and the National Dance Theatre Company of Jamaica.

1025 **Roots and rhythms: Jamaica's national dance theatre.**
Text by Rex Nettleford, photographs by Maria La Yacona. London: Andre Deutsch, 1969. 128p.

The photographs constitute an equally important part of the book. The work outlines the beginnings of the National Dance Theatre Company, formed in 1962, with Rex Nettleford as Artistic Director, describing its repertoire and the particular contributions of its choreographers, dancers and other artists.

1026 **The introduction of Jamaican music into the established churches.**
Pamela O'Gorman. *Jamaica Journal*, vol. 9, no. 1 (March 1975), p. 40-44, 47.

Traces the origins of the use of Jamaican folk music and music composed in a Jamaican idiom in church worship and outlines congregational reactions to this development.

1027 **Reggae, Rastafarianism and cultural identity.**
Verena Reckord. *Jamaica Journal*, special issue, Jamaica's 20th anniversary of independence (1982), p. 70-79, bibliog.

An informed outline of the development of reggae and other forms of popular Jamaican music since about 1950, with several group and single portrait photographs.

1028 **Possible survivals of African song in Jamaica.**
Helen H. Roberts. *Musical Quarterly*, vol. 12, no. 3 (July 1926), p. 340-58.

An account of Koromantyn songs collected among the Maroons of Jamaica during field-work sponsored by the Folklore Foundation of Vassar College and the American Association for the Advancement of Science. The author collaborated with Martha Warren Beckwith in her investigations into Jamaican folk life.

1029 **The Jamaican heritage in dance: developing a traditional typology.**
Cheryl Ryman. *Jamaica Journal*, no. 44 ([June 1980]), p. 7-13. map.

Notes on 39 traditional dances, with a tabular arrangement by categories and a map showing regions with strong dance traditions in the various types and also areas in which research has been done. Discusses Jamaican dances as preservers of the people's African heritage. The author is a principal dancer, choreographer and member of the National Dance Theatre Company of Jamaica and a Research Fellow at the African Caribbean Institute of Jamaica.

1030 **Reggae - a musical weapon.**
Garth White. *Caribe* (New York), (Dec. 1980), p. 6-10.

An outline of the development of reggae as an indigenous musical form, with some remarks on its social and religious message. Several contributors to the creation of this musical form are mentioned by name.

1031 **Reggae, Rastafarians and revolution: rock music in the Third World.**
James A. Winders. *Journal of Popular Culture*, vol. 17, no. 1 (summer 1983), p. 61-73. bibliog.

Discusses reggae as a vehicle of Rastafarianism and as 'a revolutionary impetus for change'. The author is a member of the Department of History, Appalachian State University, Boone, North Carolina.

Theatre and film

1032 **The Jamaican theatre: a preliminary overview.**
Wycliffe Bennett. *Jamaica Journal*, vol. 8, nos. 2 & 3 (summer 1974), p. 3-9.

An account of some outstanding theatrical productions in Jamaican theatre of the 20th century, being an excerpt from a forthcoming book entitled *The historical foundation of the Jamaican theatre*.

1033 **A history of theatre in Jamaica.**
Henry Fowler. *Jamaica Journal*, vol. 2, no. 1 (March 1968), p. 53-59.

An historical outline by a long-time patron and supporter of the Jamaican theatre.

1034 **Twenty years of theatre.**
Barbara Gloudon. *Jamaica Journal*, special issue, Jamaica's 20th anniversary of independence (1982), p. 63-69.

A concise review of developments since 1962, mentioning the names of several dramatists, performances and institutions connected with the theatre. Illustrated. The author is a journalist and playwright.

1035 **Thoughts about the theatre in Jamaica.**
Alex Gradussov. *Jamaica Journal*, vol. 4, no. 1 (March 1970), p. 46-52.

A lively, bantering review of Jamaican theatre when the theatre of protest was well launched, tilting at the value systems of social classes expressing themselves or reacting to contemporary Jamaican theatre.

1036 **The theatrical into theatre: a study of the drama and theatre of the English-speaking Caribbean.**
Kole Omotoso. London; Port of Spain: New Beacon Books, 1982. 173p. bibliog.

A pioneering, critical and historical study by the Acting Head of the Department of Dramatic Arts at Ife, Nigeria and Acting Director of the University Theatre. He discusses the development and themes of the main theatrical movements in the area and chapter 6, 'The performance of Caribbean theatre' (p. 78-97), is largely devoted to the theatre in Jamaica.

1037 **Old story time and other plays.**
Trevor D. Rhone. Harlow, England: Longman, 1981. 234p.

A collection of three plays by Jamaica's most popular dramatist - comedies rooted in Jamaican life which comment wittily on social and moral issues such as the harmful effects of tourism, the school system and colour prejudice in Jamaican society. The introduction by Mervyn Morris outlines Rhone's career and the development of his dramatic and theatrical work.

1038 **Revels in Jamaica, 1682-1838: plays and players of a century, tumblers and conjurors, musical refugees and solitary showmen, dinners, balls and cockfights, darky mummers and other memories of high times and merry hearts.**
Richardson Wright. New York: Dodd Mead, 1937. Reissued, New York; London: Benjamin Blom, 1969. 378p.

The most comprehensive account of the theatre and public entertainment in pre-emancipation Jamaica. The author has made extensive use of contemporary newspapers as well as primary and secondary sources. It is particularly strong on the connection between Jamaican theatre and American players in the period 1755-1785.

Folklore, literature, proverbs and songs

1039 **Jamaica proverbs and sayings.**
Collected by Izett Anderson, Frank Cundall. Kingston: Sangster's Book Stores in association with Irish University Press of Shannon, Ireland, 1972. rev. ed. 128p. bibliog.

First published 1910; revised edition 1927; reprinted 1972. Includes 1,383 proverbs and sayings, arranged alphabetically by subject, and 72 riddles. Frank Cundall was Secretary and Librarian of the Institute of Jamaica and Izett Anderson an honorary member of the Institute.

The Arts. Folklore, literature, proverbs and songs

1040 Jamaica Anansi stories.

Martha Warren Beckwith, with music recorded in the field by Helen Roberts. New York: American Folk-lore Society, 1924. Reprinted, New York: Kraus Reprint Co., 1976. 295p. (Memoirs of the American Folk-lore Society, vol. 17).

A collection of 149 stories, set down without literary embellishment, with shorter sections on witticisms and riddles, critical and explanatory notes by the collector and an index of informants.

1041 Jamaica folklore.

Collected by Martha Warren Beckwith, with music recorded in the field by Helen H. Roberts. New York: American Folk-lore Society, 1928. Reprinted, New York: Kraus Reprint Co., 1969. 95, 67, 137, 47p. bibliog. (Memoirs of the American Folk-lore Society, vol. 21).

Contains four works based on notes gathered in the course of four collecting trips to Jamaica, 1919-24, by a pioneer in the systematic study of Jamaican folklore. Contents include: Folk games of Jamaica; Christmas mummings in Jamaica; Jamaica proverbs; and Notes on Jamaican ethnobotany. Illustrated.

1042 Anancy and Miss Lou.

Louise Bennett. Kingston: Sangster's Book Stores, 1979. 82p.

Thirty-one stories, told in dialect, of Anancy, 'the trickify little spider man', hero and villain of Jamaican folklore, told by the leading folklore artist of Jamaica. The words and melodies of lullabies which form part of the stories are grouped as a final chapter. The introduction is by Mervyn Morris.

1043 Jamaican song and story: annancy stories, digging sings, ring tunes, and dancing tunes.

Collected and edited by Walter Jekyll, with new introductory essays by Philip M. Sherlock, Louise Bennett, Rex Nettleford. London: David Nutt, 1907. Reissued, New York: Dover Publications, 1966. 288p.

An unabridged and unaltered re-publication which includes an introduction by Alice Werner, appendices on traces of African melody in Jamaica by C. S. Myers, and on English airs and motifs in Jamaica by Lucy E. Broadwood. A comprehensive collection made by a folklorist and a musicologist who came to Jamaica in 1895 and remained until his death in 1929. The author lived in close touch with the countryside and country people and has transcribed the materials faithfully and accurately.

Letters from Jamaica 'the land of streams and woods'.
See item no. 39.

Black roadways: a study of Jamaican folk life.
See item no. 316.

Periodicals

1044 Folklore Bulletin.
Kingston: Folklore Studies Committee, Faculty of Arts & General Studies, University of the West Indies, 1980- . three times yearly.

The first issue supplies basic information on existing facilities for folklore research in Jamaica. Later issues are expected to extend to the whole Caribbean area.

Festivals

1045 Christmas mummings in Jamaica.
Martha Warren Beckwith, with music recorded in the field by Helen H. Roberts. Poughkeepsie, New York: Vassar College, 1923. 46p. (Publications of the Folklore Foundation, no. 2).

An investigation of John Canoe dancing and related festivities whose celebration in Jamaica dates from the period of slavery, drawing upon documentary sources as well as field observations made during visits to Jamaica in the winter of 1920-21 and in 1923. It is perhaps the first attempt to investigate these festivities within the comparative framework of similar occurrences in Africa and England. More than half the text is devoted to the words and music of songs sung on these occasions.

1046 The Hussay festival in Jamaica, with music recorded by phonograph.
Martha Warren Beckwith. Poughkeepsie, New York: Vassar College, 1924. 17p. (Vassar College Folk-lore Foundation. Publications, no. 4).

An account of a Mohammedan religious festival annually celebrated by the East Indians in Jamaica, based on interviews with two East Indians in the winter of 1922. The festival songs are transcribed with musical notation at the end of the publication.

1047 Jamaican Jonkonnu and related Caribbean festivals.
Judith Bettelheim. In: *Africa and the Caribbean: the legacies of a link*. Edited by Margaret E. Crahan; Franklin W. Knight. Baltimore, Maryland; London: Johns Hopkins University Press, 1979, p. 80-100. bibliog.

A succinct historical and descriptive account of Christmas mummings in Jamaica, the Bahamas, Bermuda, the Leeward Islands and Belize, based on research carried out in 1976, including interviews in Jamaica.

1048 **Jonkonnu in Jamaica: towards the interpretation of folk dance as a cultural process.**
Sylvia Wynter. *Jamaica Journal*, vol. 4, no. 2 (June 1970), p. 34-48. bibliog.

This article is a shorter version of a much fuller treatment of the subject. It attempts to interpret and also to tabulate the survivals of folk-dance in Jamaica.

Customs and costume

1049 **The sun and the drum: African roots in Jamaican folk tradition.**
Leonard E. Barrett. Kingston: Sangster's Book Stores in association with Heinemann, 1976. 128p. bibliog.

This is a work written for the non-specialist and for the student wishing to obtain an elementary conspectus of the folk tradition of Jamaica. The author is a Jamaican and the book 'emerges out of his own reflection on his childhood and adolescence in Jamaican bush...'. There are chapters on proverbs, medical lore, witchcraft and psychic phenomena.

1050 **Sketches of character, in illustration of the habits, occupation, and costume of the Negro population, in the island of Jamaica, drawn after nature, and in lithography.**
Isaac Mendes Belisario. Kingston: published by the artist, at his residence, no. 21, King Street... 1837[-38]. 7 leaves (text). 12 plates.

Coloured lithographs issued in three parts of four plates each. The work is of unusual interest in that it concerned itself with the social life and customs of the slaves rather than with that of their masters. Completion of the work was projected in twelve parts but long before that came about there seems to have been a petering out of support for the book. Abbey states that while the first part is occasionally to be found, the second is more rare and the third of very rare occurrence. The Institute of Jamaica reissued eight of these prints, lithographed by Stephensons, in a portfolio in 197-?

1051 **Jamaica traditions of African origins.**
Louise Bennett. *Caribe* (no. 1? 1980?), p. 32-37.

The author discusses Jamaican dialect, the pocomania cult, 'John Cunu' festivities, anancy stories and other traditional customs and dances as survivals of traditional African culture.

1052 **The folk culture of the slaves of Jamaica.**
Edward Kamau Brathwaite. London, Port of Spain: New
Beacon Books, 1981. rev. ed. 56p. bibliog.

First published in 1971, abstracted from the author's *The development of creole
society in Jamaica 1770-1820*. This edition contains some additional analysis and
an improved bibliography. The folk culture of the slaves derived
mainly from West Africa and in its creolized and inherited form has become
increasingly articulate since Jamaica became independent in 1962. This work
succinctly treats of birth and funeral customs, religious practices, music and
dance, public entertainments, houses, furniture and language.

1053 **Africa and the Caribbean: the legacies of a link.**
Edited by Margaret E. Crahan, Franklin W.
Knight. Baltimore, Maryland; London: Johns Hopkins
University Press, 1979. 159p. bibliog.

Essays on the contribution of Africa to the culture of the Caribbean, written for
specialists and non-specialists alike. An interdisciplinary and multidisciplinary
study. The contents include: 'The African migration and the origins of an Afro-
American society and culture' by Franklin W. Knight and Margaret E. Crahan;
'The cultural links' by Harry Hoetink; 'African and creole slave family patterns
in Trinidad' by B. W. Higman; 'Myalism and the African religious tradition in
Jamaica' by Monica Schuler; 'Jamaican Jonkonnu and related Caribbean festivals' by Judith Bettelheim; 'The African impact on language and literature in the
English-speaking Caribbean' by Maureen Warner Lewis; and 'The African
presence in the poetry of Nicolás Guillén' by Lorna V. Williams.

1054 **Characteristic traits of the Creolian & African Negroes in
Jamaica, &c. &c. (1797).**
Edited by Barry Higman. Mona, Jamaica: Caldwell Press,
1976. 23p.

Extracts from anonymous observations originally published in 1797 in *The
Columbian Magazine; or Monthly Miscellany* (Kingston, Jamaica: printed by
William-Smart). Interesting first-hand observations of customs relating to dress,
occupations, food, music and entertainments, providing new information on some
subjects. Limited edition.

Indian heritage in Jamaica.
See item no. 265.

Family and colour in Jamaica.
See item no. 356.

Cookery

1055 A merry-go-round of recipes from Jamaica with additional recipes.

Leila Brandon. Kingston: Novelty Trading Co., [after 1963]. new ed. 82p.

First published as *Merry-go-round of recipes* in 1963. The author disclaims any intention of producing an orthodox cookbook but rather presents a personal selection of recipes some of which she has created herself and others with which she has experimented and altered to suit locally produced edibles. It includes a number of Jamaican specialities which do not find their way into some of the more comprehensive and conventional Caribbean cookbooks. The author is a Jamaican.

1056 Jamaica run-dung: over 100 recipes.

Teresa E. Cleary. Kingston: Brainbuster Publications, 1973. rev. ed. 59p.

First published 1970. A Jamaican cookbook by a Jamaican woman who describes herself as 'an ardent cook and collector of recipes'. Unfortunately the printing is poor, being blurred and uneven in parts.

1057 Cooking our way: a course in Caribbean cookery and nutrition.

Yvonne Collymore, illustrated by George L. Glaze. Aylesbury, England: Caribbean Universities Press, Ginn, 1972. 144p.

Intended for use in schools, this work has chapters on food values, food storage, choice and care of cooking utensils, cooking processes, serving meals and safety measures in the kitchen as well as a recipe section. The author and publishers acknowledge the help of the Caribbean Food and Nutrition Institute, University of the West Indies, for their interest and help with this series, of which this is volume one. The choice of illustrations is both practical and attractive.

1058 Some fruits & recipes of Jamaica.

Judy Cuninghame. Virgin Islands: Caribbean Natural Colour, 1971. 16, [16]p.

Sixteen delicately coloured plates representing fruits of Jamaica, each with an adjacent page of text giving recipes for use of the fruit. An unusual combination of artistic and useful information.

1059 The Rastafari cookbook: ital recipes.

Margaret Ebanks, foreword by Arthur Kitchin, illustrations by Desmond McFarlane. Kingston: Antilles Book Co., 1981. 95p.

As the writer of the foreword informs us, 'ital' or natural cooking was 'started primarily as an alternative to Western-based nutritional habits which rely heavily on meats and fish' and has 'gained popularity among the wider society who, either conscious of the desirability of health foods or the need to find substitutes for imported staples, are adopting the Rastafari-influenced diets that utilise only the fruits of the soil.

1060 **The farmer's food manual: a recipe book for the West Indies.**
Prepared and published with the help and collaboration of the Jamaica Social Welfare Commission by the Jamaica Agricultural Society, Kingston. Glasgow, Scotland: printed by Robert Maclehose & Co., Glasgow University Press, 1957. 386p.

This work is not only a recipe book but a valuable and authoritative manual on nutrition and home economics in Jamaica, with historical notes on the food crops of Jamaica. Illustrated; some illustrations in colour.

1061 **Banana recipes.**
Jamaica Information Service. Kingston: reprinted by Novelty Trading Co., from originals prepared and published by the Agency for Public Information, 1975. 32p.
Originally published by the Jamaica Information Service in 1965 as a souvenir of the Culinary Arts Competition of the annual Jamaica Festival. A selection of recipes, illustrated in colour.

1062 **Jamaican cuisine.**
Kingston: prepared and published by the Jamaican Information Service [1964?]. (Face of Jamaica, 4).
An attractively illustrated brochure compiled with the assistance of some of the leading hotels, restaurants and persons trained in home economics.

1063 **Cook up Jamaican style.**
Novelette C. Jones. Kingston: Kingston: Agricultural Information Service, Ministry of Agriculture, 1977. 111p.
A book of recipes for cooking Jamaican foods. The author is a specialist in home economics and many of the recipes were prepared and tested by Home Economics Officers of the Ministry of Agriculture. Illustrations are in colour as well as in black-and-white.

1064 **Caribbean cookbook using the foods we grow.**
Elsa Miller. Kingston: Kingston Publishers, 1979. 81p.
The recipes are intended to reflect the varied cultural heritage of the people of the Caribbean. Illustrated with three coloured photographs of Caribbean fruit and vegetables and provided with a glossary. The author studied cookery in Europe, worked in the catering departments of larger hotels and managed a number of small hotels in Jamaica and elsewhere.

1065 The best of Caribbean cooking.
Elizabeth Lambert Ortiz. London: Andre Deutsch, 1975. rev. ed. 323p.

First published in United States as *The complete book of Caribbean cookery* by M. Evans & Co., 1973. A comprehensive cookbook, well produced, with clear and concise directions, a glossary of Caribbean foods and terms and coloured illustrations of Caribbean fruits and vegetables. Each recipe is identified with a Caribbean country by name and variations for other Caribbean countries are indicated in a note at the end of the recipe. The author states in her foreword that she first became interested in Caribbean cookery in Jamaica, where she lived for some years as a child, and that all the recipes have been subsequently tested in her kitchen.

1066 Caribbean cooking for pleasure.
Mary Slater. London: Hamlyn, 1970. 146, [6]p.

Although there is a brief chapter on regional recipes, including some Jamaican specialities, this book does not set out to list regional recipes as such but to give a selection of those recipes which are considered to have the widest appeal, with some suggestions of new ways of using Caribbean produce. Each chapter is prefaced by short introductory remarks including historical details relevant to culinary traditions and practices. Amply and colourfully illustrated and prefaced by a glossary.

1067 Caribbean cookbook.
Rita G. Springer. London: Evans Brothers, 1975. 2nd ed. 255p.

First published 1968. Simple, clear recipes with practical directions for the preparation of a wide range of Caribbean dishes. Includes short chapters on historical aspects of Caribbean cookery. Illustrated.

1068 The cooking of the Caribbean islands.
Linda Wolfe, Editors of Time-Life Books, photographed by Richard Meek. New York: Time-Life Books, 1972. rev. ed. 208p. map. bibliog. (Foods of the World).

First edition, 1970. A beautifully illustrated work on Caribbean cuisine, by culinary experts, presented for gourmet use. Against a background text of descriptive and historical commentary and personal anecdotes, some 85 recipes, identified with the names of individual countries, are given. There is a select list of specialities, arranged by country, a recipe index and glossary of terms. A recipe booklet containing all of the 85 recipes in this book plus 58 more, designed for use in the kitchen, was issued as an accompanying volume.

Sport and Recreation

1069 George Headley.
S. I. Burrowes, J[ames] A. Carnegie. London: Nelson, 1971. 80p.

George Headley (b. 1909), acclaimed as a hero of cricket at home and abroad. The authors have sketched his career 'mainly for young people who are separated from Headley's great cricketing days by more than a generation'. The 'Acknowledgements' indicate that the authors submitted their manuscript to Headley and many well-known authorities on cricket, both for verification and correction.

1070 Donald Quarrie: the career of an Olympic champion.
Jimmy [James A.] Carnegie. Kingston: Jamaica Publishing House, 1978. 124p.

A factual account of an internationally famous track athlete and one of Jamaica's greatest figures in the world of sports. The work also serves as an outline of track athletics in Jamaica from 1965, when Quarrie first attracted attention in school athletics at the age of fourteen, with occasional flashbacks to the early 1950s. The illustrations include interesting shots of track race finishes.

1071 The Jamaican tradition of greatness in sports.
Jimmy [James A.] Carnegie. Kingston: Agency for Public Information, 1977. 16p.

A concise review of the performances of Jamaican sportsmen during the last half-century. Illustrated.

1072 The happy warrior: biography of Collie Smith.
Ken Chaplin. Kingston: Dominion Publishing Co., 1960. 62p.

Collie Smith's life, short though it was (he died as a result of a motor accident at the age of 25) illustrates the West Indian love for cricket, both as a player and spectator. From a poor boy with a passion for cricket, with the encouragement of Boys' Town, a philanthropic club, he became perhaps Jamaica's most beloved cricketer.

1073 **Caribbean cricketers from the pioneers to Packer.**
Clayton Goodwin, foreword by Colin Cowdrey. London:
Harrap, 1980. 260p. map.

A comprehensive account of West Indian cricket from its beginnings, told in the
achievements of individuals as well as of teams in international, test and English
county matches. The statistical appendix includes detailed records of each test
match played by the West Indies from 1928 to 1979, a list of every West Indian
to have played in a test match and other records. The author has close ties with
the West Indies and is a contributor to the West Indian press.

1074 **Sport in Jamaica.**
Jamaica Information Service. Kingston: Jamaica
Information Service, [1966]. [20]p. (Face of Jamaica, 8).

An illustrated outline of the development of various forms of sport in Jamaica
and of the accomplishments of some outstanding sportsmen, including a brief
statement of government measures to promote sport. Appended is a list of autono-
mous bodies which control sport in Jamaica.

1075 **A brief historical survey of the British West Indies at
Bisley, 1902-1950.** Robert Johnstone. Trinidad: Government Printing Office,
1951. 53p.

Includes information on joint West Indian rifle shooting teams as well as Jamaican teams only, giving names of team members, scores and other data relative to
performances.

1076 **History of the inter-secondary schools championship sports,
1910-1970.** Sir Herbert MacDonald, compiler. Kingston: [1970?].
1 vol. (unpaged).

An interesting compilation, copiously illustrated, on the once most popular and
highly esteemed of sporting events. It records the sporting achievements of many
who later have occupied a prominent place in public and sporting life.

1077 **History of the inter-secondary schools football competitions,
1909-1973.** Compiled, edited and published by Sir Herbert
MacDonald. Kingston: (Stephenson's Litho Press), [1973?].
208p.

An illustrated record of teams, individuals and events, recording the achievements
of many who later have occupied a prominent place in public and sporting life.

Sport and Recreation

1078 Land of sprinters and dreamers.
Kenny Moore. *Sunday Gleaner* (3 April 1983), P. 8, 20.
reprinted from *Sports Illustrated* (14 Feb. 1983).

An account of Jamaica's accomplishments in international track athletics during the last forty years, based in part on interviews with some athletes such as Herb McKenley, Arthur Wint and Mel Spence.

1079 A history of West Indies cricket.
Gordon Ross. London: Arthur Barker, 1976. 175p.

A compact account.

1080 With rod and line in Jamaica.
A. F. Strachan. London: T. Werner Laurie, [1910]. 78, [15]p.

A guide to angling with information on equipment, baits and locales most suitable for the various types of river fish to be found in Jamaica.

1081 Herb McKenley, Olympic star.
Errol Townshend, Jimmy [James A.] Carnegie, Herb McKenley. Kingston: Institute of Jamaica, 1974. 97p. (Jamaicans of Distinction).

A life of one of Jamaica's champion athletes and hero of the 1952 Helsinki Olympic Games. This book contains much information on other contemporary Jamaican track stars with appendices, compiled by Richard Ashenheim, track and field statistician, of Jamaica's performances at various international games from 1930 to 1972.

Libraries, Archives and Information Systems

General

1082 Jamaican National Bibliography.
S[amuel] B. Bandara. *International Library Review,* vol. 13, no. 3 (July 1981), p. 311-21. bibliog.

An account of the *Jamaican National Bibliography* first published in 1975 and of its antecedents, with a critical look at its effectiveness as a national bibliography. The author is a librarian on the staff of the University of the West Indies Library, Mona, Jamaica.

1083 Private and subscription libraries in Jamaica before 1879.
Hazel Bennett. *Journal of Library History* (USA), vol. 3, no. 3 (July 1968), p. 242-49.

An exploratory foray into a little-known field.

1084 Jenkinson and Jamaica.
Clinton V. Black. In: *Essays in memory of Sir Hilary Jenkinson.* Edited for the Society of Archivists by Albert E. J. Hollaender. (Chichester, England: printed by Moore and Tillyer) 1962, p. 154-66.

Basing his discussion on the significance of the survey of the archives of Jamaica made by Sir Hilary Jenkinson in 1950 and on his report thereon, the author reviews the archives, archive administration and legislation of Jamaica, concluding that Jamaica's role of leadership in the archives field in the Caribbean 'owes a great deal to the work Jenkinson did in Jamaica, and the developments which flowed, with time, from his Scheme.' (p. 166).

1085 Our archives: six broadcast talks.
Clinton V. Black. Kingston: printed by the Government Printer, 1962. 28p.

The main purpose of these talks, by the Government Archivist, directed to a wide audience, was to stimulate an interest in archives and in the 'priceless national heritage' which Jamaica possesses in its archives.

1086 Early circulating libraries in Jamaica.
Roderick Cave. *Libri*, vol. 30, no. 1 (March 1980), p. 53-65.

This work complements an earlier study by Hazel Bennett on the development of private and subscription libraries in Jamaica before 1879.

1087 Consultation on the co-ordinated development of national information systems in the Caribbean region, Kingston, Jamaica, 19-23 May 1980. Final report and recommendations.
Paris: UNESCO, July 1980. 32p. (PGI - 80/WS/20).

This consultation of 18 participants drawn from 16 countries of the Caribbean met to consider priorities for national information development and the modes of implementation. Although focused on the particular needs of the lesser developed countries of the region it contains much that is relevant to the Jamaican situation.

1088 Library work in Jamaica.
Frank Cundall. *Transactions and Proceedings of the Second International Library Conference*, London, 13-16 July 1897, p. 173-78.

Perhaps the first account of the development of libraries in Jamaica, it remains basic to later research on this subject. This article was reproduced separately and issued as a memento on the occasion of the opening of the new library school building for the Department of Library Studies, University of the West Indies, Jamaica, 22 March 1973.

1089 Jamaica: library development.
J. P. Danton. Paris: UNESCO, 1968. 56p.

This is a photographic reproduction of the original manuscript produced for limited distribution (Serial no. 885/BMS.RD/DBA/DND). It is a brief, factual report on library development in Jamaica based on a survey carried out from June to September 1968, with a summary of principal recommendations.

Libraries, Archives and Information Systems. General

1090 **Directorio regional de unidades de información para el desarollo. (Regional directory of development information units.)**
Santiago de Chile: Naciones Unidas, CEPAL/CLADES, 1979. 3 vols.

A bilingual publication containing basic information on the holdings and services of approximately 800 libraries and documentation centres which serve experts in economic and social development in Latin America and the Caribbean. The data were collected between 1976 and 1978 by the Latin American Centre for Economic and Social Documentation (CLADES) of CEPAL (Comisión Económica Para América Latina). Volume two, p. 655-93, lists 30 units of information in Jamaica. Volume three consists of a number of indices to the publication.

1091 **The Institute's West India Reference Library from WIRL to NLJ.**
Patricia Dunn. *Jamaica Library Association Bulletin* (1979-80), p. 13-16. bibliog.

A brief account of the establishment and growth of the West India Reference Library of the Institute of Jamaica and of its collections up to April 1979 when it became the National Library of Jamaica. The author is a librarian and a former member of staff of the West India Reference Library.

1092 **A description of the role of the Schools Library Service in the development and promotion of school libraries in Kingston, Jamaica, West Indies.**
Annette K. Eng. Brookville, New York: 1970. 82 leaves. map. bibliog.

This was originally an MS thesis for Long Island University. Data were gathered by the author from the unpublished quarterly, biyearly and annual reports of the service during a visit to Jamaica. Many of the findings of this work still remain relevant.

1093 **National primary socio-economic data structures. IX: Barbados, Jamaica, Trinidad and Tobago.**
J. E. Greene, Reive Robb. *International Social Science Journal*, vol. 33, no. 2 (1981), p. 393-414. bibliog.

A concise and informative outline of the development of the major producers of socio-economic data in the three countries mentioned, the processes of dissemination of information, regional and international linkages and the inadequacies of the systems. It is useful as a source of information on the individual countries mentioned as well as for its comparative treatment of them and is particularly helpful on the role of the University of the West Indies as a producer of primary socio-economic data.

1094 The Library of the University College.
H. Holdsworth. *West Indian Medical Journal*, vol. 2, no. 1 (March 1953), p. 81-84.

A description, illustrated with photographs, of the library building occupied in May 1952, with brief indications of its collections and services, written by the first Librarian of the University College of the West Indies, who was responsible for planning the library building.

1095 Libraries and the challenge of change: papers of the International Library Conference held in Kingston, Jamaica, 24-29 April 1972.
Edited by K. E. Ingram, Albertina A. Jefferson. London: Mansell Information/Publishing for the Jamaica Library Association and the Jamaica Library Service, 1975. 266p.

The plan of the programme was to invite a panel of experts from outside the Caribbean to present papers dealing with general aspects of the various topics of librarianship chosen as the subjects of sessions and then to have a counterpart from the Caribbean treat the same topics with particular reference to the Caribbean area. Among the latter group of topics were papers on public, national, university and special libraries in the Caribbean, as well as on libraries for youth, library education and co-operation, all of which draw heavily on experience in Jamaica; also a paper on a national library development plan for Jamaica. Papers are reproduced in full, discussions are summarized and the text of resolutions and a list of participants round off the volume. This was the first international library conference to be held in Jamaica.

1096 A report on the archives of Jamaica.
Sir Hilary Jenkinson. Kingston: Government Printer, 1950; reprinted 1957. 28, [3]p.

A survey of public, semi-public, private and ecclesiastical archives in Jamaica, with recommendations of practical measures and policy for immediate implementation and long-term planning. This report laid the foundations of modern archive administration in Jamaica.

1097 The development of library service in the West Indies through interlibrary cooperation.
Alma Theodora Jordan. Metuchen, New Jersey: Scarecrow Press, 1970. 433p. bibliog. 6 maps.

A comprehensive survey of libraries done in 1960 and originally presented as a PhD dissertation to the University of Columbia School of Library Service. Chapter IV (p. 47-62) is devoted exclusively to Jamaica.

1098 The state of science and technology information systems in Jamaica.

Ouida Lewis. In: *Science communication in the Caribbean: a report of a workshop*. Edited by Victor Forsythe. London: Commonwealth Science Council, 1977, p. 27.1-27.5.

An outline of systems and services offered by some 84 STI (Science and Technical Information) collections, with a directory of addresses of the 10 most tightly organized such collections.

1099 Health information needs in the Commonwealth Caribbean: proceedings of a workshop held at the Medical Library, University of the West Indies, Mona, Jamaica, January 11-15, 1982.

Edited by Lakshmi Mansingh. Mona, Jamaica: Medical Learning Resources Unit, Faculty of Medicine, University of the West Indies, [1982]. 84p.

Includes a background paper entitled 'Growth and organization of health care, research, education and literature and trends and needs in the information retrieval system in the Commonwealth Caribbean', by Laxmi Mansingh. The individual sessions dealt in detail with various aspects of the general topic. The proceedings of the workshop embraced the theoretical as well as the practical components of planning for the health information needs of the Commonwealth Caribbean. The workshop was sponsored by the Library and the Faculty of Medicine of the University of the West Indies, Kingston, Jamaica.

1100 A history of the library of the University of the West Indies (1948 to 1966).

Sylvia G. Moss. Tylers Green, High Wycombe, England: University Microfilms, 1969. 156p. bibliog.

The only comprehensive historical study of the University Library, comprising the main libraries of the Jamaica, Trinidad and Barbados campuses of the University, albeit only up to the end of the academic year 1965-66, based on the official files of the Library and on the personal observation of the author who was chief cataloguer at the Cave Hill campus library in Barbados. Submitted to the Library Association in fulfilment of the requirements for the Fellowship of the Library Association, February 1969.

1101 Directory of information units in Jamaica: libraries, archives and documentation services.

National Council on Libraries, Archives and Documentation Services (NACOLADS). Kingston: National Council on Libraries, 1980. 177p.

Based on a wide-ranging survey of information units carried out by means of questionnaires and by personal visits to organizations by the Librarian/Researcher of the National Council, this directory provides information on 151 information units, comprising the National Library, public libraries, libraries of educational institutions, special libraries, and libraries and other information units of public and private sector organizations. Information on each unit is presented under 14

possible heads and all entries in the directory have been approved by the respond-
ing units.

1102 **Plan for a national documentation, information and library system for Jamaica.**
    Prepared by the National Council on Libraries, Archives and Documentation Services (NACOLADS). Kingston: National Council on Libraries, 1978. 83p.

At head of title: Office of the Prime Minister. The contents include: Letter of transmission; Plan... Principal recommendations; Reports of the working parties.

1103 **Regional seminar on copyright for English-speaking Caribbean States, Kingston, Jamaica, 19-23 October 1981: report and recommendations.**
    Copyright Bulletin: Quarterly Review, vol. 16, no. 1-2 (1982), p. 71-75.

The Government of Jamaica hosted the seminar and participated in formulating the recommendations. A list of participants is annexed.

1104 **Directory of Jamaican libraries. Part 1.**
    Compiled by Judith E. Richards (for the Jamaica Library Association Research & Publications Working Party). Kingston: Jamaica Library Association, 1967. 99p.

Part one gives basic library directory information for the major library systems, that is, the Jamaica Library Service and the University of the West Indies Library and for government departmental libraries however small. Part two, which was planned to cover school, college, business and technical libraries, was never published.

1105 **The West India Reference Library of the Institute of Jamaica.**
    Glory Robertson. *Jamaica Journal*, vol. 6, no. 1 (March 1972), p. 15-20.

Brief as this sketch is, with the aid of a few well-chosen illustrations, it gives a good idea of the nature of the West India Reference Library (now the National Library of Jamaica), the character of its contents, its functions and its problems.

1106 **Jamaica, Libraries in.**
    Joyce L. Robinson. In: *Encyclopedia of library and information science*, vol. 13. Edited by A. Kent et al. New York: Dekker, 1975, p. 169-205. bibliog.

An historical and factual survey of libraries mentioning holdings, services, publications and organization, with particular reference to the growth of public libraries in Jamaica. The author is a former director of the public and school library service of Jamaica.

1107 Library planning in Jamaica.
Joyce L. Robinson. *Bowker Annual of Library & Book Trade Information*, 20th ed., 1975, p. 355-60.

This report, adapted from an address to the IFLA (International Federation of Library Associations) conference in Washington, DC, November 1974, reflects many of the concerns and policies which have influenced national and public library planning in Jamaica during the last twenty years. The author is a former Director of the Jamaica Library Service and is chairman of the National Council on Libraries, Archives and Documentation Services.

1108 Jamaica Library Service: 21 years of progress in pictures, 1948-1969.
[Cynthia M. Warmington, Joyce L. Robinson, Rosalind A. McLaughlin]. Kingston: Jamaica Library Service, 1972. 376p.

A pictorial record of all aspects of the island's public library service. The Jamaica Library Service comprised at the time of writing, the headquarters in Kingston and a network of 13 parish libraries, 46 branch libraries, 139 book centres and 64 bookmobile stops. The pictures have been reproduced from the Jamaica Library Service's picture collection and are of considerable historical interest for the development of libraries in Jamaica. The captions are detailed and frequently identify by name persons in group pictures.

Periodicals

1109 Jamaica Library Association Bulletin.
Kingston: Jamaica Library Association, 1950- . approximately annual.

Provides information on activities of the Association as well as carrying articles on topics of professional interest.

Books, Book Production and the Book Trade

1110 **Educational publishing and book production in the English-speaking Caribbean.**

Alvona Alleyne, Pamela Mordecai. *Library Trends*, vol. 26, no. 4 (spring 1978), p. 575-89. bibliog.

A summary view of educational publishing at all levels in the English-speaking Caribbean, particularly in Guyana, Jamaica and Trinidad, with the exception of the publication of literary materials.

1111 **The Institute of Jamaica and publishing.**

Wenty Bowen. *Jamaica Library Association Bulletin* (1975), p. 11-12, 15.

A short account of the Institute's venture into the field of publishing for a more popular and less specialist audience than it had catered for in the past.

1112 **Printing in eighteenth-century Jamaica.**

Roderick Cave. *The Library*, 5th ser., vol. 33, no. 3 (Sept. 1978), p. 187-206.

A succinct and carefully researched paper, with fresh information on the press, printers and publications of 18th-century Jamaica. Appendix two is 'A handlist of eighteenth-century Jamaican subscription proposals and publications not in Cundall or Ingram.' The author was formerly Senior Lecturer in the Department of Library Studies, University of the West Indies.

Books, Book Production and the Book Trade

1113 **A history of printing in Jamaica from 1717 to 1834.**
Frank Cundall. Kingston: Institute of Jamaica, 1935. 63p.

The only work of its kind for the period up to the end of slavery. It consists of a short discursive section followed by brief biographical sketches of printers and a list of publications in various forms during the period covered. Reprinted from the centenary number of the *Gleaner*, 13 September 1934.

1114 **Directory of publishers, printers & booksellers in the Caribbean Community.**
[Compiled by] I. Dianand, [edited by] C. Collins.
Georgetown, Guyana: Information and Documentation Section, Caribbean Community Secretariat, 1980.

Directory divided into three sections, viz: - Publishers, Printers, Booksellers - and arranged alphabetically by names of firms within each section, listing information such as address, telephone number, name of director, ownership, type of enterprise, date established, type of equipment, size of plant, areas of specialization, size of stock, as appropriate. A country listing at the end provides an alphabetical listing by name of firm for each of the 3 categories included. Under Jamaica 16 publishers, 13 printers and 4 booksellers are listed.

1115 **Book production in Jamaica: a list of Jamaican publications.**
Compiled by the Jamaica Library Service. Kingston: [Jamaica Library Service], 1979. 83p.

A list of books published in Jamaica compiled from information obtained by a questionnaire sent to a number of organizations and publishers, selected mainly on the basis that they appeared as publishers in the 1976 annual edition of the *Jamaican National Bibliography*. Consequently, organizations which published nothing in 1976 were excluded, as also were authors acting as their own publishers. The list is restricted solely to book publishing and is arranged by publishers and title, with an index. The list includes for each title the number of copies printed, the movement of prices, if any, since publication and the level of reader for which the work is intended. Produced for a Seminar/Workshop on Book Production in the Caribbean, Kingston, 15-24 November 1978, as part of the 30th anniversary celebrations of the Jamaica Library Service.

1116 **The first printing in Jamaica... with a discussion of the date of the first establishment of a press on the Island by Robert Baldwin. With a facsimile of the earliest extant Jamaican imprint, the second edition of the *Pindarique Ode*, the only known copy of which is preserved in Chetham's Library, Manchester, England.**
Douglas C. McMurtrie. Evanston, Illinois: privately printed, 1942. 7, [5]p.

Provides a valuable corrective to Frank Cundall's dating of the first printing in Jamaica as 28 May 1717, stating that according to modern reckoning the date was 28 May 1718.

1117 **Early Jamaican printing.**
Glory Robertson. *Jamaica Journal*, vol. 3, no. 4 (Dec. 1969), p. 7-11.

Illustrations of early specimens of Jamaican printing, i.e. from 1718 to 1794, with a brief commentary, being a selection from an exhibition mounted by the Institute of Jamaica for National Heritage Week, 1969.

1118 **The spread of printing: western hemisphere: the Caribbean area.**
Bradford F. Swan. London: Routledge & Kegan Paul; New York: Abner Schram, 1970. 47p. bibliog.

Summarizes the more important dates and events in the spread of printing in the Caribbean area, including a short section on Jamaica, by a scholar and bibliographer.

Mass Media

General

1119 Communication and politics in Jamaica.
Mervyn Alleyne. *Caribbean Studies*, vol. 3, no. 2 (July 1963), p. 22-61.

An examination of the language situation in Jamaica, its effect on the political process, the operation of the communication media and their specific role in politics. The bulk of the observational research was carried out in the weeks prior to the general elections on 10 April 1962, by which representatives to the first parliament of an independent Jamaica were chosen. The author is now a professor and Head of the Language Laboratory, University of the West Indies, Jamaica.

1120 The mass media of communications and socialist change in the Caribbean: a case study of Jamaica.
Aggrey Brown. *Caribbean Quarterly*, vol. 22, no. 4 (Dec. 1976), p. 43-49.

An examination of the ownership structure of the media and their functions with a view to understanding their impact on the prevailing distribution and use of power in the Jamaican society. This is a slightly modified version of an article which first appeared in Carl Stone and Aggrey Brown's *Essays on power and change in Jamaica* (Jan. 1976).

1121 Mass media in national development: governmental perspectives in Jamaica and Guyana.
Marlene Cuthbert. *Caribbean Quarterly*, vol. 23, no. 4 (Dec. 1977), p. 90-105. bibliog.

Reviews the stated policies of government leaders and suggests models which may accommodate these views.

1122 **Some observations on the role of mass media in the recent socio-political development in Jamaica.**
Marlene Cuthbert. *Caribbean Quarterly*, vol. 22, no. 4 (Dec. 1976), p. 50-58. bibliog.

Outlines the content and ownership of the Jamaican media and their suggested role under the government's 'democratic socialist' programme.

1123 **The Jamaican press, 1789-1865.**
H. P. Jacobs. *Jamaica Journal*, vol. 6, no. 3 (Sept. 1972), p. 2-6.

An historical sketch which concentrates on the character of the information likely to be found in the Jamaican press during the period covered, with numerous illustrations cited. The author is a journalist and historian.

1124 **Third World mass media and their search for modernity: the case of Commonwealth Caribbean, 1717-1976.**
John A. Lent. Lewisburg, Pennsylvania: Bucknell University Press; London: Associated University Presses, 1977. 405p. map. bibliog.

This study examines the historical, cultural, economic and political aspects of Commonwealth Caribbean mass media, printed and electronic, from the appearance of the first newspaper in 1718 until 1972. Data for the study were collected by visits to the major islands in the area in 1970 and 1971 and the manuscript was updated on the basis of interviews conducted in January 1976 in Jamaica, Barbados and St. Lucia, the more recent information being given in footnotes. It is a well-documented study including chapters on mass media ownership, content, production and consumption and press freedom. It contains a great deal of information on the mass media in Jamaica. Particularly noteworthy are the list of newspapers in the Commonwealth Caribbean and the bibliography, both of which are subdivided by the names of countries in the region. The author was Professor of Communications at Temple University.

1125 **Development of the documentary film in Jamaica.**
M. A. Rennalls. MS Thesis: Boston University, School of Public Communication, Division of Broadcasting and Film, November 1967. 199 leaves. bibliog.

A lucid and informative account of the development of documentary film in Jamaica from its introduction in 1938 for educational purposes up to the year 1966, by one who was closely associated with that development from its early beginnings. The last three chapters evaluate what has been accomplished and make recommendations for future development with special reference to the development of a Jamaican style of film production.

1126 **Spanish American independence in the Jamaican press, 1808-25: a survey.**
Bruce B. Solnick. *Journal of Caribbean History*, vol. 17 (1982), p. 14-25. bibliog.

A view of the early 19th-century Jamaican press, its concerns and its accounts of the struggles of Spain's New World colonies' fight for independence and its reflection of the Jamaican response to these events. The author is an Associate Professor of History at the State University of New York, Albany.

1127 **Ideology, public opinion and the media in Jamaica.**
Carl Stone. *Caribbean Issues*, vol. 4, no. 2 (Aug. 1978), p. 53-70.

An examination of the impact of the mass media on public opinion in Jamaica, with reference to specific ideological issues which have much exercised the public there recently, namely, communism, the presence of Cubans in Jamaica, foreign investment and attribution of responsibility for the deterioration of economic and social conditions in the country.

1128 **The press and the law in the Caribbean: part two of the report on the workshop on Caribbean women in communication for development, UWI, Mona Campus, Jamaica, June 13-15, 1975.**
Dorcas White. Bridgetown, Jamaica: Cedar Press, 1977. 70p. bibliog.

Discusses laws relating to setting up a newspaper, libel and the publication of official information, with reference to Jamaica and elsewhere in the Commonwealth Caribbean.

Appeals by Jamaican political parties: a study of newspaper advertisements in the 1972 Jamaican general election campaign.
See item no. 410.

Periodicals

1129 **PAJ News: monthly organ of the Press Association of Jamaica.**
Kingston: Press Association of Jamaica, 1976- . monthly.

Includes items on all forms of mass media of Jamaica, as well as news and views of the Press Association of Jamaica. Likely to be especially useful to anyone studying the political events of the latter half of the 1970s in Jamaica.

1130 **Press, Radio and TV.**
Kingston: Press Association of Jamaica, [1969]- . annual. 20p.

Includes news and photographs of public media events in Jamaica, including an article on the Gleaner Company's new building. Formerly published as *Press & Radio*, the 25th anniversary issue, 1968.

General Periodicals

1131 **Caribbean Insight.**
London: Publications Division of the West India Committee, 1978- . monthly.

In addition to brief feature articles on notable events in the area, this publication provides crisp up-to-the-minute reporting on public affairs and on social, economic and political happenings in the Caribbean under the names of the individual countries and territories.

1132 **Caribbean Quarterly.**
Mona, Jamaica: Extra-Mural Department, University of the West Indies, April-June 1949- . quarterly.

The aim of this general publication is to foster the knowledge and study of the culture, history and social development of the West Indies. Current developments receive a notable amount of attention and in recent years whole issues have been devoted to a single theme or subject, such as 'Race,' 'Social change,' 'Caribbean writing,' 'Religion.' Includes book reviews and creative writing.

1133 **The Daily Gleaner.**
Kingston: Gleaner Co., 1834- . daily.

Founded in 1834. It provides good coverage of local and international news together with editorial comment, correspondence, contributed articles and advertisements. The Sunday edition appears under the title *The Sunday Gleaner*. A weekly publication entitled *The Jamaican Weekly Gleaner*, comprising a selection of items from the previous week's issues, is distributed overseas in a North American edition and a European edition.

1134 **Jamaica Inter Com: the people to people magazine.**
Kingston: Inter Com Publishers, 1974- . quarterly. (with annual supplement).

Features short articles and items of news and views under the headings: Business, education, agriculture, sport and family. Illustrated.

1135 Jamaica Journal.

Kingston: Institute of Jamaica, (vol. 1-) 1967- . quarterly.

Articles of scholarly and general interest explore the diversity of Jamaica's culture in the fields of history, literature, science, art and music. The publication observes a high standard of production and occasionally has colour reproductions of works of art. Between 1978 and 1982 the journal dropped the original volume numbering and appeared twice yearly. In 1982 it resumed quarterly publication as volume 16.

1136 Jamaica News.

Edited, printed and published in Ottawa as a newsletter for the Jamaican Embassy, Washington, DC; the Jamaican High Commission, Ottawa; and the Jamaican Consulates in Miami, Toronto and New York. March 1982- . frequency not stated.

This publication is edited by the Information Attaché to Canada with the assistance of reports from the Jamaican Information Attachés at New York and Washington. Beginning with this issue one newsletter will serve North America where previously each office had issued a separate newsletter, the publication issued by the Embassy of Jamaica, Washington, having been entitled *Jamaica Newsletter*. The superseded publication carried current news and reports on Jamaica's international relations and appeared every two months. The new publication emphasizes Jamaican news likely to be of interest to Jamaicans abroad as well as news about Jamaican nationals resident abroad.

1137 Prostand.

Kingston: Professional Societies Association in Jamaica, (vol. 1, no. 1) 1979- . quarterly.

The official publication of the Association.

1138 Sky Writings: Air Jamaica's inflight magazine.

Kingston: Creative Communications Inc. for Air Jamaica, [1972?]-. quarterly.

A colourfully illustrated periodical containing articles on subjects of historical, cultural and topical interest and other features likely to be of interest to visitors to Jamaica. Occasionally includes articles on recent developments in Air Jamaica's services.

General Directories and Handbooks

1139 **Reference book of Jamaica.**

Edited and published by Wyatt Bryce. [Kingston]: published by the editor, [1946?]. 404p. map. bibliog.

This was one of the most comprehensive directories of its day, including a substantial amount of information on business, banking, tourism, art and culture, as well as general and historical background information. Although no longer useful as a ready reference tool it is of historical interest. Amendments to the general and historical sections mainly, appeared as a supplementary work, arranged to give the completeness of a separate publication under the title *The Pocket reference book of Jamaica* (1958).

1140 **Caribbean directory of human resources in social development. Directorio caribeno de recursos humanos en areas de desarollo social.**

San Juan, Puerto Rico: Association of Caribbean Universities and Research Institutes, 1977. 186p.

Includes directory information, mainly obtained in June 1976, on persons and organizations in 24 Caribbean countries, relating to the following subjects: agriculture, Caribbean thought, community health, crime and violence, documentation and dissemination, economic development, education, fisheries, housing, labour, population policies, social development and planning, tourism. The section on Jamaica occupies p. 54-70.

1141 **Official handbook, Jamaica, 1971.**

Jamaica: Jamaica Information Services, [n.d.]. 460p. 2 maps. bibliog.

The most recent in a series begun in 1881 as *The Handbook of Jamaica* and appearing annually up to 1967, except for a break during the years 1940 to 1946. It provides factual and statistical information on the nation generally and on the public sector in particular.

General Directories and Handbooks

1142 **The Caribbean Yearbook, 1979/80 -**
   Edited by Colin Rickards.   Toronto: Caribrook, 1980- .
   annual.

The 50th edition of this work which was known as *The West Indies and Carib-bean Yearbook* from 1953-54 to 1977, prior to that as *The West Indies Year-book*, 1936-48, and prior to 1935 as *Yearbook of the West Indies and the Countries of the Caribbean*, 1926-27 to 1935. It is a useful compilation of facts, supplied on a year round basis, by many individuals. Much of the information originates from government agencies and is provided by the managers of the Royal Bank of Canada in the various countries of the Caribbean. The initial chapters relate to regional organizations, the rest of the text being arranged alphabetically by name of country or territory. The chapter on Jamaica in the latest volume examined has a map and sections on history, topography, climate, population, political geography, government, public and social services, public uti-lities, communications, natural resources, industries, finance, trade and commerce, travel and tourist information, diplomatic and consular offices, newspapers and periodicals and a business directory.

1143 **Commonwealth Caribbean directory of aid agencies:**
   charities, trusts, foundations and official bodies offering
   assistance in Commonwealth countries in the Caribbean
   region.
   Consultant editor Norman Tett, assistant editor Ronald
   Macfarlane.   London: Commonwealth Foundation, 1978.
   128p. map. bibliog.

A handbook of technical assistance, excluding capital aid, offered by organiza-tions known to be interested in the Caribbean. Included are a few scholarship award and study grant schemes open to nationals of all countries, where they are considered of special relevance to the Caribbean. Among items of information given for each organization is one on 'Relevant activities'. This frequently includes concise information on projects in specific countries of the Caribbean.

Bibliographies

General

1144 Family life education publications in the Caribbean: the report of a study and an annotated bibliography on publications for family life education in the Caribbean.
Michael H. Alleyne. [Bogotá]: CRESALC, 1980. 66p.

Includes a number of detailed annotated entries for Jamaican publications relating to the subject. The author is a member of the Board of Directors of CRE-SALC, the Spanish acronym for Regional Committee on Family Life and Sex Education for Latin America and the Caribbean, created in 1976 with funds from the Swedish International Development Authority.

1145 West Indian literature: an index to criticism, 1930-1975.
Jeannette B. Allis. Boston, Massachusetts: G. K. Hall, 1981. 353p.

A valuable key to critical writings on the literature of the Commonwealth Caribbean which have appeared in some 80 periodicals, newspapers and collections of essays published in and outside the West Indies. Access is provided by an index of authors, an index of critics and reviewers and an index of articles, with full citations. Appended is a list of books on West Indian literature. The author is Documents Librarian at the Public Library in St. Thomas, US Virgin Islands. The work is a modified version of part of a thesis toward the degree of Master of Philosophy submitted to the University of the West Indies.

1146 Theses on Caribbean topics 1778-1968.
Compiled by Enid M. Baa. San Juan, Puerto Rico: Institute of Caribbean Studies with the University of Puerto Rico, 1970. 146p.

Lists 1,242 theses of which the geographical index of countries studied indicates that 140 pertain to Jamaica. Subject and chronological indices and an index of universities (by country) are also appended.

294

1147 Root crop investigation in the Caribbean: a bibliography.
Glenys Barker. [St. Augustine, Trinidad]: Caribbean
Agricultural Research and Development Institute (CARDI),
1981. 33p.

A compilation of references on various aspects of the work done on root crops in the Caribbean region with particular reference to agronomy, economics, marketing and processing. There is an appendix of local names of fruits and vegetables in the English-speaking Caribbean (CFNI) 1971. CARDI is a regional organization serving twelve member states of the Caribbean Community. It provides for the research and development needs of the agricultural sector in the region, as identified in national plans and policies.

1148 Caribbean films.
Valerie Bloomfield. *Journal of Librarianship*, vol. 9, no. 4
(Oct. 1977), p. 278-314. bibliog.

This article traces the development of documentary and feature film production in the Commonwealth Caribbean. The types of film listed include documentaries, sponsored films, independent productions, educational films, television films, feature films on 16 and/or 35 mm. film in reels, film strips or slides. The films cover a wide range of cultural, economic and social interests. The 'Select filmography' (p. 293-314) lists some 28 films, in various formats, relating specifically to Jamaica or made in Jamaica, as well as a number of other general films on the West Indies which draw on the Jamaican experience. The author was Librarian of the Institute of Commonwealth Studies, University of London, during which period she made three acquisition trips to the Caribbean.

1149 Caribbean recordings: notes on sources with a select discography.
Valerie Bloomfield. *Journal of Librarianship*, vol. 8, no. 1
(Jan. 1976), p. 47-72. bibliog.

This article investigates the range of sound recordings, available for the study of the non-Hispanic Caribbean, describing institutional collections, identifying musical forms, surveying record guides and other sources and concluding with a select discography (p. 62-66). Some twenty recordings relate specifically to Jamaica in addition to a number of other items of general Caribbean interest which draw upon the Jamaican experience or which were recorded in Jamaica. Musical forms and types represented include folk music, cult and religious music, dance music, calypso and steel band music, reggae, ska and rock steady. There is also a short listing of poetry recordings. The author was Librarian of the Institute of Commonwealth Studies, University of London, during which time she made three acquisition trips to the Caribbean.

1150 Jamaica poetry, a checklist: books, pamphlets, broadsheets, 1686-1978.
Edward Kamau Brathwaite. Kingston: Jamaica Library
Service, 1979. 36p.

A valuable checklist of 376 publications, grouped in three divisions reflecting the development of the country from slavery through colonial dependence to greater national awareness. Each of the three divisions is prefaced by a brief commentary and there are occasional bio-bibliographical notes for some titles. The work was compiled to mark the thirtieth anniversary of the Jamaica Library Service, 1948-78, whose director, Leila Thomas, writes the foreword.

1151 **Our ancestral heritage; a bibliography of the English-speaking Caribbean designed to record and celebrate the several origins of our structural, material and creative culture and to indicate how this is being used by us to mek ah-we.**

Compiled by Edward Kamau Brathwaite for the Literary Committee of Carifesta '76. Kingston: Literary Committee of Carifesta '76, 1976. Reprinted Savacou, 1977. 194p.

Although this work is only a first draft edition of but part of the original project which is still to be completed, its arrangement, the selection of material described and the occasional annotations form a useful interpretative record of the culture of the English-speaking Caribbean.

1152 **The complete Caribbeana 1900-1975: a bibliographic guide to the scholarly literature.**

Lambros Comitas. Millwood, New York: KTO Press, a US division of Kraus-Thompson Organization, 1977. 4 vols. end-paper maps.

The most comprehensive bibliography of post-1900 Caribbeana, prepared under the auspices of the Research Institute For the Study of Man. The work concentrates on publications dealing with the mainland and insular possessions, or former possessions, of Great Britain, France, the Netherlands and the United States in the Caribbean region. It excludes Haiti, Cuba, Puerto Rico and the Dominican Republic. The organization of the material is topical or subject-oriented rather than geographical, favouring specificity over generality in the choice and number of topical chapters. The collection contains over 17,000 references to authored publications which were physically located and verified. The contents include: volume one, People (chapters 1-18); volume two, Institutions (chapters 19-40); volume three, Resources (chapters 41-63); volume four, Indices (including author and geographical indices). The geographical index indicates some 2,800 references to Jamaica. A code to geographical units allows each entry to be coded so as to identify the geographical unit(s) to which it refers.

1153 **Theses on the Commonwealth Caribbean, 1891-1973.**

Compiled by the Commonwealth Caribbean Resource Centre. London, Ontario: Office of International Education, University of Western Ontario, [1974?]. 136p.

Lists 837 theses submitted in Britain, Canada, France and the United States, of which the 'geographical index of countries studied' indicates that 203 relate to Jamaica.

1154 **Bibliographia jamaicensis: a list of Jamaica books and pamphlets, magazine articles, newspapers, and maps, most of which are in the Library of the Institute of Jamaica.**
Frank Cundall. Kingston: Institute of Jamaica, [1902]. 83p.

The author, who was Secretary and Librarian of the Institute of Jamaica, described the work more as a series of notes for a bibliography than a complete bibliography itself on the grounds that the titles had been shortened in some instances and other bibliographical details such as names of publishers and pagination omitted, and also because works which treated on the West Indies generally had been omitted except in a few instances where they dealt chiefly with Jamaica. Nevertheless, the work remains the chief bibliographical standby for works on Jamaica published up to that date, having been based on what was, and remains, the principal collection of books and related materials on Jamaica. *A supplement to Bibliographia jamaicensis*, by the same author, was published by the Institute of Jamaica in 1908 and, in like manner, *Bibliography of the West Indies (excluding Jamaica)* appeared in 1909. Notwithstanding the title of the latter work it supplements Cundall's original bibliography of Jamaica in some of its sections such as those which deal generally with the West Indies, slavery, buccaneers and parliamentary papers.

1155 **A guide to Jamaican reference material in the West India Reference Library.**
Rae Delattre. Kingston: Institute of Jamaica, 1965. 76p.

An annotated bibliography of reference works comprising bibliographies, directories, guides, handbooks, yearbooks of various forms of published material and of various subjects relating to the Caribbean area in general, or to Jamaica in particular, with author and title indices.

1156 **A directory of major statistical publications.**
Port-of-Spain: United Nations Economic Commission for Latin America, Office for the Caribbean, Caribbean Development and Co-operative Committee, 1981. 23p. (CEPAL/CARIB 81/2).

Lists the major statistical serials of the Caribbean under 10 topical headings of socio-economic interest, ranging from agriculture to tourism. Each topical heading is subdivided geographically by name of country. Some 28 titles relating to Jamaica are listed under various headings.

1157 **An annotated bibliography of agricultural development in Jamaica.**
Compiled by Frank A. Erickson, with assistance from Elizabeth B. Erickson. Washington, DC: Rural Development Division, Bureau for Latin America and the Caribbean, Agency for International Development, 1979. 197p. (Working Document Series).

This bibliography covers selected aspects of agricultural development in Jamaica, mainly for the period starting from 1962, and is based on searches made in the United States and Jamaica. Locations are given in some instances. The titles listed are of more general than narrowly technical interest, including several of general economic interest. Descriptive rather than critical annotations are given for some, not all entries. The compilers were attached to the Development Planning Group, Organization for International Cooperation and Development, US Department of Agriculture.

1158 **Caribbean writers: a bio-bibliographical-critical encyclopedia.**
[Edited by] Donald E. Herdeck, associate editors Maurice A. Lubin, John Figueroa, Dorothy Alexander Figueroa, José Alcántara Almánazar. Washington, DC: Three Continents Press, 1979. 943p. end-paper map. bibliog.

A comprehensive survey, containing biographical information on some 2,000 creative writers and bibliographical information on more than 15,000 works. The work is arranged in four major divisions embracing anglophone, francophone, Netherlands Antillean and Spanish-language literatures of the Caribbean. Some 180 Jamaican writers are included in the anglophone section which provides a biographical sketch, literary criticism and a fairly detailed bibliography for each author.

1159 **Manuscripts relating to Commonwealth Caribbean countries in United States and Canadian repositories.**
K. E. Ingram. Barbados: Caribbean Universities Press in association with Bowker Publishing Co., Epping, England, 1975. 422p. bibliog.

Includes a substantial number of entries for manuscripts relating to Jamaica, descriptions of many of which have never been published before.

1160 **Sources of Jamaican history 1655-1838: a bibliographical survey with particular reference to manuscript sources.**
K. E. Ingram. Zug, Switzerland: Inter Documentation Co. AG, 1976. 2 vols.

Discusses in broad outline the principal repositories in which these collections of source material find themselves, the nature and extent of the sources, their historical and bibliographical backgrounds with special reference to their formation, provenance, availability and the use to which they have been put, also their relationships to one another where such relationships exist. As a basis for these general considerations this survey embodies a detailed enumerative bibliography of manuscript sources. Apart from its immediate use to historians and those pursuing other scholarly disciplines, it may be viewed as a contribution whereby those who are concerned with further discovering, understanding and constructing Jamaica's identity through the study of her past and the persons and influences which have shaped it, will be guided to some of the sources for this task of discovery and understanding.

1161 **Sources for West Indian studies: a supplementary listing, with particular reference to manuscript sources.**
K. E. Ingram. Zug, Switzerland: Inter Documentation Co. AG, 1983. 412p.

This work supplements the author's earlier work entitled *Sources of Jamaican history 1655-1838*. In 1,169 entries it describes historical and literary source materials, a preponderant number of which relate to Jamaica, in British and West Indian depositories.

1162 **The catalogue of the West India Reference Library.**
Institute of Jamaica, Kingston, West India Reference Library. Millwood, New York: Kraus International Publications, 1980. 6 vols.

Contents include: part one, Catalogue of authors and titles (3 vols); part two, Catalogue of subjects (3 vols). 'The Institute of Jamaica's West India Reference Library, [now the National Library of Jamaica], is the world's outstanding collection of printed and manuscript materials relating to the history and culture of the West Indies. Rich in primary source material covering all aspects of Caribbean life and society, it provides an invaluable basis for research in the fields of Jamaican and West Indian studies.' (Introduction, p. [7]). The Library attempts to acquire all material relating to Jamaica and, in varying degrees, material relating to other countries of the Caribbean.

1163 **Jamaican government publications: a bibliography.**
Compiled from the Periodicals Collection in the [Institute of Jamaica] West India Reference Library. Kingston: Institute of Jamaica, 1971. 13p.

An alphabetical listing under corporate author or title, providing a useful conspectus of such publications and of the agencies issuing them.

1164 **Jamaica: a teacher's guide to study resources.**
London: Commonwealth Institute, April 1979. 11p. map. bibliog.

Includes a short check list of key facts, a description of the Jamaica exhibition and other resources available at the Commonwealth Institute and a recommended selection of printed and audio-visual resources.

1165 **The printed maps of Jamaica up to 1825.**
Kit S. Kapp. [Kingston]: Bolivar Press, 1968. 36p. 33 maps. (Map Collectors' Series, no. 42).

The most complete list of early maps of Jamaica, compiled by a collector as well as a student of antiquarian maps. Locations of specimens are given in one or more of eleven well-known or outstanding collections. The several reproductions of maps are an aid to identification.

1166 **Bibliography of Jamaican geology.**
Edited by Marion Kinghorn. Norwich, England: Geo
Abstracts, 1977. 150p.

This is intended to be a complete a bibliography of the subject as possible,
containing over 1,000 entries pertaining almost entirely to published works and
theses submitted for higher degrees. Geology has been given a wide definition so
as to include publications in newer fields such as geochemistry and marine geology. The editor was Librarian, Mines and Geology Division, Ministry of Mining
and Natural Resources, Jamaica.

1167 **Caribbean mass communications: a comprehensive
bibliography.**
John A. Lent. Waltham, Massachusetts: Cross Roads
Press, African Studies Association, 1981. 152p. (Archival
and Bibliographic Series).

Attempts a comprehensive listing of works on Caribbean mass communication
from the 18th century through May 1980. About 2,250 sources are listed of
which 331 deal with Jamaica. A considerable number of articles and short pieces
from the daily press and from other local publications are included. The arrangement of the material is by region, country and subject categories.

1168 **A bibliography of the Commonwealth Caribbean peasantry,
1838-1974.**
Compiled by Trevor G. Marshall. Cave Hill, Barbados:
Institute of Social and Economic Research (Eastern
Caribbean), University of the West Indies, 1975. 47p.
(Occasional Bibliography Series, no. 3).

This bibliography is a by-product of the compiler's research on the history of the
Caribbean peasantry since 1838. The material is arranged in two sections; the
first dealing with the Commonwealth Caribbean in general and the second containing lists of studies on individual territories. The sub-section on Jamaica (p.
21-29) includes material subdivided according to the following subject categories:
economic, sociological or historical. The material listed is to be found in the
libraries and archive departments of Barbados and Trinidad. The author is a
member of the Department of History of the University of the West Indies.

1169 **Women in the Caribbean: an annotated bibliography. A
guide to material available in Barbados.**
Compiled by Joycelin Massiah, with the assistance of
Audine Wilkinson, Norma Shorey. Cave Hill, Barbados:
Institute of Social and Economic Research (Eastern
Caribbean), University of the West Indies, 1979. 133p.
(Occasional Bibliography Series, no. 5).

This publication developed out of the compiler's work on the analysis of census
data on working women in Barbados, when she realized the paucity of bibliographical guidance to relevant literature on women in the Caribbean. The
material is arranged under topical headings subdivided by names of countries.
There are entries relating to Jamaica under all but two of the eleven main
divisions of the work. 'The entries are intended to reflect the state of our know-

ledge of a range of activities assumed to impinge on the lives of Caribbean women.' Locations for each item cited are noted.

1170 Legal literature and conditions affecting legal publishing in the Commonwealth Caribbean: a bibliography.
Velma Newton. Cave Hill, Barbados: Institute of Social and Economic Research (Eastern Caribbean), University of the West Indies, 1979. 108p. (Occasional Bibliography Series, no. 6).

This bibliography lists, in the main, materials received in the Law Faculty Library of the University of the West Indies, since 1973. It is intended for use along with *Bibliographical guide to law in the Commonwealth Caribbean*, prepared by Keith Patchett and Valerie Jenkins (1973). Contents include: part one, Primary sources; part two, Secondary sources; part three, Conditions affecting publishing. Includes much material relating to Jamaica.

1171 A bibliographical guide to law in the Commonwealth Caribbean.
Keith Patchett, Valerie Jenkins. Jamaica: Institute of Social and Economic Research and Faculty of Law, University of the West Indies, 1973. 80p.

A compilation for students and practitioners of law. The arrangement of primary and secondary sources under geographical headings allows for ready identification of material relating to Jamaica.

1172 A guide for the study of British Caribbean history, 1763-1834, including the abolition and emancipation movements.
Compiled by Lowell Joseph Ragatz. Washington, DC: Government Printing Office, 1932. Reprinted, New York: Da Capo Press, 1970. 725p.

A most useful bibliographical and historical tool for the period covered, distinguished by the scholarly annotations which form part of many of its entries. This guide grew out of the author's work on his study *Fall of the planter class in the British Caribbean, 1763-1833* (New York, 1928). It is based on material in 69 repositories, in seven countries, including a great many items relating to Jamaica and a list of Jamaican newspapers compiled by Frank Cundall.

1173 A select bibliography of publications and studies relating to human resources in the Commonwealth: material available in Trinidad and Tobago.
Compiled by Marianne Ramesar. St. Augustine, Trinidad: Institute of Social and Economic Research, University of the West Indies, 1981. 127p. (Occasional Papers: Human Resources, 3).

A comprehensive bibliography of published and unpublished studies undertaken within the past 35 years, on a wide range of topics including employment, population and economic development, pertinent to the Human Resources Programme of

Bibliographies. General

the Institute of Social and Economic Research. Although the bibliography lists material located in Trinidad and Tobago and consequently emphasizes studies relating to Trinidad, there are sections devoted to Jamaica under each principal topic treated.

1174 **Social and Economic Studies: author and keyword index, volumes 1-26, 1953-1977.**
Compiled by Reivé Robb. Kingston: Institute of Social and Economic Research, University of the West Indies, 1980. 280p.

A computer output cumulative index to the major journal in the field of Caribbean social and economic studies. Under the keyword 'Jamaica' or other terms beginning with Jamaica, nearly two hundred references are listed. This index is part of a larger project, known as DOERS, to improve the Institute's Data Bank and Documentation Centre.

1175 **Select bibliography of education in the Commonwealth Caribbean 1940-1975.**
Compiled by Amy Robertson, Hazel Bennett, Janette White. Mona, Jamaica: School of Education, University of the West Indies, 1976. 196p.

A select list of materials for the period 1940 to early 1976 to be found in the Documentation Centre of the School of Education, or in other public or university libraries of the region, for which location symbols are given. The emphasis is on recent educational thought and development which support the national aspirations of the countries of the region. The material is arranged in broad subject categories with a section on education in individual territories.

1176 **Jamaica music: a select bibliography.**
Gordon Rohlehr. *Caribe* (New York), Dec. 1980, p. 11-12.

Lists 31 items, mainly periodical articles, with some annotations. Includes also a short list of related reading and works on the social and political background.

1177 **Jamaica agricultural situation and prospects: an annotated bibliography.**
Compiled by Ann Thirkell Smith. Oxford, England: Commonwealth Agricultural Bureaux, 1974. 8p. (Commonwealth Bureau of Agricultural Economics Annotated Bibliography, series D, no. 2).

Lists 64 publications abstracted in *World Agricultural Economics and Rural Sociology Abstracts* (WAERSA) from 1965 to 1973. Very informative annotations.

1178 **A select bibliography of reference material providing an introduction to the study of Jamaican agriculture.**
Edgar S. Steer. Kingston: Agricultural Planning Unit, Ministry of Agriculture and Fisheries, 1970. 40p.

Lists monographs, serials and periodical articles under the following headings: General studies; Special studies and reports; Crop production; Livestock production; Fishing; Annual reports. A useful selection of relatively recent publications, though the bibliographical details relating to imprint are somewhat uneven and sketchy.

1179 **A bibliography of the Caribbean.** [Prepared by Audine Wilkinson]. Cave Hill, Barbados: Institute of Social and Economic Research (Eastern Caribbean), University of the West Indies, September 1974. 167p. (Occasional Bibliography Series, no. 1).

A bibliography compiled from sources available in the Library of ISER (Eastern Caribbean) and under each of the territories covered it lists books, articles and documents, by author, being stronger on articles than books. Its primary purpose is for use of the staff of the Institute and the emphasis is on current research in the field covered by the Institute. The section on Jamaica is at p. 44-63.

1180 **The Caribbean sugar industry: a select bibliography.** Compiled by Audine Wilkinson. Cave Hill, Barbados: Institute of Social and Economic Research (Eastern Caribbean), University of the West Indies, 1976. 87p. (Occasional Bibliography Series, no. 4).

A comprehensive, though not exhaustive, listing of material in various forms, available in established libraries in Barbados. A general section on the Caribbean is followed by geographical sections in each of which the entries are arranged by subject. The Jamaica section comprises p. 61-69. The foreword, by Trevor G. Marshall, is a concise and useful overview of writings in the Caribbean sugar industry.

A companion to West Indian literature.
See item no. 908.

Authors and areas of the West Indies.
See item no. 910.

Periodicals

1181 **Jamaican National Bibliography.**

Kingston: Institute of Jamaica, 1975- . quarterly, with annual cumulations.

This work superseded an earlier publication entitled *Jamaica Accessions*, 1964-67. The first issue, published in 1973, was a cumulative one covering the years 1964-70. The issues for 1975 onwards have appeared quarterly, with annual cumulations. It is a subject list of material relating to Jamaica received in the National Library of Jamaica (formerly the West India Reference Library of the Institute of Jamaica), arranged according to the Dewey Decimal Classification System, with author, title and series index and a list of Jamaican publishers. It includes works published in Jamaica, as well as works by Jamaicans published outside of Jamaica and works about Jamaica.

1182 **SECIN Abstracts: journal of the Socio-Economic Information Network.**

Kingston: Documentation Centre, Nation Planning Agency for the International Development Research Centre, 1982- . biannual.

The primary purpose of this service is to provide access to the socio-economic literature on Jamaica with special emphasis on locally-generated materials. The abstracts are furnished with author, subject and title indices.

Index

The index is a single alphabetical sequence of authors (personal and corporate), titles of publications and subjects. Index entries refer both to the main items and to other works mentioned in the notes to each item. Title entries are in italics. Numeration refers to the items as numbered.

319

Map of Jamaica

This map shows the more important towns and other features.

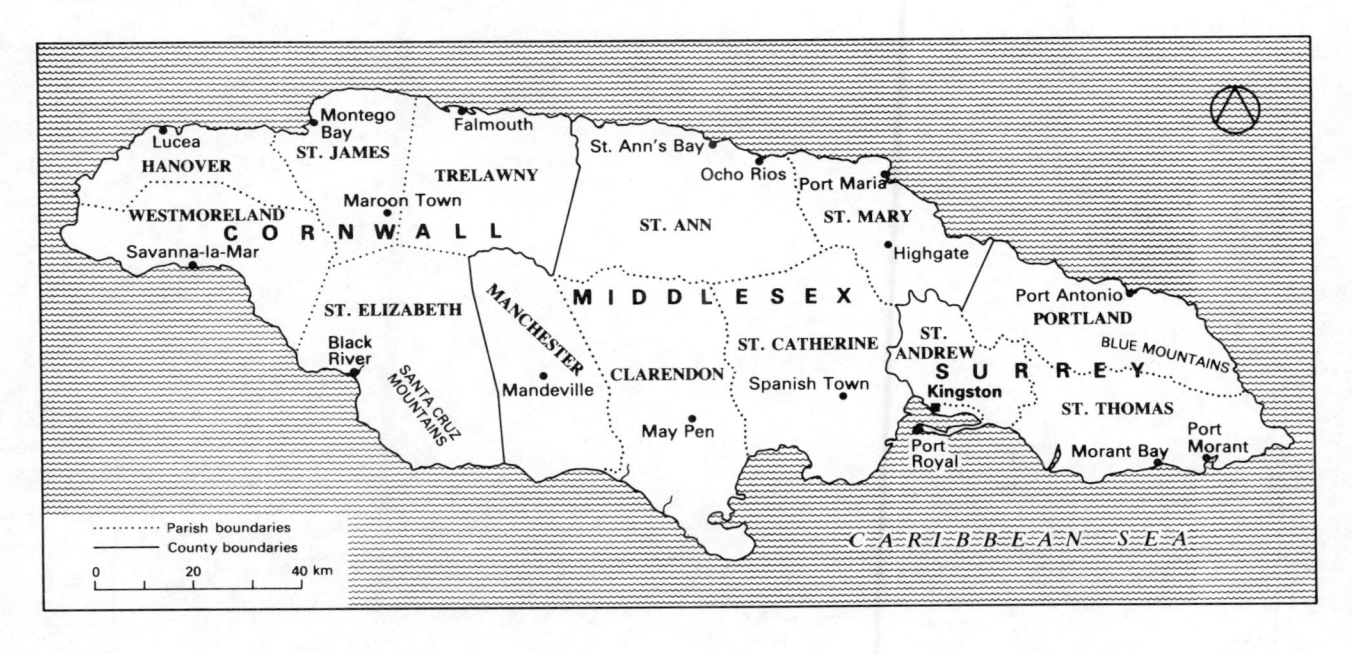